POPULAR TYRANNY

SOVEREIGNTY AND ITS
DISCONTENTS IN ANCIENT GREECE

POPULAR
TYRANNY

KATHRYN A. MORGAN, EDITOR

UNIVERSITY OF TEXAS PRESS, AUSTIN

First edition, 2003

Requests for permission to reproduce material from this work
should be sent to Permissions, University of Texas Press, Box 7819,
Austin, TX 78713-7819.

⊛ The paper used in this book meets the minimum requirements
of ANSI/NISO Z39.48-1992 (R1997) (Permanence of Paper).

LIBRARY OF CONGRESS
CATALOGING-IN-PUBLICATION DATA

Popular tyranny : sovereignty and its discontents in ancient
Greece / Kathryn A. Morgan, editor.
        p.   cm.
Includes bibliographical references and index.
ISBN 0-292-75276-8
1. Despotism.   2. Greece—Politics and government—To 146 B.C.
I. Morgan, Kathryn A.
JC381 .P66   2003
320.938′09′014—dc21

                                        2002154910

Contents

Acknowledgments

This volume emerged from the conference "Popular Tyranny: Sovereignty and Its Discontents in Classical Athens," held at the University of California, Los Angeles (UCLA) in the spring of 1998. First thanks, then, must go to the Department of Classics at UCLA, which provided the funding for the event. The initial audience of these papers also deserves mention for the depth and engagement of the comments that were made at the time. We were extremely fortunate to enjoy expert commentary from Vincent Farenga, Sander Goldberg, Ian Morris, and Greg Thalmann. Although their specific contributions are recognized in the body of this volume, it is worth emphasizing here their overall importance as respondents and interlocutors. James McGlew made helpful comments on the entire manuscript, and all contributors owe him their gratitude.

Much of the editing work on this book was done while I enjoyed a productive sabbatical year in Oxford. My work there was financially supported by a George A. and Eliza Gardner Howard Foundation Fellowship and by a University of California President's Research Fellowship in the Humanities. The Principal and Fellows of Jesus College, Oxford, made me welcome as Visiting Senior Research Fellow and supplied a most congenial atmosphere for the contemplation of the broad themes that tie this volume together.

Final thanks must go to Jim Burr, Classics Editor, and Lynne Chapman, Manuscript Editor, at the University of Texas Press, for their skill and patience in overseeing this project. Nancy Moore, our copyeditor, substantially improved the clarity and consistency of the volume; all the contributors owe her their gratitude. I would also like to acknowledge the help of Karen Gunterman, Brian Beck, and Lowry Sweney at UCLA in preparing and checking the manuscript and for their work on the indices.

Kathryn Morgan
UCLA
April 2002

K A T H R Y N   A .   M O R G A N

INTRODUCTION

The essays collected together here originated as a series of talks presented at the conference "Popular Tyranny: Sovereignty and Its Discontents in Classical Athens." This volume, therefore, possesses both the strengths and the weaknesses of collected conference papers. The strength is the vigorous debate occasioned by bringing together a group of historians, archaeologists, and literary critics to discuss a topic that exerts a lively fascination for audiences both ancient and modern. A potential weakness is unevenness of coverage. This volume does not, for example, contain a detailed treatment of the theme of tyranny in Attic oratory or provide even coverage of the Thucydidean material. Nevertheless, I made the decision not to try to extend the coverage of the volume by inviting extra contributions (with the exception of the concluding essay by Robin Osborne). The reasons for this decision were twofold. First, I am doubtful whether complete coverage is possible in a single volume, even given the focus of the majority of essays on the world of Athens. Second, I was anxious to retain the lively interaction of the original participants without dilution. The reader is left to judge the success of this decision.

The collection, for the most part, focuses on the conceptual force of tyranny rather than on historical instances of it. Although much interesting work on Archaic and Classical tyrants continues to be done, the ambition of the UCLA conference was to examine tyranny as a foundational ideological force. While not every essay focuses on Athens (indeed, one of our most important conclusions is that an overly Athenocentric approach impoverishes), all encompass themes that are crucial in our evaluation of Classical Athenian—and Greek—culture. The nature of authority and rule is a persistent worry in the construction of ancient ideology. The figure of the king or tyrant and the sovereignty associated with him provide a powerful source for political speculation and historical analysis. If tyrants had not existed, we and the Greeks would still have had to invent them as an indispensable tool for political analysis and construction.

Thus this volume starts with "Imaginary Kings: Alternatives to Monarchy in Early Greece." This is Sarah Morris' lively attack on the notion of Bronze and Iron Age kingship, in which she forces us to reconsider the strategies by which we construct an originary past. In "Form and Content: The Question of Tyranny in Herodotus," Carolyn Dewald explores the productive tension between a foundational despotic template associated with the Persian East and the stories of individual Greek despots, whose individualism seeks to escape the narrative template. This tension between an antityrannical template operating at the level of ideology and the unruly behavior of individuals and even citizen bodies is fundamental. It provides the best way to understand the conflicts and inconsistencies explored in the later essays. Kurt Raaflaub then surveys the centrality of tyranny for official fifth-century Athenian ideology in "Stick and Glue: The Function of Tyranny in Fifth-Century Athenian Democracy." This essay presents the hard-line antityrannical stance of the demos and creates a standard against which later contributions will compare different visions of the nature of democratic authority.

Richard Seaford's examination, "Tragic Tyranny," criticizes the majority of critics of tragedy for failing to understand the way tyranny operates within tragedy. This failure results from identifying the tragic tyrant with the interests of the polis and interpreting his downfall as a disaster for the community. Seaford's insistence on the aetiological importance of the tyrant as opposer of the community's best interests therefore falls into line with the ideological position staked out by Raaflaub. The two following essays, however, map out a different route over fifth-century terrain. "*Dēmos Tyrannos:* Wealth, Power, and Economic Patronage" by Lisa Kallet argues that the conspicuous use of wealth by the Athenian demos on a "tyrannical" scale reflects an aspect of tyrannical practice that the people would have found attractive and to which they could aspire. Jeffrey Henderson, too, suggests that the "acquisition of arguably tyrannical powers was considered by the majority of the Athenian demos to be a justifiable, indeed a legitimate ambition." His essay, "Demos, Demagogue, Tyrant in Attic Old Comedy" examines how conjuring with the figure of the tyrant in Attic comedy helped to strengthen radical democracy and imperialism and create its ideology. Both these essays, although acknowledging the strength of antityrannical ideology, suggest that the demos was happy to act and talk in a fashion inconsistent with that ideology. It escapes from, even while manipulating, the despotic template.

My own essay, "The Tyranny of the Audience in Plato and Isocrates," traces the process by which Plato and Isocrates pointed out and critiqued the demos' tyrannical desire for power and pleasure (despite its professed hatred of tyranny) to create new models of political and literary authority. Josiah Ober ("Tyrant Killing as Therapeutic *Stasis:* A Political Debate in Images and Texts") concentrates on the resonance of tyrannicide as a model of therapeutic civil conflict and on how this model was used both in democratic ideology and in critical political thought, which sought to redefine the tyrant as the demos. Both essays trace how a dissident tradition capitalized on competing ideologies of autonomy, desire, and legitimate authority and on the tensions that existed between these ideologies and political practice. The very freedom, however, with which accusations of tyranny can be hurled as rhetorical bombs in fourth-century political discourse indicates that the metaphor of tyranny was losing its specificity. Thus Robin Osborne's concluding contribution, "Changing the Discourse," proposes that the discourse of tyranny at the start of the fourth century was losing touch with political reality. Although this distancing of ideology from reality may have facilitated rhetorical manipulation by people such as Plato and Isocrates, it was unhelpful in solving the constitutional problems faced by the Athenians, although the topos of the tyrant did enjoy a long and fruitful rhetorical afterlife.

In the remainder of this introductory chapter, I want to move out from Sarah Morris' scene-setting essay and expand on some of the issues that draw this volume together: the construction of authority and of constitutional models, the importance of religion and ritual, and the autonomy of the individual. Even though interpretation of Greek and Athenian ideologies varies in individual essays, these themes recur repeatedly—unsurprisingly, since they are at the center of life in a community.

Morris' contribution performs two functions. It introduces some of the major themes of this volume and is itself an innovative contribution to the debate on the nature of Bronze and Iron Age systems of authority. She argues that scanty evidence for Bronze Age kingship has been over-interpreted in line with preconceptions, both ancient and modern, about development from monarchical to more democratic systems of government. The rise of tyrannies in the Archaic period should not, therefore, be interpreted as a reversion to earlier constitutional forms but as a result of increasing tensions among local elites caused by the accumulation of wealth. At least on the Greek mainland, monarchical tendencies were always a veneer upon a stronger system of communitarian government. This essay will doubtless spark spirited debate among ancient historians and archaeologists, especially in the case of the Bronze Age material, for it encourages fundamental questioning of our assumptions, even though it does not provide all the answers. How robust does the authority of an individual have to be before it counts as a monarchy? What is the nature of this authority? Does a ritual king have it?

But if the kings of the Bronze Age were imaginary kings, what relevance does this have for the chief focus of this volume, the world of the fifth and fourth centuries, particularly in Athens? Here, the qualification "imaginary" becomes important, since it is largely constructions of tyranny that form the focus of the remaining essays. In the admittedly meager evidence provided for the Bronze Age and the Archaic period by myth, art, and archaeology, we can nevertheless discern elements that resonated in the ancient imagination and may have helped to form it. This essay concentrates on four areas of importance: the role of construction in our assessment of constitutional models, ritual and cult, regional geographic variation, and crucially, the tension between communitarian and individualistic models.

First: construction. This topic resonates in both ancient and modern contexts. Morris argues that the scholarly model of development away from monarchy in most of the Greek mainland is rooted in an overly uncritical acceptance of fabricated king lists and of the relevance of the Roman and eastern models for Greek practice. This acceptance stems from a desire to credit ancient Greek accounts of their own past but also from a modern prejudice that traces a teleological development from monarchy to various forms of republicanism. The construction of mythico-historical kings satisfies a desire for tidy origins as well as for an original focus of authority from which subsequent developments are diffused. We must, then, always ask whose interests are served by a model of original kingship and hereditary descent of authority. If aristocratic elites in the Archaic and Classical periods fantasized about royal descent, this served the dual purpose of reinforcing their elite status and communicating to nonelites the (relatively) more egalitarian nature of elite influence in the polis. Thus attempts at dominance by powerful members of the elite can be cast as reversion to a superseded past. The contrast between legitimate hereditary kingship and illegitimate and tyrannical usurpation of power may thus be seen as a contrast between a quasi-official historical construction and the harsher reality of authoritarian government.

Second: ritual and cult. If Morris' emphasis on the chiefly ritual importance of the *wanax* is sustainable (even if it is not the whole story), the centrality of cult is a major area of continuity between Bronze Age and later notions of monarchic rule. Ritual kingship casts a shadow down as far as the Athenian *archōn basileus* and the heroic honors paid to ancient city founders. In most later conceptions, it is the gap between the human and the divine that is significant, as we see in much of the poetry of Pindar and also in the vase paintings cited by Morris. Religious and temporal power do not coincide. Yet the figure of the tyrant complicates this divide. Sicilian tyrants such as Gelon and Hieron were anxious to become city founders, by fair means or foul, and the Emmenids of Acragas may have used their hereditary priesthoods as a springboard for the acquisition of temporal power. Peisistratus' charade as favorite of Athena, escorted into the polis by the goddess in her chariot, is also relevant here. The ritual king of early Greece as presented in this volume does not embody standard conception of monarchic rule. While this tradition continues, we are also presented with an authoritarian ruler (the tyrant) who attempts to draw to himself the trappings of religious legitimation. This change of emphasis lies behind the Zeus-like powers of the tyrant in tragedy and comedy, as detailed by Seaford and Henderson. The *Prometheus Bound* shows that if a tyrant can be conceived as a god, a god can also be conceived as a tyrant.

Morris' focus on cult is chiefly picked up by Seaford's treatment of the tyrant in tragedy. For Seaford, one crucial aspect of the tyrant is his perversion of ritual. We see this both in the stories associated with historical tyrants such as Polycrates and in the abuse of ritual by tragic characters such as Clytemnestra. The abuse of the sacred forms part of a larger pattern in which the destruction of the royal family and the institution of a polis cult becomes a structuring principle in Greek tragedy. The contrast with Morris' picture of the Bronze Age situation is instructive. There, kingly authority *is* ritual authority. In the later period, however, ritual becomes a tool in the pursuit of power and is often perverted by that pursuit. Seaford's tragic tyrant exists in a problematic relationship with ritual, and a successful polis cult is possible only once the tyrant has been expelled. Thus religious legitimation and power have been detached from the king and attached to the polis. It seems reasonable to consider this a symptom of the considerable transformation in governmental structures after the Bronze Age. Even if, with Morris, we find traces of communitarian government in the earlier period, it is clear that there has been a reconfiguration of attitudes towards the individual figure of authority. But the area in which the tension between individual and community is played out remains constant, and that area is ritual.

Another important characteristic of tyrannical power is wealth. Seaford points out that tyrants are greedy for money and the power it allows them to exercise. Yet tyrannical greed may have a positive counterpart in lavish expenditure, and here again, the importance of religious factors is striking. As Morris notes, the capacity of sanctuaries in the Archaic period to attract tyrannical largesse and the concomitant power and influence wielded by such sanctuaries remind us of the religious significance of kingship in the prehistoric period. Historical tyrants, both Greek and foreign, seek legitimation and negotiate power in their relationships with these sanctuaries. Just as tyrannical greed is intimately connected with impiety in the world of tragedy, so tyrannical expenditure upon offerings and religious building projects attempt to realign the tyrant and reembed him in the religious sphere.

In the tragic imagination, as Seaford suggests, the use of money may mark a failure in reciprocity, but on a pragmatic level it enables successful diplomatic exchange and marks preeminence. Thus it is that the Athenian demos engages in quasi-tyrannical expenditure with its massive use of public moneys, a phenomenon analyzed in Kallet's fascinating essay. The demos both taxes and spends in a demonstration of its preeminent power. Its role as economic patron forestalls challenge from members of the elite, who do not have the resources to match it. The symbiotic relationship of tyranny, wealth, and expenditure (studied by Kallet and Seaford), taken together with the implication of the king or tyrant in religious concerns (as we see in the essays of Morris and Seaford), goes far to explain the extraordinary magnificence of the fifth-century building program on the Athenian Acropolis. While Kallet rightly sees this as an instance of public patronage, it is significant that this patronage, to use Morris' words, marks "the convergence of polis and shrine."

The third area where Morris' treatment of kingship is significant for this volume as a whole is that of regional geographical variation. This concern manifests itself in the remaining essays in two ways. It emerges as an awareness that we can best understand Athenian developments in light of a broader Greek context. Thus we note that robust forms of kingship established themselves chiefly on the margins of the Greek world, while the communitarian model had greater force in the heartland. Nevertheless, a network of economic, military, and diplomatic relationships ensured lively exchanges between widely varying constitutions. My own essay explores the notion of "constitutional slide" as a function of the close proximity of differing forms of government. The richness of constitutional variation allows both Plato and Isocrates to criticize democratic tyranny and construct political structures based on ethics rather than on the number of people in whom power was vested.

Regional variation mandates an awareness of multiple audiences and permits the development of "amphibolic" readings of texts as diverse as Isocrates' *Panathenaicus* and the funerary monument of Dexileos, the object of an unsettling analysis by Ober. He rightly points out that tyranny in the Classical period was a concern to poleis other than Athens. Our tendency towards Athenocentrism often predisposes us to ignore this wider context, but to do so is to ignore an important area of cultural exchange. Tyranny could remain a concern in Athens because the Athenians had frequent contacts with kings and tyrants in a politically unstable world. But it was an exportable concern, as Ober's investigation of the Erythrae Decree concerning repairs to the statue of a tyrannicide shows. Athens liked to export democracy to the subject cities of its empire, but its hatred of tyranny, and the concomitant iconography of resistance to tyranny, was just as real an export.

The most important geographic variation was, of course, the one to the East. As several contributors remark, the very word tyrant seems to come from the East, and early forms of royal iconography may have been eastern imports. For the historical period, the presence of the Persian empire and the unsuccessful attempt of that empire to take control of Greece in the early fifth century were decisive. The Persian Great King represented the most significant form of tyranny known to Greeks in the Classical period, and the figure of the Persian tyrant is memorably instantiated in the Xerxes of Aeschylus' *Persians* and of Herodotus. Consequently things eastern, especially eastern luxury, became suspect, at least officially.

It is clear, however, that the official story is not the whole story, for the rule of the Great King, or indeed of any successful tyrant, could be viewed as the pinnacle of human achievement and happiness (a view that Plato combats energetically). Kallet's interpretation of Pericles' statement in Thucydides' Funeral Oration that the Athenians "love beauty with economy" suggests how Athenian imperial power and the luxurious perquisites that came with it could be seen as an example of eastern excess, an interpretation that Pericles wants to suppress. Similarly, the evocation of eastern luxury in the figure of rejuvenated Demos in Aristophanes' *Knights* and the Persian garments of Philocleon in the *Wasps* intimates a complicated Athenian love-hate relationship with the trappings of tyrannical eastern power.

In Herodotus, however, the significance of what Carolyn Dewald calls the eastern "despotic template" is most pronounced. Her essay documents a bifurcation in Herodotus' narrative structure. On the one hand, his researches use the activities of eastern monarchs to establish a despotic template of abuse of power, distance between ruler and ruled, and an inherent momentum towards violence. On the other hand, Greek despots, despite cruel acts, are very much like other "ferocious and highly intelligent" individuals. In this picture the Greek tyrant represents the desires of the individual writ large, a representation consistent with the popular beliefs about the happiness of tyrants we see expressed gnomically in tragedy and in the mouths of ambitious supermen in the making, such as Plato's Callicles.

We might be inclined to see here, in the narrative tension between system and individual, a reflection of Greek individualism versus an imagined collectivist eastern mentality, but this would be an oversimplification, for it would fail to take into account the context in which Herodotus writes. We must imagine a world in which the Archaic imagination of tyranny and historical memories of elite opportunists are modified by the events of the Persian Wars into creating a model of the eastern tyrant. This image is then further modified by the events of the late fifth century, when the imperial ambition of Athens created the opportunity to apply the template at home. All the while, the individual drive for power remained. Conceiving the demos as an individual in the late fifth century allowed the paradigms of the tyrannical individual and of the community to merge. Thus the system of empire could be viewed as the expression of the desires of the Athenians conceived as a coherent citizen body: the Demos, the individual that is Athens and whom we see crowned by Democracy in the relief atop the Eucrates Decree of 337/36. Greece's eastward glance allowed it to construct a paradigm it wished to reject, but the paradigm both repelled and attracted. Like eastern clothes and other imports, it was not easily excluded.

The question of the tension between individuals and a larger system returns us to the Bronze Age. Despite the strength of the Bronze Age autonomous local communities, Morris also traces evidence of a conflict between the collective and the individual. The conflict is not between the **da-mo** and the **wanax** but between the **da-mo** and a priestess over land ownership. On one level, this is unsurprising: wherever there is a collective, there will be antagonism between it and individuals. Nevertheless, the standoff between community and authority figure is important. In spite of this possibility of communal autonomy in the prehistoric period, investiture scenes in art show the attraction of powerful individuals. So too for a later period, Morris remarks (following the lead of McGlew) that "the myth and cult of a founder hero celebrated individual autonomy that was soon subverted into an image of 'collective sovereignty'." Thus the authority of the polis exists in a dynamic tension with individual drives and desires. In his Funeral Oration Pericles celebrates the happy convergence of individual and collective goals in Classical Athens, but in less idealistic visions the tension was expressed less optimistically.

Seaford's essay brings out this tension clearly. Much is at stake in our interpretation of tragic tyranny: nothing less than our conception of the tragic hero and the community with which he or she interacts. Seaford believes that interpreters of tragedy have been insufficiently historical, particularly in the widespread belief that the tragic tyrant embodies the community. In this picture the Greek tyrant represents on a larger scale the desires of the individual, and disaster for one would be disaster for the other. Not so, says Seaford. The tragic tyrant embodies the Athenian experience of tyranny, belongs to the aetiological past, and is adapted to the needs of the polis in the present. This means that the Athenian polis reinvents the hero of myth as the antitype of polis values, the tyrant, who both emerges from and controls the polis. Tragedy projects anxiety about the autonomy of the individual citizen "onto its most extreme embodiment, the horribly isolated autonomy of the tyrant" (p. 107). It may thus be the case, as Vincent Farenga (1981) has suggested, that conceptualizing the tyrant had an important part to play in the construction of an idea of the individual. Two different approaches to the tragic hero thus present two alternate ways of understanding the individual as he or she emerges from the background of the community. The dispute between Seaford and those with whom he disagrees represents an alternatively pessimistic or optimistic view about the inevitability of conflict between the autonomous individual and the polis. Must the ruler figure be a Pericles or an Alcibiades?

When we ask whether the individual hero is a king or a tyrant and conceive preeminent, even aggressive, individuality positively or negatively, we are asking a question analogous to the one that concerns a number of essays in this collection: would it have been possible to think positively of the Athenian demos or polis as a tyrant? For some politicians and intellectuals, the answer is a resounding "no." Isocrates, Plato, and Aristotle use the metaphor of the people as tyrant to lay bare the flaws of Athenian democracy. This dissident discourse is examined by Ober. He suggests that in developed Athenian democracy, the demos was "sovereign" and democratic authority was viewed as continuous, tyrannical aberrations notwithstanding. The dissidents, however, viewed this authority as spurious: "Legitimate (i.e., nontyrannical) government can arise only when the demos has been deposed from its tyrannical position and political authority returned to those few who actually deserve it and are capable of its appropriate exercise" (p. 230). On this interpretation the demos is not sovereign but tyrant; popular ideology is the *hēgemōn* and can be combated only by reeducation. The desire for tyranny must be expunged from individual and polis.

My own contribution explores further the notion of misplaced authority as set out by Plato and Isocrates and the strategies by which they attempt to construct nondemocratic sources of authority. Democratic rhetorical culture tyrannically privileges (audience) desire over rational calculation of appropriate ends. Plato and Isocrates resist this tyranny and attempt to install an austere rationality as ruler in the city and the soul. Whereas democratic ideology, as expressed in tragedy, rejects tyranny as inimical to polis values, this philosophical discourse rejects democracy as an embodiment of tyranny. I use the word "embodiment" advisedly, for Plato in particular conceives the soul as a polity. The analogy between city and soul means that the individual can be seen as a collective and the collective as an individual. This blurring of distinctions breaks down the polarity between individual and polis and allows a range of interpretative moves, the most important of which is the emptying out of traditional democratic antityrannical ideology. It also bestows political authority on the author of the philosophical text, since the relationship of author and audience is political and parallel to that between politician and audience. Political, rhetorical, and philosophical authority converge in the individual who has knowledge, but this authority is that of the king and rightful ruler.

The issue of blurring between individual and group is relevant to one of the most vexing problems discussed in the volume: to what extent could the demos conceive of itself as a tyrant? The issue is laid out in Raaflaub's masterly survey of the role of tyranny in fifth-century Athens. His analysis encompasses the ideologization of tyrannicide, the political measures enacted against tyranny, and the references to tyranny in literature. It establishes that tyranny was a pervasive theme in literature and politics and that the official democratic ideology viewed tyranny as almost uniformly negative. Although a minority tradition might have seen tyranny as desirable, this view never entered the ideological mainstream. He thus mounts a challenging attack against Connor's (1977) influential thesis that tyranny is bad for the city but good for the tyrant and that this notion lies behind references to Athens as a tyranny in Thucydides.

What, then, are we to make of the analyses of Kallet and Henderson? Both stress that the acquisition and exercise of quasi-tyrannical power might be seen as desirable by the ordinary Athenian citizen. Kallet focuses on the demos as tyrant in the realm of internal politics and uncovers a complex network of democratic ideologies connected with the spending of public monies in a lavish display of *megaloprepeia* (magnificence). She suggests that the Athenians might positively assess themselves as tyrannical in the following ways: They possessed and spent 'tyrant-scale' wealth, they had economic power greater than any others and used it to express and strengthen their political power, and they were free, unaccountable to anyone but themselves. At the same time, she detects in our literary sources two conflicting attitudes towards such a connection. Pericles, with his vision of an aristocratic democracy, adopted a rhetoric that implicitly denied any link between the demos and a tyrant: the Athenian love of beauty and expenditure is not seen as excessive. Aristophanes, however, is pleased to associate his reformed democratic heroes such as Demos and Bdelycleon with eastern luxury. Henderson further teases out the nuances of Aristophanes' attitudes towards popular power and democratic leadership. In his reading of the comic poets, power is always seen as a good, as long as it is exercised collectively. While the tyranny of the demos as a corporate body is desirable, fear of tyranny is focused upon the problem of leadership: is it the elite or the demagogues who threaten to curtail the sovereignty of the people and impose a tyranny upon them?

The disagreement between Raaflaub on the one hand and Henderson and Kallet on the other is extremely fruitful. It underlines the complex implications of the image of tyranny in the Classical period. The difficulty of sorting out this complexity shows how central a topic the evaluation of tyranny is and was for our understanding of Classical Athens. As McGlew points out, "Tyranny functioned not simply as a liminal construct providing graphic images of incorrect citizen behavior, but as a defining model of political freedom, and as a bond between individual citizens."[1] Rather than attempt to arbitrate a solution to the opposing positions, I shall explore how the opposition between the two positions helps us understand the importance of the figure of the tyrant for collapsing a variety of boundaries, those between public and private, individual and collective, ideology and practice.

A tradition concerning the enviability of tyranny had existed since the

Archaic period. While disclaiming interest in private sentiments, Raaflaub admits that on a personal level, individual Athenian citizens may have envied the wealth, power, and freedom of the tyrant. It was this tradition on which the comic poets drew: "Comedy could draw out aspects of the collective Athenian character that would otherwise show up in private rather than public contexts" (p. 78). But effective rhetoric and cultural policy does not deal with official ideology alone. If a strand of popular culture spoke of desires for magnificence and unrestrained freedom, it comes as no surprise that the comic poets and some politicians could play on these desires. Politicians could not do so explicitly, but Kallet's analysis of what was at stake in Pericles' offer to finance personally the building program on the Acropolis shows how such desires could be manipulated.

Despite the negative picture of tragic tyrants such as Clytemnestra and Aegisthus (in the *Oresteia*) and Zeus (in the *Prometheus Bound*), Plato in the next century could still write that the testimony of tragic poets makes tyranny out to be a good thing. At *Republic* 568b3–8 the tragedians are banned from the ideal state specifically because they hymn the praises of tyranny. Clearly, it was not in Plato's interests to be a subtle interpreter of tragedy. Nevertheless, his comment illustrates that statements in tragedy such as "tyranny is the greatest of gods" might have been thought to express a popular sentiment.[2] This is not to dispute that the dominant Athenian ideology of tyranny was negative but to recognize that a complete account of a culture must acknowledge the gap between ideology and practice or, rather, the coexistence of several competing ideologies. The work of Margaret Miller on the Athenian reception of Persian culture provides a good example of this. As Kallet, following the lead of Leslie Kurke, points out, the cultivation of eastern luxury by aristocrats in the Archaic period fell into disrepute after the Persian Wars. Miller's study, however, reveals that the social culture of Athens was not monolithic: "Athenian receptivity to Persian culture contradicts the contempt for the Oriental as expressed in public rhetoric."[3] This example is particularly apt, since the conceptual link between Persia and tyranny was so close. Athenians may claim to despise effete Persian culture, but they adopt Persian fashions. They condemn tyranny but glory in tyrannical or quasi-tyrannical power.

I suggest that this paradoxical attitude was facilitated by the blurring of the boundary between individual and collective. As Henderson notes, the negative Athenian image of the tyrant becomes more ambiguous when we move from the individual to the corporate demos (p. 156). As several essays acknowledge, if we want to conceive of the demos as a tyrant, we must ask over whom it would rule. It is possible to answer that the demos is the entire citizen population of Athens (the official line) or that it is an interest group within that population, opposed to the elites (the dissident line). We could then infer that the demos, as the corporate body of the Athenians, tyrannizes over the subject cities in its empire. If conceived as a special interest group, however, it would tyrannize the elite. Because the demos can imagine itself as a body politic, it can block any move to criticize its internal rule; it was left to Plato to imagine a way around this block. To the question, "Whom does the demos rule?" he replies, "Itself." Because he hypothesizes parts to the soul (which are analogous to those in the city), he can imagine tyrannizing oneself. But he can do this only because the citizenry has previously conceived of itself as a corporate individual. A tradition going back to Solon argues that tyranny is the supreme good for the individual, the supreme evil for the community.[4] This polarity breaks down, however, when the term is applied to a collective. As a community, the Athenians reject tyranny; as an individual, they aspire to it. They can be all things to all people, especially themselves.

The paradox of collectivity entails a conceptual slippage between demos the faction, demos the people, and the individual citizen. Similarly, I agree with Henderson (p. 159) that "though the distinction drawn by Kallet between tyrant demos (domestically) and tyrant polis (abroad) is real, it seems more a distinction drawn by outsiders and theoreticians than by the comic poets, for whom the demos' tyrannical power is all of a piece." Indeed, the scope of the remark may be extended beyond the comic poets. The assumption of collective identity makes different realms overlap: public and private, polis and self, internal civic and external Hellenic politics—all interpenetrate, and several truths combine.[5] Competing ideologies and desires struggle for space in cities and their citizens.

This lack of uniformity within the body politic means that different political arenas, different genres and text, express differing ideologies of tyranny, both from each other and within themselves. The heterogeneity of conclusions drawn in this volume is partly an index of scholarly disagreement (over, e.g., the interpretation of Thucydides' Funeral Oration or *Oedipus Tyrannus*) and partly an indication of a lack of uniform ideology in our sources. Such heterogeneity is important when we evaluate the effect of the rhetoric of tyranny on audiences, both Athenian and non-Athenian. These audiences are not uniform. In my own essay I emphasize the multiple and Panhellenic audiences of Plato and Isocrates as well as suggest that these authors see the human soul as an unpredictable audience whose potential range of response must be tamed by reason. Such an audience may conceive itself now in one role, now in another. Such versatility is especially typical of the Athenian citizen. Thus a reference to tyranny will resonate differently in Sparta, Macedon, and Athens, differently among the various factions within Athens, and differently within a single Athenian citizen when he thinks of Peisistratus, the Athenian empire, the Persian empire, and his own power and comfort. Kallet makes a similar point in her analysis of Pericles' use of the tyranny metaphor in Thucydides: the perspective of the speaker and of the audience is of paramount importance and influences reception of any remark. The Athenian empire may seem to be an unjust tyranny to Athenian quietists, but this attitude need not be generalized to all Athenians.

The question of audience brings us back, unsurprisingly, to tragedy. If we sidestep for a moment the problems associated with specifying the precise makeup of the audience in the Theater of Dionysus, and imagine an audience whose ideologies and desires create a shifting play of attitudes, we may be better able to come to grips with the complexity of tragic tyranny. Let us consider Seaford's disagreement in this volume with Bernard Knox (1957) over the interpretation of *Oedipus Tyrannus*. I have already referred to this problem in general terms: does the tyrant represent the city, or does his autonomy represent the audience's deepest fears? In the case of *Oedipus Tyrannus*, the issue is especially pointed, given Knox's hypothesis that Oedipus is a reference to imperial Athens and his fall predicts Athens' own. Oedipus the tyrant is Athens the tyrant. Seaford's objections to this hypothesis are well taken; we are given no explicit textual indications that this is the line of interpretation we are meant to pursue. What we might call Seaford's ideology of tragedy would oppose such a reading. Even if the tragic tyrant is the autonomous citizen writ large, he must still function as the scapegoat whose expulsion is necessary to ensure the correct functioning of the polis. Nevertheless, without denying the force of this powerful paradigm, one may still suggest that Oedipus in his glory before his fall embodies what must have been many people's ambition. What is more, Sophocles' Oedipus is separated by only a few years from Aristophanes' old man Demos, who needs to be rejuvenated into the monarch of Greece.

It did not take much to see the demos as a collective individual, and the Athenian resonances of Oedipus are facilitated when we consider him not as a crude allegory of the polis but as a possible aspect of the demos. It is not an aspect that can be explicitly recognized, and thus Oedipus pollutes himself and the city and ends his life as an exile. Tragedy endorses the ideology of democratic Athens, expressed in mythological aetiology, yet it also reveals the underside of that ideology as an expression not just of the demos' deepest fears but of its desires. If, as one is so often tempted, one succumbs to the lure of reading the Peloponnesian War as the tragedy of Athens, the determination of the demos to do just what it wanted in the trial of the generals after Arginousae (a classical tyrannical characteristic) can appear as the quintessential act of tragic autonomy, taken to the extreme with no regard for consequences.

The ambivalence in the conception of the tyrant noted by several contributors matches the manifold contradictions in the demos remarked by intellectuals both ancient and modern. At the end of the fifth century, Parrhasius painted the famous picture of Demos described by Pliny (*NH* 35.36.69). The figure was

> *varium iracundum iniustum inconstantem, eundem exorabilem clementem misericordem; gloriosum excelsum humilem ferocem fugacemque et omnia pariter*
> changeable, angry, unjust, inconstant, but also capable of being moved by entreaty, clement, merciful; boastful, lofty, humble, aggressive, prone to flight—and all at the same time (my translation).

Charlotte Schubert connects this portrayal with Plato's depiction of the democratic man at *Republic* 560d–561a.[6] Yet we should also think of the puzzling character of Demos in the *Knights*. He is shown to be foolish and gullible, easily deceived by the machinations of the Paphlagonian/Cleon. Yet towards the end of the play, he declares that he has never really been hoodwinked but has seemed so only to catch those who do not mean him well (cf. Henderson, this volume). Opinions may differ on the accuracy of this self-representation; this justification after the fact may be merely misguided complacency or else, as the chorus speculates, deep cunning. Nevertheless, if the exchange is not to fall flat, there must be some sense in which both interpretations of his conduct are valid. Demos' behavior embraces the extremes of simplicity and guile. Similarly, the tyrant is a cunning political manipulator and the victim of base flattery who is unable to act in his own best interests. The tyrant and the demos, conceived as a collective, are both plagued by internal contradiction. The sovereignty to which both aspire can express itself as the authoritative exercise of power (thus desirable) and as uncontrolled recklessness and indulgence. The tyrant is thus a fruitful metaphor to apply to the democratic citizen body precisely because of the range of characteristics, both positive and negative, with which he can be associated. A full appreciation of the importance of tyranny for Classical Athens must seek to preserve this ambivalence.

Osborne's concluding essay reveals how, despite its promise for ideological self-identification, the contrast between democracy and tyranny was beginning to lack descriptive power at the beginning of the fourth century. Although the charge of tyranny provided a useful stick with which to beat oligarchs at the end of the Peloponnesian War, and although the paradoxical identification between democracy and tyranny was to remain a potent weapon in the dissident arsenal, Osborne argues that ideological focus on tyranny had obscured the reality of the need for constitutional change. As this need was recognized and acted upon, doctrinaire polarities began to break down, and some constitutional change was enacted. This analysis goes some way towards explaining the terminological slippage described in my paper on Plato and Isocrates, where constitutional distinctions break down and are subsumed into an ethical focus.

What it leaves unexplained is the continuing hostility on the part of intellectuals such as Plato and Isocrates towards even a somewhat reformed democracy. They do not seem to acknowledge any change in democratic culture between the radical democracy of the fifth century and that of their own time. One might interpret this intransigence in two ways. One might (with Ober) maintain that no real change of constitutional emphasis has taken place, or one might conclude that fifth-century democracy made a clearer and more identifiable target, especially for critics predisposed to see no good in any form of Athenian democracy after, say, Ephialtes. The emptying out of constitutional terminology in Plato and Isocrates may have been enabled by a popular perception of the inadequacy of current ideology of tyranny in the wake of the revolutions of 411 and 404, but they still seize upon tyranny as an indispensable rhetorical weapon.

Indeed, Osborne's analysis of the reactions to constitutional experimentation in the last part of the fifth century exposes the same tension between ideology and practice that has been a recurring theme in this introduction, although in a slightly different form. Whereas some essays have presented (or doubted) the gap between a democratic ideology that rejects tyranny and a practice that seems to reveal aspiration towards tyrannical power, Osborne posits a political reality at odds with the rhetoric used to describe it; attacks on and changes in the democracy were interpreted as tyrannical in retrospect, although they may not have been tyrannically intended. The function of tyranny as "stick and glue" described by Raaflaub had become so fundamental an aspect of Athenian thought that it could hardly be abandoned. The need to organize political thought in polarities overrode a more nuanced appreciation of constitutional realities. For all the reasons gathered together in this introduction, the polarity between demos and tyrant was useful, especially since the polarity could veer towards analogy. One can see why oligarchy occupied a rhetorically unappealing middle ground. It resisted easy personalization and easy grasp as an extreme. It could not easily be adapted to express the Athenian obsession with the individual and autonomy.

The question of whether we are to regard tyranny or oligarchy as the chief threat to developed Athenian democracy thus depends on the attitude we take to expressed ideology. According to one rhetoric, the Athenians continued to hate and fear the possibility of the imposition of a tyranny above other political dangers. The figure of the tyrant was a convenient repository in which to load fears about political change and about one's own darker impulses. But we must not allow rhetorical convenience to make us oversimplify a complex situation. Dominant ideology cannot be the whole story, and we can tease out a different narrative of oligarchic threat. Similarly, we can trace the construction of an antityrannical political self-image that was at odds with the dictates and temptations of tyrannical desire as traced by Aristophanes, Thucydides, and dissident thinkers of the fourth century. We must not, however, oversimplify the distinction between ideology and practice. It is clear that the counter image of the tyrannical demos is itself ideologically motivated, whether as an expression of a dissident agenda or an expression of the imperial ambitions and self-confidence of the democracy. The analysis of the intersection and interaction of these two competing ideological practices presents us with our best hope of a nonreductive cultural history.

The issues that are at the center of tyranny are also those at the center of life in the polis: money, relations with family and friends, the relationship of the individual and the collective, and the autonomy of the individual and the demos. Does individual autonomy threaten the existence of the collective? One way to attempt to solve this problem is to conceive the individual as a collective, and the collective as an individual. This solution brings its own problems with it, however. Chief among these is the further blurring of the already unstable division between public and private. Here again, the figure of the tyrant is paradigmatic. He notoriously treats the city as his own private household and therefore invites disaster.[7] Yet this blurring is not the unique characteristic of tyranny, since we see it again and again in the attitude of the democracy to its politicians. The distrust of Alcibiades' (proto-tyrannical) private life felt by the Athenians led to his disastrous recall from Sicily. Any candidate for public office had to be prepared for similar scrutiny. Indeed, one of Isocrates' chief complaints about Athens in his time was that the citizens did not exercise the same care with affairs of state as with their own private affairs (*On the Peace* 13; cf. 133).

In a successful democracy, then, the public good becomes the private good, while in a city that is lapsing into tyranny, the private good is imposed upon the public good. The danger of confusion is great, however. If one treats the city like one's household, one could do it either in an exploitative fashion (as in tyranny) or benevolently (as in idealized democracy). The same caution applied to an Athenian demos that claimed authority over the empire. The problem does not lie with sovereignty or authority but with how authority is exercised. That exercise will always be implicated in, but escape from, the ideologies that underlie it.[8] The complex and unstable relationship between democracy and tyranny is a reflection of the instability inherent in the use of power.

Notes

1 McGlew 1993: 183.

2 Xen. *Mem.* 1.2.56 states that Socrates was accused of making his students "tyrannical" (*tyrannikoi*) by citing renowned poets.

3 Miller 1997: 243.

4 Lévy 1976: 137; Connor 1977.

5 Cf. Lévy (1976: 123) on the confounding of internal and external rule.

6 Schubert 1993: 69.

7 Cf. Lanza 1977: 81, 138.

8 Aristotle complains of Plato that he confused political authority with the mere exercise of power (cf. Annas 1999: 100, n. 12). If this is so, it is clear that Plato was very much a creature of his time in this failing, since fifth- and fourth-century ideology seems to map the private onto the public, the personal onto the civic.

S A R A H   M O R R I S

Imaginary Kings: Alternatives to Monarchy in Early Greece

When Hellas became stronger and placed even more emphasis on acquiring wealth, tyrannies were set up in most of the cities as a result of increased revenues (*previously, there were hereditary monarchies with formally restricted powers* [ἐπὶ ῥητοῖς γέρασι πατρικαὶ βασιλεῖαι]) (Thuc. 1.13, Lattimore translation; italics mine).

The function of my contribution to this volume is to set the scene for discussing images of Greek tyranny, by recalling the peculiar history of early Greece. Behind the confident picture of early Greek history rendered by Thucydides, or the selective narrative histories of Greek city-states in Herodotus, rests evidence based largely on archaeology, mythology, and a set of prehistoric texts (Linear B) difficult to fathom. Nowhere in this record can we discern any robust institution we might call monarchy, a hereditary succession of rulers wielding supreme power in military, economic, ideological, and/or political spheres.[1] Thus the specter of tyranny—which I define here as the illegal seizure or use of power by an individual (and/or his family) or by one state over its people or another state—does not exist against any plausible background of a native, legitimate version of absolute, hereditary power. This makes all the more clear how tyranny surfaced as an occasional extreme result of (or even solution to?) aristocratic *stasis,* and that government in Greek communities never either transcended a developed form of chiefdom or descended broadly enough to be a real government by, of, and for the people. Curious throughout this history is how and why Greek thinkers maintained a serious flirtation with autonomous rule(rs) in practice and rhetoric, myth and tragedy, whether they feared, admired, or simply exploited sovereignty for dramatic effect and in political argument.

I propose to examine this interesting tension between imagined monarchs and real tyrants (later inverted by history and rhetoric into a dialogue with historical monarchs and fictional tyrants) for its relevance to the treatment of tyranny in ancient sources. This analysis will unfold in three parts: 1, a reassessment of the prehistory of Greek leadership, including its relationship to communal and collective institutions since the Bronze Age; ii, a look at survivals of certain conditions of prehistoric authority in Archaic and Classical society, particularly in cult; and iii, an assessment of what inspired visions (and lists) of past monarchies and potential tyrannies, and their connection to actual or attempted royal powers peripheral and external to the Greek world. My analysis aims to dovetail with those that follow on Archaic tyrants and their foreign counterparts (by Dewald), on *Dēmos* and *tyrannos* (by Kallet, Ober, and Raaflaub), and on imagined or distant rulers in discourse, drama, and history (by Henderson, Seaford, and Morgan).

PART I. THE BRONZE AGE: THE MISSING RULER?

The ancient and modern notion that early Greek kingship declined, disappeared, or was actively dismantled for a more "democratic" system is partly fostered by mythical king lists, enhanced by assumptions comparing Hellas to the early history of Rome. In Italy, a tradition of early (Etruscan) kings who cede to a republic has some basis in history, if embellished by myth and by antimonarchic sentiments that arose much later in Roman history than during the transition to a republic.[2] Thanks to several recent studies[3] (in fact, since Jacoby's earlier deconstruction of Greek king lists), many Hellenists now question the idea of a series of kings abolished in early constitutional reforms inching Greek culture ever onward towards "democracy." Meanwhile, studies of Homeric kingship must understand the society of the *Iliad* and the *Odyssey* as an imaginary one, projected back into prehistory, not strictly equivalent to early Greek history or its Bronze Age past.[4]

What remained unquestioned in these models until recently, and is sustained in mythology, is the idea that some form of kingship did prevail in the Bronze Age. Archaeologists probed prehistory in search of the legends of Minos and Agamemnon, and found these figures too easily in excavation: the "face of Agamemnon" appeared to Schliemann in a gold mask found at Mycenae; the "palace of Minos" was soon named as it was uncovered by Evans.[5] These early and romantic claims were eventually substantiated, it appeared, by the decipherment of Mycenean Greek in tablets that name a **pa-si-re-u** and **wa-na-ka,** ancestors of Greek *basileus* (king) and *wanax* (lord). How plausible are they as terms for early rulers?

I will attempt an answer to this question by comparing the evidence for Bronze Age kingship in myth, text, and archaeology with traces of an early demos, then consider the survival of prehistoric roles in Classical cult and

Fig. 1.1. Male figure with staff, urban landscape. LMIb clay sealing found in Chania, Crete. Chania Museum KH 1563. After drawing of impression by Poul Pedersen (Hallager 1985: fig. 11), courtesy of Erik Hallager.

some reasons for ancient and modern inflation of Greek monarchy's minimal past.

In Bronze Age archaeology, a convergence of recent scholarship agrees on the peculiar ambiguity, or even absence, of figures of authority in prehistoric Aegean art.[6] Those from Crete once entertained by Evans have been literally deconstructed, like the Priest- or "Lily"-king assembled from fragments of relief sculptures found at Knossos.[7] More recent candidates include a striking figure who appears on a lump of impressed clay discovered in connection with the palace beneath modern Chania, in western Crete, which depicts a young man with staff (?) before an architectural landscape (Fig. 1.1). But his role is more likely to have entailed ritual powers than any political ones, according to most scholarly opinions.[8] The best candidate for an image of authority in Mycenean art comes from the shrine area at Mycenae, where a figure in a shaggy cloak with a sword faces a female in a flounced skirt.[9] If the figure on the left is male (only a pair of white feet are preserved, and human flesh painted white is at best gender-ambiguous in Aegean prehistory) and faces a goddess, then we may have a scene of investiture so common in Near Eastern art. On the walls of the Old Assyrian palace at Mari (eighteenth century B.C.), the figure of the king (Zimri-lim) receives royal insignia from the gods.[10] If we allow the Mycenean figure in a shaggy cloak to be a *wanax,* it confirms two aspects of kingship claimed in this paper, its extra-Aegean origin and its association primarily with ritual activities, the chief function of the *wanax,* as we shall see, in Mycenean texts. The same context characterizes another potential image of royalty, in the procession of offering bearers painted in the vestibule of the palace at Pylos. The largest figure in front has been identified as the *wanax* of Pylos, perhaps even one named **e-ke-la-wo** or Echelawon, who contributed the largest offering to Poseidon—a bull—in an offering tablet from the same site (Un 718).[11]

If royal images are scarce in art or confined to ceremonial contexts, archaeological "thrones" are equally misleading. The stone seat at Knossos has long been reassigned to the figure of a goddess or someone dressed like her, taking part in an elaborate enactment of a divine epiphany.[12] The "throne" at Pylos is largely restored (in wood) to look like the one in Crete, on the basis of a single square patch or low base found against the east wall of the megaron, without further evidence.[13] Thus it appears that according to the latest consensus, Aegean Bronze Age archaeology offers minimal evidence for images of rulers or their thrones. Instead, individual power seems confined to the ritual sphere—one aspect of the ideological category—and even here one suspects the influence of foreign traditions from the Near East.

Turning to the evidence of prehistoric texts, here we find crucial terms and relationships relevant to prehistoric society and its organization. Hooker pointed out many years ago how thin the evidence was for royal power or identity in the corpus of texts.[14] In a more recent look at Mycenean dimensions of kingship, Palaima reminds us that neither *wanax* nor *basileus* has a secure Indo-European ancestry in etymology or function.[15] Like the word *tyrannos* itself, borrowed from Anatolian or Semitic traditions, Greek terms loosely understood as "king" and applied to legitimate rulers or usurpers have no native ancestry, an interesting complement to the non-Greek nature and image of monarchy. According to the hierarchy implied by ownership of land and goods in Mycenean texts (and a single text from Pylos, Er 312, a document describing land tenure among high-ranking individuals, is crucial here), the *wanax* occupies the peak of the socioeconomic pyramid, with certain commodities (oil, wine, perfume, and textiles) marked as his property, and draws a larger yield from his *temenos* (piece of land) than that of *lawagetas* ("leader of the *laos,*" or of an armed body of the people) or *basileus.* But his function (and he is by far the most prominent person in these tablets) is largely manifest in ritual activities, where he is the figure closest to, and most actively involved in, ceremonies and property concerning the *potnia* ("lady," or goddess).[16] Outside this domain, military, economic, and even local judicial powers seem to be in other hands: even if the *lawagetas* is not a military figure, he occupies an important leadership function in name and action. The *basileus* wields local powers in supervision of metallurgy but shares his status with other figures (e.g., **ko-re-te, te-re-ta, e-qe-ta**).

One official is appointed by the *wanax* in a tablet where he names a **da-mo-ko-ro**. The *damos* elsewhere contributes offerings to religious events, an equal partner to *wanax* and *telestai* (local officials). Following earlier studies, I consider **da-mo** a regional community group and collective of landowners, anticipating certain functions of a deme, without the inclusive powers of a classical demos in the sense of an assembly representative of "the people."[17] A glimpse of its local powers emerges in a land dispute between the priestess "E-ri-ta" and the **da-mo** over land she has (**e-ke**: = *exei*) and claims (**e-ke-ta** = *euxetai*) that she holds from (?) the deity; the **da-mo** protests she actually has the land from public holdings (**ke-ke-me-na ko-to-na**).[18] Other than the tablet itself recorded by and for the palace, there is no role for the *wanax* in this dispute, debated instead between an individual and a collective entity, the **da-mo**. This appears to be a record of a demos, whatever its Bronze Age identity, in conflict with an individual over matters of property, implying both public ownership or management of land and the resolution of a conflict between an individual (a priestess) and her community. We cannot speculate further on the powers and activities of this demos, beyond those visible in issues of land ownership, contributions to common feasts, and some regulation by the palace through a *damokoros* ("keeper of the *damos*," appointed by the king in one tablet).

Here it helps to consult the wider historical background of these terms and functions in the tablets. According to scholars such as Deger-Jalkotzy, the palatial system of the Late Bronze Age was a short-lived phenomenon, partly imported from Crete and modeled on Near Eastern systems, imposed on a network of strong local communities that retained essential autonomies.[19] Palace, throne, and *wanax* topped a far more widespread system of regional communities (sixteen districts around Pylos), still visible in practice even within the centralized system recorded in palace tablets. Even the random and incomplete documents we have for a single year from a few palaces record some form of a collective body at work, recognized by the palace. Thus the tablets add an element of communal life hard to trace in the elite

Fig. 1.2. "Camp-Stool" fresco, Minoan Palace, Knossos. Color restoration by E. Gilliéron. After Evans 1935/1964, IV: pl. XXXI. LMIIIA mature?

art of frescoes and seals, and offer some ingredients essential to later polis culture.

These epigraphic details encourage a closer look at certain Aegean images. One of the latest frescoes at Knossos is the so-called Campstool Fresco, where men sit on folding stools at small tables and lift cups in a ceremony presided over by a larger seated female, perhaps a goddess (Fig. 1.2).[20] Partly by analogy to this composition, the megaron fresco at Pylos has been restored with a scene of men seated at small tables lifting cups (only two small groups of two men are partially preserved, their drinking vessels entirely restored). Here the famous figure of a poet in the same field, at a much larger scale, gives meaning to their gathering. In recent interpretations of these frescoes, a bard entertaining drinking men not only is highly Homeric but anticipates that most essential and aristocratic of Greek institutions, the symposium.[21]

These figures could be an early group of *basileis,* assembled for social purposes (drinking and listening to song, even epic poetry?), while the *wanax* is preoccupied with a different kind of ceremony, in the vestibule fresco.[22] Here lies the kernel of the Greek polis, in small groups of elites, equals among themselves, neither showing domination by a greater power nor sharing their own with a larger franchise. Somewhere among them sits an ancestor of the Neleids and perhaps of Messenia's first tyrant (if Sparta had allowed an autonomous Messenia to unfold its local history).

The weak picture in material culture and text for dynastic power in Bronze Age Greece is further enhanced in Greek mythology, however treacherous a source, by the strong tradition of a line of descent through daughters of kings, not sons or princes. In Greek legend, most Greek royal dynasties are founded by an outsider, even a foreigner—Pelops of Lydia, Cadmus of Phoenicia—or at least sustained by uxorilocal exogamy. Menelaus marries Helen and becomes king of Sparta; Agamemnon offers Achilles a daughter and a choice of kingdoms in the *Iliad* (9); Jason seeks the throne of Corinth through marriage; Oedipus was (almost) the perfect bridegroom for widowed Jocasta at Thebes, just as Odysseus appeared to the Phaeacians as the ideal "gentleman caller" for their daughter Nausicaa. Atchity and Barber, then Finkelberg, have analyzed these patterns in terms of their preservation of an older, pre–Indo-European pattern whereby the queen and her daughter are the key to the succession, while the king's son must move away and seek his fortune and a foreign bride.[23] They trace the power of this female line to women's role in prehistoric cult, manifest in the Minoan and Mycenean cult of the Potnia and the role of the priestess, which remains hereditary in later Greek religion.[24] As cautious as we must be in pressing myth into the service of history, the consistency of this pattern has interesting implications for the image of monarchy later, as we shall see (Part II).

Equally significant for later paradigms, the most reliable witnesses to Aegean Bronze Age kingship come from abroad. The possible image of a king being "invested" by a deity, considered above as explanation for a fresco from Mycenae, may be Near Eastern in origin. Indeed, many features of the Mari scene of investiture, flanked by palm trees and sphinxes, resemble Aegean ceremonial room decoration, where such images flank "thrones." In historical (textual) sources, direct references to Aegean kings may survive only in Anatolia. Since the fifteenth century, Hittite texts record relations with "the king of Ahhiyawa" (variously a people or a place), if only we could decide who are these "Achaeans," whether mainland Myceneans speaking Greek or residents of the eastern Aegean.[25] At least one genuine Hittite object made its way into the Shaft Grave burials at Mycenae: the silver vessel in the shape of a stag has recently been certified as Anatolian in both form and silver content.[26] This kind of object resembles a royal gift called a *bibru* in Akkadian, often described in diplomatic correspondence: a silver, stag-form example was sent as a gift from the Hittite ruler Suppiluliumas I (1344–1322 B.C.) to the king of Egypt (El Amarna letter 41 [Moran 1992: 114–115], lines 39–40). The one found at Mycenae had been pierced through the nostrils to serve as an Aegean rhyton and was buried in the same grave with other, Aegean rhyta (the gold lion's-head, the silver bull's head, and the silver conical rhyton engraved with scenes of a city-siege). Among these Aegean shapes, the Hittite *bibru* was imported, perhaps as a gift to a "king of Ahhiyawa" from a Hittite ruler.

By coincidence, it is in Anatolia where features of Aegean kingship survive in striking ways. Here I am thinking not of Troy, where locals and Greek migrants shaped an Iron Age Ilion on the ruins of Troy, but of Troy's neighbors (and allies in epic), the Phrygians. The king of the Phrygians, a homonymous sixth-century successor of Midas (d. 696 B.C.), termed himself not only *wanax* but *lawagetas,* in a singular survival of two titles peculiar to Bronze Age Greece.[27] These offices had virtually disappeared from Greece except as poetic titles or glosses and must have migrated to central Anatolia with Phrygians from the northern Aegean or survived as vestiges of Bronze Age Aegean life in western Anatolia. The Greeks returned the compliment paid by Midas' use of their (?) royal titles, by reconfiguring him into a king with asses' ears, an old Anatolian royal attribute.[28]

The afterlife of such "royal" phenomena is striking, in their singularity and isolation from the more widespread development of polis culture, and specific to certain locales. Arcadia, refuge of Bronze Age Greek language if not culture, is characterized in antiquity as an *ethnos* rather than a polis and develops different institutions.[29] Farther afield, kingship survives and even thrives in Arcadia's linguistic cousin (and fellow refuge from Bronze Age collapse) Cyprus, with full use of Bronze Age titles (both *wanax* and *basileus*) and many trappings of monarchy, including palaces and kingly attributes such as thrones and scepters found in "royal" burials with sacrificed servants, dogs, and other figures.[30] Here the proximity of Levantine or Mesopotamian kingdoms, and the presence of Phoenicians, may have helped foster such emulation of kingly status, in life or death.[31]

Similar geographic configurations may help explain why monarchy also flourished outside the Mycenean heartland, in areas such as Epirus, Thrace, and Macedonia.[32] These zones north of Thessaly, at times in contact with their southern neighbors, did not develop a local version of Mycenean culture, which was characterized by fortified citadels, palaces, and tholos tombs. For this reason, the latest arrivals—northwest-Greek speakers, Macedonians—were able to establish a robust system of kingship independent from central and southern Greek traditions of strong local leaders. These are areas also distinguished by "tribal" structures and late or secondary urbanism without a true polis, eccentric to Greek patterns of local elite councils with their safeguards against individual concentrations of power. Hence hereditary dynasts with close-knit groups of nobles (the Macedonian *hetairoi*) lasted until Roman campaigns ended local rule. It is equally striking that no "tyrant" in the strict sense arose here, outside of kin-based challengers, precisely because these areas were already ruled by kings. Monarchy flourished here, much as later foreign despots did, on the fringes of the Greek world.

Summing up the early picture, we find a striking absence of ruler ideology (as opposed to heroic but anonymous figures in hunt or battle) in Aegean art and of distinct royal functions outside of ritual and related royal wealth in texts. Memory in myth gives wives and daughters of kings an explicit role in determining royal succession, and "foreign" men priority in that succession, while non-Greek sources may be responsible for inspiring the only identifiable royal imagery (if the Mycenae fresco indeed represents an investiture). In other words, evidence does not allow us to reconstruct historical monarchies of a conventional kind in prehistoric Greece.

This conservative view is now widely shared among prehistorians, but its implications rarely reach those who study post-Homeric Greece. My summary serves to remind us that the Archaic phenomenon of tyranny was, more than ever, no resurgence of monarchy but the latest twist in an intra-aristocratic drama that could itself be older than the age of Mycenean "palaces." That is, it recalls struggles for power among earlier Bronze Age chieftains or those that led to the formation of early Mycenean society.[33] In terms of the representation of tyranny that is the focus of this volume, the concept may have borrowed from an imagined past but also participated in its construction, as Seaford notes in his analysis of kingship in tragedy.

PART II. THE ARCHAIC PERIOD: STRONG TYRANTS, SHADOWY KINGS?

As we move to the first millennium, I will sidestep in a deliberate and controversial way the testimony of Homer and the Homeric *basileus,* a well-developed and closely studied phenomenon but one that, in my view, transcends history and ignores the actual rise of tyrants. This may seem all the more perverse, when the codification of epic poems was rumored in antiquity to be the work of tyrants (in Sicyon and Athens), and the historicity of that notion has been revived in recent scholarship.[34] But if the Homeric corpus was inspired by memories of prehistory, strongly shaped by Archaic ambitions,[35] it did not directly contribute to history or image of tyrants. Moreover, the Homeric world may reflect certain *realia* of Greek "Dark Age" history and archaeology (e.g., at Lefkandi) in its picture of chieftains, without informing us more closely about kingship or tyranny.[36] An aggregate of chiefdoms, as defined by anthropologists from Elman Service (1962) to Timothy Earle (1997), appears in nearly every landscape: archaeologically, in elite burials from the Shaft Graves to Lefkandi; in literature, in the *basileis* of Homer and Hesiod, a collective of leaders rather than "kings"; and in history, where aristocrats trace their heritage back over many generations, as Hecataeus tried in Egypt or the Peisistratids in Athens, claiming descent to Nestor.

My emphasis is complicated by my skepticism on the rise of the polis as an exclusively eighth- or even ninth-century phenomenon, a notion cherished since Snodgrass' celebration of this twenty-five years ago. I have never shared the view of a polis as an innovation of the eighth century, however fertile that period was for the rise of large extra-urban sanctuaries, an increase in colonization, the adaptation of the alphabet, and the related redaction of the Homeric poems. I suspect we have been misled by an artificial concentration of "events"—destructions, foundations, graffiti—in the late eighth century B.C., thanks to Late Geometric ceramic chronology (once adjusted as it needs to be, data would redistribute more evenly into the next century). To some degree, evolution, and not only revolution or renaissance, was responsible for certain phenomena. I continue to separate the polis as an early Greek term for city that essentially means an *akropolis* (Van Effenterre 1985: 29–30) from the civic institution that preoccupies ancient and modern scholarship, a Classical and post-Classical concept. It is much more likely that some form of small, collective community existed at the local level in the Bronze Age and survived the so-called Dark Ages, once the veneer of a palatial system collapsed around 1200 B.C.[37] This is sustained by prehistoric documents on the activity of a **da-mo** in local, land-based hierarchies, as argued above, and its prominence in Homer, Hesiod, and archaeology.[38]

My view of the polis enhances the emergence of the first tyrants by framing them not as some resurgence of kingship but as an event precipitated by an accumulation of power and wealth within the governing elite, as Thucydides treated them. Thus those achievements acclaimed by tyrants and their fans—populist measures, largesse, sponsorship of public buildings and festivals—emerged as novelties of leadership, not ones borrowed from popular monarchs. Likewise, the negative image of tyranny was never a fear of reversion to monarchy, an institution new to Archaic Greece and alien in most places.

One important Archaic phenomenon promotes monarchy as an illusion fostered by artificial king lists, a response to historical methods of record-keeping in neighboring, non-Greek kingdoms (Lydia, Egypt and Persia).[39] The deconstruction of early Greek history in terms of a series of kings, initiated by Drews (1983) and confirmed recently by Barceló (1993), is further certified in Burkert's analysis of how such imagined dynasties were constructed. Such research further emphasizes the absence of powerful kings in history, underscoring the fragility of king lists constructed by later aristocratic families and their myth-makers. Here the alien element enters the picture once again: it was foreign monarchs and their claim to historical succession through a line of ancestors that encouraged local Greek communities to endow themselves with similar pedigrees, as Burkert argues. In Archaic Greece, invented king lists designed for individual poleis often fail to override a stronger (heroic) genealogical tradition, where descent through a single *line* is more secure a memory than a sequence of rulers in a single *place* (like the Neleids of Athens, who trace their descent to a Messenian dynasty, with relevant names in the Pylos tables).[40] In the passage from Thucydides quoted at the beginning of my text, his reconstruction of hereditary Greek kingship as a contrast and prelude to tyranny—the blueprint for modern narratives of early Greek history—may be encouraged by the exceptional patterns (Sparta?), not the rule.

Just how alien the notion of mortal kingship remained is often vivid in Greek myth and art, where the hierarchy on Olympus offers a more solid picture of monarchical status than secular rule. To illustrate one striking example, the François vase, that comprehensive encyclopedia of early Greek mythology (ca. 560 B.C.), offers us the image of Zeus and Hera enthroned on Olympus, awaiting the return of the drunken god Hephaestus (Fig. 1.3). The king and queen of the gods sit on elaborately decorated seats with footstools, clearly meant to suggest wooden furniture inlaid with luxury materials such as amber and ivory. Elsewhere on the same vase, framing a scene of Achilles

Fig. 1.3. Return of Hephaestus: Zeus, Hera on throne. "François Vase," black-figured volute krater, from Chiusi. Florence Museum 4209. 560 B.C. After Furtwängler and Reichhold 1904: pl. 11.

ambushing Troilus at a fountain, Priam sits outside his palace or city on a more modest seat, baldly labeled *thakos* (seat) by the artist, the painter Cleitias (Fig. 1.4).⁴¹

Few documents portray more vividly the distance between sacred and secular authority, where the glamor of the former was never attained in Greek reality by the limited powers of the latter.⁴² Further confusion reigns in scenes from the fall of Troy, where the image of Priam attacked by Neoptolemus is poised on an altar (contributing to the element of sacrilege), in the absence of native Greek familiarity with a throne as a prop in mythohistory.⁴³ Ironically, it was easier to promote a living individual to cult status than to political power: hero-cults were more safely bestowed after death than secular powers could be granted in one's lifetime in a constitutional polis. Herein lie some roots of Hellenistic ruler cult: it was easier to honor an individual with divine privileges than have him rule as king.⁴⁴

One area shared by prehistoric kings (the *wanax*) and early *basileis* involves a role in community ritual. It is no accident that an archon called *basileus* retained responsibility for cults important to the city in Athens, and his wife became the symbolic consort of Dionysos, neatly transferring royal succession, along with other powers, to the gods. Other palatial traditions devolved to the gods: Susan Langdon has explored how elite gift exchange in prehistory was translated into contractual arrangements to attract the favor of the gods.[45] Priesthoods were often hereditary (in Athens, the Eumolpidae and Eteoboutidae) and linked to power (in Samos: Hdt. 3.142), as elite families retained privileges in civic ritual that offered avenues to power and popularity or used them to gain power (Gelon of Sicily, son of Telines the priest: Hdt. 7.153–154). Recent studies have sought to trace how religious activity survived Mycenean palaces and migrated to sanctuaries, new spheres of power in the Early Archaic period.[46]

Ritual activity for Bronze Age kings without extensive other privileges further helps suggest why the sanctuary rather than the polis proper became the locale of intrastate and international power in the Archaic period. In the absence of hereditary political status in civic communities that could be cultivated by foreigners, both Greek and non-Greek, gods and their representatives offered permanent partners for international relations. Difficult for foreign potentates were negotiations with Greeks, in the absence of monarchy: elected or rotating officials were not open to *xenia* (guest-host friendship) relationships or to bribery through gifts. For these reasons, Greek sanctuaries rather than cities attracted foreign largesse, as those who dealt

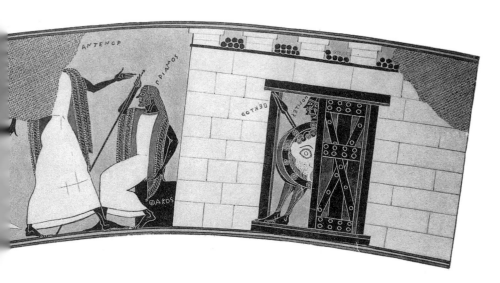

1.4. Priam on *thakos* outside walls, gate of Troy. "François Vase," black-figured volute krater, from ...usi. Florence Museum 4209. After Furtwängler and Reichhold 1904: pl. 11.

with Greeks sought to impress them in other ways.[47] Croesus showers Apollo at Delphi with gold treasure (Hdt. 1.50–54): was his real motive impressing Greeks for the sake of their military support? When the same Lydian king approaches the Spartans for a military alliance (1.69: *xenia kai summachia*), they remember his gift (*dotinē*) to them of Lydian gold for their statue of Apollo at Thornax, when they came to buy it and received it as a favor (*euergesia*). Their return gift to the Lydians was a huge bronze krater with a capacity of 2,500 gallons. The krater never made it to Lydia but ended up in the sanctuary of Hera at Samos. Herodotus reports (1.70–71) that it was stolen or sold en route to Sardis, then dedicated on Samos. But one wonders if the sanctuary played some role in diplomatic transactions between Lydia and Sparta, with the krater being dedicated as some public expression of the alliance it sealed. This episode may reflect a striking instance of foreign kings cultivating Greek cities through gifts to gods, also implied in certain artifacts.[48] Even ambitious Greeks exiled from their own cities used sanctuaries this way. Thus the Alcmeonids endowed the sanctuary at Delphi with a lavish marble pediment for the temple of Apollo in a successful bid for support in returning to power in Athens (Hdt. 5.62).

It is equally significant that when individuals develop *xeniai* with foreign kings, they are tyrants or aristocrats in exile. For example, Croesus won the favor of exiled Alcmaeon at Delphi and later rewards him at Sardis (Hdt. 1.50–54, 6.125); Darius adopts Syloson, exiled brother of the Samian tyrant Polycrates, as reward for his gift of a cloak in Egypt (3.139–140); Hippias married his daughter to the tyrant of Lampsacus (Thuc. 6.59); Pausanias, the Spartan general later accused of Medism and "love of tyranny" (Hdt. 3.48–53), married the daughter of a Persian commander and cousin (if not daughter: Thuc. 1.128) of Darius. Periander of Corinth sent Alyattes of Lydia three hundred eunuchs from Corcyra, captured from noble families and castrated in vengeance, as only a tyrant would do (Hdt. 3.48–53). Here I anticipate Carolyn Dewald, who will trace the fascinating intimacy, in Herodotus if not in history, between tyrants (or those rejected from a polis) and foreign, royal powers and behavior.

In fact, Greeks themselves used sacred places as customs and arrival areas for foreigners. On a famous Corinthian krater in the Vatican (Fig. 1.5), a Greek embassy (Odysseus, Menelaus, and the herald Talthybius) has arrived at Troy to negotiate for the return of Helen: an important diplomatic prelude to the Trojan War from the lost epic poem, the *Cypria*. They do not approach palace or king but wait on the steps of an altar or temenos wall: their first

Fig. 1.5. Greek ambassadors at Troy: embassy for Helen. "Astarita" krater, Museo Gregoriano-Etrusco, Vatican, no. A 565. Ca. 560 B.C. Courtesy of Monumenti Musei e Gallerie Pontificie.

encounter is with cult personnel (absent from the version in *Il.* 3.205–224). For coming to meet them are Theano, chief priestess of Athena at Troy and wife of Antenor (prominent in city ritual: *Il.* 6.297–311), followed by two female servants and an old nurse. A cavalcade of Trojan men on horseback follows at a safe distance, on the other side of the krater.[49] A sanctuary was a safe haven for visitors and travelers, and negotiations between city-states took place there. Many a Greek tragedy makes this clear, most poignantly in the *Supplicants* of Aeschylus, whose political refugees, women caught between Greece and Egypt, seat themselves on an altar just outside the city and in fact appeal to their Classical audience as *metoikoi* (resident aliens).[50] For Greeks and foreigners, a sanctuary is clearly a safe place, while for foreign kings, a Greek sanctuary remained the place to make oneself popular. Philip II of Macedon knew this as well as Croesus, when he negotiated his way into central Greece via the Delphic amphictyony and cultivated favor at Olympia by participating in Panhellenic games and building the lavish Philippeion and its ivory statues.

Reviewing how tyrants embellished Archaic cities, while foreign kings and aristocrats enriched Panhellenic sanctuaries, helps to see in the Classical period the convergence of polis and shrine in the building program of the Acropolis. Just as Athens perfected the fusion of demos and tyrant in a fascinating process Lisa Kallet (this volume) traces, the Acropolis became a fusion of Archaic Panhellenic shrine with imperial city. The citizens themselves acknowledged this, when they agreed to pay the costs rather than have Pericles do so and take full credit, like an Archaic tyrant (Plut. *Per.* 14). Allied tribute to Athens, once a contribution to a religious league centered on Delos, was technically a gift to Athena, now displayed in processions[51] and stored in the Parthenon, as the city absorbed the role of Panhellenic sanctuaries in an imperial stratagem. The Athena Parthenos now wore the wealth of gold once displayed as treasure by a monarch like Croesus. In a much-discussed phrase of Pericles urging Athenians to become *erastai* (lovers) of the city (Thuc. 2.43) rather than lovers of tyranny (as in Archilochus frs.; Hdt. 1.96, 3.53, 5.32), a new demotic *erōmenos* (love object)—however passive and greedy on the comic stage (Ar. *Knights* 732)—displaces Archaic objects of desire as well as fear. In multiple ways examined in the papers that follow, Archaic patterns associated with tyrants are subverted into discourse both praising democracy and dissenting from it, admiring tyrants and warning against them. Here I would add visual persuasion to the verbal arguments marshaled by others. Could this fusion help explain the peculiarly Archaic, aristocratic figures on the Parthenon frieze? If meant to seduce citizens into desiring the city while celebrating a new democratic ideology, young and idealized men on horseback, however reminiscent of oligarchic families and tyrants, may have delivered a more familiar message than the hoplites responsible for victory at Marathon and Salamis. Likewise, the statues of the tyrannicides, unmistakably a pair of aristocratic lovers, could celebrate democracy without a trace of irony (here, see Ober's essay).

PART III. ALIENS, ABROAD: THE MOVE OUT?

In my final section I pick up two different but related threads: how neighboring traditions of royalty shaped Greek images of monarchy and how distant locales devoid of such monarchs also encouraged experiments in leadership alien to native democracy.

The most familiar and fascinating images of kings remained foreign ones. Herodotus calls Midas the first foreigner to honor Greek gods; his gifts at Delphi were displayed next to those of Gyges of Lydia and near those given later by Croesus (1.14). We can detect such foreign interest in Greek gods among Anatolians as early as the Bronze Age, if Mursilis ii indeed needed the "gods of Ahhiya" and of "Lazpa" (Lesbos) to cure his loss of speech (KUB 5.6.ii, lines 57–60). Thus Midas may not have been the first to show interest in Greek gods, and like his royal titles (*wanax, lawagetas*) and his asses' ears (above, nn. 27–28), he inherited this attitude from Bronze Age Anatolian kings. When Greek colonists found dynasties, they become hereditary monarchs in the image of their barbarian hosts and neighbors, as scholars have observed in the image of Arcesilas of Cyrene supervising transactions in wealth like an Egyptian overseer (Fig. 1.6).[52] Haunting all these stories is the grander image of the "Great King" of Persia, who dominated Greek history from Cyrus the first to Darius the last (Fig. 1.7).

As Greek artists and poets imagined them, foreign monarchs in myth and history, like Midas, Priam, or Busiris, became gradually more Persian in appearance, and the same foreign trappings, both fascinating and feared, were applied to native tyrants (on stage, for example) and prehistoric rulers.[53] Meanwhile, the education of proper rulers borrowed as well from alien traditions of elite conduct (Xenophon's *Cyropaedia*). This fascination with royal biography and personality from Herodotus to Xenophon anticipates philosophical discourse (Plato, Aristotle) on ideal rulers, much as Americans fought wars to reject a foreign monarchy, yet remain as fascinated by contemporary royal misadventures as any tabloid reader in England.

Not only does the portrait of the successful and enviable foreign ruler derive from Persia and Lydia, but so does the negative image of kingship. I remain convinced that the tragic pattern of the fall of a great man on stage is generated by historical experience: the fall of foreign dynasts in Lydia and Persia best exemplified in the fate of the Lydian king Croesus (Fig. 1.8). At this point the timing of the Persian Wars is either decisive or unfortunate: our first fallen hero on stage (Aeschylus' *Persians* is our oldest surviving tragedy) also happens to be a foreign king, Xerxes. Moreover, the first Greek king whose rule and image are tainted with Oriental imagery is the same poet's Agamemnon, literally caught in Oriental trappings (see Seaford's analysis in this volume).

Turning this around, the exception to Greek patterns of strong collective leadership, disrupted by tyranny, clearly stems from abroad. Away from

Fig. 1.6. Arcesilas of Cyrene, loading of cargo (silphion?). Laconian cup by the Arcesilas Painter, ca. 560 B.C. Paris: Cabinet des Médailles 189. Courtesy of Bibliothèque Nationale de France, Paris.

home, in Greek colonies in Magna Graecia, the northern Aegean or Black Sea, and North Africa, tyranny makes a fresh start, as it were, without the usual obstacles to advancement. I have already mentioned Cyprus and northern Greece, where a form of monarchy flourished without competition from strong local communities or chieftains: the *wanax* without competing claims by any *basileis* (although both titles were absorbed into a single dynasty in one instance in Cyprus). These settings nourish monarchs who become patrons of poets (Pindar, Aeschylus, and Euripides) in Sicily and Macedon and attract the encomia of Solon (Hdt. 5.113) and Isocrates for monarchs on Cyprus and the counsel of Plato (as Morgan traces in her essay, this volume). In such "barbarian" locales, the absence of local land-based aristocracies, tenacious in their genealogies as old as prehistory, allowed new dynasties to take root and made founder heroes and their successors (e.g., Fig. 1.6) the substitutes for mythical king lists cherished at home. This also makes them closer associates of foreign kings, as Dewald argues in her essay (this volume) on tyrants in Herodotus. In one famous example, the Macedonians Amyntas and his son Alexander I married Alexander's sister to a Persian, Bubares, whose son then ruled a city in Phrygia (Hdt. 5.18–21, 8.136). Did the Persians find these northerners more congenial to royal manipulation in forming their satrapy of "Skudra" than Ionians and central Greeks? From the south, Athenian activity in the northern Aegean, whether Peisistratids in the Troad or the Philaids in Thrace, gave tyrants and tyrant-wannabes a chance to flex monarchical powers abroad (the "heart of darkness" model). Here motives are largely commercial and capitalist: these areas offered resources for enrichment that could lead to tyranny, as they enabled Peisistratus to return to power in Athens with a private army or recapture Sigeum in the Troad as a family fiefdom. In this volume, Kallet defines tyrants as men with means (literally, to raise and sustain an army),

1.7. King Darius I, scenes at Persian court. Made ca. 340 B.C. Darius Painter, name vase: Naples 3253, n Canosa. After Furtwängler and Reichhold 1909: pl. 88.

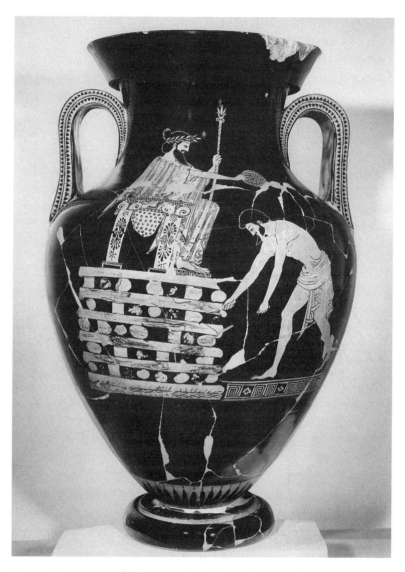

Fig. 1.8. King Croesus of Lydia on pyre. Red-figured neck amphora, Myson.
Ca. 490–480 B.C. Courtesy of Musée du Louvre, Département des Antiquités
Grecques, Étrusques et Romaines, G 197. Réunion des musées nationaux.

the source of such means often lay abroad in locales independent of polis or peers. Even in Greek colonies sanctioned by a demos, the myth and cult of a founder hero celebrated individual autonomy that was soon subverted into an image of "collective sovereignty."[54]

What effect does the unchallenged rule of such non-Greek or meta-Greek kings have on political thought and practice at home? How does a "tyrant" celebrated by Pindar differ from an aristocratic victor from Aegina or Thebes? How close in terminology and image are foreign king and Greek tyrant? How early does the dangerous slippage noted by the fourth century (see Morgan's paper, this volume) become a matter of practice and discourse? I pose these problems as questions, deliberately, in seeking to redirect modern discourse "outwards," as Morgan does in her investigation on Plato and Isocrates in this volume. Can we keep our perspective open to events and cases outside Athens to prevent all discussion from collapsing into the inevitable polarities of Athenian discourse? Dominated by critical and rhetorical sources of Classical Athens, we should recall that Aristotle surveyed the constitutions of 158 different city-states, a depressing reminder of how confined we are, in Greek history and political thought, to one city. Measures against tyrants in distant cities (see Ober and Raaflaub, this volume, on laws enacted by Erythrae in Ionia), even if coerced by Athens, are another reminder of the wider world that shared the same experience and specter of tyranny.

To conclude with one final thought on Greek tyrants, it is the anomaly of a culture, so peculiar in history, which resisted? avoided? never knew? monarchy in government, if never democratic enough for modern tastes. At the same time, the paradox with which I began—the Greeks never had real kings yet imagined them incessantly—is matched by modern experience. Here I mean not just American fascination with the British royal family it rejected as rulers two centuries ago but the imposition of kingship on Greece itself. After liberation from Ottoman rule, a Bavarian dynasty was installed in Athens, and architects designed palaces for them on the Acropolis. King Otto entered Athens in the same century in which Queen Victoria and the Kaiser dominated Europe, just before Minos and Agamemnon became targets of archaeology, which is where I began. And just as *wanakes* reigned briefly in Mycenean Greece, a national referendum eliminated kingship from Greece in 1974, after a similarly brief reign (ca. 150 years). If the mirage of tyranny is our focus, its chief partner a demos, it changed its shape from an accident of aristocratic *stasis* to an image both feared and desired, still informed by contact with imaginary kings.

[1] Here I follow categories defined by Max Weber, modified by Michael Mann (Mann 1986: 22–28), as recommended by Ian Morris in his comments at the conference.

[2] Raaflaub 1986: 38; Barceló 1993: 36, 38. An archaeological twist on these circular arguments compares the architecture of early "regal" buildings in Greece and Italy (Scheffer 1990). But Building F in the Agora at Athens (probably a workshop: Papadopoulos 2003: ch. 5) was itself rehabilitated as the house of Peisistratus on the analogy of the Regia at Rome.

[3] Drews 1983; Carlier 1984.

[4] Homeric kingship: see Lenz 1993. I. Morris 1986 (following Snodgrass' doubts on an "historical" Homeric society) is an important corrective to treating Homeric society as a reflection of an historical age rather than of specific social ambitions.

[5] For a recent summary of these explorations, see Fitton 1995.

[6] See especially the essays in Rehak 1995 and Laffineur and Niemeier 1995.

[7] Coulomb 1979 and Niemeier 1988 have reconfigured the "king" as the legs of a figure moving left, the torso of a bull-grappler, and the head of a sphinx, while Shaw 1999 sees the figure as a victorious athlete (a successful bull-leaper?) crowned with lilies.

[8] Hallager 1985; Davis 1995. See Laffineur and Niemeier 1995: 380 for a discussion of the meaning of this figure.

[9] For a drawing and (different) analysis of the Mycenae shrine fresco, see Marinatos 1988.

[10] Pelon 1995 compares the throne room at Mari and other images to Minoan art.

[11] Palaima 1995: 132–133.

[12] Mirié 1979; Niemeier 1986.

[13] Lenz 1993: 56, n. 9, points out that a hearth, not a throne, is consistent in Mycenean "megaron" halls.

[14] Hooker 1979, 1987.

[15] Palaima 1995; cf. Shelmerdine 1999.

[16] Carlier 1984: 40–134, esp. 130–132; Ruijgh 1999; Lupack 2001.

[17] Donlan (following Lejeune 1965, Maddoli 1970) 1970, 1989: 13–15, 18–20; Carlier 1984: 130; Deger-Jalkotzy 1995; Shelmerdine 1999: 24. Ian Morris (2000: 100–101) is skeptical about a prehistoric **damos,** following Finley (1957: 158–159), but historians as well as prehistorians must come to terms with its implications for civic power.

[18] Sutton 1970, ch. 10, for a close analysis of this text, its draft, and its controversies.

[19] Deger-Jalkotzy 1995, and earlier arguments (Van Effenterre 1985).

[20] For a discussion of this ceremony, see Wright 1996: 294–295. For the date of the Camp-stool fresco (from the type of cup depicted, "not current before mature LMIIIA"), see

Hood 2000: 193, 206. A. Evans first dated (1935; IV. 2, 379–390) the same cup to the Shaft Grave period, based on a restoration of the fresco now corrected by Hood.

[21] McCallum 1987; Carter 1995: 294–296; Wright 1996: 295.

[22] Killen 1994; Mazarakis-Ainian 1997, on communal feasting; cf. Palaima (n. 11).

[23] Atchity and Barber 1987; Finkelberg 1991 (cf. I. Morris 1986 on Homeric marriage); Figes 1976: 36–41; these patterns not noted by Griffith 1998.

[24] On priestesses, see Turner 1983, esp. ch. 2 on inheritances, and Kron 1996.

[25] See Bryce 1998: 394–407.

[26] Koehl 1995.

[27] Lejeune 1969; de Graaf 1989.

[28] Hawkins and Morpurgo Davies 1998 discuss this Luwian onomastic. I shall argue the connection to Midas in a forthcoming article.

[29] Drews 1983: 71–74.

[30] For an excellent discussion of Cypriote kingship in its Mycenean, Phoenician, and Persian contexts, see Zournatzi 1996, now supplemented by essays in Buitron-Oliver and Herscher 1997. Cf. Woodard 1997: 217–224 on continuities of Mycenean culture on Cyprus.

[31] As argued by Rupp 1988; against Demand 1997 on Cypriote origins for the polis.

[32] Cambitoglou and Papadopoulos 1993; Tartaron 1996, 73–95 and 435–448 on Mycenean Epirus; and papers in Best and De Vries 1989 (Thrace), Phroussou 1999.

[33] Wright 1995, and discussion in *Politeia*.

[34] Nagy 1996: ch. 3, on the Peisistratid recension as a "definitive" phase for epic.

[35] As argued by I. Morris 1986.

[36] Lenz 1993; Mazarakis-Ainian 1997.

[37] As argued by Van Effenterre 1985 and Deger-Jalkotzy 1995, who emphasize a Bronze Age polis as kernel of the later city-state. Lenz 1993, ch. 7, likewise emphasizes origins for the polis both earlier (in the Dark Ages) and later, in the sixth century, than the overemphasized eighth century. Cf. Muhly 1999 on the decline of the Dark Age as a historical barrier; Thalmann 1997: ch. 5 and Ruzé 1989.

[38] The Geometric settlement under excavation at Skala Oropou (Attica), with its apsidal buildings and metalworking establishments, adds greatly to our view of such early communities: *Archaeological Reports 1996–1997*: 14–15; reports in *To Ergon* since 1996.

[39] Burkert 1995 analyzes well the manipulation of king lists in Greek tradition, under the influence of those in Lydia, to create the illusion of a venerable past.

[40] Conflict between heroic and royal lineages is discussed by Finkelberg 1991: 304, 313.

[41] Compare the square seat of Priam (or Poseidon?) on the Archaic pediment of the temple of Artemis, Corfu: Rodenwaldt 1939: pls. 1–2, 25. At the conference, Raaflaub compared Priam's seat to Homeric descriptions of ξεστοῖσιν λάεσσι ("polished stone [seats]").

[42] Compare how Dionysus absorbs other privileges of authority or Prometheus suffers the tyrannical behavior of Zeus, both in tragedy (see Seaford's essay, this volume).

[43] S. Morris 1995, citing earlier work by Touchefeu.

[44] Price 1984: 27–40 captures well how Hellenistic ruler cults accommodated the alien institution of monarchy in a Greek city, and allowed citizens to classify and represent power in a way that was Greek. Compare founder cults in Greek colonies (below, n. 54).

[45] Langdon 1987. The gods also inherit perfumed and oiled clothing once reserved for the elite (Shelmerdine 1995) among other divine privileges once mortal, but royal.

[46] C. Morgan 1996; Sinn 1996.

[47] Linders 1987 on sanctuaries as substitutes for sovereign guardians of treasure; S. Morris 1992: xvi. In Hellenistic times, building donations are redirected at cities (most famously by the Attalids of Pergamon to Athens) in an age of monarchy and empire.

[48] S. Morris 1992 (citing earlier work by Muscarella); Sinn 1996.

[49] Beazley 1957, a visual document not considered in Raaflaub 1997b: 4–5, 21, to whose analysis of the early Greek community add Carlier's Mycenean **ke-ro-si-ja** (*gerousia*): Carlier 1984: 112, n. 649, and 1995.

[50] Bakewell 1997.

[51] See Wesenberg 1995: 168–172 for the suggestion that the *hydriaphoroi* on the Parthenon frieze are carrying Athenian tribute in the form of silver coin stored in hydriai.

[52] Boardman 1999: 149. The king (or a *dokimos anēr*) of Cyrene married his daughter to Pharaoh Amasis of Egypt: Hdt. 2.181.

[53] Miller 1997, 2000, for the progressive Medism of Priam, Midas, and Busiris.

[54] McGlew 1993, ch. 5, "Narratives of Autonomy: Greek Founders," explores the relationship between the founder and tyrant as "alternate images of power" (173); cf. Ogden 1997.

CAROLYN DEWALD

FORM AND CONTENT: THE QUESTION OF
TYRANNY IN HERODOTUS

At the moment there does not seem to be much scholarly consensus on the
Archaic Greek tyrants and what they meant to their cities' political development.[1] The tyrant as a moral monster and tyranny as the lowest form of
government, autocracy unconstrained by law or custom, was a fourth-century
construct. Plato, Aristotle, and their contemporaries fashioned it out of earlier
hostile formulations of the idea of the tyrant, but they were also responding
to early fourth-century political contexts and theoretical issues.[2] When we
turn back to the extremely scanty and mostly poetic contemporary evidence
for the Archaic Greek tyrannies themselves, the picture becomes no clearer.
It is not certain where the word *tyrannos* itself came from or what its original semantic field was.[3] Nor is our sense of a general development in Archaic
Greek political structures as definite as it might be. There is little convinc-
ing evidence for the widespread phenomenon of an eighth-century *basileus*
as a reigning monarch unseated by aristocratic clans. It is also hard to document the specifics of a seventh-century "hoplite revolution"; in particular, we
can no longer link that revolution with some sort of newly enfranchised or
newly wealthy body of citizens forcing change on a traditional aristocracy.[4]
Whether and/or how the Archaic tyrannies were relevant to the development
of a civic consciousness, the rule of law, the creation of mass politics, or even
a money economy—all these issues currently remain under discussion.[5]

Given the uncertain parameters of what was after all a historical phenomenon of real interest, it is not surprising that historians turn with particular attention to Herodotus. Herodotus gives us the first extensive prose
narrative about the Archaic tyrannies, and he is the first extant Greek author
to describe them in their social and political contexts. But historiographers
continue to debate whether Herodotus' *Histories* present a portrait of the Archaic and Early Classical tyrannies that is systematically hostile (in effect,

anticipating the more elaborately constructed schemata of Plato and Aristotle) or whether his *logoi*, stories, about tyrants and tyranny do something else that is more complicated and ambiguous.[6] The problem of tyranny in Herodotus is a particularly useful and interesting one, because it allows us to look closely at some of the ways in which narrative history shapes its material and in shaping it, necessarily creates patterns in the data it presents.

Here we will first look at how the *Histories* taken as a whole produce a strongly negative pattern of despotism and what it does to people and institutions. In this development the Archaic Greek tyrants certainly play a role: they share in the negative thematic connotations of the pattern of autocratic tyranny and its coercive powers. But if we focus instead on the portraits that Herodotus constructs of the Greek tyrants as individual actors in events, the picture that emerges is rather one of idiosyncratic personal achievement of the very sort that Herodotus thinks large-scale autocracy threatens. Thus if we are trying to tease out the notion of Greek tyranny in Herodotus, the foregrounded portraits of tyrants in the individual *logoi* and the diachronic, larger thematic patterns about monarchical autocracy in general do not carry the same message, although Greek tyrants figure in both. The resulting ambiguity or doubleness of Herodotus' treatment of despotism and despots is encoded in the basic doubleness of Herodotus' narrative structures. As Charles Olson, one of the founding fathers of postmodernism, opined: "Form is never more than an expression of content."[7] Herodotus' work is both an ongoing narrative with substantial thematic continuity linking together its various parts and a paratactic progression of individual *logoi*. The tension or inherent contradiction between the overarching structure of the ongoing narrative and the idiosyncratic autonomy of the individual *logoi* qua *logoi* both reproduces and reflects upon the tension between despotism as an organizing theme in the *Histories* and the individual portraits of highly autonomous Greek tyrants within the narrative.

THE TYRANT AS DESPOT

The case for Herodotus' deliberately negative presentation of tyrants and tyranny has four basic components: the despotic template, eastern despotism as a structuring device in the *Histories,* the negative uses of *tyrannos* and its cognates, and the treatment of the Greek tyrants themselves, all of which figure as parts of an overall thematic development.

THE DESPOTIC TEMPLATE

In three extended passages, the *Histories* of Herodotus present a static, quasi-systematized picture of the drawbacks of autocratic, monarchical government. The three passages are found in books 1, 3, and 5; in all of them, the absolute rule of a single man is referred to as a tyranny, and it is presented as a negative phenomenon.

THE DEIOCES MODEL In book 1 Herodotus creates a diachronic but extremely schematic portrait of how autocratic rule was first established in Media. At the conclusion of the Croesus episode, Herodotus backtracks to give the developments in early seventh-century Media that led to the reign of Cyrus, grandson of Astyages the Mede. He begins by describing how the Medes first came to be ruled by a king, Deioces (1.96–100). By telling a story of how Median kingship arose, Herodotus also tacitly analyzes and critiques the development of monarchical power.[8] Without assuming we know what the word *tyrannis* means in the Deioces story, we should note that Herodotus uses it three times in this brief passage, twice at the beginning and once at its end.

Deioces is a clever Mede who, Herodotus says, returns the Medes to tyranny after they have won freedom from Assyrian rule (1.96.1). Deioces himself is *erastheis tyrannidos,* "in love with tyranny."[9] He first makes himself indispensable as a just judge in legal cases but claims that he has no time to do anything else, and he quits, because there is nothing in it for him personally. His supporters call for him to be king so that the country will be well governed, and the rest of them can go about their business. Deioces is then chosen king (*[hoi Mēdoi] . . . peithousi heōutous basileuesthai*), and he isolates himself from his peers (*hoi homēlikes*) so that they will not be tempted to plot against him, thinking him no better than themselves.[10] Immediately he establishes a fixed seat of government, gets a bodyguard, and develops a royal stronghold, Ecbatana, with seven circles of differently colored walls around it. He becomes inaccessible to the people with a series of regulations. Lawsuits now must be submitted in writing, and a system of spies is instigated so that although still dispensing justice, he does so in a harsh and despotic fashion (*chalepos,* 1.100.1).[11]

The various aspects of the Deioces story are articulated as a series of causally connected steps in a historical process, indeed almost as a recipe for how to found an autocratic government. The story begins with the need for justice and one man's desire to rule autocratically; it ends with the acknowledgment that with an efficient system of justice administered by one man is likely to come distance between the people and their ruler, and oppression. Thus it articulates a paradox about monarchical justice itself: by allowing one individual to dispense justice, the people also in effect create one man who operates in a fashion that is distant from themselves and independent of the system he enforces. If they want a legal system with teeth in it, they have to acquiesce in the harsh rule of the man who controls it.[12] We should note that this power has not been exercised violently or illegally. Its development is even ostentatiously a matter of persuasion and rational decision-making. But the result is a permanent distance established between ruler and ruled and consequent oppression. This begins an important thematic movement in the *Histories:* what Herodotus calls tyranny here is not the result of personal violence but of systemic changes that have been undertaken to protect and extend the power of the ruler. The word Herodotus uses to mark the phenomenon at both the beginning and end of the account is *tyrannis.*

The placement of the Deioces story within the *Histories* is also significant, since it acts as a marker of transition. With the Deioces episode we have left the sphere of Croesus, the genial although misguided philo-Hellene Lydian who conversed with Solon. Deioces represents a different sort of autocracy, formed further north and east in the harsh uplands of the Iranian plateau. The idea of a distanced, harsh, tyrannical rule developed in this passage will define the outlines of the reigns of the four Persian kings to come, Cyrus, Cambyses, Darius, and Xerxes. Through their subordinates, hereafter Cyrus the Persian and his heirs will enforce a sterner and more systematic rule on the Greeks as well as their many other subjects (1.141, 153, 177). In this sense, the Deioces story is the first installment of Herodotus' description of the evils of autocratic rule, what we may call "the despotic template."[13] In this version of it, a *tyrannis* is a bureaucratic autocracy, and it is marked by an institutional harshness and distance between ruler and ruled.

THE CONSTITUTIONAL DEBATE The second version of the despotic template, and its most classic formulation, occurs in book 3.[14] Like the Deioces episode, it contains as an implicit premise the notion that at base, people (at least, the important people) choose their form of government. After the death of Cambyses and the murder of the usurpers, in 522 B.C., the seven Persian co-conspirators meet together to decide what government to adopt for Persia. Three of them, Otanes, Megabyzus, and Darius, take an active part in the debate (3.80–82). Two, Otanes and Megabyzus, criticize autocracy, and they call it both monarchy and tyranny.

Otanes (3.80) argues against monarchy and for democracy. He asks a central question: "How could single rule (*mounarchiē*) be a well-ordered matter (*chrēma katērtēmenon*), when it is possible for the ruler to do what he wants and not be accountable?"[15] Otanes is not particularly concerned with some of the major issues of the Deioces model, the harshness of despotic rule, for instance, or the distance between ruler and ruled. His definition of the problem is that the monarch or single ruler is himself unconstrained (*aneuthunos*). The lack of restraint reveals itself in several ways: in personality, the autocrat is full of hubris and envy; in act, he violates ancestral custom, outrages women, and kills people without trial; in judgment, he prefers evil men to good, welcomes slander, and despises flatterers while he resents those who treat him only with due respect: "Although a man who is a tyrant ought to be without envy, since he has everything good, the opposite is true concerning his fellow citizens" (3.80.4).

It is not surprising, given the immediate narrative context, that Otanes makes the judgment he does, since Cambyses' reign, just ended, has exemplified most of these traits. In the debate with his peers after Cambyses' death, however, Otanes' picture does not stand uncontested. Megabyzus, though agreeing with Otanes' assessment of autocracy (*tyrannis*), goes on to argue for aristocracy and dismisses Otaines' favorable picture of democracy (*plēthos archon*) as mob rule. At least, Megabyzus says, the autocrat (*tyrannos*) has some plan in mind when he acts, while the *plēthos* or *homilos,* the crowd, is always rushing witlessly hither and yon, *cheimarrōi potamōi ikelos,* like a torrential river. It is rather the rule of the best men deliberating together that will, Megabyzus thinks, bring forth the best counsel.[16]

Otanes argues for democracy and Megabyzus for aristocracy, but it is the third debater, Darius, who has the last word. Darius agrees with Megabyzus' criticism of popular rule, but he criticizes Megabyzus' portrait of aristocracy, called by Darius *oligarchiē.* In an oligarchy, Darius says, there is rivalry and consequent strife, leading to *stasis,* and it comes out as *mounarchiē,* rule of the autocrat, in the end.[17] Rule of the people also leads ultimately to *mounarchiē,* because evil is done by the faction of bad men in power, someone rises up to champion the demos, and then he becomes a single ruler. If one simply picks the best man as monarch or single ruler in the first place, one has done far better than one would accepting the monarch that is the product of rule of the people or rule of an oligarchy. Besides, he ends by asking, which system brought us Persians our freedom? *Mounarchiē* (3.82.4).

Herodotus is not very interested anecdotally in the workings of democracies and oligarchies in the *Histories,* but he is interested in autocracy.[18] The observations Otanes makes about the lack of restraint intrinsic to autocracy/tyranny, and the violent thoughts and acts that flow from it, become an important thematic constant as the main narrative of the *Histories* continues, since this behavior is found not just in Cambyses but in other despots as well, Darius himself among them. For after the Constitutional Debate, the Persians do vote for monarchy. The procedure through which despotism is chosen and the individual despot selected is, if not democratic, elaborately planned and agreed upon by all the co-conspirators. But in order to become the individual chosen as king, Darius has initially violated ancestral custom by lying and even justifying the need to lie (3.72); he then uses a trick dreamed up by his groom.[19] And although it is not narrated until Herodotus has interrupted his narrative to survey the gigantic tax base that the Persian empire attained under Darius, the first recorded act of Darius' reign is the killing of one of his co-conspirators, Intaphrenes, along with much of the man's family (3.119).[20]

The Constitutional Debate is not presented by Herodotus in the *Histories* as something intended definitively to solve the puzzle of the best form of rule or to criticize autocracy alone. In context it is if anything an exercise in irony, because all the negative arguments of Otanes, Megabyzus, and Darius are relatively cogent, while none of the positive ones convince in theory or are borne out by subsequent events. Darius' argument for monarchy is to the point only if one can, anticipating Plato, pick the best human being possible as king.[21]

THE SPEECH OF SOCLES Where the Deioces model of the despot is one of bureaucratic harshness and distance, and Otanes' argument focuses on the despot's lack of restraint and subsequent violence of thought and deed, the third theoretical critique of tyranny is harder to interpret unequivocally. It is the only one of the three overtly to concern genuine Greek tyrants. As the Lacedaemonians convene their allies, hoping to lead a movement to reinstate tyranny in Athens in the last years of the sixth century, a Corinthian by the name of Socles gets up and gives a long speech about the Corinthian tyrants Cypselus and Periander, who had ruled Corinth ca. 657–587 B.C. The purpose of Socles' speech (5.92) is to discourage the Lacedaemonians and their allies from reinstating tyranny in Athens: "If it seems to you to be so useful that cities be ruled by tyrants, set up a tyrant for yourselves first and then think about setting one up for others." Socles' approach is anecdotal; he gives a vivid and highly selective history of the Cypselid presence in Corinth.[22] His implicit point is, like that of Otanes, a structural one.[23] It is not an intrinsically evil personality that makes the tyrant and the tyrannical family bad, in Socles' thinking. The real horror of it is the inevitability of a process. In Socles' sequence of anecdotes, tyranny is like kudzu in one's garden or like Aeschylus' lion cub: it grows, like the lion cub, from charming infant weakness to mature domination of others. When grown, tyranny is unjust and bloodthirsty as well as extravagantly wasteful of resources.[24]

A number of ironic elements arise from the way this speech is integrated into the surrounding narrative. The central irony is pinpointed by Socles himself: the freedom-loving Spartans, mirabile dictu, are imposing tyranny on others! But for Herodotus' audiences it must also have been odd to have the Corinthians depicted as vigorously protecting Athenian democracy in about 504, since by the 430s, Athens and Corinth were sworn enemies (something the exiled Hippias predicts, 5.93.1). Socles' speech seems to have succeeded in its objective. Because Socles speaks *eleutherōs*, like a free man, the allies refuse in the end to help the Lacedaemonians to mount an allied campaign against Athens. Actual tyrannical rapine and murder directed against Corinthian citizens, although certainly mentioned in Socles' speech, are much less vivid than the depictions of trickster behavior on the part of Cypselus' mother, Thrasybulus, and Periander himself; this is a point to which we shall return below.[25]

The final irony to the Socles speech is one that remains entirely unspoken by Herodotus but obvious to his audiences throughout Greece and Magna Graecia in the 440s and 430s: in the late 500s Socles is arguing against the imposition of tyranny in Athens, but it is Athens itself that has become a tyrant state in Herodotus' own day. Herodotus' interest in the structural implications of large empires and the theme of tyrannical despotism throughout the *Histories* may in fact have seemed to many of his audiences quite directly, even if tacitly, aimed at contemporary Athens.[26]

Although their dynamics are somewhat different, the vivid accounts of tyranny in books 1, 3, and 5 all focus on a variety of evils incurred in autocratic rule. As we have seen, only the last of the three, and that ambiguously, concerns tyrants as Plato and Aristotle define them. Deioces in book 1 is a "constitutional monarch" and the Constitutional Debate in book 3 concerns Persian kingship. But it is important to acknowledge an underlying thematic coherence. In all three passages, a ruler unconstrained in his power is called a *tyrannos* and/or his rule a *tyrannis*. Negative aspects of this form of individual absolute rule are more or less systematically explored, so that the resonances of these stories are bound to affect our understanding of other passages in which Herodotus uses the term "tyrant."[27] Moreover, all three occur at important points of pause in the narrative: the Deioces story, as the introduction to the four Achaemenid reigns that will constitute the narrative backbone of the *Histories;* the Constitutional Debate, as the introduction to the reign of Darius, the most powerful Achaemenid and the one who first systematically turned his attention toward the conquest of the Greeks; the Socles speech, as part of the (itself highly ironic) introduction to a long, complicated, and ultimately ambiguous narrative about the growth of Athenian democracy. This in turn is the prelude to the Athenians' acceptance of the proposal of Aristagoras the Milesian, which will eventually bring the wrath of the Persians down on all of Greece (5.97.3).

The three passages make different but connected points: the distance between the despotic ruler and the people he rules, the autocratic ruler's violent lack of restraint, and the tendency of despotism to begin by looking innocent and attractive and end by brutality and the wasting of resources. Spaced as they are, the three portraits of the negative value of autocratic rule suggest that they have been carefully placed to articulate facets of a basic theme, and one that provides a dynamic continuity in Herodotus' narrative: the tendency of powerful autocratic regimes to become more powerful still and to transgress more and more against the persons of those they rule in the process.[28]

EASTERN DESPOTISM AS A STRUCTURING DEVICE IN THE *HISTORIES*

As we have already seen in looking at the despotic template, "tyranny" is a concept that involves far more than Herodotus' depiction of Archaic Greek tyrants. The very first episode of the *Histories,* concerning Croesus king of Lydia, introduces Croesus as *tyrannos* of all *ethnē,* people, west of the Halys river (1.6). The use of the term *tyrannos* to describe Croesus (its first usage, we may note, in the *Histories*) is suggestive, because immediately we launch into the story of Croesus' great-great grandfather, Gyges, a former spear-carrier who chose to kill King Candaules and take the rule of Lydia (1.10). The narrative context almost begs us as readers to ask at the outset the following question: is Croesus called a *tyrannos* in 1.6 simply because *tyrannis* was originally a Lydian term for autocratic monarchical rule, used by Archilochus in a poem in close connection with Gyges himself (fr. 19.3 West), and for Herodotus' contemporaries, virtually another word for monarchy? Or rather because the whole Croesus story will hinge on the fact that Croesus is

Gyges' great-great grandson and will have to pay for Gyges' assumption of an illegitimate rule? In other words, does the use of *tyrannos* in 1.6 by itself foreshadow the violence and betrayal depicted in the Gyges story? Herodotus does not answer this question directly. He does say that after the slaying of Candaules, the Mermnads, Croesus' family, hold the *tyrannida* of Lydia (1.14) and that Gyges' son Ardys is *tyrannos* of Lydia in turn (1.15). The first extended *logos* of the *Histories* describes how Croesus must pay for Gyges' mistake in judgment by losing his kingdom to Cyrus; perhaps Herodotus chooses to introduce the Mermnads in general and Croesus in particular as *tyrannoi* to suggest associations of illegitimacy and usurpation that already in Archaic Greek poetry cluster around the term.[29]

I lowever, it is not just the descendants of Gyges who are called *tyrannoi*. As we have already seen, in the *Histories'* more theoretical discussions of despotism, it is not crucial for Herodotus' understanding of regimes he calls "tyrannies" that the accession of the ruler in question be irregular. It is much more important that the rule is autocratic. Within the story of Croesus, Candaules, the man Gyges kills, is also called a *tyrannos* in 1.7, despite the 505 years that his family has ruled in Lydia. A little later, the Medes Cyaxares (1.73) and Deioces (1.96, 100) and the Babylonian Labynetus (1.77.2) are called *tyrannoi* as well, and Astyages' rule is called a *tyrannis* by Harpagus (1.109). Thus in the early parts of book 1, a number of important and largely legitimate eastern potentates—two Lydians, three Medes, and a Babylonian—are all called "tyrants." The subsequent Persian kings Cyrus, Cambyses, Darius, and Xerxes will not be called *tyrannoi* in the narrative, although Xerxes refers to his own reign as a tyranny in 7.52. Their behavior as autocrats, however, will create the central and unifying theme of eastern despotic imperialism in the *Histories,* an ongoing pattern in which the Greek tyrants will play a smaller and much more ambiguous role.

Part of what the *Histories* explore, in the stories of Croesus and subsequent eastern monarchs, is a broad picture of what kinds of things happen to those who wield vast autocratic power and what casts of mind they tend to have.[30] If we "look to the end," as Solon teaches us to do (1.32), it is worth noting that the largest outlines of the narratives of Croesus, Cyrus, Cambyses, Darius, and Xerxes reinforce some aspects of the despotic template. All the five major monarchs in the *Histories* begin with great power, overreach themselves, and end unhappily, as Herodotus portrays them. A brief outline of each career shows this trajectory in action.

Croesus of course neglects Solon's good advice and believes he is the happiest man in the world. He loses his son, is humiliated by Cyrus, and is compelled by the force of his changed circumstances first to unman his own people and ultimately to flatter and grovel in fear of his new master, Cambyses. We learn at the description of his dedications that he has had an enemy "carded" to death (1.92). We last see him scuttling from the room in fear that Cambyses will shoot him, as he has already shot his cup bearer (3.36).

Cyrus, a wonderfully successful king for most of his reign, overreaches himself (misled by his phenomenal earlier successes, 1.204) and is decapitated, with his head stuck in a bag filled with blood, by the warrior queen of the Massagetes, Tomyris (1.214).

His son, Cambyses, most completely fulfills all the items in Otanes' picture of the despotic template. Although conqueror of Egypt, he proceeds to outrage Egyptian custom. He marries his own sisters (legally, since his royal judges declare that although there is no law that a brother may marry a sister, there is a law that the king of the Persians can do what he wants, 3.31). He also engages in a disastrous expedition against the Ethiopians, murders his brother and one of his sisters, and violently mistreats an Egyptian god (3.25–32). Cambyses dies with the Persian state in chaos.

Darius, the most competent and successful of the five, nonetheless kills one of his seven co-conspirators (3.119) and fails completely in Scythia (4.134–135). Although he quells the Ionian revolt, the last thing Herodotus tells us about him before moving on to the reign of Xerxes is that he dies with both Egypt and Greece unsubdued (7.4).[31]

The final monarch of the five, Xerxes, fails miserably in his attempt to conquer Greece, because of a series of serious misjudgments brought on by bad advice (and also by the will of the gods). He is last seen trying to seduce his sister-in-law and having an affair with her daughter (married to Darius, Xerxes' own son and heir). At the end Xerxes is forced by his own misdeeds to kill his brother's whole family (9.108–113).[32]

As these five reigns develop, we see a basic misjudgment arising in all of them that has to do with the distance from others that also insulates the autocratic ruler from hearing good advice, or acting on it if by chance it is heard. In Herodotus' narrative this misjudgment is definitively associated with imperialism. Croesus misjudges and tries to conquer Cyrus and the Persians; Cyrus, misled by his successes, tries to conquer the Massagetes; Cambyses does conquer Egypt but goes mad in the process, embarking on a bizarre attempt to conquer the Ethiopians that results in cannibalism among his troops and then leaving for Persia to stem a usurpation that has apparently succeeded while he is away in Egypt; Darius tries to conquer Scythia and although he subdues the Ionians, dies with Egypt and Greece left unsubdued; Xerxes loses the Persian Wars and kills a cadet branch of his own royal family. The lack of judgment exhibited by the despot is, in Herodotus' eyes, the most important explanation for the failure of Xerxes' massive campaign against Greece in the Persian Wars.

Something in the nature of autocratic imperialism prevents despots from taking seriously their own fallibility and mortality and also the real dynamics motivating others. Autocratic rulers misjudge the motives and strengths of uncivilized but hard opponents: most notably, Tomyris the Massagete in book 1, the Ethiopians in book 3, the Scythians in book 4, and the Greeks of books 7 through 9. Moreover, talented but opportunistic clients or underlings like Syloson, Democedes, Histiaeus and Aristagoras, the Peisistratids and Mardonius repeatedly flatter the autocratic ruler and/or manipulate the imperial structure to their own private advantage.[33] If we fit this pattern of imperial misjudgment in practice together with the analyses articulated in the despotic template, it is clear that Herodotus thinks the personal failures of despotism occur for structural reasons: the way despotism works leads it to overreach itself.

OTHER NEGATIVE USES OF THE TERMS *TYRANNOS, TYRANNEUEIN, TYRANNIS*

Herodotus additionally presents, scattered through his text, a number of quasi-aphoristic observations, either his own or enunciated by various actors in events. These observations take as a given the negative aspects of tyranny developed in the larger despotic template and the plot line formed by eastern despotism. They thus reinforce their thematic importance. Some of these aphorisms, of course, occur in the Constitutional Debate and Socles' speech. One of Otanes' observations we have already looked at: "How could single rule (*mounarchiē*) be a well-ordered matter (*chrēma katērtēmenon*), when it is possible for the ruler to do what he wants and not be accountable?" Otanes goes on to say: "Put the best man of all in this position, and he will have thoughts unlike his normal ones. Arrogant violence arises from his good fortune, and envy is there from the beginning in human nature." "Tyranny" and "monarchy" are used interchangeably by Otanes, and he thinks both of them a terrible idea. A little later, he states, "Now, although a man who is a tyrant ought to be without envy, since he has everything good, the opposite is true concerning his fellow citizens. He envies the existence of the best men, while he takes pleasure in the worst of them. He is unparalleled at taking in slander, and his own behavior is the most outrageous of all." Socles, in book 5, takes up this theme, stating that "there is nothing in human experience more unjust or bloodthirsty than tyranny."[34]

Socles is talking about tyranny in a Greek and civic context. Other comparable statements are made by other actors in the *Histories* concerning a Greek context as well. Histiaeus in Scythia tells the Ionian tyrants as a self-evident fact that "each city would prefer to rule themselves (*dēmokrateesthai*) rather than be ruled by a tyranny" (4.137); the Lacedaemonians ask the Athenians to ignore the advice of Alexander of Macedon, stating the truism that "a tyrant is always out to support his fellow tyrants" (8.142). Herodotus himself, in 5.66, 5.78, and 5.91, develops the idea that the Athenians, weak under their tyrants, became formidable warriors when they were fighting freely for their own benefit and that, therefore, participatory government is a desirable thing (*hē isēgoriē . . . chrēma spoudaion,* 5.78). In 6.5.5, he remarks in passing that the Ionians were not at all eager to have tyrants, since they had tasted freedom (*hoia eleutheriēs geusamenoi*).[35]

Twice Herodotus puts in the mouths of Spartans a comment on the excellence of freedom and the rule of law, phenomena that militate against the presence of the kind of autocracy associated with tyranny. In 7.101, Xerxes asks the exiled king of Sparta for his opinion on whether the Greeks will oppose Xerxes' massive force. Demaratus replies: "Poverty has always been a factor in the rearing of the Greeks, but their courage has been acquired as the product of intelligence and the force of law. Using it, Greece has warded off both poverty and despotism (*desposunēn*). . . . Although they're free, they are not entirely free, for law is their master, and they are far more afraid of this than your men are of you" (7.102, 104; cf. 7.234–235). In 7.135, two Spartan heralds are asked by the satrap of coastal Asia why on earth they do not become vassals of the king, like himself. They reply, "Although you know what it is like to be a slave, you've never tried freedom and don't know whether it's sweet or not. If you had tried it, you would not be counseling us to fight for it with spears but even with battle axes." None of these passages, or others like them, argues the terribleness of the despotic template at length; they rather glancingly assume it. Their cumulative impact, however, is worth noting.[36]

GREEK TYRANTS AND DESPOTIC VIOLENCE

Greek tyrants are certainly a part of Herodotus' treatment of despots. Like Gyges, Croesus and the other eastern monarchs in book 1, Greek tyrants are called *tyrannoi* and are autocrats in their cities; like the five great eastern monarchs, they do commit outrageous deeds, which Herodotus duly mentions.[37] Details in their stories thus reinforce the cumulative impact created by the thematic development implied in the three versions of the despotic template, the larger plot lines of the five great eastern autocracies, and the single-line aphorisms examined above. What follows sets out the kinds of tyrannical violence described by Herodotus for the four Greek tyrannies that figure most prominently in the narrative, those of Athens, Corinth, Samos, and Miletus.[38]

The Peisistratids, the sixth-century tyrants of Athens, are introduced into the Croesus narrative in book 1 (1.59–64) to explain why the Athenians were weaker as potential allies of Croesus than the Lacedaemonians. The Athenians, Herodotus says, were in the time of Croesus held down and fragmented by their tyranny (*katechomenon te kai diespasmenon*, 1.59). Peisistratus himself, as we shall note below, does not behave at all according to the despotic template. But the various ingenious machinations of his family in trying to obtain and then regain power in Athens are noted in books 1 and 5, and Hippias the deposed Peisistratid tyrant shows the Persians the way to Attica and Marathon in book 6 (1.59–64, 5.55–65, 6.102 and 107); the sons of Peisistratus have Cimon the father of Miltiades killed, after too many Olympic victories (6.103). The Peisistratids also play a key part in encouraging Xerxes to mount his massive expedition to Greece in book 7 (7.6).[39]

Periander of Corinth is introduced in book 3, in the context of background information about Samos in the sixth century. Periander, the same seventh-century tyrant of Corinth that Socles describes in book 5, had killed his wife and, because of that deed, had alienated his son (3.50). In the story that follows, the father and son remain at odds, despite the clear advantages of the son sharing in the benefits of the tyranny his father exercises. Eventually the son is killed by the Corcyraeans because they do not want Periander among them (3.53), and in vengeance, Periander proposes to have three hundred boys from good Corcyraean families sent off to Samos and castrated, to be sold as eunuchs (3.48).[40] We have already noted that the Socles speech in book 5 refers generally to the story of Periander's misdeeds, as well as those of his father, Cypselus (5.92).[41]

The Samian tyrants are treated in three narrative units that all fall in book 3. While Amasis was still in Egypt, Polycrates took power on the island of Samos, first with his brothers and then by himself, after killing one of them and exiling the other. His wealth, military success, and unscrupulousness are noted. Herodotus says, "He attacked and plundered everyone, sparing

nobody—for he said that a friend would have more gratitude if he got back what had been taken than if it hadn't been taken in the first place" (3.39).⁴²
Polycrates conquered Ionian cities of both the mainland and the islands and had prisoners from the island of Lesbos dig a trench around the wall of Samos, in shackles.

The heart of the account, however, is not Polycrates' military successes or treatment of his captives but the famous story of his ring (3.39–43).⁴³ After losing his ring, Polycrates continues in his tyrannical ways, now helping Persia rather than Egypt. Ostensibly to help Cambyses in his conquest of Egypt, Polycrates fills forty triremes with his enemies and sends them off, hoping they will not return from Egypt.⁴⁴ He shuts their wives and children up in the shipyards and threatens to burn them all alive, and then fights a war with the alienated Samians, the Lacedaemonians, and the Corinthians. Money figures largely in the Polycrates story as a whole. At the end, led astray by greed, he is killed by the unscrupulous Persian satrap Oroetes, shortly before Darius comes to power (3.125).

Tyranny in Samos does not end with Polycrates. Although his secretary, Maeandrius, wishes to make the island free, to save himself, he is forced in the end to become a tyrant also. When the Persians clear him and his family out, Polycrates' relatives resume tyrannical control, until the Ionian revolt. During the revolt, they work on Darius' behalf, persuading the Samians to betray the Ionian cause.

For the largest plot line of the *Histories,* the most important Greek tyrants apart from the Athenian Peisistratids are Histiaeus and Aristagoras of Miletus. They initiate the Ionian revolt (books 5 and 6). Here a new negative quality connected fairly pointedly to the theme of Greek tyranny emerges, because, as the power of Persia grows, the implications in the *Histories* of what it means for a Greek city to have a tyrant change. From book 3 onward, tyrants in the Greek world have been increasingly portrayed as looking to the Persian king to establish, maintain, or reestablish their power and as being unscrupulous about asking for Persian military support if necessary.⁴⁵ Polycrates is the first intimation of this new trend; he dies because he has become embroiled in the ambitions of Persian satraps. In book 5, we also see the recently exiled Athenian tyrants, the Peisistratids, positioning themselves well with Persia, in the hopes of returning to power in Athens (5.96).⁴⁶ But the fullest statement of this theme comes in the account of the tyrants of Miletus.

According to Herodotus, the Ionian revolt of 499 B.C. begins because Aristagoras, the deputy tyrant left behind in Miletus by his uncle Histiaeus, wants the Persians to help him win the island of Naxos. He offers them an easy conquest of the Cyclades as a springboard towards Euboea. It is only when this plan backfires and Aristagoras is in danger of punishment from his Persian overlords that he makes the eastern Greeks rise in revolt, precipitating Greco-Persian hostilities that lead to real suffering and enslavement for the region and ultimately to Xerxes' massive invasion in 481. From the later sixth century onward, the Samians, Athenians, and a number of other Greek cities in Ionia are depicted as vulnerable to the imposition (or reimposition) of local tyrannies backed up by the threat of Persian power.

The most pointedly ironic analysis of this new phenomenon, that is, the growing connection between Greek tyranny and eastern despotism, occurs as the Ionian tyrants in about 610 B.C. are waiting for Darius' return from Scythia. In the meantime they have been set to guard the bridge across the Ister for him (4.137). The Scythians want the Ionians to destroy the bridge, leaving Darius and his army to be picked off in Scythia, and the Ionians agree—until Histiaeus the tyrant of Miletus makes the comment we have already looked at above: "It is through Darius that each one rules his city as tyrant; . . . if Darius were overthrown, neither would he be able to rule Miletus nor would any of the rest of them remain in power either, because each city would prefer to rule themselves (*dēmokrateesthai*) rather than be ruled by a tyranny (*tyranneuesthai*)."[47] After Histiaeus' speech, the other tyrants realize that it is in their self-interest to bring Darius safe back from Scythia, and they decide to guard his bridge very, very carefully.

The idea of eastern autocracy creating and savagely sustaining local despotisms reaches its most horrific point in the narrative of the preparations for the battle of Lade. At the Persians' behest, the Ionian tyrants gather like vultures before the battle, secretly undermining the morale of their various cities (6.9). Some of the Samians listen to the threats and bribes of their erstwhile tyrant and deliberately betray their comrades, so that the Ionian cause is lost. Ionian young men are, as earlier threatened, castrated and their sisters shipped off into eastern slavery, while their cities are burned and their temples plundered (6.13, 19, 32).[48]

Earlier Herodotus is dryly ironic about tyrants' and potential tyrants' aspirations, as he shows in the quasi-humorous story of 5.12. There, a couple of Paeonian rustics decide to try to attract Darius' attention to their people, in the hopes of being made tyrants of their region (*autoi ethelontes Paionōn tyranneuein*). In Darius' presence, they make their sister walk along busily, leading a horse, spinning flax, and carrying water on her head at the same time. Their plan backfires when, instead of establishing a satrapy in the region of the Strymon with them in charge, Darius is so impressed with all this industry that he ships the whole Paeonian people off to Phrygia to work for him instead. The Ionian revolt of books 5 and 6, whose initial stages occur almost immediately after this episode is, in some respects, the story of the Paeonians writ large, with Aristagoras and Histiaeus cast in the role of the two rustics, Pigres and Mastyes. The ironic humor with which the pretensions of the two Thracians' local ambitions have been treated is gone, however, in the longer Ionian narrative.

Part of the horror of the Ionian revolt lies in the way Aristagoras and Histiaeus, although not particularly evil in themselves, create out of their relatively local and reasonable ambitions real evil for the cities of Ionia and, more than twenty years later, potentially even greater evil for mainland Greece. Despotism is, it turns out, no laughing matter. Its drives and aspirations as embodied in the plans of various ambitious Greeks no longer involve merely the subjection of the individual city for a generation or two. Instead, it may well in any particular instance bring in the permanent establishment of the Persians and in doing so call into question for everyone the very survival of traditional Greek ways of managing civic affairs. By the later sixth century, Greek tyrants are depicted as dangerous, not necessarily as instances of harsh despotism in themselves but as potential wicks drawing foreign domination and real, systemic autocracy, the kind based on the Deioces model, down into Greece. In Herodotus' text the theme of the threat posed to Greek communities by the specific despotism of the Persian empire is an important organizing principle.

THE TYRANT AS INDIVIDUAL

Here, however, I want to make an abrupt volte-face. I began this paper with a question about Archaic Greek history and how Herodotus perceived tyrants as part of that history. If we return to this problem, that is, how the Archaic tyrants are depicted in Herodotus' *logoi* about them, the conclusions arrived at just above do not entirely account for the evidence of the text. We start with the word tyrant itself. In a handful of passages Herodotean rulers and friends of rulers refer to their own reigns as tyrannies and themselves as tyrants. In these instances tyranny seems to be used neutrally to signify *archē* (rule), and these comments are our best evidence that the semantic field of *tyrannis, tyrannos,* and *tyranneuein* in Herodotus does not necessarily carry with it a negative connotation, however Herodotus usually deploys it.[49] The autocratic monarchs and their friends who refer positively or neutrally to their reigns as tyrannies can be either Greek tyrants or eastern monarchs who have legitimately inherited their thrones. Xerxes tells Artabanus, "Guard my house and my tyranny" (7.52.2). Croesus tells Cyrus that Solon is someone "I would give a lot of money to have all tyrants have a conversation with" (1.86). Periander sends his daughter to persuade her brother to value the family's tyranny, and she pleads: "Tyranny is a difficult matter, and many lust after it (*autēs erastai eisi*). . . . Don't give your benefits to others" (3.53). Aristagoras' deputy to the Paeonians marooned by Darius in Phrygia tells the Paeonians that Aristagoras, the tyrant of Miletus, is offering them protection in their return home (5.98).

When rulers and their friends speak neutrally of a *tyrannis,* this could merely be an instance of Connor's formulation: tyranny as something good to have for oneself, very bad and shameful to have exercised over one by someone else.[50] It is more important that in the ongoing narrative as well we find the terms *tyrannos* and *tyrannis* used as synonyms for *basileus,* king, and *archē,* rule. In 8.137, telling the story of the origins of the Macedonian royal house (a *tyrannis,* 8.137.1), Herodotus mentions that the first Perdiccas and his brothers had their food cooked by the king's wife (*hē gunē tou basileos*), and he adds as an explanation that in those days, both the common people and *hai tyrannides* were poor. Other rulers to whom the narrative applies the terms *tyrannis, tyrannos,* or *tyranneuein* without any apparent negative overtones include Philocyprus of Cyprus, who is singled out because Solon praised him above all other tyrants (*ainese tyrannōn malista,* 5.113);[51] Argathonius, the king of the Tartessians (1.163); Procles the tyrant of Epidaurus (3.50); Telys, the tyrant of Sybaris (5.44); the valiant assembled tyrants of Cyprus, offering the Ionians their choice of whether to fight Persians by land or Phoenicians by sea (5.109); Cleisthenes of Sicyon throwing his year-long house party (6.126–130); Artemisia, the high-hearted tyrant of Halicarnassus (7.99); and Aridolis, the tyrant of Alabanda (7.195).[52] The semantic field of the term tyranny per se does not account for the way Herodotus analyzes the dynamics of despotism in action.

The most important issue is not a semantic one but arises if we look at Herodotus' treatment of the great eastern despots and the Greek tyrants as individual actors within specific *logoi.* What the self-contained Herodotean *logos* focuses on is the immediate context, an individual's goals, and his or her consequent actions within that *logos.* Whether the individual depicted is a poor herdsman, someone's wife or mother, royal courtier, Greek citizen, prostitute, eastern potentate, or Sicilian adventurer, his or her actions in the

Herodotean narrative are first defined by the constraints of external circumstances. Within these constraints, he or she is shown acting out of a desire to obtain some particular objective through whatever means are realistically available.[53]

The literary critic who to my knowledge was first sensitive to this feature in the Herodotean text, disliked it intensely. Plutarch felt that Herodotus had no real sense of the dignity or nobility of character that he, Plutarch, was sure attended the Greek heroes of such great movements of history as the Persian Wars. It is true that this trait, exhibited across a wide variety of different individuals, means that people in Herodotus' *Histories* are mostly, so to speak, bourgeois rather than heroic, depicted as focusing on private benefits for themselves and their families, and exhibiting a disconcerting tendency to become unscrupulous, even ignoble trickster figures when they have to be, in pursuit of getting what they want.[54] Put more neutrally, most of the actors in the *Histories,* small characters and large, are shown working with considerable resourcefulness to attain their own idea of individual happiness within the constraints that their circumstances create.

One of Herodotus' more habitual narrative choices for a plot line shows us a particular character, overlooked by other ostensibly more important individuals in the narrative, but busy making private choices that for the moment determine the course of important events. Gyges the spear carrier of the king "chooses to live" and founds a new dynasty in Lydia. Cyno wants a burial for her baby and to raise baby Cyrus, who ultimately brings Persian rule to Media. Democedes the Crotoniate physician wants to get home to Croton and turns Darius' attention toward Greece. Megacles the Alcmaeonid is offended at Peisistratus' treatment of his daughter and therefore becomes resolutely antityrannical. In the narrative of the later books of the *Histories,* Amompharetus wants only to be loyal to his narrowly Spartan set of ideals in battle and nearly costs the Greeks the battle of Plataea. Cleomenes' feud with Demaratus ends up gaining the Persian king an extremely valuable new advisor, because Demaratus flees to Persia. Miltiades needs to leave the Chersonese and evades the Phoenicians at sea and his political enemies at home, just in time to win the battle of Marathon for Athens. Amestris needs to protect her status as queen and destroys her brother-in-law's family, effectively bringing an end to the Persian Wars.[55] On a basic narrative level, Herodotus has made the choice to have the larger trends of human history mostly shaped by the search for personal happiness undertaken by both great and small individuals.

In a way this is Darius' project too as he reports it

In this general picture, one major exception occurs: the portraits of the great eastern despots. They are not cartoon despots. Only Cambyses, of the five, acts as the Compleat Tyrant, according to the model of the Constitutional Debate.[56] The others appear as reasonably distinctive personalities making occasional idiosyncratic moves. In each case, however, their actions are substantially defined by their positions as autocratic rulers, at the head of large imperial governments, and their repeated acts as autocrats create the onward movement of the despotic theme in the *Histories*.[57]

Croesus the Lydian is the only one of the five whose story precedes the Deioces model. He is to some extent as much Everyman as he is an instance of the despotic template in action, because his story contains both real changes of circumstance and Solon's meditations on that theme. Nonetheless, his role in the *Histories* is defined by his royal position and subsequent loss of it. Cyrus and Darius resemble each other in the trajectories of their careers: the account of Cyrus' reign in book 1 is mostly one of methodical conquest, while Darius, whose reign takes up much of book 3 and all of books 4 through 6, is also for most of the narrative an anonymous, distant figure, not much in evidence personally after his initial trickster accession to the throne.[58] Finally, Xerxes' portrait is the most vivid and nuanced of the five. The Persian Wars come to an end in large part because Xerxes' bad personal choices and consequent passivity and upheaval on the domestic front distract him from continuing systematically to pursue the military campaign in Greece (9.108–113). As Cyrus opines at the very end of the *Histories,* "Soft countries make soft men." Xerxes is weakened by the traits of self-indulgence, irresolution, and bad judgment in the choice of advisors and advice, and he proves personally unequal to the demands of the gigantic despotic empire that he heads.[59]

We earlier saw that the stories of Croesus, Cyrus, Cambyses, Darius, and Xerxes, taken together in order, provide both a strong thematic structure and a strong diachronic thrust to the narrative as a whole, conveying the limitations of oriental and imperial despotism.[60] Greek tyrants, however, are a very different story. Many of them are, as we saw above, described as arbitrary and brutal, in some ways that make them thematically part of the despotic template. Nonetheless, within the individual and idiosyncratic narrative frames of the *logoi* that tell their stories they remain, in the binary terms that Herodotus uses at the end of the *Histories* in the Cyrus anecdote, "hard." That is, they are in the main capable and realistic if ruthless individuals, treated, like other actors great and small in the *Histories,* as having very distinct and individual plot lines, each working to maximize his own advantages in difficult and idiosyncratic circumstances. On the whole the anecdotes about them are not structured around the traits that according to Otanes, define a despotic ruler, and their plot lines do not resemble that of systematic autocracy, as the despotic template articulates it.

Periander of Corinth enters the *Histories* as the benefactor of Miletus, in its unequal struggles against Alyattes of Lydia (1.20) and as a conscientious magistrate in the Arion story shortly thereafter (1.24). In 5.95 he is again a respected figure, an arbitrator. Although the *logos* about him in book 3 could have been organized around the Cambyses motif of tyrannical family violence and transgressive excess (these are certainly part of the larger story), what the narrative vividly depicts instead is paternal forbearance and frustration (3.52–53).[61] In the Socles speech in book 5, Periander is presented as a trickster figure, and one moreover whose family has been imposed on Corinth by the gods. His behavior, though violent, principally shows the fierce cleverness in pursuit of particular objectives that we find in many other talented individuals, whether Greek (like Hermotimus of Pedasa, King Cleomenes the Spartan, or Themistocles the Athenian) or foreign (Amasis the Egyptian, for instance, or both the Egyptian and Babylonian Nitocris).[62]

Although the story of tyranny in Samos begins with Polycrates' violence as a pirate and warlord, its main narrative outline concerns a Lacedaemonian attack on Samos (3.39–47, 54–56). As the account continues, the major focus is on Polycrates' futile attempt to evade the disaster that Amasis of Egypt has foreseen for him, by throwing his most priceless possession, his ring, in the sea. The second Polycrates story concerns his terrible end (3.120–125).[63] Oroetes, the Persian satrap of Sardis, tricks Polycrates into coming to Magnesia to discuss revolt from Persia; Polycrates is killed by Oroetes gruesomely, Herodotus says, "in a way that does not bear talking about." Here Herodotus' sympathy is overt: "Arriving in Magnesia, Polycrates was killed horribly, coming to an end worthy neither of himself nor of his ambitions. For with the exception of the tyrants of Syracuse, not one of the other Greek tyrants is worthy of being compared to Polycrates for magnificence (*megaloprepeiē*)" (3.125). After Polycrates' death, the story of Samos continues in a highly ironized vein, since Maeandrius, the lover of *isonomiē* (equality before the law; 3.142.3), finds himself compelled to become a tyrant and institute a brief and ill-organized reign of terror of his own. It is in the context of Maeandrius' failed effort to give up the tyranny that Herodotus' mordant conclusion about the Samians is enunciated: "They did not want, as it seems, to be free."[64]

Corinth and Samos are depicted as cities governed by autocratic rulers. The autocracy they exercise, however, is not an institutional, systemic one on the Persian model but is rather held in place by the personal qualities of the individual strong-willed ruler himself.

Herodotus' treatment of Greek tyrants becomes more complex as it moves toward the end of the sixth century. As we have already seen, neither the Peisistratids in Athens nor the Milesians Histiaeus and Aristagoras can be considered apart from the diachronic plot line of Persian imperialism that impinges on their stories. What we get in the story of the Athenian and Milesian tyrannies, however, is also a highly idiosyncratic account of ambitious individuals maneuvering their way through the larger structural constraints that confront them.

Only in book 1 do the Peisistratids have the focus of a *logos* to themselves (1.59–64). There, Herodotus tells the story of Peisistratus' tyranny, ostensibly to explain why the Athenians, held down by tyranny, were weaker than the Spartans and hence not Croesus' choice as allies in 546 B.C. (1.59).[65] Peisistratus, however, unlike either Periander or Polycrates, is given praise for the way he governed. Herodotus says that he ruled "neither disturbing existing rights nor changing the laws; using what was already in place, he controlled the city, ordering it well and attractively" (1.59). The bulk of the story in book 1 concerns Peisistratus as a sort of sixth-century Robert the Bruce, elaborately persistent in his efforts to "root" his tyranny. His accession is clever in its avoidance of violence; as far as we know, Peisistratus ends his days peacefully.

Tyrants' sons have problems. Socles says that Periander in Corinth was harsher than Cypselus (5.92.η). In the comments about Athens' tyranny mentioned in books 5 and 6, Peisistratus' sons in Athens are depicted as harsher than their father, Hippias especially so after Harmodius and Aristogeiton have murdered Hipparchus, his younger brother (5.55, 6.103).[66] Ober shows us the powerful iconographic and generally symbolic use to which the story of the tyrannicides will be put in the fourth century, but in book 5, Herodotus deflates the story, making it clear that it was not Harmodius and Aristogeiton but a combination of credulous Spartans and wily Alcmaeonids who really rid Athens of Hippias in 510 B.C. (5.63).[67] The Peisistratids themselves are not again the dominant focus of the account. They appear on the margins, first, of the story of how the Alcmaeonids try to unseat them (5.62–65, 70, 76, 90), and then, hanging around as onlookers while others (first the Spartans [5.93] and later the Persians [5.96, 6.94, 7.6]) try to reinstate them through a variety of efforts.[68] We last see Hippias in 490 as a pathetic old man, coughing out his tooth on the shore of Marathon in the company of his Persian friends (6.107); Herodotus does not use the word "tyrant" in that episode.

Of all the Greek tyrants Herodotus discusses, the Milesians Histiaeus and Aristagoras are the ones most intimately bound up with Persian imperial ambitions. Histiaeus first appears in book 4, persuading the other Ionian tyrants to remain faithful to Darius at the Ister, by appealing to their self-interest as tyrants. Without the support of Darius, he says, their own tyrannies would soon collapse (4.137). Histiaeus is rewarded with property in Thrace, at his own request (5.11), but after Megabazus tells Darius that Histiaeus threatens Persian control of Thrace (5.23), Histiaeus is brought to Susa to dance a flattering but impotent attendance on the king. The plot is narrated from Darius' point of view. It illustrates what we have seen to be one of the major weaknesses of despotic rule: talented underlings (Histiaeus is *deinos te kai sophos*, 5.23) are perceived as a threat to the stability and spread of that rule, even if they have expressed no overt disloyalty. The activities of Aristagoras, Histiaeus' regent, provide the largest organizing narrative structure for the rest of book 5, as he first tries to win Naxos for the Persians and then, when that fails, attempts at Sparta and Athens to win support for an Ionian revolt from Persia.

Neither Aristagoras nor Histiaeus is used to focalize the long narrative of the Ionian revolt that follows. Although they begin it, their actions precipitate a narrative that is about a complex and changing array of armies and cities. The machinations of Histiaeus and Aristagoras are most decisively responsible, Herodotus believes, for the chain of events that leads to the Persian Wars, but they themselves vanish somewhat ignominiously (5.126, 6.30). After Lade, Mardonius, the nephew and son-in-law of Darius, desposes all the Ionian tyrants and institutes democracy in the cities of Ionia (6.43).

What emerges from narrating the structural high points of the four major tyrannies of Corinth, Samos, Athens, and Miletus is the specificity of Herodotus' portraits of Greek tyrants. Two are from mainland Greece, and two are from Ionia, but in almost every other respect their stories are structurally and thematically distinctive, and the larger causal nexuses in which they are separately embedded are very idiosyncratic.[69] Some themes do emerge: rivalry between the tyrants and other aristocrats in their individual cities, problems handing a tyranny from one generation to the next, plotting by and against political enemies, either at home or abroad. All the tyrant families in these stories except the Corinthians at least flirt with Persia. Once Persia

has made its presence known in the Aegean basin, the Greek tyrants are embroiled in its doings but more as pawns or victims than as despots themselves.
Each Greek tyrant except Peisistratus and perhaps Histiaeus is depicted with
bad features of some sort, but, as we have seen, Herodotus structures their
stories quite differently from the stories of eastern despotism that the despotic template is designed to explain. They remain talented, aggressive, and
(except for Aristagoras and perhaps Polycrates at the end of his life) realistic and in that sense "hard" individuals. Their problems are not in the main
those of the great eastern autocrats, working out the dynamics of an imperial
structure.

THE DOUBLENESS OF HERODOTUS'
PICTURE OF TYRANNY

Thus there is a profound bifurcation in our reading of Herodotus' text.
"Tyranny" and "tyrants" on the one hand are among Herodotus' standard
terms for despotism, and one of the ongoing themes of the *Histories* is a general exploration of despotism. Despots, whether Greek tyrants or eastern
autocrats, are often hard on their communities and sometimes on their families. They are not bad on the whole because their rule is illegitimate. Despite
the example of Gyges, first despot in the *Histories,* the legitimacy of their
rule is not, on the whole, the issue. Two of the three despotisms described
in what I have called the despotic template are monarchies, and the monarchs in them are chosen in an elaborate Hobbsian social contract. Even the
third, the Corinthian tyranny of Cypselus and Periander, has been foretold
and validated by Delphi. Many of the despots Herodotus describes commit
violent acts. On the whole, however, Herodotus avoids portraying any of
them as an immoral or amoral horror, like the Aegisthus, Clytemnestra, or
Creon of tragedy, or the tyrant of Plato's *Gorgias.* Cambyses, who comes the
closest to this model, is assumed to have a disease that accounts for much of
his behavior.

It is the negative portrait of eastern despotism that really occupies Herodotus in the *Histories.* Systemically, the great eastern monarchs illustrate the
problems set forth in the despotic template: the distance necessarily established and maintained between the autocratic ruler and his subjects; the despot's tendency to abuse his position's opportunities for violence; and, finally,
the tendency of despotism to involve a momentum that ends in violence
and the waste of resources, no matter how neutrally it began. Dynamically,
across the ongoing narrative of the *Histories,* other subtler processes emerge

empirically within the individual descriptions of the great eastern despots, in particular, the way the absolute power of the despot subverts the desires of those beneath him and is subverted in turn. Almost no one is honest or realistic in the eastern despotic context, since the underling must hide ambition, and the despot consequently and most unrealistically assumes a loyalty that is not in fact there or does not mean what the despot thinks it means. The talents of the despot's most dynamic subjects, like Histiaeus, are wasted or finally turned against the state. As Herodotus presents it, what is dangerous about eastern imperial despotism is not the wickedness of the individual despot, but the way he is, like everyone else, enmeshed in a structure that takes on a life of its own, that moves inexorably in the direction of its own further growth (7.8).

Those in Herodotus' audiences alert to such topics might well be thinking this theme relevant to Greek experience, not so much in the context of the Archaic tyrannies, however, as in the foreign affairs of democratic and imperial Athens. Although Herodotus notes when the Archaic Greek tyrants come to power through violence, like Polycrates, or commit violent deeds like Cypselus, Periander, Polycrates, and the sons of Peisistratus, he does not depict them necessarily coming to a bad end. More generally, these tyrants and others like them are not examples of the larger systemic violence of imperial despotism. When Greek tyrants become part of the story of Persia, like the rest of the Greek world, they appear to be caught in a larger picture in which they play relatively insignificant and marginal parts.

Herodotus is not a fan of the Archaic Greek tyrants. The Athenian, Samian, and Milesian tyrants opportunistically try to bring Persia into the affairs of their cities. Nor does he give them credit for the kinds of progress, material and social, in their states that modern scholars often assign to them. The closest he comes to this idea is the statement in Megabyzus' speech in the Constitutional Debate, that a despot at least has a plan in mind, while the demos merely rushes witlessly hither and yon (3.81). Herodotus also, in passing, compliments Peisistratus on his beautification of Athens (1.59) — but not for initiatives in trade, colonization, or for developing the fabric of Athenian governmental administration that ultimately had a great deal to do with Athens' contributions to the war against Persia. Periander is not credited with bringing Corcyra under Corinthian control or building the diolkos and the harbor at Lechaeum; Polycrates is not given credit for the three great building projects in Samos that Herodotus pointedly admires. The Greek tyrants are rather put in the context of the same ferocious and highly intelligent individualism with which other independent and talented individuals are endowed in the *Histories*. In the *Histories* as a whole, the Greek tyrants in their violent acts contribute anecdotal material to the ongoing theme of despotism. Within their own *logoi,* however, the accounts of the Greek tyrants are highly individual, and the details about the tyrants themselves are not shaped according to an easy or predictable narrative template.

This essay began by noting that form in Herodotus' narrative intimately supports and reinforces content. The doubled narrative structure I have described here, with its tension between the viewpoints of the individual *logoi* about the Greek tyrants and that of the overarching and unifying theme of imperial despotism, in a curious way itself becomes a meditation on the themes explored in this paper. Herodotus does not, like Plato, draw a contrast between the desires of the despot and the more noble aspirations of superior self-controlled individuals or, like Thucydides or the later Euripides, exalt the actions of particular noble or self-sacrificing individuals. We may wonder if, in this respect, Herodotus intends Deioces as well as Croesus as a model of Everyman: *erastheis tyrannidos* (1.96.2). In any case, Herodotus in general presents a picture of human political desires that resembles the dynamic equilibrium prevailing in the spheres of geography and natural history. Each man or woman in Herodotus wants as much scope for following his or her personal objectives as he or she can get. Each one, however, is ultimately held in check by the existence of all the others and their competing and contradictory desires.

In the Constitutional Debate Darius argues that all government ultimately ends in despotism. It is an equally compelling truth of the *Histories* that despite his huge resources, Xerxes retreats, undone by Athens, Sparta, and the other small but "hard" Greek states led by talented individuals who want their own freedom. The reality the Greek tyrants represent on the level of the individual *logos*—the desire for power on the part of talented individuals—is as fundamental a truth in the *Histories* as is the dynamic growth of imperialism. This is why the Greek tyrant in Herodotus both acts as an instance of and also tacitly suggests the limits inherent in the notion of imperial autocracy. This doubled set of movements is encoded not just in Herodotus' portrait of despotism but in the doubleness of the basic narrative structures of his *Histories*.[70]

Notes

[1] Stahl (1987: 1–2) notes that the publication of Berve's magisterial 1967 study of Greek tyranny stimulated a newly intense reconsideration of tyranny as a social phenomenon, one necessarily connected to the aristocracies of the Archaic Greek poleis. Cf. Hammond 1982: 341–351; Stein-Hölkeskamp 1989, reviewed by Donlan 1992. Of earlier studies of tyranny, Andrewes 1956 and Pleket 1969 remain influential. For more recent studies, see Kinzl 1979b; Murray 1993: 135–158; Snodgrass 1980: 111–116; Starr 1986: 80–86; McGlew 1993; Raaflaub 1993: 41–105, esp. 73–74, and this volume. Osborne (1996: 192–197) is particularly useful in systematically distinguishing the evidence of the material record from that of the literary sources; see also Raaflaub 1997b: 15–18 and nn. 7–12, this vol., stressing the scantiness and unreliability of our available extant evidence, based as it is largely on oral memory.

[2] For early hostile formulations of the tyrant, see V. Parker 1998: 155–157 and Nagy 1990: 280–292. For the particular case of Athens, Griffith (1995: 84, n. 80) remarks: "'Tyranny' in any case exists constantly in the Athenian imagination to be invoked as the dreaded extremity, and opposed to *any* version of the civic ideal: thus excessive demagoguery is as likely to incur accusations of 'tyranny' as are excessive elitist displays."

[3] For the possible etymology of *tyrannos* and its cognates, see V. Parker 1998: 145–149, but also Hegyi 1965; Labarbe 1971; Berve 1967: 3, 517. See also Raaflaub, this vol., n. 3.

[4] For the earlier *basileus*, see Morris, this vol.; for the eighth century, see Donlan 1980, 1985, 1997; I. Morris 1987; Osborne 1996: 70–160; Raaflaub 1988b and 1997b; Thalmann 1998: 243–305. For the hoplite revolution, see Raaflaub 1997d. For democratic and even populist attitudes in Athens as early as the Cylonian revolt, cf. Wallace 1997b: 16–17, 25.

[5] It may well be that in the shifting alliances of aristocratic families in the seventh and sixth centuries B.C., the Archaic and Early Classical tyrannies were in the main ad hoc affairs, one form of temporary aristocratic conflict resolution. This is in the main the view of Berve 1967 and, with important modifications, Stahl 1987 and Stein-Hölkeskamp 1989. See Osborne 1996: 190–193, Stein-Hölkeskamp 1989: 72–93, and van Wees 1999 for the violence endemic not just in Archaic tyrannies but in Archaic elite culture in general. Van Wees would call such elites "timocracies" rather than true "aristocracies."

[6] See Lateiner 1989: ch. 8 and esp. 164–166 for a discussion of the historiographical issues involved and some of the important contributors to the scholarly debate, notably Waters 1971, Ferrill 1978, and Gammie 1986; see also Hartog 1988: 322–339 for Herodotus' depiction of tyranny as the mirror image of barbarian and monarchical power, "a factor of disorder in the kosmos" (328). Although this essay does not attempt a return to Waters' "value-free" portrait of kings and tyrants in Herodotus, it does suggest reasons why Waters' approach also avoids some of the limitations that more monothematic arguments exhibit.

[7] C. Olson 1966: 16, cited by P. Anderson 1998: 11.

[8] I am here using the term monarchy in its modern sense. Herodotus does not call the

reign of Deioces a *mounarchiē,* although he uses this term both in the context of Croesus and of a number of Greek tyrannies (1.55, 5.46, 6.23–24, 7.154, 7.165), and both Otanes and Darius use it in the Constitutional Debate (3.80, 82) to mean rule by an autocrat; cf. Hartog 1988: 325–326. For the close connection in Archaic poetry of *mounarchiē* with tyranny, see Cobet 1981: 51–52; Nagy 1985: 42–46 and 1990: 182; McGlew 1993: 65–66 and n. 27. Herodotus uses the same technique of analysis through aetiology in the story of the origins of the Sauromatae (4.110–117).

[9] *Erōs* in Herodotus is used only for sexual desire and the longing for despotic power: Benardete 1969: 137, n. 9 and Hartog 1988: 330. For the wider appeals and ambiguities of tyranny in late Archaic poetic thought, see Nagy 1990: 274–313.

[10] Herodotus comments that his fears are reasonable enough, since they have been reared with him, have lineages as good, and are just as brave. Such passages suggest the way the single ruler in Herodotus is tightly and competitively connected to a network of aristo-cratic courtiers and even kin. This issue often comes up with rulers; Amasis the Egyptian deals with it most directly (2.172). Cf. Atossa's comments to Darius (3.133) and Xerxes' worries (7.6.α). In Plutarch's *Life of Pericles* (7), Pericles behaves like Deioces; he avoids partygoing or, if he has to attend, leaves the party once the drinking starts: "Conviviality tends to undermine authority, and it is hard to maintain an appearance of gravity in the midst of familiar social intercourse." Cf. Vickers 1997: 2, n. 8 for contemporary charges of tyranny against Pericles.

[11] See Steiner 1994: 127–166 on the connection between autocracy and making things fixed, pinning them down, especially in writing. Kurke (1999: 323) points out that the boy Cyrus, playing in the village, will recreate the founding acts and institutions of Deioces (1.114.2).

[12] The paradoxes of this double movement of legality created by a ruler above the law are well developed by McGlew (1993: 83–86), although it is unclear that the historical tyrants played quite the central role in the Archaic Greek development of notions of law and the state that McGlew more generally claims for them.

[13] Gammie (1986) and Lateiner (1989: 172–179) are very helpful in determining the out-lines of the despotic template. Lateiner structures his extensive chart listing autocrats and their behavior in the *Histories* around the traits mentioned by Otanes in the Con-stitutional Debate (3.80), itemized by personality traits, actions, and judgment. See also Hartog 1988: 330–339 and Munson 1993: 39, n. 2, which gives the whole nexus of despotic behavior a somewhat more restricted extent and calls it the "monarchical model."

[14] For some of the immense bibliography on the Constitutional Debate, see Lasserre 1976: 65, n. 1; Evans 1981: 79; Lateiner 1989: 272, nn. 11–15.

[15] *Katartān,* "to adjust," 3.80. For *katartizein,* "to set in order," see 5.28, 5.30.1, 5.106.5, 9.66.2. Cf. a *katartistēr,* 4.161.2, 5.28. In 5.28–30 the Parians reestablish Miletus after civil war by taking the Milesians who manage their own farms well and putting them in charge of the city. In 5.106 Histiaeus promises to set things right. In 4.161.2 the Cyrenians get an arbitrator from Mantinea. Hartog (1988: 325) comments that in 3.80 Otanes is "speaking

Greek." The later reinstitution of Greek democracies by Mardonius (6.43) shows that democracy as a system of governance is uniquely applicable to Greek cities.

[16] It is not clear that Herodotus disagrees with Megabyzus. In the two places where Athenian democratic political behavior is described (5.97, 9.5), the governing body acts like a large crowd, lacking judgment.

[17] For the connection between *mounarchiē* and tyranny, see n. 8 above. Pelling (2002) highlights Darius' emphasis on the inevitability of autocratic monarchy, since other forms of government all evolve into it.

[18] See Giraudeau 1984: 107 and Lateiner 1989: 169, n. 18 for Herodotus' neglect of oligarchies. Presumably, aristocratic oligarchies were the most common form of Greek government in Herodotus' world. They would also have been quite challenging to write about, because to narrate their doings intelligently would have meant narrating complex negotiations among various important families.

[19] Lateiner 1989: 274, n. 19 and 275, n. 31; Evans 1991: 57–58. Erbse (1992: 62) pertinently asks: "Was soll man von einem Herrscher halten, der mit solchen Mitteln zur Macht aufsteigt?"

[20] Darius has the three sons of a man asking for their release from military service killed by "those responsible for such things" (4.84). For his wholesale transfer of subject peoples, see 3.149, 4.205, 5.15, 6.20, 6.119; cf. 6.32. See further, n. 58 below. Kurke (1999: 68–89) well develops the connection between Darius' tyrannical impulses and his acquisitiveness. His son Xerxes is led astray by flatterers (7.5–6), like his father has the offspring killed of a man who asks for the release of his eldest son from military service (7.39), has an affair with his son's wife, and has his brother's family killed (9.108–113). See further, Lateiner 1989: 172–175.

[21] See Lasserre 1976 and Lateiner 1989: 272, n. 13 for the presence of Greek sophistic thought in the Constitutional Debate. Bleicken (1979) emphasizes the practical impact of contemporary politics, especially Athenian. See Pelling (2002) for the possibility that Herodotus expected his audience to recognize a tension between Greek and Persian ways of thinking about tyranny, one that is implicit in the way the various arguments of the Constitutional Debate are relevant to their larger nearby narrative contexts, both Greek and Persian.

[22] Some of the main elements of Socles' speech (5.92) are Cypselus' mixed ancestry; the prediction by Delphi; the power of Cypselus' smile as a baby; his confirmation as *basileus* by another oracle; the fact that he grew up to force large numbers of Corinthians into exile and to kill many others and confiscate their property. Socles goes on to say that Periander was initially less cruel to his countrymen than his father Cypselus, but then, after the advice from the tyrant Thrasybulus of Miletus (to top all the tallest ears of grain), "whatever Cypselus had left undone in the way of killing and persecution, Periander finished," treating his people with utter brutality. Socles' speech ends with the story of how Periander also stripped all the women of Corinth of their clothes to placate his dead wife Melissa.

[23] Stahl 1983: 215–217; Gray 1996: 386–387. Van der Veen's (1996: 86–87) objections to Stahl's structural argument seem implausibly over-subtle.

[24] Gray 1996: 379.

[25] Stahl 1983: 212–213 cites Andrewes 1956: 47 and Zörner 1971: 261ff. for the common scholarly assumption that Herodotus simply mixes two traditions about Periander, one positive and one negative, not noticing how different the *Tendenz* of Socles' own argument is from that of the stories he recounts. See also Gray 1996: 362–363.

[26] For the relevance of the fifth-century Athenian empire to 5.92, see Stahl 1983: 218–220 and Gray 1996: 386. For the essential connections that link Athenian democracy of the 430s to imperialism, see Raaflaub 1994: 111–112 and the extensive discussions by Raaflaub, Kallet, Henderson, and Morgan (introduction), this volume. For Herodotus' own larger interest in the implications of contemporary Athenian imperialism, see Strasburger 1982; Fornara 1971b: 37–58; Raaflaub 1987: 224, 241–248; Stadter 1992; Moles 1996.

[27] Herodotus does not invent tyranny's negative connotations (cf. V. Parker 1998: 155–157 and Nagy 1990: 280–292), but he is one of the first to link the term "tyranny" closely to an analysis of the dynamics of despotic empire. Cf. Hartog 1988: 339: "We may perhaps seize on a transition from the constitution of the *Histories* (the grid for them) to the *Histories* as an institution (used as a grid). From now on, in the shared knowledge of the Greeks, the king is a despot and the tyrant is a despot . . . who is moved by hubris and who behaves as a master among his slaves."

[28] See Immerwahr 1966: 61–62 and 145 for the importance in the narrative of points of structural pause.

[29] See n. 2 above. Certainly Gyges' de facto illegitimacy in the story, as a regicide and usurper, points up Croesus' feeling of entitlement more sharply as a mistaken one (1.33).

[30] See n. 13 above; see Evans 1991: 9–40 for a survey of imperialism in the *Histories* and the extent to which the "imperialist impulse" is for Herodotus the result of human choice (35); cf. Immerwahr 1966: ch. 4, esp. 187–188. Fornara's 1971: 29 strictures are, however, well taken: the repetition and prominence of this theme in the early books of the *Histories* do not mean that Persian imperialism is the subject of the first six books of Herodotus.

[31] Evans 1991: 60 points out that Herodotus' Darius bears little resemblance to the elder statesman of Aeschylus' *Persians*. See also Immerwahr 1966: 169: "The Herodotean principle noted for the other Persian kings, namely, that their fall is due to the conditions of their rule, applies to Darius as well." See also nn. 20, 58. However, Fol and Hammond (1988: 234–253) make the case that historically, Darius' European conquests were quite substantial and that Herodotus' account of the purposes of the Scythian expedition in particular may mislead, since it is structured so as to bring out parallels with Xerxes' later invasion of Greece (see also Hartog 1988: 35–40).

[32] Both Xerxes and Darius would be killed in August 465 B.C., and another of Xerxes' sons, Artaxerxes, would assume the throne. Herodotus' final narrative about Xerxes assumes his audience's awareness of these later events.

[33] 3.133, 3.140, 5.35, 5.106–107, 7.6, 7.9, 8.100; also in the reign of Darius: 3.134, 5.12–15, 5.30, 6.30. Eastern rulers are concerned about the possibility of trouble coming from beneath: 3.134.2, 5.23. In stories about the Greek tyrants, Herodotus almost never tells of flattery or manipulation from beneath, and consequent retribution (but see 6.103). He puts the most vivid statement of tyrannical defense against the threat posed by over-competent or ambitious underlings, however, in a Greek context: Thrasybulus swishing off the heads of grain for the young Periander's benefit (5.92.ζ).

[34] 3.80.3, 3.80.4, 5.92.α.2.

[35] Cf. 6.127 and 7.164.1 for more understated expressions of the same values. Herodotus calls Pheidon of Argos a tyrant, although he was a legitimate hereditary *basileus,* presumably because of despotic acts (6.127); cf. Arist. *Pol.* 1310b26–28.

[36] Cf. 5.32 and 9.116.

[37] For a complete list of Greek tyrants in the *Histories,* see Waters 1971: 42–43; for Herodotean bibliography, see n. 6 above. Lateiner 1989: 176–179 lists outrages committed by Greek tyrants along the lines described by Otanes in the fourth and fifth columns of his chart.

[38] Other tyrants considered at some length by Herodotus but not to the extent of the four analyzed here include Cleisthenes of Sicyon (5.67–69, 6.126–131), Miltiades the elder and younger (4.137–138, 6.34–37, 39–41, 103–104) and Gelon of Syracuse (7.145, 153–168), who seems to have surpassed Polycrates in magnificence (3.125).

[39] Thucydides (1.17) agrees with Herodotus' point that a tyrant weakens his city. The extent to which the tyranny of the Peisistratids differed from other Archaic tyrannies, or laid a necessary groundwork for what came next in Athens, is much debated: see, e.g., Jeffery 1976: 94–99; Murray 1993: 268–274; Osborne 1996: 283–285 but also Lavelle 1993; Stein-Hölkeskamp 1989: 139–153; Stahl 1987. See the extensive bibliography in Berve 1967: 543–563, esp. 563, and Raaflaub, this volume, nn. 9–11, 15. For the later significance of the slaying of Hipparchus by Harmodius and Aristogeiton, see the essays of Raaflaub and Ober, this volume.

[40] Both Plato (*Resp.* 336A) and Aristotle (*Pol.* 1313a–b) use Periander, the earliest of the tyrants of whom substantial stories were retold, as "the type of tyranny," and Aristotle makes him (along with the Persians!) the originator of most of the conventional devices by which tyrants repress their subjects: "suppression of outstanding personalities, forbidding the citizens to live in the city, sumptuary legislation, prevention of assemblies, anything that will keep the city weak and divided" (Andrewes 1956: 51). See further Berve 1967: 525–526, and, for the way 3.48 positions Periander at the margins of Greek civic life, Schmitt-Pantel 1979.

[41] See n. 25 above.

[42] "This is an epigram rather than a serious statement of policy. Samos was no backward pirate state but a developed commercial city where trade cannot have been merely insecure, and Polycrates' seizures are to be connected with the wars which he waged for most of his reign": Andrewes 1956: 119. Kurt Raaflaub points out to me, however, that

the concept of a "Samian empire," suggested by Herodotus and Thucydides, has been substantially challenged in recent scholarship; see Shipley 1987: 94–95.

[43] The story of Polycrates' ring probably displays some Samian bias for their tyrant, since it is far more likely historically that Polycrates actually abandoned Amasis for a more powerful Persian-Phoenician alliance in the 520s. On its thematics, Kurke (1999: 101–121) convincingly argues that the Polycrates story as a whole and the ring story in particular concern the issue of failed reciprocity, raising the questions: "What constitutes value? What are Polycrates and his rule worth?" (121). See n. 63 below.

[44] Cf. Osborne 1996: 276: "It no doubt served well the purpose of those Samians who went to Sparta to ask for help in getting rid of Polykrates to claim that Polykrates had dispatched them to their death fighting against Amasis, but a high degree of collaboration between Polykrates and the élite, rather than an élite constantly in terror for their lives, would seem best to fit the evidence."

[45] Osborne 1996: 319–322.

[46] They are not the only Athenians to do so; the Persians, however, reject the approaches of the young democracy (5.73). Martin Ostwald points out to me that the evidence for Peisistratid pro-Persian sympathies before their expulsion from Athens is quite weak. Thucydides 6.59.3 mentions the marriage of Hippias' daughter to a Lampsacene tyrant, but this attempt to curry favor with Darius takes place after Hipparchus' murder, when Hippias is already thinking in terms of a safe haven in the north.

[47] The terminology is probably that of Herodotus' own day: Raaflaub 1997c: 35–37. Cf. Hansen (1991: 69–71), who argues that *demokratia* might well have been a Cleisthenic term.

[48] Darius does not, however, reinstitute tyrannies in most of Ionia, presumably because they have proved inadequate to the task of keeping local populations docile (6.43).

[49] Cf. the different conclusion of Lateiner 1989: 276, n. 34. See n. 3 above for the etymology.

[50] Connor 1977.

[51] In the same passage Herodotus calls his son, Aristocyprus, a *basileus*. See n. 8 above for the connection in Herodotus between *tyrannoi* and *mounarchoi*.

[52] Cleisthenes, however, is called a stone-thrower in 5.67, where the implication is that his rule was illegitimate and also that in changing Athenian tribal names, his namesake, Cleisthenes the Athenian Alcmaeonid who invented democracy, was behaving in as high-handed and arbitrary a fashion. One of the Cypriot tyrants betrays the Ionian cause in 5.113, and even Artemisia is admired somewhat ambiguously, since she exhibits the same double-edged qualities that Athens does (Munson 1988: 98–106). Cf. 5.11 and 8.67, where the Persian king rewards and consults the tyrants who are loyal to him; these passages can be read as neutral or negative, depending on the narrative context one frames them with (cf. 4.137–138). For a strong statement of potential beneficial aspects of tyrants, kings, and despots in the *Histories,* see Flory 1987: 120–143.

[53] Approximately a thousand different people are mentioned in the *Histories;* Waters (1985: 140) estimates that thirty to fifty of these are significant. Despite Homeyer's (1962) contention that biography can be found in Herodotus, Momigliano (1971: 33–40) is right to stress that biographical sketches per se in the fifth century are eastern in inspiration and come to the Greeks through Ionia, while history as Herodotus and Thucydides conceive of it is collective in its impulse. True Greek biography—interest in personality for its own sake—has to await the language and self-conscious persuasive techniques of the fourth-century development of rhetoric (102). See also Evans 1991: 43, n. 8.

[54] Plut. *de Malignitate,* passim. Cf. Hdt. 1.61, 3.148, 5.51, 6.72, 6.75, 6.84, 6.134. A few individuals in Herodotus renounce power and/or are outstandingly noble, altruistic, or honest. The degree to which they impress and surprise Herodotus is itself revealing: e.g., 2.139, 3.83, 3.138, 6.24, 7.164, 8.79, and of course 7.204–208, 222–228.

[55] 1.11, 1.61, 1.112, 3.129–134, 6.70, 6.104, 9.55, 9.112.

[56] Even Cambyses' final account of his misdeeds is both lucid and principled (3.65). Cambyses' behavior is presented as aberrant, despite his being a despot, and a physiological explanation is advanced for it (3.33).

[57] See Christ 1994: 168, n. 4; Evans 1991: 9–40; Erbse 1992: 10–92 for more extended discussions of the Herodotean kings. Christ (1994: 169–182) acutely distinguishes the investigatory impulse of Herodotus himself from that of the kings in his *Histories,* which has its root in greed and self-aggrandizement. Looked at schematically, the most prominent traits of the great eastern rulers form a pattern of ring composition. Croesus and Xerxes at the beginning and end are men with a lot of human qualities, brought to a bad end that is not entirely but partly the result of their choice of actions. Cyrus and Darius, falling second and fourth in the pattern, are just but ruthless and highly competent autocrats, responsible for exploiting the autocratic regime's opportunities for growth. In the middle, third of the five, stands Cambyses, the violent and unstable autocrat, the conqueror of Egypt.

[58] After killing Intaphrenes, Darius is rarely shown interacting with his subjects; he tends to be manipulated by ambitious subordinates (n. 33 above). We do form some idea of a personality: for his acquisitiveness, see Kurke 1999: 80–89. In books 3 through 5 we learn of his curiosity about other peoples, perhaps again as an extension of his cupidity (3.38, 4.44, 5.12; Christ 1994: 177–179). He is violent (n. 20 above) but, although he kills Intaphrenes and most of his male relatives, he spares Intaphrenes' brother-in-law and eldest son (3.118–119); although he sacrifices seven thousand of his own troops and impales three thousand of the captured enemy in Babylon, and abandons the weak and the sick from his army in Scythia (3.157, 159, 4.135), he also generously acknowledges the virtues of the courtiers Zopyrus and Megabazus (3.160, 4.143). Reflecting over an errant official's comparative merits and demerits, he orders the man, Sandoces, taken down from the stake on which he has been left to die (7.194; cf. 5.25 for Cambyses' very different behavior). Ruthless but civilized, he is generous to the Greeks under his patronage (3.140, 5.11). He expresses regret at Histiaeus' murder and buries him with honor (6.30). Kurke's (1999) larger project, however, raises an interesting problem for the issue of the

historicity of some of these details. Her argument makes it clear that even the most vivid accounts of kingly personal characteristics might have been retained in Greek anecdote because they were meaningful in the context of larger sociological and ideological issues (the invention of a money economy, for instance) rather than because they accurately revealed specific and historical personality traits of a given ruler.

[59] Xerxes comes on the scene as the youthful heir of Darius, and his decisions and actions are clearly shaped by the imperial successes of the past. He is described as eager to live up to the expectations for royal accomplishment, which Darius' achievements had raised. Evans (1991: 66, n. 84) comments that Xerxes' own surviving inscriptions show this concern to be historical.

[60] See n. 30 above.

[61] Periander does attempt savage retribution against the Corcyreans who have killed his son (3.49). Stahl (1983: 208–210) comments that Periander's assumptions about the *agatha*, benefits, connected with tyranny are being punished in the same way as Croesus' expectations of permanent happiness are in book 1.

[62] See Camerer 1965.

[63] Polycrates' earlier exploits have had quite a lot to do with money. His emerald ring conveys a sense of his wealth; he also owes his power to the money he has gotten from systematic brigandage, and he is said to have tricked the Spartans into lifting their siege by bribing them with lead coinage covered with gold (although Herodotus does not believe that part of the story, 3.56; Osborne (1996: 259) does not either). Cf. Kurke (1999: 105, n. 9; 115, n. 37), whose discussion of the Samian tyranny and electrum-coated lead slips actually found in Samos forms part of her larger and fascinating argument about money and its role in the transformation of Archaic value systems. See n. 43 above.

[64] Irony pervades the narrative of Samian governance; the Persian who strips Samos of its population for Darius ca. 515 B.C. and reestablishes Syloson on Polycrates' throne is Otanes, the same Otanes who propounds the superiority of democracy and the horrors of tyranny in the Constitutional Debate (3.80).

[65] Cf. n. 39 above.

[66] The need of cities to break free from their tyrants' families with violence is discussed suggestively by McGlew 1993: 157–182 in terms of civic foundation legends.

[67] The account does not narrate the doings of the Peisistratids themselves in Athens but rather the machinations of the Alcmaeonids and the activities of the Lacedaemonians. After their children are captured in leaving the country, the Peisistratids flee to their properties at Sigeum on the Hellespont (5.65). The Lacedaemonians, when they see they have been tricked, change their minds and try unsuccessfully to reinstate the Peisistratids in Athens in about 504; this is where the speech of Socles comes, delivered to discourage the reinstatement of tyranny in Athens (5.92).

[68] The one exception to their lack of center stage is a surprisingly sympathetic account of Hipparchus' dream, the night before he is killed (5.56).

[69] Gray 1996: 366: "Herodotus is creating their images out of a variety of patterns that do not conform in their details or even in their outlines to any one stereotype." I would go somewhat further; perhaps the very idiosyncrasy of the details preserved gives us some grounds for hoping that they often represent (admittedly approximate) memories of genuine data. See also nn. 53, 59, and the ends of nn. 1, 58 above.

[70] All translations from the Greek text in this essay are my own, although I have borrowed felicities from the Waterfield and Marincola/de Selincourt translations when they seemed particularly apt. The piece has greatly profited from the comments of audiences at the University of California at Los Angeles, the University of Leeds, the University of North Carolina, Brown University, Northwestern University, Amherst College, and the University of California at Berkeley. I would like particularly to thank Kathryn Morgan and Kurt Raaflaub. Thanks are also due Roger Brock, Michael Clark, Walter Donlan, Simon Hornblower, Leslie Kurke, Martin Ostwald, Christopher Pelling, Ronald Stroud, Philip Stadter, and Robert Wallace for generous scholarly and editorial assistance at the various stages of its writing.

KURT A. RAAFLAUB

STICK AND GLUE: THE FUNCTION OF TYRANNY IN FIFTH-CENTURY ATHENIAN DEMOCRACY

"Popular Tyranny" can mean either tyranny that is popular or tyranny by the *populus,* the people. Both aspects are relevant for my present investigation. I will argue for three points. First, in their capacity as citizens, Athenians in the second half of the fifth century were accustomed to thinking of tyranny in a very negative way, although privately many of them might have held different views and we know that elite circles disgruntled with democracy did so. If we talk of "popularity of tyranny," we thus mean an elite and dissident phenomenon or one rooted in popular culture.[1] These aspects are explored further in this volume by Lisa Kallet, Jeffrey Henderson, and Josiah Ober. For my present purpose, it is important to distinguish rather sharply between public and private, official and personal, although in reality these perspectives may often have overlapped or been somewhat blurred. My focus here is strictly on the Athenians' official views and self-representation, their political ideology.

Second, this official, negative concept of tyranny played a useful, perhaps even indispensable, role in providing the citizens with a contrast against which they defined their shared civic identity and virtues. This was especially important in a system that was unprecedented and remained extraordinary (hence "glue" in my title).

Third, because the citizens, conditioned by decades of antityrannical ideology, were broadly familiar with this negative concept of tyranny, it offered itself to easy use in comparison and metaphor, culminating in the concept of "tyranny by the people," as it was expressed in slogans such as *dēmos tyrannos* and *polis tyrannos.* Such slogans, like the earlier and more general accusation of tyrannical behavior, were powerful tools with which skilled demagogues could attack and discredit their opponents or "whip" the citizens into accepting their proposals and rejecting those of their rivals (hence "stick" in my title). Even in such metaphorical use, therefore, "tyranny" was normally understood negatively.

Ironically, according to a view not uncommon in recent scholarship, what I am proposing to discuss here is a virtual nonissue. For example, the entry "tyranny" in the new *Oxford Classical Dictionary* mentions only "real" tyrants. The index of volume v of the new *Cambridge Ancient History* refers under "tyranny" to the Peisistratids, Sicily, and cultural influences of tyrants but mentions nothing under *lemmata* such as polis, democracy, demos, empire, or imperialism (the latter two do not even exist there). John Davies' *Democracy and Classical Greece* is interested in tyrants only as fourth-century "opportunists," while the volume on Classical Greece in the Nouvelle Clio series, edited by Pierre Briant and Pierre Lévêque, and Christian Meier's important "portrait of Athens" are concerned with tyranny and the Tyrannicides but not with the issues to be discussed here. Even Jochen Bleicken's comprehensive analysis of democracy and Russell Meiggs' authoritative history of the Athenian empire offer no more than brief references in passing. To be sure, others have taken the matter more seriously: for instance, Martin Ostwald and Vincent Rosivach discuss the role of tyranny in domestic politics, James McGlew considers it vital for the self-perception of the Athenian citizens, and the interpretation of *polis tyrannos* has prompted a variety of analyses, although in his review of this issue, Christopher Tuplin insists that the most remarkable aspect of the phenomenon is precisely its rareness and unimportance.[2] Overall, then, a new look at this complex problem seems overdue.

I begin with a few general comments on tyranny, limiting myself to aspects that are important for my investigation.[3] Tyrants played a significant role in Greece from roughly the mid seventh to the late sixth century and again, at least in certain areas, in the fourth century.[4] "Tyranny" is an umbrella term used both in antiquity and by modern scholars for a variety of types of sole rule with different origins and characteristics.[5] It was originally and could always be used indiscriminately with other terms for monarchy (especially *basileia,* kingship). A precise and strict functional separation, in which *basileia* was the term for legitimate and good forms, *tyrannis* that for illegitimate, violent and bad types of monarchy, is a late phenomenon, first occurring in Thucydides.[6]

The earliest historians writing on tyranny drew on oral memory. As a general rule, such memory is able to cover somewhat reliably a period of up to three generations or one century; information surviving from earlier periods tends to be scarce, anecdotal, and "mythical" rather than historical.[7] The period when tyrants were most frequent lies substantially before this critical threshold; hence what Herodotus and later sources tell us about early tyrants can rarely be accepted at face value.[8] In Athens, indeed, somewhat reliable oral memory reached back at most to Peisistratus' "third" and lasting tyranny, the tyranny of his sons, and its fall.[9] The traditions about earlier conflicts, events, "parties," and "tyrannies" are likely to have been distorted or misinterpreted, perhaps more than once. Their nature and historicity are uncertain, perhaps unrecoverable, intense modern debates notwithstanding.[10]

Nor does the potential of oral memory to reach back to the tyranny of Peisistratus and his sons guarantee that extant narratives based on such memory are historically reliable. The Athenians of the mid to late fifth century drew on firmly established, although conflicting, traditions. Like all oral traditions, whatever their origin and historical core, these too were subject to distortion by more recent experiences, changing political perspectives and needs, partisan interests (particularly of elite families), and the fabrication of new "myths."[11] Moreover, the earliest historians wrote not only in conditions that were very different from those in the seventh and sixth centuries but also with a concept of history that differed greatly from ours. In particular, I think, what Herodotus tells us about Archaic tyrants illuminates his concerns and those of his late fifth-century contemporaries as much as it does Archaic tyranny.[12] Bad though this is for our efforts to reconstruct Archaic history, for the purposes of the present volume it is quite useful.

Nonetheless, traditions about Archaic tyranny are far from worthless. One important aspect, amply confirmed by independent evidence, is a marked ambivalence in the contemporaries' reactions to it. Tyranny in general as well as specific tyrants could be viewed both highly favorably and unfavorably, and the dividing line could run both between classes and within the elite. Some tyrants were counted among the "Seven Sages"; others were despised for their cruelty. Those who praised Peisistratus' rule as the "Age of Cronus" presumably were not identical with those who spent years in exile.[13] Even at a time when Hippias' tyranny turned oppressive, his exiled elite opponents failed to rouse the Athenian demos against him. Pittacus, according to Aristotle an "elected tyrant," was hated by those members of the elite who, like Alcaeus' faction, had lost out in their struggle for power, but he was popular among the people of Mytilene. The important role these and other tyrants played in integrating their community helps explain tyranny's paradoxical role in preparing the ground for a more egalitarian political system.[14]

On the other hand, the tyrant monopolized power; hence status and opportunities of others were vastly reduced, and the traditional competition for influence in the community was suspended. The tyrant's elite rivals had no choice but to submit, go into exile, or seek opportunities elsewhere, with or without the tyrant's support. Miltiades did so in the Chersonese, the Alcmeonids in Delphi.[15] In fact, although attested only indirectly in the sixth century, terms denoting political equality (*isonomia* [equality of participation], *isēgoria* [equality of speech]) are likely to have been coined in aristocratic circles as slogans to express what the elite had taken for granted previously but lost through the tyrant's seizure of power and were striving to regain.[16] (Such terms, flexible as far as the extent of equality was concerned, were to feature prominently in fifth-century Athens, as it evolved from partial or proto- to full democracy.) At the same time, as Solon's poems illustrate, even here the judgment on tyranny depended on the judge's perspective. Because of the power and wealth it promised its holder, it appeared immensely attractive to many an ambitious elite person but was categorically rejected by those, like Solon himself, who considered its impact on the rest of the elite and the community as a whole. Robert Connor suggests that such ambivalence persisted through the Classical period.[17] It perhaps explains as well why *tyrannos* could long be used synonymously with *monarchos* and *basileus*.[18]

By the mid to late sixth century, tyrannies virtually disappeared in the main areas of Greek settlement. This development was paralleled by and probably causally connected with the spreading of egalitarian phenomena in the social and political life of Greek poleis.[19] Exceptions remained, for different periods of time and specific reasons, especially in Persian-ruled Asia Minor and in Sicily, where Greek interests collided with those of the Carthaginians.[20] In Athens, with Hippias in the Persian army at Marathon and other Peisistratids in Xerxes' entourage, the danger of a restoration of tyranny remained a political issue, reflected not least in the ostracisms of the 480s.[21] After 479, however, tyranny was no longer a realistic possibility.

Nonetheless—and this brings us to the core of this chapter—the Athenians continued to be preoccupied, at least intermittently, with the danger of tyranny, and tyranny played a significant role in the political discourse of democracy.[22] This discourse surfaced mostly in accusations, leveled against specific politicians, of tyrannical behavior or aspirations, in expressions of general fear of tyranny, and in the comparison of the demos' rule in democracy or Athens' rule over its allies with a tyranny (the slogans of *dēmos tyrannos* and *polis tyrannos*). The question is how serious all this was and how it is to be explained, especially since, at least from our perspective, tyranny itself was not a serious threat at the time.[23]

In this chapter I shall first survey briefly the honors bestowed upon the Athenian tyrannicides, political measures enacted against tyranny, the use of tyranny as a slogan in domestic politics, "metaphorical" uses of the concept of tyranny, and the function of tyrants and tyranny in drama, historiography, and political theory.[24] All this will help us to reconstruct the ideological context of the discourse on tyranny in late fifth-century Athens, to determine the scope and intensity of this discourse, and to get a feeling for the degree to which the citizens must have been familiar with it. This in turn will make it possible to answer, on a more solid basis than before, the question of what role exactly the concept of tyranny played in the thinking and politics of Athenian democracy, what its function was, and why.

THE IDEOLOGIZATION OF TYRANNICIDE

I begin with memories (or what was later perceived as such) and measures related to the overthrow of tyranny, grouped here together under the label of "the ideologization of tyrannicide." The first item to consider, of course, is the statue group of the Tyrannicides, Harmodius and Aristogeiton. The group we know was created soon after the Persian Wars by Critius and Nesiotes. An earlier group, by Antenor, was carried away by Xerxes' troops; what it looked like and when—or why and by whom—it was set up is much debated.[25] Whatever the contribution of these two men to the liberation from tyranny, the fact that Xerxes had these statues removed makes it probable, and their prompt replacement with a new group fully proves, that the Athenians themselves placed exceptional value on them already at the time of the Persian Wars.[26] Much could be said about the stance and characterization of the two later statues. Although, most likely, different groups among Athenian citizens interpreted them differently, they also represented crucial civic values that were shared by the entire community, such as responsibility, equality (*isonomia,* celebrated in the "Harmodius Song"), and collaboration across age and social groups.[27] They were placed in the Agora—the first and for roughly a century the only citizens to receive this honor—along the Sacred Way. The site may have been chosen originally because it was believed to be the site of the assassination, but it was also close to the orchestra, that is, in a central and highly symbolic location.[28] Even later, when the demos permitted the erection of other honorary statues in the Agora, a respectful distance from the Tyrannicides was ordained in the authorizing decrees.[29]

We do not know the full wording of the dedicatory epigram. The first two lines are preserved in a late source and attributed to Simonides, while the ends of both distichs were discovered on a statue base that probably belonged to the later group. Hence this is what we have:

> A great light rose for the Athenians when Aristo-
> geiton and Harmodius killed Hipparchus;
> . . . . .
> . . . . [? politically equal (? *isonomon*)] made their fatherland.

We would especially like to know in lines 3–4 what exactly the Tyrannicides were supposed to have accomplished for their fatherland. Similarity to line 4 of the two relevant stanzas in the "Harmodius Song" (p. 65) recommends *isonomon*. The light metaphor in line 1 is equally intriguing: in Aeschylus' *Libation Bearers* it explicitly refers to the liberation of the polis from tyranny. This may well have been its intended meaning in the epigram, particularly after the Persian Wars, when the newly discovered concept of liberty as a political value was immediately applied to the domestic sphere as well; but Homeric allusions are frequent here, and in the *Iliad* the image is that of "light of deliverance."[30]

What matters more here is the monument's overall significance. As Tonio Hölscher puts it well,

> Familiar with the monuments of Washington, Garibaldi or Bismarck that furnish our modern squares, we find it difficult to imagine what an unprecedented act the erection of this one was: neither cult statues nor votive dedications to a deity nor sepulchral statues, [the tyrannicides] did not belong to any traditional category of sculptures. Their meaning is revealed by their placement on the edge of the orchestra, the meeting-place of the citizens' Assembly. There the tyrant-slayers stood not only as praiseworthy heroes but above all as concrete examples of behavior for the citizens during the *ekklesia* and the *ostrakismos*. Its paraenetic character is particularly evident from the fact that this monument recognizes not a successful achievement but a political attitude. . . . Harmodios and Aristogeiton were supposed to encourage [the citizens] to embrace the ideology of the tyrannicides.[31]

Much later, indeed, the killers of Phrynichus, hawk among the Four Hundred, were publicly honored; so were the "men of Phyle" for having overthrown the "Thirty Tyrants."[32] All this would have been particularly significant if the statues were indeed set up soon after 510, when the Assembly was still meeting in the Agora—although even after the construction of Pnyx and Theater of Dionysus, the Agora remained the civic center of the community, visited daily by thousands of citizens for public and private purposes—*and* if the statues were set up by the community and with this paraenetic purpose. For the later monument of 477/76 this was most probably the case; for the earlier, it is at least possible.[33]

The Tyrannicides received cult honors at their tomb in the Ceramicus, which was probably located at the northern end of what became known as the *dēmosion sēma* (public cemetery). The Archon polemarchos (the official responsible for matters of war) arranged the appropriate offerings. It seems highly probable, therefore, that Harmodius and Aristogeiton were put on the same level as those who died in war for their polis. This cult may well have been established early on (perhaps initially on a private basis), but no evidence survives to confirm this explicitly.[34]

The Tyrannicides' deed was celebrated in songs (*scolia*).[35] Two stanzas (893, 896) praise Harmodius and Aristogeiton for having killed the tyrant and realized *isonomia* in Athens:

> I shall bear my sword in a branch of myrtle
> like Harmodius and Aristogeiton,
> when they killed the tyrant
> and made Athens *isonomos.*
> Your fame shall be throughout the world forever,
> dearest Harmodius and Aristogeiton,
> because you killed the tyrant
> and made Athens *isonomos.*

Another stanza (894) associates the Tyrannicides, on the isles of the blessed, with the famous Trojan War heroes Achilles and Diomedes. Comparison with Achilles strongly signals the heroization of the Persian War dead in Simonides' Plataea elegy.[36] Again the martyrs of the fight against tyranny seem to have been treated like those fallen in Athens' "national" wars. The date of these *scolia* is uncertain: I tend to agree with Ostwald and others that they express sentiments formulated close to the events,[37] which, if correct, would indirectly confirm that the specific political interpretation we can confidently assume for the second Tyrannicide monument applied to the earlier one as well. Such songs point to an aristocratic environment, but allusions in several

Aristophanic comedies suggest that by the late fifth century they were familiar and popular far beyond the elite. Thus they probably were an important medium to propagate the Tyrannicides' fame.[38]

The paradigmatic role of the Tyrannicides is visible not least in imitations of the monument. Especially Theseus, the liberator from oppressive monsters and abusers of the weak and helpless, "came to symbolize," as David Castriota puts it, "a selfless commitment to the public good in much the same way that Harmodius and Aristogeiton had paved the way for better times." In architectural sculpture and vase painting, representations of Theseus' labors began to imitate the stance and gestures of the Tyrannicides. Castriota is probably right in concluding that all this resulted in a "deliberate attempt to equate Theseus and the Tyrannicides ideologically as analogous founders and *re*founders of democracy," especially when in the last third of the fifth century, at the latest, Theseus was also discovered as leader (*prostatēs*) and founder of democracy.[39] Nothing illustrates better the popularity of the Tyrannicides and the Athenians' familiarity with their typical poses than a set of regulations, enacted at an unknown date, that protected them from slander and prohibited use of their names for slaves, and the discovery of a red-figured wine-bowl, dated ca. 470, showing a drunken pair striking the familiar pose.[40]

Extraordinary honors were extended to the Tyrannicides' direct descendants. Among these, the right to receive meals at public expense in the Prytaneion (*sitēsis*) is confirmed for the mid fifth century; *ateleia* (exemption from taxes) and *prohedria* (special seats at public events) are attested later and are of uncertain date.[41] Such honors were otherwise awarded, for example, to persons with special merits about the polis or to war orphans but, as far as I know, not to their descendants. Again, the Tyrannicides seem to have occupied a very special place in the community's honor gallery.

Despite some uncertainties, it seems safe to assume that by the last third of the fifth century, at the very latest, the myth of the Tyrannicides as the liberators was firmly established and widely popular.[42] Then came the historians. Describing the Athenians' reaction to the scandals of 415 (the mutilation of the Herms and the profanation of the Mysteries), Thucydides emphasizes that the matter was taken very seriously because it was thought to be part of an oligarchical and tyrannical conspiracy aimed not only at sabotaging the Sicilian expedition but at revolution and overthrowing the democracy (6.27.3; cf. 28.2, 53.2, 60.1). For the people "knew through having heard it (*akoēi*) how oppressive the tyranny of Peisistratus and his sons had become before it ended, and further that the tyranny had been put down at last, not by themselves and Harmodius, but by the Spartans, and so were always in fear and took everything suspiciously" (53.3; cf. 60.1; transl. Strassler 1996 with modifications). This provides the occasion for the famous digression on the fall of tyranny (54–59), which raises many difficult questions.[43]

What matters here is Thucydides' insistence that at the time the Athenians were greatly concerned about tyranny anyway and that such concerns were based on oral information (*akoē*) they had received about the true nature of Peisistratid tyranny and the causes of its fall. What was the source and nature of such *akoē*? We think of an event bringing into focus alternative oral traditions that contradicted the Tyrannicide myth or, as Kenneth Dover suggests, agitation by ruthless demagogues who frequently used the specter of tyranny to arouse the demos' suspicion against powerful rivals; the latter is supported by well-known comments in Aristophanes' comedies. Alternatively, as Jeffrey Henderson (this volume, p. 175) concludes, "the historical refutation of popular beliefs was a weapon not of the demagogues but rather of their elite opponents." It is even possible that popular belief in the Tyrannicide myth had been shaken recently by recitation specifically from Herodotus, whose report on the events was the first serious attempt at establishing the historical facts about the fall of the tyranny and the role of the Tyrannicides in it.[44]

Herodotus emphasizes in book 5 that the tyranny continued for four years after Hipparchus' assassination, more oppressively than before (5.55). The Alcmeonids and other Athenian exiles failed in effecting their return by force of arms (62). The tyrants were eventually expelled by Spartan intervention, at the urging of Delphi, supposedly at the instigation of the Alcmeonids, who had gained the oracle's favor by magnificently rebuilding Apollo's temple (63–65).[45] In book 6 the historian returns to this issue (6.115, 121.1, 123.1): after the battle of Marathon, the Alcmeonids were suspected of having flashed a treasonous shield signal to the Persian fleet.[46] Very unlikely, Herodotus concludes: their family was greatly honored in Athens—hence they probably held no grudge against their city (124)—and they were among the most avid tyrant haters and thus would hardly have desired to subject their city to the barbarians and Hippias (121). In fact,

they spent the whole era of the Athenian tyrants in exile, and were responsible for the Peisistratids losing their tyranny—and so played a far greater part in winning Athens' freedom than Harmodius and Aristogeiton, in my opinion. After all, the assassination of Hipparchus by Harmodius and Aristogeiton only served to enrage the surviving

Peisistratids, without checking their tyranny in the slightest. However, if it is really true that, as I explained earlier, the Alcmeonids were the ones who persuaded the Pythia to tell the Lacedaemonians to free Athens, it is obvious that they were the liberators of Athens (123; trans. Waterfield 1998, with modifications).

Why was Herodotus so eager to correct current traditions? A long-held view, that he was on a crusade to vindicate the Alcmeonids' honor against vicious anti-Alcmeonid propaganda, is no longer plausible.[47] The intensity of his protest, comparable to that about Athens' role in 7.139, is perhaps easiest to understand if he felt provoked by widespread and deep-seated prejudices that his own inquiries had led him to recognize as fundamentally flawed *and* if he believed that the episode had specific significance for his own time. Although it is no longer obvious to us what exactly Herodotus intended to imply here, his discussion of who was responsible for the fall of tyranny in Athens was almost certainly a direct response to popular views held at the time. It is very likely, therefore, that the issue of the liberation of Athens from tyranny was not a dead and merely historical issue but a live issue in Athens when Herodotus collected this material and wrote his *Histories*. His report in turn intensified awareness and heated up debate, prompting suspicion and emotional reactions, as Thucydides attests.

At any rate, in the late fifth and early fourth century, Athenian elite families routinely claimed to have been committed antityrannists and leaders in the "movement" to expel the tyrants. This tendency is visible already in the Alcmeonids' claim, reported by Herodotus, to have "spent the whole period of tyranny in exile" (6.123.1). This claim conveniently omits Cleisthenes' archonship in 525, revealed by a fragment of the archon list, and thus his temporary reconciliation with the tyrant family.[48] Other pertinent evidence comes from defense speeches preserved from the post–Peloponnesian War period. I cite the defense of Andocides in 399:

Those were dark days for Athens when the tyrants ruled her and the democrats were in exile. But, led by Leogoras, my own great-grandfather, and Charias, whose daughter bore my grandfather to Leogoras, your [the demos'] ancestors defeated the tyrants in battle near Pallenion and returned to their country. Some of their enemies they put to death, some they exiled, and some they allowed to live on in Athens without the rights of citizens (1.106; trans. Maidment 1968, modified).

This obviously is a bad case of distorted history, caused by loose memory (the battle of Pallene by which Peisistratus seized power has become an imaginary battle sealing the end of tyranny) and by recent reinterpretation in the light of Thrasybulus' and the democrats' overthrow of the Thirty.[49]

At this late stage, the disputes about whether the Tyrannicides, Alcmeonids, or Spartans bore the main merit for overthrowing the tyrants had receded and been replaced, under the impression of the events of 403, by the collective merit of the Athenian demos under the leadership of rival elite families. The question now was, so to speak, who was the true Thrasybulus of 510. There is no reason to assume that this type of competition was new after 404. Herodotus mentions in passing a much earlier debate about who had been the greatest tyrant hater in Athens: it was Callias who expressed his opposition by buying up the tyrants' properties. Hatred obviously did not cloud his sense for good business (6.121). Such claims probably counted in courts and politics; ancestral opposition to past tyranny strengthened a politicians' credentials. What Thucydides' Alcibiades opportunistically says in Sparta to justify his family's distinguished record of democratic leadership plays on Sparta's antityrannical tradition but needed little modification to be valid in Athens: "My family has always been opposed to tyranny; democracy (*dēmos*) is the name given to any force that opposes absolute power (*dynasteia*); and on that fact has been based our continuous leadership of the masses" (6.89.4; trans. Warner 1954).

POLITICAL MEASURES AGAINST TYRANNY

Thucydides (6.55.1–2) mentions a stele erected on the Acropolis that listed the members of the tyrant family who were expelled for wrongdoing (*adikia*) against the Athenian people. Presumably, Dover writes, "the purpose of the stele was to outlaw for ever the surviving Peisistratidai and their issue and everyone who might be found to be a descendant (even an illegitimate descendant) of those members of the family who were already dead." This stele was easily accessible and, as Thucydides attests, well known. *Adikia* describes offenses against the demos, often associated with tyranny, on an ostracon of the 480s and in several other documents throughout the century.[50] Aristophanes *Birds* 1074–1075 ("whoever kills one of the long-dead tyrants shall receive a talent") is usually taken to be "our sole evidence for recitation at the Dionysia of a decree proclaiming a reward for killing 'any of the (Peisistratid) tyrants'." If so, the specific exemption of the Peisistratids from the general amnesty of 413, after the Sicilian disaster, seems less absurd and attests a continuing fear of tyranny after 415.[51]

Furthermore, before every Assembly meeting, a curse was pronounced, echoed in Aristophanes' *Thesmophoriazusae* (338–339), against any who aspired "to become tyrant or to join in restoring the tyrant." The oath of the heliasts (members of the panels of judges) contained a clause against tyranny and, although the evidence is late and distorted, by the mid fifth if not the late sixth century, such a clause was probably part of the councillors' oath as well.[52] From way back (some think Draco or Solon), there existed laws against attempts at subversion or establishing a tyranny. Such a law, supposedly reinstituting a Solonian regulation but in fact broadening the scope of the violation to fit the experiences of 411/10, was enacted in 410/09 upon the restoration of democracy (the Demophantus Decree) and repeated in the fourth century (the Eucrates Decree).[53] A similar law apparently was applied to cities in the empire as well: a clause in the regulations imposed on Erythrae before the mid fifth century sets the death penalty for anyone caught betraying the city to the tyrants. As Brian Lavelle concludes, "It appears that by the end of the fifth century the Peisistratidai had become mythic symbols of dire menace to the democracy even as the tyrannicides had been canonized as its saviours."[54] Ostracism too was believed to have been instituted out of fear of tyranny. Whatever the real purpose, several of the persons threatened or exiled by an ostracism were accused of relations to tyrants or of tyrannical aspirations (members of the Peisistratid family in the 480s, Pericles and Alcibiades later; see below), and indications are that whenever an ostracism was actually held, tyranny featured prominently in popular debate.[55]

Hence, as Vincent Rosivach observes, in many ways "the figure of the tyrant was woven into the institutional fabric of Athenian democracy. Since Athens' democracy was mass-participatory, the repeated use of these institutional forms could not fail to have an effect on the consciousness of the citizen body as a whole."[56]

TYRANNY IN POLITICS AND LITERATURE

All in all, then, at numerous locations, at political and religious occasions, if not at parties, the Athenian citizens saw monuments and images, sang songs, heard personal and political statements, and observed events associated with the heroization of the Tyrannicides, just as they heard and read curses against tyrants on monuments, at festivals and in assemblies, where they also passed laws against tyranny. All this reminded them regularly of their civic duty to fight would-be tyrants when and in whatever shape they might appear. Alan Sommerstein concludes rightly that this "helped to keep the fear of tyranny alive in the popular mind, enabling politicians to use the word as a stick with which to beat their opponents."[57]

Such fears were mobilized against Alcibiades in 415, as attested amply in Thucydides, and earlier against Pericles, as echoed in comedy and perhaps tragedy, and for both elaborated in Plutarch's *Vitae*. In Alcibiades' case, fear of tyranny was compounded by danger of war and betrayal.[58] In the 420s, especially Cleon seems to have exploited fear of conspiracy and tyranny as a political tool and was ridiculed for it by Aristophanes. Even if this was mere agitation, a crude means to arouse the people's emotions, Cleon would hardly have used it unless it promised political gain.[59]

What is important here is the remarkable pervasiveness of these themes in comedy and, as many have demonstrated, in tragedy and historiography.[60] Two sets of questions need to be answered in each case. One concerns the function of tyranny and related topics in each individual work and in each author's oeuvre as a whole: to what purpose does this particular author use the motif of tyranny, what does he achieve with it, why does he exploit it in this or that specific way, or perhaps even, who or what prompts him to be so concerned with tyranny? Such questions have been addressed quite frequently, although not always in very sophisticated ways. A different set of questions, more crucial for my present purpose, aims at elucidating the whole picture: why is it that at a time when tyranny was extremely rare in the core areas of the Greek world and, with few and brief exceptions, democracy seemed deeply entrenched in Athens, so many authors in so many genres dealt so frequently and centrally with tyranny? Why this collective intellectual concern about tyranny, and how does this phenomenon relate to that of enduring popular and political concern about tyranny?

Looking over the evidence I have assembled, two aspects leap out. One is precisely the *pervasiveness* of concerns about tyranny in Athenian political and intellectual life. The Athenians must have been deeply familiar with this concept, in all its dimensions. Hence authors could "play" with it, politicians exploit it. Hints and allusions would suffice to conjure up the whole picture and produce the expected reactions among the audience. General familiarity with a concept makes it suitable for metaphorical use. Hence the Persian king could be described as a tyrant, even become the tyrant par excellence. A new generation of gods could be accused in the *Eumenides* of virtual tyranny — that is, of having established their rule by violence and of ignoring traditional laws and rights—and Zeus could be presented, effectively and provocatively, as tyrant in the *Prometheus Bound,* in both cases forcing the audience to reflect on political tensions troubling their polis at the time.[61] The audience was perhaps even expected and able to recognize in Sophocles' characterization of Oedipus as tyrant a collective portrait of the Athenians and hence of Athens as *polis tyrannos,* which does not appear unlikely, given the pervasive concern scholars have found in all tragedians about Athens' imperial rule.[62]

Trained for decades in the skills of recognizing political allusions, the Athenians would have picked up hints of tyranny much more frequently and easily than we suspect it. Hence it seems methodologically too rigid to limit our discussion of the metaphorical use of tyranny in Athenian politics to passages where the connection is made explicit.[63] For example, as Hermann Strasburger points out, Herodotus must have intended Hippias' prophecy, uttered against the Corinthians' rejection of the Spartan plan to reinstate him in Athens, as an implicit allusion to the Corinthians' role in 432 in denouncing Athens as *polis tyrannos:* Hippias "swore that the Corinthians would be the first to miss the Peisistratids when the time came, as it surely would, for them to suffer at Athenian hands" (5.93.1).[64]

The second notable aspect is that this pervasive concept of tyranny was overwhelmingly *negative.* All the phenomena I have discussed so far, be they monumental, political, literary, or ideological, combined to instill in the Athenian citizens hatred and fear of tyrants. Their civic duty was to be tyrant haters and killers rather than admirers or emulators. Leaders and citizens defined their civic virtues and identities, their democracy and their liberty in opposition to tyranny, past and potential. It seems a priori unlikely, therefore, that a change of perspective and a positive view of tyranny could easily be accommodated in this political and civic setting, for whatever reasons.

Hence I have doubts about Robert Connor's widely influential interpretation of the *polis tyrannos* metaphor. The interpretation is based on the assumption that the concept of tyranny continued to be ambivalent, that tyrants were admired as much as detested among elite and commoners alike throughout Greek history, and that the notion of having a tyrant's power oneself remained a strong and attractive one, especially in Athens. Connor further argues that Athenian leaders, when characterizing Athens as *polis tyrannos,* exploited such ambivalence and the Athenians' tendency to be attracted to tyrannical power, presented Athens' imperial tyranny as enviable and desirable, and thus pressured the demos into holding on to it by every means possible.[65] To check this out more thoroughly, we need to examine whether the Athenians had reason, at least occasionally, to think positively of Peisistratid tyranny, whether there is evidence, in the second half of the fifth century, for a positive or at least ambivalent assessment of tyranny in general, and whether the evidence Connor adduces is strong enough to support his thesis.

LATE FIFTH-CENTURY ASSESSMENTS OF TYRANNY

What, then, did late fifth-century Athenians actually know about the sixth-century tyranny? Herodotus and Thucydides say little about this, Aristotle not much more beyond anecdotes and generalities.[66] Thucydides' references to the inscriptions of Peisistratus son of Hippias on two altars and to the *adikia* stele on the Acropolis show that things could be known if one went to examine monuments.[67] But one of the two Peisistratus inscriptions was obliterated even by his time. Many of the monuments the Peisistratids erected and the useful things they did had either largely disappeared by the second half of the fifth century (for example, the Olympieum or the buildings they initiated on the Acropolis) or were perhaps not identifiably marked as products of Peisistratid initiative. Thanks to later antiquarians and modern archaeologists, we know much about these initiatives (such as the preparation of the Agora as a public square, the great drain on the Agora, and the impressive system of water supply and fountains), but did the contemporaries of Pericles and Socrates know about them?[68] Likewise with cultural and religious innovations: as Carolyn Dewald points out, if Herodotus is representative, it is not primarily the tyrants who were credited with the great achievements of sixth-century Corinth and Samos.[69]

To be sure, in the fourth century and probably much earlier, the age of Peisistratus was remembered as a Golden Age. By the time Herodotus and Thucydides wrote, positive things could be said about his rule and that of his sons before 514, including their moderation, respect for law and religion, and beautification of the city. There are, however, good reasons to think that both these historians, eager to correct firmly entrenched popular views about the Tyrannicides' merits in overthrowing tyranny, deliberately enhanced the contrast between the character of the tyrants' rule before the murder of Hipparchus and that of Hippias after this event. It is unlikely that such positive judgments of the earlier period were shared by other historians or by the public at large.[70] Yet what prevailed in the general assessment clearly was the oppressive last phase of tyranny, probably enriched by other negative traits of tyranny and condensed into a schematic abstraction that had little to do with any specific person or place.[71] I suspect therefore that, if asked, the average citizen might have admitted that Peisistratus' rule had its positive sides but insisted that his sons were cruel and rotten; they deserved what they got, and that was all that mattered about Athenian tyranny.

Nor did knowledge of other tyrannies or similar phenomena (such as Persian monarchy) prompt the Athenians to revise this assessment, some at least partially positive exceptions (such as Pittacus or Periander) notwithstanding. To most of them, thinking in their capacity as citizens, the notion of tyranny must have been predominantly bleak, abhorrent, and negative. Ethical stereotypes reinforced this view: after all, tyrants were known to be suspicious of the best citizens, kill men without trial, rape women, subvert ancestral custom, and behave arrogantly and abusively.[72]

Context and purpose are certainly important, and we need to differentiate. Naturally, when necessary and expedient, the Athenians were able to maintain good relations with monarchs and tyrants, wherever they existed. Personally and privately, the average Athenian might have thought of tyrants admiringly and with envy: what a life they had! Just so, even staunch democrats in William Tell's Switzerland and George Washington's U.S.A. used to harbor romantic illusions of royalties, until recent scandals and disasters prompted an onslaught of unfavorable reports. With good reason, Xenophon's Hieron insists that the reality in a tyrant's life is different. Moreover, tyrants were "supermen," and admiration for supermen was probably widespread, then as now, among the average citizens no less than among young and ambitious aristocrats. As Victoria Wohl shows in her work on the "erotics of democracy," such admiration had strong and strange erotic overtones as well. Hence the demos' attitude toward tyrants was certainly not simple and straightforward.[73] But was this enough to balance the official and deeply ingrained ideology and to create an ambivalence of attitudes in political contexts as well?

Again, it is true that in a slightly later period, political theory discovered monarchy as a potentially or ideally positive phenomenon that was discussed in biographies and fictitious debates, speeches and letters of exhortation, historical novels, and philosophical discussions of ideal states.[74] Such works, however, often had a paraenetic and educational purpose and emerged from a background of intense worry about the negative aspects and excesses of democracy, on which even reasonable critics could agree. At least in part, they belonged to a genre, concerned with the education of kings ("Fürstenspiegel"), which was to have a long life throughout the Hellenistic and Roman periods and far beyond. As Walter Eder points out, they aimed at preparing the elite for a more responsible and constructive role as leaders in their communities, whether democratic or not, and in the wider Greek world that was increasingly torn apart by *stasis,* hegemonial rivalries, and wars.[75]

Precursors of such thinking and exhortations to leaders and kings (even tyrants) are known from earlier periods (we think of Hesiod and Pindar), but in political thought and the beginnings of political theory in the second half of the fifth century, we find few hints at a positive assessment of monarchy.[76] True, tragedy offers positive examples of kings, especially Athenian ones, but the Athenian mythical kings, as opposed to their Theban counterparts, were not considered tyrants, and in several cases (especially that of Theseus) they are portrayed as ideal democratic leaders (*prostatai tou dēmou*) rather than kings. True, too, some sophists seem to have idealized the tyrant, with applause from some quarters, but, as we shall see, this was a small minority, out of tune with the vast majority of Athenians. A negative typology of tyranny had emerged in the first half of the century (visible, for example, in the *Prometheus Bound*), and these negative stereotypes dominate the historians' and dramatists' presentation of tyranny as well.

It suffices to mention, in Herodotus, the speech of the Corinthian Socles against reinstating Hippias in Athens (5.92) and the story about the origins of monarchy, exemplified by the case of the Mede Deioces (1.96–100): neither conveys a positive picture.[77] Most of all, in the famous "Constitutional Debate" (3.80–82), the threeway discussion between proponents of monarchy, aristocracy, and democracy is de facto reduced to a comparison of monarchy and democracy. Its function is twofold. As Carolyn Dewald observes in this volume, it illustrates the "despotic template" by offering "a static, quasi-systematized picture of the drawbacks of autocratic, monarchical government." At the same time, as I have shown elsewhere, monarchy serves as a foil to highlight the strengths and weaknesses of democracy.[78] A similar piece in Euripides' *Suppliants* (403–455) confirms that the emphasis in such constitutional debates was placed on democracy. Accordingly, the critique of monarchy is schematic, based on the negative typology of tyranny (Hdt. 3.80.2–5), and supports democracy by establishing a stark contrast: democracy "is entirely free of the vices of monarchy" (3.80.6). Conversely, the praise of monarchy focuses on aspects that are suitable to bringing out contrasting faults of democracy (3.82.1–5).

Herodotus was no Athenian, which is significant for the type of historiography he developed,[79] and he did not write specifically for Athenians.

But, surely, much of what he has to say about constitutions in general and democracy in particular is based on and directed at Athens. Thucydides was an Athenian but a victim of democracy, an exile for many years, and thus able to observe his city from and with some distance. Writing at the very end of the century, he saw oligarchy as the real opponent of democracy,[80] but he had strong views about tyranny as well, which he used skillfully for interpretative purposes.

Early on, he comments that with the exception of Sicily, tyrants were in the habit "of providing simply for themselves, of looking solely to their personal comfort and family aggrandizement." This attitude "made safety the great aim of their policy and prevented anything great proceeding from them" (1.17). As Connor observes, apart from playing down the significance of earlier wars (Thucydides' purpose in the entire "Archaeology") this particular comment implies a sharp contrast between the real tyrants of old and the new *polis tyrannos* paradigm of interventionism (*polypragmosynē*), which delights in taking great risks (1.70) and has accomplished far more than any other Hellenic city (2.64).[81]

Next, Sparta, the model of *eunomia,* was uniquely able to avoid tyranny altogether. Aristocratic "good order" (*eunomia*) thus is as starkly opposed to tyranny as is democratic equality (*isonomia*). More than that: Sparta acquired the reputation of being a tyrant killer (1.18.1), a reputation that was greatly enhanced, if not invented, in the fifth century. But this reputation is revealed to be illusionary in the course of the war: as happened in the case of Athens, here too the liberator turns into a tyrant.[82]

Finally, the famous digression on the fall of the Peisistratid tyranny (6.54–59), foreshadowed in the "method chapters" at the very end of the "Archaeology" (1.20.2), again uses historical tyranny to reflect upon and interpret behavior patterns in contemporary Athens. Overall, nothing can be found in Thucydides' concept and use of tyranny that might reflect a positive assessment of tyranny by the author himself or his contemporaries.[83]

What the historians provide, at least to some extent, is "applied theory." What about the early political theorists themselves? According to Plato, some sophists developed theories, based on the contrast between *nomos* (custom, convention) and *physis* (nature), which idealized the tyrant. In the *Prometheus Bound,* where Zeus is denounced as a tyrant, we find the line, "No one but Zeus is free" (50). Similarly, some sophists presented the strong, totally self-centered individual, who shatters all the fetters of conventional norms, follows only the impulses of his natural desires, and has the power to realize such desires, as the freest and happiest man in the world. The tyrant can be seen as the ultimate realization of such tendencies; to be a tyrant thus is the most desirable condition imaginable. These are the views, argued for by Polus, Callicles, and Thrasymachus, that Socrates refutes in the *Gorgias* and the beginning of the *Republic*.[84]

No doubt, such views were discussed in late fifth-century Athens, and they enjoyed some popularity especially among young members of the elite, in what sometimes has been interpreted as a veritable conflict of generations.[85] But those who fostered such a positive image of tyranny belonged, I am sure, among a small minority, comprising especially those who were frustrated by democracy's strict egalitarian ideology and the limitations it imposed on the elite, as Athenagoras states explicitly in Thucydides 6.38.5 and the "Old Oligarch" attests clearly as well ([Xen.] *Ath. Pol.* 1.1–9).

This positive concept of tyranny thus was created in reaction to democracy and directed against democracy. Neither these views nor the persons who promoted them could have been attractive to the vast majority of Athenians at the time, and they were fully discredited soon enough by the experiences of 411/10 and especially 404/03.[86] I find it hard to imagine that *this* concept of tyranny could easily have been integrated into democratic ideology or served as the basis for a positive interpretation of the concept of Athens as a *polis tyrannos*.

POLIS TYRANNOS

Such a positive interpretation, however, is what Connor finds in some texts and tries to explain. It is time, therefore, to reexamine his argument and the evidence he adduces to support it. He begins with some well-known passages in Thucydides. The Corinthians urge the Spartans twice to liberate Hellas from the *tyrannos polis* (1.122.3, 124.3). Pericles then accepts the Corinthian charge by admitting that the Athenians now in fact hold a rule (*archē*) that is "something like a tyranny" (2.63.2: *hōs tyrannida . . . echete autēn*), and Cleon later repeats this, without qualification: "Your empire is a tyranny" (3.37.2: *tyrannida echete tēn archēn*). (Another Athenian speaker, Euphemus, alludes to the same comparison in 6.85.1; see p. 80.) Since independent evidence suggests that Athens was indeed compared to a tyrant at the time, the comparison is not Thucydides' invention.[87]

But why would an *Athenian* speaker have adopted terminology specifically used by critics of the empire? In Connor's view, it "seems to concede too much to the opposition. It acknowledges not only the unpopularity of the empire, but also its injustice and its irreconcilability with Athenian values. If the speaker wished merely to stress the danger of relinquishing the empire, there were many other ways in which he could vividly and persuasively make his point." The explanation Connor proposes is that the concept of tyranny was ambivalent throughout Greek history and thought: baldly stated, "Tyranny is bad for the city but good for the tyrant, for the tyrannical life is the most enjoyable and desirable way of life." Hence every Athenian, though officially a tyrant hater, was also an admirer of tyrants, and the thought of being one himself conjured up all kinds of positive associations and could serve as a powerful incentive.[88]

The evidence Connor cites ranges from statements in Archaic poetry to the praise of old man Demos in Aristophanes' *Knights,* a number of passages in tragedy where the ambivalence helps make sense of the use of the word *tyrannos,* and criticism voiced in Socratic circles (represented by Plato and Xenophon) against the positive assessment of tyranny advanced by some sophists.[89]

Of these, the testimony of Archaic poetry is clear: Solon and Archilochus confirm, as does the history of tyranny itself, that parts of the Archaic elite *did* consider tyrants enviable and tyranny highly desirable.[90] Nor, as I said before, do I doubt — or want to contest the explicit testimony of Xenophon and others — that something of a "conventional view of the desirability of tyranny" continued throughout Greek history, sweetened the dreams of average citizens, and may even have helped shape the thinking of elite persons who were disgruntled with Athenian democracy.[91] The question simply is how widespread such views were and what impact they had on political thought and decisions.

Comedy could draw out aspects of the collective Athenian character that would otherwise show up in private rather than public contexts. It could parody the average Athenian's love of power and empire as well as his propensity to build and expand the polis' empire and to meddle in other people's affairs, as in the *Birds,* performed in 414, during the Sicilian expedition. It could crack a good joke now and then even about the demos' tyrantlike rule in polis and empire, as in the *Knights,* but the skins to be flayed here are those of the demagogues. The eventual triumph of old man Demos, who turns out to be smarter than all and fearsome, "just like a tyrant," to all people in his worldwide empire, however ironical, is necessary to balance the poor impression he makes at the beginning and to show that the demos, not the demagogues, are in control or, at any rate, should be. Elsewhere in comedy, the *dēmos-despotēs* metaphor seems to be used in a somewhat critical sense.[92] Still, comedy probably *does* reflect a degree of contemporary ambivalence about tyranny or at least shows that the demos' omnipotence was enough of an accepted fact that jokes could be made about it.

Tragedy usually dramatizes general contemporary concerns, not specific politics. Again, we need to be careful. For example, in the debate between Oedipus' sons and their mother about power and equality in the *Phoenician Women,* Eteocles praises tyranny as the "greatest of goddesses." Are we supposed to interpret this positively? Certainly not. Rather, we are reminded, surely intentionally, of sophistic arguments as they reappear in Plato's *Gorgias* and *Republic* I. Moreover, I suspect, context and intention dictated the choice of terminology: by that time, *tyrannis* usually was not interchangeable with *monarchia* and *basileia.*[93]

Finally, as we have seen, sophistic idealizations of tyranny appear in a context (frustration about and opposition to democratic egalitarianism) that is completely different from that which fostered tyranny in the Archaic period. I thus tend to doubt the significance of long-term continuity in ambivalent attitudes toward tyranny. Conditions had changed fundamentally from the times of Archilochus and Solon, and what looks superficially similar should be recognized as essentially different. More importantly, the circles that voiced such views, and their motives, would have made their arguments highly suspect to the large majority of prodemocratic citizens, which in turn made these views unusable in democratic discourse, be it domestic or imperial.

For all these reasons, I disagree with Connor. Pericles and Cleon did not use the metaphor of *polis tyrannos* to flatter the Athenian demos and remind them of the pleasures of being rulers over a great empire.[94] What, then, was the purpose of this metaphor? It might be best to preface my response by emphasizing an important distinction. According to Thucydides' assessment (1.70), with which Euripides' comments (for example, in *Suppliant Women*) and Aristophanes' parody (in *Birds*) accord, in their pursuit of foreign policy the Athenians were restless activists, interventionists, and imperialists. They were perfectly aware of the advantages they gained from their empire, they did not hesitate to mention them, and they had no qualms about calling their empire an empire and to boast about the power of their city. Hence, for example, even in official inscriptions, the poleis of the empire, normally called *xymmachoi,* allies, could appear as "the cities over whom the Athenians have power (*kratos*)." But they were not officially called subjects (*hypēkooi*) or even slaves (*douloi*), even though such terms were used by the victims and other non-Athenians, by authors intending to emphasize the specific nature of the Athenians' rule, and by Athenians themselves in very specific contexts.[95] Hence, too, the Athenians countered the Spartan "battle cry of freedom" at the outbreak of the war with their concept of "the greatest and freest city," which combined freedom from tyranny and foreign rule with rule at home and abroad. This concept comes close to that of *polis tyrannos,* but no Athenian would have admitted it in this particular context.[96]

I could even imagine a debate in the Assembly (along the lines of the famous confrontation in the 440s, described by Plutarch). Thucydides son of Melesias attacks Pericles: We Athenians are behaving like tyrants, decorating our city, at the expense of the allies, as if it were a vain woman. Pericles responds: So what? If we have the power and the means, and as long as we meet our obligations toward the allies as agreed upon in our treaties, who is to keep us from acting as we want, even from behaving like tyrants? The point is that this would be nasty polemics, not normal political discourse nor, of course, part of the official ideology and the way the Athenians liked to think and speak of their community.[97]

Terminological differences, then, do matter: *archē* and *kratos* are compatible with leadership and hegemony; *tyrannis* usually is not. Because Athens' *archē* is called a *tyrannis* in a few very specific contexts, we are not free to hear *tyrannis* every time someone says *archē*.[98] Euphemus, the unusually outspoken Athenian envoy to Camarina in Sicily in 415/14, juxtaposes empire and tyranny so closely that they appear virtually identical: "For a man who is tyrant and a polis that has an *archē* (*andri tyrannōi ē polei archēn echousēi*), nothing that is expedient is unreasonable" (Thuc. 6.85.1). Yet he does not say, "for a man or a polis that holds a tyranny" (*andri ē polei tyrannōi*): the words he uses still preserve the distinction. Nor do the Athenian ambassadors to Melos in 416 mention the word *tyrannos,* as much as they emphasize that by law of nature they, the stronger, seek to rule over the weaker (5.89, 105; cf. 111), which is precisely the basis of the sophists' idealization of tyranny. The Athenian ambassadors to Sparta in 432 equally stress their city's right to rule because of its supreme merits and by natural law (1.73–78). Yet they call their city's empire an *archē* they assumed without force (*elabomen ou biasamenoi*), motivated by fear, honor, and advantage, on the basis of the initial hegemony offered them by the allies. "Finally, there came a time when we were surrounded by enemies, when we had already crushed some revolts, when you had lost the friendly feelings that you used to have for us and had turned against us. . . . :

At this point it was clearly no longer safe for us to risk letting our empire go. . . . And when tremendous dangers are involved, no one can be blamed for looking to his own interest" (1.75; trans. Rex Warner). This is precisely the context in which Pericles uses the tyrant metaphor: the empire confers honor (*timē*) upon the citizens, but they need to accept the burden (*ponos*) of defending it. The war is not only about slavery or freedom (which is roughly equivalent to being ruled or ruling themselves) but "also about the loss of the empire and the danger from those whose hatred you have incurred through the empire. It is no longer possible for you to abdicate from it. . . . You now possess the empire like a tyranny, and, though it may be considered unjust to have acquired it, to renounce it would be dangerous" (2.63.1–2; trans. Rhodes). Clearly, the tyrant metaphor has the purpose of prompting fear, not happy feelings; so does the passage in which Cleon uses it (3.37.2). In both cases the message is: Like it or not, you Athenians rule like (or as) tyrants; your subjects hate you and aim at overthrowing you; you can survive only if you hold on to power, ruthlessly and uncompromisingly. An imperial power that is perceived as, and has become, a tyranny cannot afford to abdicate. Nor can an individual tyrant do so, as Herodotus lets the Samian Maeandrius discover just in time (3.142–143).

Concerning the polis, then, the tyrant metaphor, evoking the negative associations inherent in the concept—above all, the constant danger from resentful subjects—serves, in extreme situations, to arouse the citizens' determination to pursue their city's harsh policy of imperial domination. In the hands of Athenian leaders, it is a stick, not a carrot, intended to force the citizens to accept an unwelcome reality. The same set of negative associations is implied when politicians accuse their opponents of tyrannical aspirations or warn the demos of conspiracies and tyranny threatening them everywhere and anytime.

DĒMOS TYRANNOS

What about *dēmos tyrannos*? I defer here to Lisa Kallet's and Josiah Ober's detailed exploration of this issue elsewhere in this volume but still formulate my position very briefly, for the sake of discussion. The explicit use of this concept is attested in the fourth century; implicitly and in comedy, it appears in the fifth.[99] It is essentially a critical and negative concept. Normally, it could not be used positively in democratic politics or ideology (all I am concerned with here) because of the powerful tradition of antityrannicism I discussed earlier, and for two additional reasons.

On the one hand, according to democratic ideology, *dēmos* is an inclusive concept, comprising all citizens, high and low alike. The democratic demos as a tyrant in the polis would lack subjects over whom to rule. From this perspective, the demos can be tyrant only over the subject cities of the empire. It is no accident, therefore, that in *Knights* the demagogues are the slaves of master Demos in an Athens imagined as *oikos* (household) and that, when the chorus praises Demos as a tyrant, the perspective immediately broadens to include the *archē*, the empire.

On the other hand, in the oligarchs' perspective, *dēmos* is an exclusive concept, comprising only the lower classes. Hence the demos can be represented as tyrant over the elite, the latter as enslaved by the demos, and vice versa. The concept of *dēmos tyrannos* is by necessity an elite and oppositional concept: it presupposes acceptance of the dichotomy of elite and demos, as we see it in the "Old Oligarch." Operating with the same dichotomy, as Aristotle shows, political theory, too, uses the concept of *dēmos tyrannos* for analytical and interpretative purposes. Only by assuming the oligarchs' exclusive perspective, however, and only in defensive terms, can the democrat speak of the danger of the demos' enslavement by an oligarchy.[100] Moreover, since those who aim at overthrowing democracy have by definition excluded themselves from the inclusive democratic community, the charge of aspiring to tyranny can be aimed at would-be oligarchs as well.[101]

All this does not preclude, as Kallet shows, that the demos could be perceived then, and can be now, as assuming attitudes and behavior patterns typical of tyrants, just as it did with elite values and behavior. My point is that this perspective was mostly that of the critics and opponents of democracy. To the extent that Athenian citizens themselves felt this way, which in my view remains elusive, it had its place outside official politics and ideology and played a role, however consciously, in popular sentiments and culture.[102]

CONCLUSION

The role of tyranny in the context of fifth-century democracy was complex. From a position outside and opposed to democracy, tyranny could be represented as positive. From a position within and identifying with democracy, especially in political discourse and ideology, it was seen as entirely negative. It served various purposes, depending on the speaker's perspective and intention. It could be used as a stick, by outside critics to beat up democracy and its policies, by democratic leaders to hit rivals and their policies, and to whip the citizens into determined action. But theory and political polemics do not fully explain the strong tradition of antityrannicism that, as we saw earlier, pervades the literature and politics of the time.

Tyranny was greatly useful to democracy for two other reasons. It helped the Athenians define what they were not and did not want to be: the hostile Other, which helped them confirm, by contrast, what they were or did want to be.[103] To put it simply, tyranny was good to think with. Hence "tyranny" encompassed everything that was hostile to democracy, including and especially oligarchy, which goes a long way to explain its prominence in the late fifth century. In addition, and partly because of this broad antithetical function, the ideology of antityrannicism was the glue needed to hold together a large and complex community that virtually from the fall of tyranny in the late sixth century, embarked on a new and uncharted course, a course that led it to unprecedented heights of power exerted in unprecedented ways by the entire citizen body both within their polis and over many other poleis but that also caused deep anxieties, insecurities, and strong tensions.[104]

The overthrow of tyranny in 510 was followed by a period of civil strife that was in turn overcome by demotic revolt, constitutional reform, and broad communal reorganization (known as the reforms of Cleisthenes). Despite their incisive nature and far-reaching consequences, we do not hear of any major resistance to these changes. The contrast to the violent reactions prompted by the Ephialtic reforms some forty-five years later is most remarkable.[105] Apparently, in the time of Cleisthenes, virtually all Athenians, high, middle, and low, found common ground in their shared opposition to tyranny and elite *stasis*. This new system, broadly integrative as it was, enabled them to focus on their shared responsibility to ward off the return of tyranny, threatened first by Sparta and its triple coalition in 506, then by the Persians in 490 and again in 480/79.

In those twenty-five years, the complementary ideologies of *isonomia* and antityrannicism glued the community together. As a result, the Athenians came to define their civic identities and virtues, their democracy, equality, and liberty in opposition to tyranny, past and potential, real and fictitious. Hence the lasting "ideologization of the tyrannicide," the execration of the Peisistratids, and the curses against would-be tyrants. Hence, too, the tendency to express concerns about powerful and domineering leaders and about oligarchic opposition in terms of tyranny, in both politics and drama. Such concerns, intermittent during the fifty years between the wars, were greatly intensified during the long and painful Peloponnesian War, when democratic leadership promised exceptional opportunities to gain power and influence, when democracy gradually lost legitimation that was based largely on success, when criticism and opposition increased, and when new theories of power and natural law raised new worries and threats. The results, including tyrant hysteria and specific antityranny laws, are abundantly visible in the extant late fifth-century sources.[106]

[1] Although I am not going to discuss the broader picture, I suspect that the assessment of tyranny was similar all over Greece; against this view: V. Parker 1998: 168–172. All translations are mine, except where otherwise indicated.

[2] Davies 1993: ch. 13; Briant and Lévêque 1995; Meier 1998; Bleicken 1994: 326; Meiggs 1972: 288; Ostwald 1986: index s.v. Tyranny; Rosivach 1988; McGlew 1993: esp. ch. 6. On *polis tyrannos:* Hunter 1973/74; Schuller 1974: index s.v. Tyrannis, 1978; Connor 1977; Raaflaub 1979, 1984; Tuplin 1985.

[3] For other general comments, see Morris and Dewald, this volume. The word itself (first attested in Archil. 19, 23.17–21; cf. Semonides 7.69 West [all these references are to West 1971–1992; trans. in West 1993]; etymology: see Dewald, this volume, n. 3) seems to come from the East. Yet, in my view, even if some Greek tyrants adopted eastern trappings (West 1997: 14–19; see Morris, this volume) and imitated eastern despots, the "institution" itself was certainly not imported or inspired from the east (as Hegyi 1965; Drews 1972: esp. 136–139; Fadinger 1993: 265–266, among others, believe; against this view: e.g., Walser 1984: 16; Pintore 1983; Graf 1985: 80; Giorgini 1993: 49; cf. Davies 1997: 33–34) and not similar or related to old Greek kingship (as V. Parker 1998: 168–172 suggests; against this view: Morris, this volume).

[4] For surveys, see Andrewes 1956; Mossé 1969; Berve 1967; Giorgini 1993. For the "older tyranny," also Kinzl 1979b; von der Lahr 1992; de Libero 1996. Carlier 1984; Barceló 1993; and V. Parker 1996 discuss tyranny as monarchy. The new *Cambridge Ancient History,* organized by regions rather than topics, lacks a systematic chapter on tyranny (see Hammond 1982: 341–351 on Archaic Peloponnesian tyrannies; Andrewes 1982; Lewis 1988 on Peisistratos and his sons); the Italian "equivalent," *I Greci,* has one (Stein-Hölkeskamp 1996); see also Murray 1993: ch. 9; Osborne 1996: index s.v. Various aspects are discussed in Pircher and Treml 2000. The fourth-century tyranny lies beyond the scope of this chapter; see, e.g., Frolov 1974a; Carlier 1984: pt. 3; Giorgini 1993: ch. 7, and Morgan and Ober, this volume.

[5] E.g., Berve 1954; Pleket 1969. Variety: Kinzl 1979a.

[6] V. Parker 1998 with bibliography; further bibliography in Dewald, this volume, n. 8.

[7] Vansina 1985; for Athens: Raaflaub 1988a; Cobet 1988. See Osborne 1989: esp. 313, on how few events of the seventh century were remembered in Athens.

[8] Stahl 1987: ch. 1; see also Gammie 1986; Walter 1993.

[9] Even in these reports, much is of doubtful historicity; see esp. Stahl 1987; Welwei 1992: 229–265. Various aspects are discussed in Sancisi-Weerdenburg 2000. Brian Lavelle is preparing a monograph on the tyranny of Peisistratus and his sons.

[10] See Hdt. 1.59–61; [Arist.] *Ath. Pol.* 14–15.1; recently Rhodes 1981: 189–207; Andrewes 1982; Stahl 1987: pt. 2; Asheri 1988b: 301–305 (with earlier bibliography); Stein-Hölkeskamp 1989: 139–154; Welwei 1992: 221–229; Giorgini 1993: 107–118; Lavelle 2002.

The famous "Phye episode" (Hdt. 1.60.3–5) is a case in point; see Connor 1987: 42–47; Blok 2000; Fadinger 2000.

[11] See esp. Thomas 1989; Lavelle 1993. Forsdyke 1999 offers an interesting example of democratic reinterpretation.

[12] See, e.g., Strasburger 1955; Fornara 1971b; Raaflaub 1987, 2002; Lateiner 1989; see also Dewald, this volume, and many pertinent observations in Kurke 1999.

[13] "Age of Cronus": [Arist.] *Ath. Pol.* 16.7; cf. Rhodes 1981: 217–218. Cruelty: esp. Phalaris of Acragas; see Berve 1967: 1.129–132, 2.593–595. Sages: Periander and Pittacus; see Griffiths 1996: 1397 with bibliography.

[14] Stahl 1987: pt. 3; Eder 1988, 1992; Giorgini 1993: 114. Mytilene: Arist. *Pol.* 1285a35–b1 with Alc. Fr. 348 Campbell and the comments by Romer 1982; for discussion of Alcaeus' statements, see Page 1955: pt. 2; Rösler 1980; Podlecki 1984: 62–82. Athens: Hdt. 5.62.2 with Nenci 1994: 245–248; [Arist.] *Ath. Pol.* 19.3 with Rhodes 1981: 234–235. Like others before him, Zahrnt (1989: 297, nn. 2–3) tries to date these failed attempts before 514.

[15] See Stahl 1987: 106–136; Robinson 1994; Brandt 1998: 201–204. On the continuing tradition of the tyrant-elite opposition, see Gentili 1979. For an attempt to reassess the tyrant's relationship to the community, see McGlew 1993.

[16] Raaflaub 1996: 143–145; see also Fornara 1970: 171–180; Rosivach 1988: 47–52.

[17] Solon 32–34 West; discussed recently by Giorgini 1993: 88–99. Ambivalence: Connor 1977; Dewald, this volume, discusses its reflection in Herodotus; its persistence is questioned, pp. 77–81.

[18] Emphasized recently by Giorgini 1993: 81–82; V. Parker 1998: 149–154.

[19] As discussed by I. Morris 1996, 1998; Robinson 1997.

[20] Asia Minor: Berve 1967: 1.89–122; Walser 1984: ch. 4; Graf 1985; Austin 1990; Briant 1996: index s.v. "Tyrans grecs"; Luraghi 1998; Georges 2000: 10–23. Sicily: Berve, 132–154; Asheri 1988a; Luraghi 1994.

[21] Raaflaub 1985: 99–100 (with bibliography); Ostwald 1986: 176–177; Siewert 2002.

[22] I use "discourse" here in a general and unspecific sense.

[23] Seaford, this volume, p. 108 and n. 68, and especially Osborne, this volume, disagree, but fear of tyranny, enhanced by political polemics, does not suffice to establish that any one person could realistically have hoped to succeed in establishing a tyranny (in the strict sense of the word) in democratic Athens before the Sicilian disaster. To put it differently, tyranny as an institution was dead, but fear of tyranny was not.

[24] The literary and theoretical aspects are discussed in this volume in more detail by Dewald, Henderson, Morgan, Ober, and Seaford.

[25] For discussion, see esp. Jacoby 1949: 152–168; Ehrenberg 1950, 1956; Podlecki 1966b; Fornara 1970; Brunnsåker 1971; Taylor 1991: ch. 2; Lavelle 1993; Castriota 1997: 202–209; J. Shear 1997 (whom I thank for kindly sharing this unpublished paper with me); Anderson forthcoming. Martin Ostwald (written communication) points out that the

years after 510 are also the period in which the murder of Aegisthus becomes a favorite theme of vase painters.

[26] E.g., Hall 1989: 67 on Xerxes' action symbolizing "his intention to deprive Athens of her liberty"; Taylor 1991: 18–19 on the connection between the tyrannicide and Marathon.

[27] Song: p. 65 below. See, generally, Taylor 1991: 15–16, and the excellent observations of Fehr 1984; Ober, this volume; furthermore, Day 1985: 44; Monoson 2000: ch. 1.

[28] Wycherley 1957: nos. 260, 276. Recent discussion in Taylor 1991: 16–18; J. Shear 1997. This placement suggests that it was a public monument from the beginning. A private monument would probably have been dedicated on the Acropolis, as was that of Leaina, supposedly the lover of one of the Tyrannicides who died under torture but did not betray the conspirators (I thank Ross Holloway for this suggestion). This monument, however, probably dates to a much later period, and the story may well be a legend spun from it: see Geyer 1925 with sources and bibliography.

[29] Wycherley 1957: nos. 278, 279.

[30] *Il.* 6.6, 8.282, 11.797, 15.741, 16.39; cf. Taylor 1991: 33. Aesch. *Cho.* 809–810, 863; cf. 1046. Epigram: Simon. Fr. 76 in Diehl 1925 (from Heph. *Ench.* 4.6); Wycherley 1957: no. 280 (whence part of the transl.); for discussion, see Meritt 1936: 355–358; Podlecki 1966b: 135–137; Page 1981: 186–188; Day 1985: 30–44; Taylor 1991, 32–33; see also, for related documents, n. 34 below.

[31] Hölscher 1998: 158–160; cf. Ober, this volume.

[32] Phrynichus: ML no. 85. Men of Phyle: Aeschin. 3.187–190; Raubitschek 1941; Krentz 1982: ch. 7, esp. 111–112; cf. 16, n. 2 on the designation "Thirty Tyrants." See further nn. 35, 42 below.

[33] See n. 28 above and n. 34 below. Agora: Hölscher 1996: 171–178.

[34] Cult: [Arist.] *Ath. Pol.* 58.1; Dem. 19.280. Location: Clairmont 1983: vol. 2, fig. 1 and index s.v. Harmodios. Heroic honors: doubted by Rhodes 1981: 651–652, but see (with discussion of the date) Kearns 1989: 55; Taylor 1991: 5–8; J. Shear 1997 (with discussion of the occasion at which the offerings were made); G. Anderson forthcoming. Whether an epigram found in Chios (*SEG* 16.497, 17.392, dated to the third/second century B.C.; see Trypanis 1960: 71–72; Podlecki 1973: 31–34; Day 1985: 34–44; G. Anderson forthcoming) is a copy of the Athenian funeral epigram remains an open and, on present evidence, unanswerable question. The discovery of related fragments in Olbia (dated to ca. 400 B.C.; see Lebedev 1996) has further complicated the problem. Both documents are discussed in Raaflaub 2000: 262–265.

[35] Ath. 15.695a; *Carmina convivialia* 893–896 in Page 1962; Fornara 1983: no. 39 (as quoted below, adapted). According to Philostr. *VA* 7.4.28–30, from the end of the fifth century at the Panathenaia, songs celebrated both the Tyrannicides' deed and that of the heroes from Phyle who brought the "Thirty Tyrants" down.

[36] Simon. 11.1–20 West; cf. Boedeker 2001.

[37] Ostwald 1969: 121–136; cf. Bowra 1961: 373–397; Fornara 1970: 158. Fornara and Samons 1991: 42–50 argue that the text of the *scolia* was transformed over time and, as preserved, reflects sentiments of the late fifth century.

[38] For sources and discussion, see Ehrenberg 1956; Lavelle 1993: esp. ch. 2.2; Taylor 1991: 85–92; G. Anderson forthcoming.

[39] Eur. *Supp.*; cf. Castriota 1997: 209–213 (cit. 211); Mills 1997: ch. 3. For detailed discussion of the Tyrannicide motif in vase painting, monumental painting, and sculpture, see Taylor 1991: chs. 4–5; see further Ober, this volume.

[40] Slander: Hyp. *Ag. Philokrates* 3; this perhaps indicates "a certain measure of opposition to what they represent" (Boedeker 1998a: 202). Slaves: Gell. *NA* 9.2.10; Lib. 5.53; Taylor 1991: 9. Drunken pair: Kinzl 1978: 125 with Fig. 11.

[41] *Sitēsis: IG* I² 77 = I³ 131.5–7; for sources and discussion of the other privileges, see Taylor 1991: 1–5; G. Anderson forthcoming.

[42] As attested by numerous allusions in Aristophanes: Lévy 1976: 138. For detailed discussion, see R. Thomas 1989: ch. 5. As symbols of liberation and democracy, the Tyrannicides appear on Athena's shield on several Panathenaic prize amphoras of the end of the fifth century, celebrating the overthrow of the "Thirty": e.g., Beazley 1956: 411, no. 4; 412, nos. 1–2 (middle); Beazley 1986 (1951): pl. 99, nos. 2–4; Boardman 1974: fig. 304, no. 1 (I thank Julia Shear for this reference).

[43] E.g., Fornara 1968b; *HCT* IV: 317–329; Connor 1984: 176–180; Ostwald 1986: 323–333; R. Thomas 1989: 243–245.

[44] Thus Munn 2000: 114–118; cf. Fornara 1968b: 422–424; Fornara and Samons 1991: 43 n. 22: "Thucydides is probably alluding to Herodotus's account of these events." Whether Herodotus visited Athens only in the 440s (Ostwald 1991: 138) or spent much time there even much later (thus already Meyer 1892: 156, 196–201) is unknown. That he was still working on his *Histories* after 424, if not during the Peace of Nicias, seems to me established (Fornara 1971a, 1981, whose view, of course, is far from uncontested: see, e.g., Cobet 1977; Evans 1979, 1987; Hornblower 1996: 25–28). The source of the Athenians' *akoē* might thus have been personal recitation, his recently published work, or an otherwise circulating "prepublished" section or lecture (on the last, Evans 1991: 89–90 and ch. 3; R. Thomas 1993: esp. 228–230; R. Thomas 2000: esp. 20 and ch. 8). Dover, in *HCT* IV: 329, also cited by Connor 1984: 178: "The seed from which the digression grew must have been the use in 415 of the argument: 'Beware, men of Athens, of the would-be tyrant; for nothing is easier than to give yourselves into the hands of a tyrant, *but nothing harder than to escape him again. Why, not even the tyrannicides. . . .'*" (author's emphasis). See also Rawlings 1981: 115–116 on the specific significance of Thucydides' emphasis on *akoē*. Henderson, this volume. On Aristophanes, see n. 59 below.

[45] Stahl 1987: 120–133; Nenci 1994: ad loc.; Robinson 1994.

[46] See Gillis 1979: ch. 5.

[47] R. Thomas 1989: 247–251, with a different explanation (250–251) that, I think, complements mine.

[48] Hdt. 6.123.1; ML no. 6c.3 with commentary; already Thucydides (6.59.4) corrects this detail: not all the Alcmeonids were in exile at the time; see Fornara 1967: 294–295. On Athenian family traditions: R. Thomas 1989: ch. 2.

[49] See also the defense of Alcibiades Junior in 397: Isoc. 16.25–26. Pallene: Hdt. 1.62–64; MacDowell 1962: 1, 140, 212–213 defends Andocides' version.

[50] Lavelle 1988; quote from Dover, in HCT IV: 324–325; see also Lavelle 1984.

[51] Quote from Dunbar 1995: ad loc. Exemption: Marcellin. Vit. Thuc. 32. See also Sommerstein 1987: 272; Henderson, this volume, pp. 171–173.

[52] Ostwald 1955: 112; Rhodes 1972: 194–195; 1981: 156 on Ath. Pol. 8.4. Heliastic oath: Dem. 24.149. Curses: see Rhodes 1972: 36–37, with an attempt at reconstruction.

[53] Ostwald 1955; 1986: 8, 414–415; Rhodes 1981: 220–222; Gagarin 1981; Lavelle 1988: 34–37; see also Ober, this volume, pp. 222–224.

[54] Lavelle 1988: 38. Erythrae: IG I³ 14; ML no. 40.32–34; Fornara 1983: no. 71; cf. Highby 1936: 27–32. See also Ober, this volume, pp. 227–228.

[55] Even though Thuc. 8.73.3 does not mention this motive for the last known ostracism (of Hyperbolus at some time before the Sicilian expedition; Rhodes 1994). 480s: Ath. Pol. 22.3–4; see Rhodes 1981: ad loc. for other sources and discussion; Lavelle 1988: 25–27 with bibliography. Purpose of ostracism: Thomsen 1972; Dreher 2000; Forsdyke 2000; and generally, Siewert 2002.

[56] Rosivach 1988: 45.

[57] Sommerstein 1987: 272.

[58] Alcibiades: esp. Thuc. 6.15.4, 28.2, 61.1–4; cf. Seager 1967; Woodhead 1970: ch. 4; de Romilly 1995: ch. 5. Pericles: Berve 1967: 1.198 with 2.627–628; Schwarze 1971: index s.v. Perikles, Tyrannis; Stadter 1989: index s.v. Pericles, Tyrant; Kagan 1991: 183–184; Henderson, this volume. For both: Vickers 1997: index s.v. Pericles, tyranny, charges of; Alcibiades, tyrannical disposition.

[59] Wasps 345, 417, 463–507, 953; Knights 236, 257, 452, 476–479, 628, 862; Lys. 619, 630; Thesm. 338, 1143. See also Lévy 1976: 138–139; Taylor 1991: 85–92; Giorgini 1993: 239–245; Lenfant 1997; and esp. Henderson, this volume.

[60] Tragedy: e.g., Lanza 1977; Griffith 1995; see also Ehrenberg 1954: 84–91; de Romilly 1969; Seaford, this volume, with bibliography. Herodotus: e.g., Waters 1971; Ferrill 1978; Gammie 1986; Dewald, this volume, with further bibliography. Thucydides: Scanlon 1987; Farrar 1988: 144–152; Barceló 1990, and, more generally, de Romilly 1963; Woodhead 1970. See also Berve 1967: 1.190–206; Lévy 1976: esp. 136–144, and the corresponding chapters in Giorgini 1993; Barceló 1993. Seaford, this volume, p. 104, suggests that tragedy may even reflect an increase in the anxiety about tyranny in the last decades of the century.

[61] Thomson 1929; Podlecki 1966a: chs. 5–6; Cerri 1975; Meier 1990: 98–119; Meier 1993: 108–112, 143–159; Raaflaub 1988c: 290–291, 293–294; see also Seaford, this volume. Per-

sian king: Raaflaub 1985: 123–124 with n. 251; see now Hall 1989: esp. 154–159, 192–200, 208–210; Georges 1994, index s.v. Tyrants.

[62] Raaflaub 1988c: 284–286, 294–295, 298–299; Rosenbloom 1995 (Rosenbloom is currently working on a broad study, "Playing the Tyrant: Athenian Drama and the Logic of Athenian Imperialism"); Mills 1997. Oedipus: Knox 1954; against this view: Seaford, this volume, pp. 107–110.

[63] As does Tuplin 1985.

[64] Strasburger 1955: esp. 590–604; see also Van der Veen 1996: ch. 5.

[65] Connor 1977. On the continuing ambivalence of tyranny, see also Adkins 1960: e.g., 164–165, 234–235; Lévy 1976: 137–145; the latter's conclusions, however, rather support my own. Meiggs 1972: 288 and ch. 21; Schuller 1974: 120–122, accept the brutal realism of political language reflected in Thucydides; against this view: Smart 1977: 254–255.

[66] Hdt. 1.59.6; Thuc. 6.54.5–6 [Arist.] *Ath. Pol.* 16 offers the most detailed assessment. See further n. 70 below.

[67] Thuc. 6.54.6–7, 55.1–2 (p. 69 above).

[68] For Peisistratid building activities, see T. L. Shear 1978; Camp 1986: 39–48; Camp 1994; Tölle-Kastenbein 1994; Boersma 2000, and bibliography cited by Kallet, this volume, n. 23. Kallet (this volume, 126) points out that "considerable visual evidence lay before them" (in form of column drums of temples incorporated into the north wall of the Acropolis and the Themistoclean city wall: see Travlos 1971: 143, 402), but, again, we need to ask whether the Athenians, fifty years later, knew the origins of such evidence.

[69] See the end of Dewald's chapter in this volume. The characterization of Pericles' building program as "tyrannical" by Thucydides son of Melesias (p. 80 with n. 97), if authentic, presupposes, however, that magnificent building was seen as typical of tyrants. Both Herodotus and Thucydides (see next note) emphasize this aspect as well; see Kallet 1998 and this volume.

[70] Peisistratus' rule as "Age of Cronus": n. 13 above; cf. Her. 1.59.6 (quoted by Dewald, this volume, p. 45; and see Kallet, this volume, p. 125). On Peisistratus' sons, see Thuc. 6.54.5–6: their *archē* was not burdensome (*epachthēs*) and caused no hatred (*anepipthonos*); they displayed *aretē* and intelligence (*xynesis*); they were moderate, beautified the city, were successful in wars, observant in religion, and generally respected the existing laws. The oppressive last phase: 59.2; cf. Hdt. 5.55, 6.123. This positive assessment was picked up by some Atthidographers and Aristotle. Ephorus (Diod. Sic. 10.17) and Idomeneus, historian of the late fourth–early third century (*FGrH* 338 F3), made no such distinction; neither, as Thucydides' polemic suggests, did Hellanicus of Lesbos: see Jacoby 1949: 158–159; Fornara 1968a; Fornara 1968b: esp. 402, 418–420; Day 1985: 27. On the interpretative purpose of Thucydides' positive characterization, see also Rawlings 1981: 105–106.

[71] Thus Rosivach 1988: 46–53. For factors possibly prompting the negative picture, see Lavelle 1993.

[72] See esp. Hdt. 3.80; Eur. *Supp.* 444–455; and Lanza 1977: 233–236 with further evidence; Rosivach 1988: 53–56.

[73] Wohl 1999. Xen. *Hier.* passim. I suspect, however, that such popular admiration of tyrants was vague and "generic," specifically excluding the Athenian case.

[74] Examples are, in the sequence of the genres listed, Xenophon's *Agesilaos* and *Hieron;* Isocrates' *Philip, Euagoras,* and *Nicocles;* Xenophon's *Cyropaedia;* and Plato's *Republic* and *Laws.*

[75] Eder 1995; cf. Frolov 1974b; Barceló 1993: ch. 7.

[76] Hesiod: Martin 1984; Pindar: Bowra 1964: 117–158, esp. 126–141; Young 1968: ch. 1; see also Kurke 1991: pt. 3. On the beginnings of monarchical theory, see Stroheker 1953/54.

[77] Dewald 1998: 606, and this volume. On Socles, see also Wecowski 1996.

[78] Dewald, this volume; Raaflaub 1989: 41–49; cf. Bleicken 1979; Lateiner 1989: ch. 8; Osborne, this volume.

[79] Boedeker 1998a.

[80] See esp. Athenagoras' speech in Thuc. 6.38–40 (cf. Raaflaub 1989: 47–48) and the historian's description of the oligarchic coup of 411 in book 8.

[81] Connor 1977: 105–106; see also Farrar 1988: 148–149.

[82] Raaflaub 1985: 251–257. Reputation: Bernhardt 1987. On 1.18, see Hornblower 1991: 51.

[83] For bibliography, see n. 60 above. Digression: Connor 1977: 107–108; Rawlings 1981: 100–117; Farrar 1988: 146–148; Wohl 1999 with recent bibliography. See also Hunter 1973–1974.

[84] For evidence and discussion, see, e.g., Guthrie 1969: ch. 4; Kerferd 1981: ch. 10. For the reflection of such views in late fifth-century literature, see Lévy 1976: 137–144.

[85] Forrest 1975; Ostwald 1986: 229–250; Handley 1993.

[86] See Osborne, this volume.

[87] See n. 62 above; de Romilly 1963: 125–126; on the passages in Thucydides, see also Tuplin 1985: 351–357. Significantly, in Thucydides *polis tyrannos* appears only in speeches.

[88] Connor 1977: 98. For further discussion of my disagreement with Connor, see Kallet, Henderson, and Morgan (Introduction), this volume.

[89] Connor 1977: 98–104.

[90] Esp. Archil. 19; Solon 33 West.

[91] Xen. *Hier.* 8–9: if indeed, as Hieron emphasizes, the tyrant's life knows far fewer pleasures and far more and greater pains than that of the average citizen, why is it that "many desire to be tyrant . . . and why would everybody (*pantes*) envy the tyrant?" See also Hdt. 3.52–53 with Stahl 1983; for Euripides, see Nestle 1901: 295–299; de Romilly 1969.

[92] *Knights* 1111–1114, 1329–1330, 1333; for all this I defer to Henderson, this volume, with

bibliography, who emphasizes rightly that it is always the demagogues, not the demos, who are blamed for abuses of power, and who (p. 156) questions Connor's view.

[93] For further discussion of tyranny and tragedy, see Seaford, this volume, who at pp. 107–111 discusses *polis tyrannos* in tragedy, though, in my view, far too restrictively.

[94] So too Tuplin 1985: 361–362.

[95] Raaflaub 1985: 162–171. Activists: Raaflaub 1989: 51–52; Raaflaub 1994. Inscriptions: Meiggs 1972: 227; Schuller 1974: 121 with n. 232; Mattingly 1992: esp. 136–138.

[96] I here modify what I said in 1984: 73–76, where I accepted Connor's view uncritically (as pointed out rightly by Tuplin 1985: 362). The overall argument I presented there, on Athens' ideology of absolute freedom, is not affected by this modification.

[97] Plut. *Per.* 12.1–3 with the comments by Stadter 1989. On the largely anachronistic nature of this debate, see also Andrewes 1978; Ameling 1985; Ostwald 1986: 185–188. See further Kallet, this volume.

[98] Isoc. 8.91 differentiates sharply between *archein* and *tyrannein*.

[99] For sources and bibliography, see Ober, this volume. For an early allusion, see Cratinus, Fr. 171.22–23 *PCG* IV, with bibliography (from *Ploutoi,* soon after 443); Klein 1979: 505 with n. 30.

[100] On the divergent interpretations of *dēmos,* see Raaflaub 1985: 267–271; 1989: 37–38, 60–61. Ostwald (written communication) suggests that perhaps "the expression *dēmos tyrannos* was driven home by the behavior of the *ekklēsia* at the trial of the Arginousai generals" (on which see Xen. *Hell.* 1.7 and Ostwald 1986: 434–445).

[101] Lévy 1976: 135–144; Ober and Henderson, this volume.

[102] Kallet 1998 and this volume. It seems to me that in her thoughtful and original contribution to this volume, Kallet demonstrates impressively in how many ways critics of democracy and of the demos' role in democracy could and probably did equate this role with tyranny. But I do not think that she succeeds equally in showing that in the fifth century the Athenian people actually saw themselves in this way and took pride in doing so. My doubts are based on the following observations that I state, by necessity, very briefly and, again, for the sake of further discussion. Aristotle's comments, written a century later, are important but irrelevant for the present purpose. [Xen.] *Ath. Pol.* 1.6–9 stresses the contrast to oligarchy. This author, like others at the time (e.g., Eur. *Supp.* 352–353, 403–408), emphasizes (a) that democracy means, logically, rule by the demos and (b) that, given that democracy and oligarchy are two mutually exclusive constitutions, the demos can preserve their freedom only if they share and control power (Raaflaub 1985: ch. VI). The terminology used in such passages may be pointed (*archein,* even *monarchia*) but does not include *tyrannos.* Of the passages Kallet cites and interprets, Eur. *Tro.* 1169 is explained sufficiently by its eastern connotations; Xen. *Symp.* 4.32 is critical of democracy; Ar. *Wasps* 496–507 belongs in the context of political polemics leveled against ambitious leaders (p. 71 above) and does not juxtapose rich elites and the demos. Pericles' Funeral Oration (Thuc. 2.40.1), as Kallet sees herself, reacts precisely to criticism voiced against democracy, not to the demos' self-perception

or self-presentation. Kallet's most compelling evidence comes from comedy, on which see pp. 78–79 above and Henderson, this volume. Conspicuous spending, I think, was integrally connected with holding power in a Greek polis. Democracy thus followed in the tradition of elite families and tyrants without necessarily perceiving itself as being a tyrant. If democracy tried consciously to prevent wealthy individuals from reaping the benefits accruing from such spending and thus from accumulating too much prestige, popularity, and influence (in polemical diction: from reaching tyrantlike power), this does not automatically mean that the demos saw itself as actually holding a tyrantlike position.

[103] See, e.g., Lanza 1977: 190–191.

[104] Meier 1993, 1996; Hölscher 1998; Boedeker and Raaflaub 1998: 339–344 suggest that culture and the arts played an important role in this same context.

[105] On the reforms of Cleisthenes and subsequent developments, see Ober 1993, 1997, and Raaflaub 1997c.

[106] Earlier versions of this chapter were presented, after the UCLA conference, in the George Washington University Seminar on Cultures and Religions of the Ancient Mediterranean, in the Brown University Seminar for Ancient Religions and Cultures, and at a conference on "Democracy and Tyranny" organized in April 1999 by Robert Wallace at Northwestern University. I thank the participants in discussions at all these events for helpful comments. I owe special thanks to Greg Thalmann, Carolyn Dewald, Kathryn Morgan, Richard Mason, Hans-Joachim Gehrke, Hans van Wees, and my colleagues at Brown University, Alan Boegehold, David Konstan, Ross Holloway, and William Wyatt.

R I C H A R D   S E A F O R D

TRAGIC TYRANNY

There has been some interest in comparing or combining the tyrant of Greek
tragedy with the picture of the absolute autocrat to be found in historical and
literary texts, notably the monarch described in Herodotus' famous Persian
debate on forms of government and the tyrant described by Plato in the *Republic*. But there is much still to be said. This is partly because the division of
intellectual labor has meant that the interpreters of tragedy have not been
sufficiently historical, and the historians have not shown much understanding
of tragedy. A recent book that can call itself *Die politische Kunst der griechischen
Tragödie,* by Christian Meier, has nothing of interest to say about tyranny and
contains not a single reference to tyranny outside the tragic texts. The still
more recent collection of twenty-nine essays entitled *Tragedy and the Tragic,*[1]
including one by me, does not contain "tyrant" or "tyranny" in the index,
though it does of course contain "hero." One exception is George Thomson's (1932) pioneering work on the *Prometheus Bound,* and another is Bernard
Knox (1957) on the *Oedipus Tyrannus.* But Knox's work seems to me to be
misconceived, as I will go on to explain. The discussion that best transcends
the division between history and literature is by Diego Lanza (1977), but even
this fails to do justice to the theme.[2]

A small portion of the blame for this interpretative blind spot can be
ascribed to Nietzsche, who in *The Birth of Tragedy* explicitly excluded the
sociopolitical from tragedy, and another small portion to Aristotle, who in
his *Poetics* implicitly excluded it.[3] This exclusion makes it easier for Aristotle
to concentrate on the similarity between tragedy and Homer, in which he
is at one with some ancient anecdote and much modern criticism.[4] But the
Homeric monarch could hardly be more different from the tragic tyrant. Suffice it to say here that the tyrannical practices that I will show to be intercon-

nected and central to tragedy—killing family, abuse of ritual, power through money—are almost entirely absent from Homer.

Another way literary critics have of failing to understand the tragic tyrant is to imagine that he somehow embodies the community/polis and that his destruction or exile is somehow a disaster for the community/polis. This preconception I will illustrate in my discussion of *Antigone* and *Bacchae*.

For the Athenians the tyrant did not embody the polis. Tragedy reflects, among other things, the Athenian experience of, and continuing preoccupation with, tyranny. Their attitude to it was generally hostile and at best ambivalent. Further, projected onto the extreme figure of the tragic tyrant may be anxiety at the general tendency towards the autonomization, notably through money, of the individual. I must emphasize at the outset that my concern is largely with representations of tyranny in various texts rather than with what the tyrants actually did.

THREE TYRANNICAL CHARACTERISTICS

Among the typical characteristics of the tyrant are impiety, distrust of his close associates (*philoi*), and greed. I begin by defining each of these characteristics more narrowly, relating each of them directly to the obtaining and maintaining of tyrannical power. This point can be illustrated from the rise and fall of Polycrates, tyrant of Samos in the sixth century B.C.

In an account preserved by Polyaenus, Polycrates seized power during a sacrifice for the whole people (*pandēmos*) at the temple of Hera, which was preceded by an armed procession. He collected as many arms as the festival provided a pretext for and instructed his brothers Syloson and Pantagnostus to take part in the procession. After the procession, with the Samians about to sacrifice, most men laid aside their arms by the altars as they attended to libations and prayers. But those who formed a coherent group around Syloson and Pantagnostus retained their arms and killed everybody.[5] Herodotus (3.39) adds that Polycrates then divided up the polis with Syloson and Pantagnostus but subsequently exiled the former, killed the latter, and controlled the whole island himself. He was eventually lured to his death by the governor of Sardis, who, according to Herodotus, promised him "enough money to get control of the whole of Greece." Polycrates accepted, says Herodotus, because he used to desire money greatly.[6] His tyranny coincided in fact with the early and rapid development in the Aegean of an especially convenient form of money, coinage, and Polycrates himself certainly produced coins. One use of the coins might have been to pay the numerous mercenary soldiers mentioned by Herodotus.[7]

The typical characteristics of the tyrant are generally represented, in Herodotus,[8] Plato, and elsewhere, as if they were defects of character. But what we can see in the case of Polycrates is that his impiety, distrust of *philoi,* and greed all belong to the logic of obtaining and maintaining tyrannical power. We can define each of them more narrowly. His impiety is specifically the use (or rather abuse) of ritual to obtain power. His distrust of *philoi* takes the extreme form of exiling and killing family, his brothers, whose close relationship qualified them to be trusty associates in the coup, with the result that they become associates in power and so obstacles to Polycrates' absolute power.[9] The claims of family, as of the sacred, are annulled by the individual desire for power that depends on violence—and on money, for his greed for precious metal money is not simply the vice of greed but, more specifically, the desire for the means of tyrannical power. All three of our tyrannical characteristics are not therefore just defects of character but instruments of power.

It is moreover important to see the interconnection between the distrust of *philoi* and the greed. Control over the relatively new phenomenon of money allows the tyrant to dispense with the ancient principles of solidarity through kinship and of reciprocity, for he is able to create his following by paying them. Of course, paying mercenaries involves reciprocity in the broad sense that the mercenaries fight in return for pay. But if we look at the means of creating a following in Homer, we do not find money, which (on any sensible definition of money) does not exist in Homer. We do not indeed find any single thing binding the Homeric leader to followers but a range of factors that include his accepted right to redistribute booty, his charisma, his martial prowess, his interpersonal relationships with his followers, and his ability to lead, all of them creating a sense of gratitude or indebtedness among his followers.[10] What the mercenaries value, on the other hand, is the objective power of a single thing, money.

The presence and interconnection of our three specific tyrannical practices—abuse of the sacred, killing family, and power through money—can be found in various historical and philosophical texts. Herodotus said that Periander the tyrant of Corinth killed his wife Melissa, and suffered in consequence the hostility of his son, but also sent to his dead wife the clothes of all the women of Corinth by telling them to come to the temple of Hera. When they came in their best clothes "as if for a festival," he had them all stripped.[11] The festival is used to despoil the citizens. At Athens it was said that Cylon tried to become a tyrant by seizing the Acropolis and robbing the temple of Athena (of its precious metal) during a festival of Zeus (schol. Ar. Eq. 445). And Peisistratus was said by Herodotus (1.60) to have reobtained his tyranny through the trick of having himself led into the city by a woman dressed as Athena, an action designed to evoke a festival procession.[12] When Peisistratus subsequently has to leave Attica again, Herodotus stresses the importance of money to hire soldiers in both the final reobtaining and the successful entrenchment of the tyranny.[13] The Hellenistic historian Baton of Sinope tells us that Pythagoras (the tyrant of Ephesus ca. 600 B.C.) combined "unlimited passion for money" with the practice of killing people in temples.[14] Various tyrants were said to have killed their opponents at sacrifices.[15] Croesus, Cambyses, and Cleisthenes the sixth-century tyrant of Sicyon were said to have killed their own brothers.[16] Many tyrants, it is claimed in Xenophon's *Hieron,* have killed, and been killed by, their own children and their own brothers, and many have been destroyed by their own wives and close companions.[17] In the description of the tyrant in Plato's *Republic* our three practices combine: the tyrant becomes like a wolf by virtue of tasting "kindred blood" (566a1, *phonou suggenous*) and eventually has to rely on the worst sort of people, people who "will fly to him of their own accord in great numbers if he provide their pay" (567d). He supports them with sacred money (*hiera chrēmata,* i.e., temple treasures) and the property of his victims (568d) and then, when these run out, with the property of his begetter, the people, with the result that he becomes a kind of "parricide" (569b). Plato also associates the tyrant with eating his children (*Resp.* 619c).

In a famous fragment of Sophocles, money finds *philoi,* honors, and "the seat of highest tyranny, nearest to the gods,"[18] and is "strangely clever (*deinos*) at getting to things not-to-be-trodden (*abata*) and things profane (*bebēla*)."[19] What exactly is this power of money? The concrete polarity seems to imply the more abstract notion that money has power to reach the sacred and the profane *indiscriminately,* to ignore or transgress the distinction between them.[20] We think of the tyrant using ritual and temple treasures to obtain and extend his secular power.

As for money obtaining the seat of tyranny nearest to the gods, the same triad—money, tyranny, deity—appeared in the very first reference to tyranny, by Archilochus (Fr. 19 West), "I do not care about Gyges and his much gold, nor did jealousy yet take me, nor do I envy the works of the gods, nor am I in love with great tyranny.[21] In Euripides tyranny is called "equal to the gods" and "the greatest of the gods."[22] It is unsurprising that the tyrant Polycrates was warned (by Amasis) of the resentment of the gods.

PROMETHEUS BOUND AND ORESTEIA

Just as the wealth and power of the tyrant may make him seem like a god, so the idea of deity may be shaped by the experience of the monetary power of tyranny. The most obvious case of god as tyrant is Zeus in the *Prometheus Bound,* who is not only repeatedly called *tyrannos* but also, it has been shown, embodies several of the typical characteristics of the tyrant: he is harsh, a law unto himself, suspicious of his friends, implacable, and violent.[23] I want to take this point further by observing the manner in which Zeus comes to power. Prometheus, appropriately for the god of technological forethought, knew that the struggle between the Titans and Zeus would be decided not by force but by guile. Being unable to persuade the Titans of this, he allied himself instead with Zeus. "By my advice," continues Prometheus, "the deep dark cavern of Tartarus covers Cronus together with his allies. And it is having had this benefit of me that the tyrant of the gods requited me with this foul punishment. For tyranny somehow has the disease of not trusting in its *philoi.*"[24] Prometheus and Zeus are united not only as allies but also by kinship.[25] We are reminded of Polycrates acquiring tyrannical power with the key assistance of his brothers, whom he then destroys. Zeus too can abandon the principle of reciprocity and dispense (once in power) with his closest allies. The report in Herodotus, cited by Dewald in this volume, of Polycrates robbing friends (so as to make them grateful when he returned what was seized) also expresses tyrannical trampling on the principle of reciprocity.[26]

This detail does not occur in the much earlier, pretyrannical version of the story to be found in Hesiod. Nor do two other details of the tragic version, each of which implies the abandonment of reciprocity by the tragic Zeus. One is his desire, after coming to power, simply to eliminate humankind. In Hesiod and in Homer, as in much of our evidence for Greek religion, the relations between mortals and immortals are imagined as shaped by reciprocity. A mortal may give sacrifice to deity and receive the goodwill of deity in return.[27] For Zeus in the tragic version to want to eliminate humankind is in effect to declare himself beyond the need for this reciprocal arrangement. Already in the sixth century B.C., Xenophanes had probably[28] maintained that the gods do not need anything, and the same view was certainly put in the fifth century by Antiphon and by Euripides' Heracles.[29]

If deity does not need anything, it is beyond the reach of reciprocal relations with humans. It is made explicit by one Aristodemus, in conversation with Socrates, that the gods neither need sacrifice nor care for humankind.[30] Xenophanes lived during the high tide of tyranny, and I would suggest that his concept of deity is influenced by the experience of tyranny. The tyrant, in contrast to the Homeric leader, is to some extent freed from the principle of reciprocity by his control of money. The invisible but ubiquitous power of money was in the sixth century a strange and radical novelty, which is reflected, I suggest, in numerous aspects of sixth-century philosophy, including Xenophanes' strange and radically new notion of a single nonanthropomorphic deity staying in the same place while nevertheless agitating all things by the thought of his mind and (probably) needing nothing.

The third detail to imply the tragic Zeus' abandonment of reciprocity is as follows. In Hesiod Zeus defeats the Titans because he has the thunderbolt, given him by the Cyclopes in return for his freeing of them from captivity, and because he has physically powerful allies, the Hundred-handers, whom he obtained as allies by the service of freeing them (too) from captivity.[31] Zeus announces to the gods that whoever joins him in the fight against the Titans will keep or obtain honors and privileges.[32] In the tragic version, by contrast, the only ally of Zeus mentioned is Prometheus, who joins Zeus not in return for benefit but as representing the principle of guile that will prevail in the conflict. The Hesiodic Zeus is not without intelligence, but he defeats the Titans by what he has obtained through *charis,* reciprocity. The tragic Zeus on the other hand defeats them by guile; but the conflict itself is simply omitted from the narrative, and so we never learn how it was that the principle of guile prevailed. Of course, the king of the gods cannot be said to control the supply of money. Nevertheless, this fifth-century version, with its privileging of unidentified guile, reflects a world in which autocracy is no longer simply obtained, as it is in the world reflected by Hesiod, by doing favors to obtain allies in a conflict of mere physical force.

The only other extant plays attributed to Aeschylus in which the words *tyrannos* and *tyrannis* occur are *Agamemnon* and *Choephori,* notably of the regime established by Clytemnestra and Aegisthus. The chorus, as the murder of Agamemnon is being perpetrated, fear a tyranny (*tyrannis*) but are unable to prevent it.[33] The corpses of Aegisthus and Clytemnestra, slain by Orestes, are called a "double tyranny," and Orestes is said to have "liberated the whole polis of the Argives."[34]

Aegisthus' and Clytemnestra's tyrannical coup involves in fact all three of our tyrannical practices: killing family, power through money, and the abuse (or perversion) of ritual. That killing family is involved is obvious: Clytemnestra kills her husband. As a result, the tyrannical couple does not seem to have any allies. They will, say the chorus, be hated by the people (1409–1411, 1615–1616); Clytemnestra will be "away from the city" (1410, *apopolis*). How then are they to maintain their tyranny? When, as the play ends, violent conflict with the chorus seems imminent, Aegisthus tells his squad of guardsmen to be ready, and the captain of the squad repeats the order.[35] The presence of these guardsmen, whether on stage or off, with a single crucial line spoken by the captain, is both highly dramatic and politically startling. Suddenly we are reminded that history, unlike myth, is decided by what Plato calls the worst kind of people, in the pay of ruthless autocrats. Aegisthus has said: "I will try to rule the citizens by means of this man's money."[36]

As for the abuse of ritual in the acquisition of tyranny, this is fairly obvious in Clytemnestra's invitation to Cassandra, just after the entry of Agamemnon into the house, to join the sacrifice that is just about to be performed there. Indeed, Clytemnestra subsequently uses sacrificial language to describe her murder of Agamemnon. But in fact she kills him in the bath, covering him with a cloth like a net. However, this too is abuse of ritual, of the ritual bathing and clothing of a dead man by his wife. Moreover, boasting of her deed, Clytemnestra says, "An unlimited covering, like a (net) for fish, I set around him, an evil wealth of cloth" (1382–1383). The cloth is "unlimited" (*apeiron*) because, unlike the garments of the living, the shroud is wrapped around the hands and feet of the corpse and sometimes even the head and so can like a net trap the living Agamemnon. Now this cloth is also in various ways[37] associated in the drama with the cloths on which Agamemnon hesitantly walked into the house, cloths that were "bought with silver" (949, *argyrōnētous*). They are, Clytemnestra attempts to reassure Agamemnon, replaceable, for the sea, from which the dye comes in an ever-renewed gush "equal to silver," is, she says, inexhaustible, and the household does not know how to be poor. So, in the astonishing imagination of Aeschylus, the cloth that Agamemnon walks on is a concrete embodiment of the unlimited money of the household, and so is the cloth that covers him in death, described as an "unlimited covering . . . an evil wealth of cloth." And so all three of our tyrannical practices—abuse of ritual, killing family, and power through unlimited money—combine in a single object displayed on stage, the murderous unlimited wealth of the shroud in which Agamemnon's corpse lies wrapped.[38]

"No mortal," says Euripides' Hecuba, "is free. For he is the slave either of money or of chance; or the mass of people in the polis or the written laws prevent him from acting as he wants" (*Hec.* 864–867). In general the hero of myth (for instance, as represented by Homer) is constrained neither by money nor by democracy nor by written laws and so in these respects has an individual autonomy that is not found in the democratic polis. The major exception is tragedy, which represents the hero of myth in a world that is inevitably the world of the polis. How then can he continue in tragedy to have the autonomy that he has in myth? Only by being identified with the historical figure who both emerges from the polis and controls it, the tyrant. Tyranny, says Antigone, can say and do what it wants (she means unlike the Theban citizens, represented by the chorus).[39] In tragedy the word *tyrannos* (and its cognates) occurs more often than the Homeric word *basileus* (and its cognates), and this cannot be attributed merely to the greater metrical convenience of *tyrannos*. The autonomous hero of myth, when imagined in the polis, can retain his autonomy only by becoming its *tyrannos*. And so the tragic hero embodies the Athenian experience of tyranny.[40]

That experience is ambivalent. On the one hand, the *tyrannos* is made possible by the polis. His kind of power is made possible by the advanced degree of political and economic organization of the polis, which he himself may well advance still further.[41] Yet, certainly from the fifth-century Athenian perspective, his absolute personal power makes him antithetical to the polis. Indeed, the Athenians regarded their democratic polis as emerging out of the elimination of tyranny. It may well have been shortly after this elimination that tragic performances were organized at the City Dionysia, in honor of Dionysos Eleuthereus.[42]

This sense of ambivalence combines with this sense of transition from tyranny to create the tragic tyrant. The members of tyrannical families in tragedy frequently kill each other[43] and frequently abuse ritual. This also happens in the tyrannical families of historiography and philosophy. But there is a difference. Tragedy was a creation of the democratic polis and was performed along with elaborate polis rituals (in honor of Dionysus). The tragic tyrants are not permitted to abuse the rituals of the polis. Rather, their abuse of ritual tends to be expressed in their killing of family. The tyrannical horrors of family killing and abused ritual coalesce, as we have seen with the tragic killing of Agamemnon. Polis ritual in tragedy is typically instituted at the end of the action, like the cult of the Furies in Athens at the end of the *Oresteia*. This gives as a typical pattern of tragedy family killing associated with abuse of ritual, projected outside Athens (notably onto Thebes) and ending in the foundation of polis cult still celebrated by fifth-century citizens.[44] What I want to stress here is the historical genesis of the tragic tyrant, his derivation to some unknown extent from the actual experience of tyranny but more importantly from the reconfiguration of tyrannical practices by the democratic imagination. The result is that the isolation of the tyrant, even from his nearest and dearest, with the abuse of the rituals in which those close ties should be expressed, is taken to an extreme. Out of this situation emerges finally a polis cult in which the tragic victim, say Ajax or Heracles or Hippolytus, may seem to his devotees no less ambivalent than in the tragedy itself, inspiring the same mixture of awe, pity, and relief that the time of the *tyrannoi* has been superseded.

Aetiological myth provides a basic pattern of perceiving the past. Once copulation occurred indiscriminately, and nobody knew who their father was, until marriage was instituted by Cecrops.[45] The original state of affairs is the opposite of civilized order. Once women voted, and outvoted the men on how Athens should be named (Athens not Poseidonia), and so Poseidon devastated the land and had to be mollified by the institution of patriliny and the removal of political rights from the women.[46] Here civilized order is preceded both by its reverse and by divinely caused havoc. In some aetiological myths the reversal and the havoc may be the same: the daughters of Proetus reject a deity and so are made to wander around the Peloponnese, frenzied, imagining themselves to be cows, or diseased, before being released at a place where a cult is founded. In the *Bacchae* the royal rejection of Dionysus causes him to impose a multiple and chaotic reversal of the civilized order (women as men, humans as animals, and so on), which ends in the founding of his cult.

Tragedy was created, in my view, out of the ritual enactment of aetiological myth in Dionysiac cult, and a dominant pattern of tragic action derives from this genesis. I have even gone so far as to define tragedy as aetiological myth adapted to the needs of the polis—manifestly incomplete as in any definition of tragedy, but useful to correct an imbalance. In the *Oresteia*, for example, the divine embodiments of reciprocal violence, the Furies, threaten Athens with devastation before being persuaded by Athena to acquiesce in the civilized institutions of patriliny and the lawcourt and to accept for themselves a polis cult. Clearly the Athenian audience was anxious about the devastation that might be visited on its city by the ever-present threat of reciprocal violence, which is in the *Oresteia* projected back onto what might be called the aetiological past.

I suggest that tyranny too belongs to the aetiological past. Three factors cohere to put it there. One is that the Athenians believed that the present democratic order had indeed actually been created out of its tyrannical opposite. The second is the anxiety that the Athenians did feel about their democracy reverting to tyranny.[47] It may even be that the far greater presence of *tyrannis* and the *tyrannos* in Sophocles and Euripides than in Aeschylus reflects an increase in this anxiety in the last three decades of the century (e.g., Ar. *Wasps* 489–491). Particularly interesting for my argument is that it was abuse of the sacred (mutilation of the Herms and profanation of the Eleusinian Mysteries) that exacerbated in the Athenians anxiety about the possibility of tyranny.[48] The fact that the Eleusinian Mysteries were an emotional polis ritual open to all may explain the democratic anxiety at their hubristic (*eph' hybrei*) performance in private houses.[49] Third, even if there had been no such anxiety, tyranny serves anyway to clarify and confirm the democratic order by signifying its opposite. This is particularly clear in the debate in Euripides' *Suppliant Women* between good king Theseus and the arrogant Theban herald, with Theseus pointing out the various respects in which democracy is the best system and tyranny, the worst.

DOES THE TYRANT EMBODY THE POLIS? ANTIGONE AND BACCHAE

In my introduction I mentioned the scholarly preconception that the tragic tyrant somehow embodies the polis. Here, for example, are Oudemans and Lardinois on Thebes at the end of the *Antigone:* "The city can only continue its existence by sacrificing those who are its most respected representatives, and there is no end to this persistent *self*-sacrifice" (emphasis mine).[50] Charles Segal, defending his account of the *Bacchae* against my account, writes: "It is . . . true that the destruction of Thebes is reflected primarily in the ruin of the royal family."[51] This is phrased as a concession to me, but still refers to "the destruction of Thebes." Let me emphatically repeat: there is no destruction of Thebes. Dionysus has come to establish his cult in Thebes.[52] If Thebes is destroyed, he will have no cult. I will now look at the *tyrannoi* of these plays, *Antigone* and the *Bacchae*.

Creon in the *Antigone* embodies the historical ambivalence of the tyrant, as well as combining our three tyrannical practices. First, extreme isolation from *philoi*. Early on, he expresses his disdain, commendable from a civic and even from a democratic perspective, for whoever puts his *philos* above his fatherland.[53] After all Polynices, to whom he denies burial, is his nephew. His principle is soon to be tested again. Faced with the infringement by his own niece Antigone, he says, "But even if my sister's child, or nearer to me in blood than my entire Zeus Herkeios (i.e., my entire household), she and her sister will not escape the worst fate" (486–489). But in the end, the principle is as a result of his actions realized in its extreme form, with the hostility and suicide of his closest *philoi,* his wife and son. The isolation of the tyrant from his *philoi* becomes his catastrophe. What seemed at first to be civic principle turns into tyrannical vice.

Second, money. Early on, Creon expresses the view to which he constantly returns, that those who act against him have been bribed to do so, and he delivers a comprehensive attack on the evil effects of money. Here too the high-sounding principle becomes tyrannical vice. It was generally known that tyrants obtain and maintain their position at least partly through money. "Oh wealth and tyranny . . . how much are you envied," says Oedipus in the *Oedipus Tyrannus* (380–382), and he tells Creon (541–542) that tyranny is obtained by a mass of people and by money (*plēthei chrēmasin*). This must represent a general view because it is not in fact how Oedipus became a tyrant.[54] Oedipus also assumes that the power of money was behind the murder of the previous king (124–125). In the *Antigone* Creon claims that the polis belongs to him (738). Teiresias, when accused by Creon of venality, responds, "No, it is tyrants who love disgraceful gain,"[55] and Teiresias is never wrong.[56] When Creon persists in the accusation, Teiresias says in effect, in a line (1062) that has never been properly understood, that he appears to Creon to be intent on gain, because that is how Creon himself is, that is, in effect, Creon is projecting his own desire for gain onto him.[57] And then Teiresias says, again in words that are generally mistranslated, that soon "you will yourself have given from your own inward parts one corpse (his son Haemon) in exchange for corpses, and as a result of the exchange you have one of those above, having put below and lodged a living soul ignominiously in a tomb (Antigone), and you have up here one of those who belongs to the gods below (Polynices)" (1066–1071). This passage is often cited as embodying the dual abuse of death ritual that is somehow at the heart of the play. It does that, but it also presents this abuse as an *economic transaction* (*echeis . . . balōn* does not mean, as it is usually translated, "you have put" but rather "you possess, having put," just as the second *echeis* also means "have" or "possess"). Creon will have given one (*hena*), and gained two. His tyrannical abuse of the death rituals of his own family is unmasked as being also a kind of hideous material gain: a metaphor but based on the reality of the devastating all-importance of money for tyranny. This description then, like that of the evil wealth of cloth in the *Oresteia,* combines our three (tyrannical) practices: killing family, abuse of (death) ritual, and power as material gain.[58]

Towards the end of *Bacchae* Cadmus gives a kind of funeral speech praising his grandson Pentheus. Here, if anywhere, it would be appropriate to praise the dead king for his championing of the polis. But Cadmus does not do so. Rather, he praises him for holding together the household (despite his conflict, in the drama, with all its living members over the new cult) and proceeding vigorously against the enemies of his grandfather in the city. "To the polis," says Cadmus, "you were a terror (*tarbos*)" (1310). This *tarbos* has been in evidence earlier, when the chorus says, "I dread (*tarbō*) to say free words to the tyrant. But nevertheless it will be said. Dionysus is second to none of the gods" (775–778). There is no indication anywhere of Pentheus representing the interests of the polis. He does rather illustrate the principle pronounced by the admirable Theseus in Euripides' *Suppliant Women:* "There is nothing more hostile to a polis than a tyrant."[59] It is true that Teiresias says to Pentheus, "You rejoice when many stand at the gates, and the polis magnifies the name of Pentheus" (319–320). But his next words are "[Dionysus] too, I think, takes pleasure in being honored," words that prefigure the polis festival of Dionysus founded at the end of the drama.

It is politically significant that Thebes does not seem to have room for both Dionysus and the tyrant. After the tyrant has been killed by his own mother in a kind of perverted sacrifice, Dionysus will replace him at the center of the polis festival. At the Athenian City Dionysia, Dionysus was accompanied by a throng through the gates of the city, as he was also at another polis festival, the Anthesteria, on his way to the ancient house of the *basileus.* In a demonstration of his power to reverse the potential autonomy of the royal household, he copulated there with the wife of the *basileus.* At the City Dionysia the tragedies themselves were performed, and the tribute from the allies, which was so important to Athenian power, was displayed in the theater.[60] It was the demise of the democratic polis that subsequently allowed powerful individuals to reverse the defeat of Pentheus, as it were, by identifying with the god in the festival: it is because of his absolute power that a century later, Demetrius Poliorcetes is welcomed into Athens as Dionysus.[61]

MIGHT THE TYRANT SYMBOLIZE THE POLIS?
OEDIPUS TYRANNUS

Negative characterization of tyranny seems to have been a feature of Athenian tragedy throughout the period from which plays are extant. To the plays I have already discussed, which cover a period of more than fifty years, we should add in particular Euripides' *Suppliant Women* (probably of the late 420s)[62] and his *Phoenician Women* (of 411, 410, or 409 B.C.). This negative characterization seems to express an anxiety about tyranny that, it has been claimed, was for at least some of this period not justified by the political situation. One response to this tragic preoccupation with tyranny might be, I suggest, to suppose that anxiety about a new kind of autonomy of the individual citizen, favored by social developments that include the increasing monetization of human relationships, is in tragedy projected onto its most extreme embodiment, the horribly isolated autonomy of the tyrant.[63]

Another response is what Bernard Knox argued for the *Oedipus Tyrannus*. When the play was written, tyranny as an institution was, claims Knox, a "dead issue" (1957: 58). Moreover, Oedipus is not a typical tyrant: he does not banish or kill his co-regents, defy ancestral laws, outrage women, put men to death without trial, plunder his subjects, live in fear of his people, or have an armed bodyguard; he is in direct touch with the Thebans, calls an assembly (*OT* 144), and so on (1957: 58–59). And yet the words *tyrannis* and *tyrannos* are especially common in this play. Knox's solution to this paradox of a democratically minded tyrant is that "Oedipus' peculiar *tyrannis* is a reference to Athens itself," as the *polis tyrannos* known especially from Thucydides. Oedipus is like Athens: they both have wealth, skill, power given to them freely, vigor, faith in action, courage, speed of action and decision, intelligence, self-confidence, versatility, fear of conspiracy, anger (64–77). Oedipus' hunt for the murderer of Laius "is presented in terms of Attic private and public law" (78–98). His fall "suggests . . . the fall of Athens itself" (99). The second *stasimon,* with its famous association of tyranny with the hubris that comes to grief, is, Knox argues, a prediction that the tyrannical behavior of Athens will lead inevitably to its downfall (99–106).

This case is worked out in great detail but is unconvincing. Of course, tragedy is not incapable of an analogy between individual and city. Knox might have quoted Euripides' *Suppliant Women,* in which the people of Thebes, ruined by their own hubris, are explicitly compared in this respect to a man with newly gotten wealth (741–744). But this passage would not have helped his case, for it confirms how easy it would have been for Sophocles to make explicit the analogy between *tyrannos* and tyrannical city. In the entire play, however, there is not the slightest suggestion of the idea of a tyrannical city.

Of course, the logic of tyranny may be the same whether the tyrant is individual or polis. Both, for example, depend on money.[64] An example of a detail that I have not seen pointed out is as follows. You hold your empire like tyranny, says Cleon in the Mytilenean debate (Thuc. 3.37). Your subjects do not like it and plot against you, and you will not make them obey you by doing them a favor that will injure you. Your power over them depends on your strength, not on their goodwill. Compare the words of Creon in the *Medea,* as he fatefully agrees to Medea's request to stay one more day in Corinth: "My resolve is not at all tyrannical" (348). But elaborate political allegory is, in my view, quite alien to Greek tragedy. The notion of Athens as *tyrannos* polis in Thucydides is used either to denigrate Athenian foreign policy[65] or to persuade the Athenians or others to recognize the Athenian empire as a tyranny so that they may act realistically.[66] In either case, it has a quite specific political point, which would be out of place in Sophocles.

Less implausible is the weaker claim, also made by Knox, that the qualities of Oedipus make him similar to the typical Athenian citizen (as described by, e.g., Thucydides). But this similarity, set in the anti-Athens of Thebes,[67] can hardly imply (ingenious) criticism of Athens. Rather, I have suggested, the tragic tyrant is indeed in a sense the autonomous citizen writ large. But he is also a tyrant, and Knox is in fact crucially wrong to suppose that at the time of its production, tyranny was a "dead issue."[68]

Can we, from our perspective of etiological myth and the typical characteristics of tyranny, make better sense of Oedipus as a democratically perceived tyrant?[69] The play ends with implicit benefit for the polis (the cause of the plague is removed) but not with the founding of an institution or cult of the polis. That is left to the *Oedipus at Colonus,* in which the polis to be benefited by the cult of Oedipus will be Athens. Yet polis cult is also important for understanding the *Oedipus Tyrannus.* This is, first, because the influence of cult etiology is, in my view, on tragedy in general, even on those tragedies in which no cult is founded. The second respect in which polis cult matters is as follows. I earlier noted, and so do other contributors to this volume,[70] the *ambivalence* of the tyrant: he is sometimes admired for his freedom or energetic beneficence to the polis and yet is almost universally detested; he is a creation of the polis and agent of its development and yet antithetical to it. This ambivalence of the tyrant is embodied, to the extreme degree characteristic of myth, in the tragic Oedipus, who is savior of the city, then would-be savior but polluter (*Oedipus Tyrannus*), then savior (*Oedipus at Colonus*). Here again, historical experience resembles, and so becomes shaped by, a mythico-ritual pattern: the ambivalence of the tyrant becomes assimilated to the extreme ambivalence of the *pharmakos,* the scapegoat, a slave or a king, whose expulsion or death brings salvation to the community. Indeed, it has been argued that the play contains allusions to the polis ritual of the expulsion of the *pharmakos.*[71] Similarly, the only point in the *Bacchae* at which the tyrant Pentheus is said to benefit the polis evokes the expulsion and killing of the *pharmakos:* it is when Dionysos says to him as he leaves the city for his death: "Alone you *kamneis* on behalf of this polis, alone" (963), with *kamneis* meaning both "toil" and "suffer."

Another factor making for the notion of Oedipus as *tyrannos* is admitted by Knox himself: Oedipus is not (or rather does not seem to be) the hereditary successor to the throne of Thebes; he "is an intruder, one whose warrant for power is individual achievement, not birth."[72] To this we may briefly add our three interconnected tyrannical characteristics. Firstly, we have already seen how Oedipus associates tyranny, and the obtaining of tyranny, with money. The disposal of the previous ruler was, however, contrary to what Oedipus first assumes, not down to the power of money. It was rather another of our three characteristics: in his ascent to power, the tyrant kills family. At the end of the play Oedipus' tyrannical isolation from his closest *philoi,* even his daughters (1521–1522), is total. It also, thirdly, involves a ritual (marriage to the queen) that turns out to be the opposite of what it should be, an *agamos gamos* ("nonmarriage marriage"), with the wedding song a howl of pain, the wedding *makarismos* reversed, Oedipus' self-blinding at the bridal bed assimilated to the sexual act, and so on.[73] Incest, we may add, is another extreme version of a historical instrument of tyrannical power, namely, endogamy.[74]

Finally, we must return to the second *stasimon,* with its famous association of tyranny with the hubris that is filled to excess with many things and falls to disaster. In arguing that this is about Athenian imperial policy, Knox focuses on the words, "But if one goes on his way, contemptuous in action and speech, fearless of justice, not revering the seats[75] of the gods, may an evil destiny seize him, in return for his ill-fated proud luxury. If he will not gain profit justly and refrain from impious actions, or if he recklessly lays hold of the untouchable," he will suffer divine punishment.[76] "There is nothing in the play," writes Knox, "which makes the remark about profit fit Oedipus" (104).

The reference is in fact, he claims, to the tribute unjustly forced by Athens from its empire. From this tribute the Athenians had adorned the statue of Athena with gold, which Pericles said he was prepared to use for war purposes if necessary, thus (according to Knox) "laying hold on the untouchable."

Against this I insist on the typicality of the choral moralizing. As we have seen, tyranny is generally associated with unjustly gained wealth, and Oedipus himself has at this point in the play already said how important money is in obtaining tyranny and associated his own tyranny with wealth. Secondly, the combination of tyrannical excessive wealth with abuse of the sacred is elsewhere implicit not only in the passages we have discussed from *Agamemnon* and *Antigone* but also, for example, in the choral moralizing of the *Agamemnon*[77] of 458 B.C., where it would be even more odd to regard it as a comment on the Athenian empire.

This does not mean, however, that the notion of Athens as a tyrannical polis is never relevant to the tragic *tyrannos*.[78] In Euripides' *Phoenician Women*, produced at a time when the *polis tyrannos* may have seemed to be suffering the consequences of its own hubris, Eteocles and Jocasta debate Eteocles' unwillingness to alternate sovereignty with his brother (499–567). I would do anything, says Eteocles, to have Tyranny, the greatest of the gods. It is cowardice to take the less, and shameful to yield. I will not yield the tyranny, even at the cost of war. If one has to be unjust, the best thing is to be unjust for the sake of tyranny and pious in everything else. Jocasta replies that love of honor, *philotimia,* is the worst of gods, unjust and destructive. Equality, on the other hand, binds people to people and city-states to city-states, and lasts, whereas the less is always hostile to the more. Equality has created number, weights, the mutual yielding of day and night. Tyranny is an empty name. The wealth obtained by mortals really belongs to the gods, who take it back when they wish. The wealth you seek will be painful for Thebes.

This broad debate sees tyranny not just as rule by an individual but as a phenomenon to be located in the ethical and natural world. Euripides wrote it not long after the Melian debate (416 B.C.), in which—in Thucydides' account (5.105)—the Athenians justify from a similarly broad perspective their domination of their empire as in accord with the divine and with the law of nature.[79] Notice that equality, the implied opposite of tyranny, is said by Jocasta to bind city-states to each other and to be lasting. The implication therefore is that relations between city-states may be tyrannical and so unstable. Here at last we do have in tragedy the notion (albeit by implication) that a polis may behave tyrannically.

It is tempting to suppose that Euripides has been influenced in this by the tyrannical and currently unstable relation between Athens and the city-states of her empire. I am happy to yield to the temptation, provided that I am allowed to qualify it as follows. I have said that the Athenians' anxiety about the constant potential for tyranny within their own polis contributes to the projection of tyranny, in tragedy, onto the past and onto the elsewhere as a means of clarifying and confirming the current democratic order. The time of the *Phoenician Women* (411–409 B.C.) was certainly a time for such anxiety, perhaps also for anxiety at the consequences of Athenian tyranny over other city-states.

These anxieties may seem to us in a sense contradictory, for it was the democratic polis that had behaved tyrannically. Yet in the logic that projects tyranny onto the traditional Theban other, the two anxieties may cohere. Athens may project both the potential internal tyranny that it fears and the tyrannical foreign policy that it fears to give up, onto Thebes, where they cohere very nicely. In the *Phoenician Women,* as in the contemporary *Oedipus at Colonus* and the earlier *Suppliant Women,* it is the arrogance of internal Theban tyranny that produces conflict between city-states. It is contrary to the current spirit of the academy, and to the privilege we naturally accord a certain kind of complexity, to suggest that Euripides does not here imply criticism of Athens. But it may indeed be that the novel, irresolvable, and perhaps unbearable contradiction of a democratic *polis tyrannos* sought some symbolic resolution in a reassuringly traditional form of projection onto the chaotic past of a hostile city.[80]

Notes

[1] Silk 1996.

[2] He does cover the greed and impiety of the tyrant but not the themes on which I focus: money, abuse of ritual, and kin-killing, with concomitant isolation. See also, e.g., Funke 1966; Cerri 1982: 137–155; Vernant 1982: 19–38; Saïd 1985; and most recently Barceló 1993; Georgini 1993; and the interesting remarks in McGlew 1993: 190–206.

[3] See Hall 1996.

[4] Seaford 1994: 275.

[5] Polyaenus *Strat.* 1.23.

[6] 3.123: ἱμείρετο γὰρ χρημάτων μεγάλως. See also Diod. Sic. 10.16.4.

[7] 3.45: ἐπικουροί τε μισθωτοὶ καὶ τοξόται οἰκήιοι ἦσαν πλήθει πολλοί (there were numerous paid auxiliaries and native archers); also 3.54. Herodotus also recounts a "silly story" (3.56) that Polycrates bought off an invading force of Spartans with gilded lead coins. Polycrates also attracted the doctor Democedes by offering him a larger salary (two talents) than that offered by the Aeginetans (one talent) and the Athenians (100 minas) (Hdt. 3.131).

[8] On the complex representation of tyranny by Herodotus, see Dewald, this volume.

[9] Cf. esp. Eur. Fr. 605; Arist. *Pol.* 1312b9–17.

[10] See most recently Donlan 1998.

[11] Hdt. 3.49, 5.92; Diog. Laert. 1.94. At Diog. Laert. 1.96, he plays the festival trick because he is short of gold.

[12] Connor 1987: 42–46.

[13] Hdt. 1.61, 64; [Arist.] *Ath. Pol.* 15.2.

[14] *FGrH* 268F3: ἔρως τε χρημάτων ἄμετρος.

[15] Amphitres at Miletus (Nic. Dam. *FGrH* 90F52); Callippus at Syracuse (Plut. *Dion* 56–57); Clearchus at Byzantium (Diod. Sic. 14.12.3).

[16] Hdt. 1.92, 3.30; Nic. Dam. *FGrH* 90F61.

[17] 3.8; similarly, Isoc. 8.113. Thucydides (6.85.1) makes the Athenian Euphemus state that for a tyrant, as for an imperial city, self-interest is logical, and nothing is οἰκεῖον (his own) unless trustworthy; that is, reliability not family association is the criterion for association.

[18] Soph. Fr. 88. "to the gods" translates Connington's (in my view, near certain) conjecture θεοῖσιν for the MSS ἄκουσιν (SM) or τ᾽ ἄγουσιν (M).

[19] βέβηλα is a generally accepted emendation of the MSS' unmetrical τὰ βατά.

[20] Dem. 18.122: βοᾶς ῥητὰ καὶ ἄρρητ᾽ ὀνομάζων.

[21] Fr. 19 West: οὔ μοι τὰ Γύγεω τοῦ πολυχρύσου μέλει, / οὐδ᾽ εἷλέ πώ με ζῆλος, οὐδ᾽

ἀγαίομαι / θεῶν ἔργα, μεγάλης δ'οὐκ ἐρέω τυραννίδος· / ἀπόπροθεν γὰρ ἐστιν ὀφθαλμῶν ἐμῶν.

22 *Tro.* 1169; *Phoen.* 506; cf. Fr. 250.

23 Thomson 1932: 7–10; Saïd 1985.

24 219–225; see also 305–306.

25 Prometheus is the son of Earth (210); Zeus is her grandson; cf. 14, 289.

26 Hdt. 3.39.4; cf. also 3.47.1, 3.48.2; Kurke 1999: 102–103.

27 See most recently R. Parker 1998.

28 The "dubious authority" of the *Stromateis* in Eusebius to this effect (DK 21A32) is, Guthrie argues (1962: 373), vindicated by Eur. *HF* 1341–1346.

29 Antiphon DK 87B10; Eur. *HF* 1345–1346.

30 Xen. *Mem.* 1.4.2, 10.

31 *Theog.* 501–506, 620–663.

32 392–396; for the Hundred-handers, cf. 735, 815–819.

33 *Ag.* 1355, 1365, 1633.

34 *Cho.* 973, 1046; cf. 824, 863–864.

35 Unfortunately, most texts attribute line 1650 to the chorus, which is most unlikely.

36 1638–1639: ἐκ τῶν δὲ τοῦδε χρημάτων πειράσομαι ἄρχειν πολιτῶν.

37 See, e.g., Taplin 1978: 79–82; Seaford 1998: 130.

38 For this argument in more detail, see Seaford 1998: 123–131.

39 Soph. *Ant.* 504–507.

40 This experience may have been unusual: it is argued by V. Parker (1998), on the basis of Thucydides and Athenian drama, that the Athenians were unusual in making a sharp distinction between kingship and tyranny, as a result of remembering their tyranny as being distinct from their monarchy, which had melted away at an unusually early date.

41 Thuc. 1.13, 6.54; Arist. *Pol.* 1314a29–1315b10. The ambivalence of tyranny is reflected in Aristotle's account of the two "opposite" ways for a tyrant to stay in power (1313a34), one hostile to the community and the other beneficial to it.

42 See Connor 1989: 7–32.

43 Belfiore 2000.

44 I have argued this at length in my book *Reciprocity and Ritual.* For Thebes as representing the "other" in Athenian tragedy, see Zeitlin 1990.

45 Schol. Ar. *Plut.* 773.

46 Varro ap. August. *De civ. D.* 18.9.

47 See Henderson and Raaflaub, this volume.

48 Thuc. 6.28, 53, 60.

[49] Note also that Thucydides' subsequent digression into the fall of the Athenian tyranny includes the abuse of a festival procession both by Hipparchus to insult Harmodius and by Harmodius and Aristogeiton to avenge the insult by killing Hipparchus.

[50] Oudemans and Lardinois 1987: 159.

[51] Segal 1997: 383. Cf., e.g., R. Friedrich in Silk 1996: 274: Dionysus in the *Bacchae* is "destroyer of the polis." But the only communities lastingly damaged in extant tragedy are barbarian (Aesch. *Pers.;* Eur. *Tro*). When Phrynichus dramatized the sack of Miletus, the Athenians fined him.

[52] On this, see further Seaford 2000.

[53] 182–183; cf. 187–190.

[54] Cf., e.g., Arist. *Pol.* 1311a9–11. The association of tyranny with wealth is very common and begins with the very earliest mentions of tyranny (Archil. Fr. 19 West; Solon Fr. 33.5–6 West).

[55] 1056: αἰσχροκέρδειαν, the word used of Darius' motive for violating a tomb at Hdt. 1.187; see further Kurke 1999: 84–86.

[56] Moreover, disgraceful gain is frequently attributed to tyrants: e.g., Eur. *Supp.* 450–451; Xen. *Symp.* 4.36, *Hier.* 7.12; Pl. *Grg.* 466b; Arist. *Pol.* 1311a4; Diod. Sic. 10.16.4.

[57] Rather as Oedipus in the *Oedipus Tyrannos* projects his own love of tyranny onto Creon.

[58] For this argument in more detail, see Seaford 1998.

[59] 429; see also *Phoen.* 560. For the tyrant serving his own interests as opposed to those of the polis, see, e.g., Arist. *Pol.* 1295a19–23.

[60] R. Parker 1996: 259.

[61] Plut. *Demetr.* 12; Douris *FGrH* 76F13; Parker 1996: 259; Mark Antony was also welcomed into Athens (and Ephesus) as Dionysus by the whole community.

[62] On tyranny in this drama, see Raaflaub, this volume.

[63] I show in my forthcoming book on money among the ancient Greeks that the interconnection of our three tyrannical practices is observable also in the individual citizen of Classical Athens.

[64] See Kallet, this volume.

[65] 1.122.3, 124.3.

[66] 2.63.2, 3.37.2, 6.85.1.

[67] For this idea, see Zeitlin 1990.

[68] Knox relies on the odd argument that Aristophanic parody of accusations of tyrannical ambition shows that nobody took such accusations seriously. But cf. Henderson and Raaflaub, this volume.

[69] A referee observed that my "reading . . . does not take into account the complexity of the play." I readily admit that my brief discussion fails to perform this impossible task.

[70] See especially the contributions by Dewald, Raaflaub, and Kallet, this volume; also McGlew 1993.

[71] Vernant 1990: 113–114; Guépin 1968; on the ruler generally as *pharmakos,* see Ogden 1997.

[72] Knox 1957: 54.

[73] 420–423, 1275–1284; Seaford 1987: 119–120.

[74] Gernet 1981: 289–302; cf. Hdt. 3.31; Pl. *Resp.* 571d; Diog. Laert. 1.96; Vernant 1982.

[75] Knox (1957: 103–104) translates ἔδη here as "statues," in an implausible attempt to relate it to the impeachment of Pheidias for carving the portrait of Pericles on Athena's shield.

[76] 883–889: the words referring to the divine punishment are corrupted and are here merely paraphrased.

[77] See esp. 367–384 (N.B. 371 ἀθίκτων, as at *OT* 891), 773–780.

[78] As well as *Phoen.* one might mention Eur. *Hel.* 395 and *Or.* 1168, both associated by de Romilly (1969: 178) with Athens in relation to her empire.

[79] Thuc. 5.105.

[80] My thanks go to participants in the UCLA conference for lively discussion, and in particular to Greg Thalmann for his formal response.

L I S A   K A L L E T

DĒMOS TYRANNOS: WEALTH, POWER, AND
ECONOMIC PATRONAGE

The party line in fifth-century B.C. Athens on tyrants and tyranny is not difficult to find. The image of the tyrant as antithetical to, indeed the polar opposite of, the free community in general, and democracy in Athens specifically,
is ubiquitous. The tyrant as ideological Other pervaded the discourse and life
of the democratic polis, as several of the essays in this volume make clear.
Euripides' formulation in the *Suppliants,* when Theseus expresses the view
that "nothing is more harmful to a city than a tyrant," is typical:[1] the presence of a tyrant means the absence of equality. The metaphor of the tyrant,
and the historical memory of both the sixth-century Peisistratid tyranny and
the threat of Persian domination, served to define Athenians and were reflected not only in genres like tragedy but in the daily realities of democratic
Athenian life.

Such prominence has seemed surprising to some, for the Athenians had
been free from tyranny since the late sixth century, and the institution of
ostracism in theory effectively eliminated the possibility that tyranny might
reappear in the polis. Yet, as Vincent Rosivach has pointed out, the figure of
the tyrant was woven into the institutional fabric of the democracy, by means
of procedures like the heliastic and bouleutic oaths (though we do not know
exactly when these were initiated) and the heroizing of the "tyrant slayers,"
Harmodius and Aristogeiton.[2] In fact, these public reminders of tyranny bring
out an essential point, namely, that tyranny was central to *collective* Athenian
identity; it was something about which all Athenians could agree as represented in "official" discourse and therefore could serve as a crucial binding
agent in a polis with otherwise conflicting and competing interests and ideologies, like those of the farmer, rower, trader, and wealthy landowning elite.

Yet at the same time, Greek writers, mostly Athenian, played with the
identity of Athens as a tyrant: thus not who we are not, but who we are.

The evident usefulness of the metaphorical image of the tyrant in contemporary discourse extended to both the polis' role as ruler of an empire and the demos' role as sovereign of Athens. Two questions immediately present themselves: first, in what way were the polis and the demos like a tyrant, and, second, was such a metaphor universally negative? Scholars examining the deployment of the metaphor of Athens the tyrant city have been concerned primarily with its imperial context of Athens as a tyrant ruling over its subjects in the *archē* (empire).[3] This makes sense, given that the conception of the city as tyrant appears explicitly in connection with Athens' rule over its allies. Less attention has been paid to the notion of the demos as tyrant in a domestic context, which is what I shall focus on here. I shall suggest in what follows that when we look at one remarkable feature of democratic Athens, namely, the demos' control over and use of its massive public moneys, the conception of the demos as tyrant becomes more ambiguous, ranging (depending on context, speaker, and audience) from formulations that resist the identification to those that flirt with—if not broadcast—the notion, making it seem even appealing and empowering.[4] Thus my approach and argument will differ substantially from those of Kurt Raaflaub and Josiah Ober in their essays, who view the metaphor of the tyrant as unequivocally negative by the fifth century (Raaflaub) or, relatedly, see its application to the demos emanating from democracy's critics (Ober).

Three points need to be made clear at the outset. First, *dēmos tyrannos* and *polis tyrannos* are clearly interrelated, in the same way as are Athenian democracy and *archē*.[5] Thus the focus here on *dēmos tyrannos* aims not to create an artificial distinction but rather to give weight to the deployment of the metaphor in the domestic, political realm in an attempt to appreciate more fully and accurately its nuances in both democratic and imperial spheres. Second, the argument that the metaphor of tyranny was not deployed in a negative context alone does not deny or necessarily weaken the potency of the "official" antityranny party line, central as it is to fifth- and fourth-century democratic ideology. Rather, the metaphor is used and viewed in complex and subtle ways, not in a uniform and transparent, negative sense alone. Finally, though I shall suggest that this strand of thinking about the demos as tyrant would have been embraced by ordinary Athenian citizens, itself constituting a democratic self-representation, my argument is, nevertheless, largely implicit (and therefore speculative). This is necessarily so precisely because of the integration of the tyrant as Other in dominant democratic ideology.

To argue for something that is largely unspoken, but felt by many, requires consideration of context, genre, and audience: we have no grounds for assuming a cohesive citizen body that thought the same—Pericles' Funeral Oration is a prime example of the presence of constituent groups and attitudes within the polis to which Pericles nods—or individuals or groups who over time maintained a consistent outlook toward their world.[6] Thus, when a viewpoint seems polemically expressed in a text, it presupposes at least one alternative way of thinking. Accordingly, we may be able to infer other attitudes.

Because my argument depends on much that is implicit, some background is necessary to establish the conceptual framework in which an Athenian might think of tyranny as a metaphorical concept within the democracy. I shall consider the following themes as preliminary to my main topic, *dēmos tyrannos* and the uses of its wealth: the ambiguity of the tyrant and tyranny; the connections between democracy, the demos, and tyranny; and the connections between wealth and tyranny. Then we shall be adequately positioned to examine the notion of *dēmos tyrannos* as spender and economic patron and to explore the connotations.

THE AMBIGUITY OF THE TYRANT AND TYRANNY

On the face of it, given the distaste for tyranny at this time, it would seem that the metaphor of the tyrant city would be unequivocally negative. Not so, according to W. R. Connor in his important study on the conception of the tyrant city. He argues that contemporary allusions to tyranny reveal the ambiguity of the metaphor. As he notes, "When the word reflects upon the situation of the ruler it is commonly neutral or positive in tone; when it reflects upon the situation of the tyrant's subjects it is commonly hostile in connotation."[7] Kurt Raaflaub agreed with part of this in his 1984 study on the role of the tyrant metaphor in the ideology of power in Athens: the absolute freedom shared by tyrant and Athens could be represented as similar, and the metaphor would therefore not necessarily be negative.[8] He now, however, argues that any ambiguity essentially disappeared by the fifth century, at least in Athens, and in his essay vigorously contests Connor's thesis. As this debate is directly relevant to the interpretations and arguments of this essay, I want briefly to address the issue of connotation.

As mentioned above, the context of allusions to tyrants and tyranny is important to appreciate as well as the differing reception to and interpretation of a comment or statement that would have depended on the perspective of the listener as well as of the speaker. A famous passage often cited as an unequivocally negative comment about the *polis tyrannos* comes from Pericles' last speech to the Athenians in Thucydides (2.63.2), in which the statesman comments, "Your *archē* is like a tyranny" (echoed by Cleon without the qualification in 3.37.2: "Your *archē* is a tyranny"). He continues by warning against the danger in disbanding it. As Raaflaub notes, this is a comment designed to instill fear in the audience. But what audience? Pericles' assertion is not a blanket statement about the empire (or the city of Athens), nor is it directed at all Athenians. Further, it has a specific rhetorical purpose for this occasion. Pericles directs his comments specifically at *apragmones,* "uninvolved ones" (in this context, those who want peace), not all Athenians. The statesman makes a pointed comment about the *archē* that likens it to a tyranny but in a rhetorical argument with the specific, limited purpose of making them see the danger in giving it up. These individuals, the *apragmones,* would be those who believe that it was wrong (*adikon*) to acquire the *archē;* but that would not necessarily have been a view shared by all. Thus this comment is not reflective of a widespread sentiment and does not in fact tell us all we need to know about attitudes toward tyranny, which may be more varied.

Consider a passage from Euripides' *Trojan Women* of 415. When Hecuba speaks to the dead Astyanax, lamenting his premature death, she reviews the blessed life in store for her grandson had he lived to maturity. His death is "unfortunate": he will never have known manhood, his wedding, nor "godlike tyranny" (*isotheos tyrannis,* 1169). While these words come from the mouth of a foreign, eastern queen, and by itself the phrase might therefore have a negative connotation, the linkage with the positive circumstances of manhood and wedding, and the sympathetic nature of Hecuba's character and position as grandmother (and mother), make the reference to "godlike tyranny" more ambiguous, if not positive.

Finally, even sources critical of tyranny can make positive statements about specific tyrants: Aristotle, for example, could call the tyrannies of the Orthagorids in Sicyon and Peisistratus "moderate" (and long lasting) because of their respect for the existing laws (*Pol.* 1315b13–32),[9] a sentiment that, concerning Peisistratus, is reflected in the fifth-century texts of Herodotus (1.59.6) and Thucydides (6.54.5–6, referring to both Peisistratus and Hippias), to which I shall return.

There are more passages that do not neatly fit the negative interpretation of the tyrant and tyranny, some of which I shall examine below.[10] These few prefatory illustrations, however, suffice to demonstrate that positive, ambiguous, as well as negative interpretations of and attitudes toward tyranny could coexist in Athens.

DEMOCRACY, THE DEMOS AND TYRANNY: THE CONNECTIONS

The notion that democracy and tyranny shared features appears frequently in Aristotle's numerous comparisons between the two forms of government in the *Politics*. One common formulation is that unbridled democracy leads to tyranny (e.g., 1296a1–5, as does oligarchy; cf. 1310b3–4 and 1312b32–38). Democracy and tyranny are held to share characteristics like "independence [lit. *anarchia*] of slaves . . . and women and children and letting one live as he likes" (1319b28–30; cf. also *Pol.* 1313b32–38). Consider the similarity between the private freedoms to which Aristotle refers and those mentioned by Pericles in the Funeral Oration, whose context is fundamentally different and not intended to liken democracy to tyranny. In a description of Athens' *politeia,* he asserts, "As free men we administer our public affairs and with respect to mutual suspicion in our daily pursuits, we do not get irritated at our neighbor for doing whatever he likes" (2.37.2).

The metaphor of the tyrant is applied to the demos, as opposed to the abstract *dēmokratia,* in *Politics* 1274a5–7, in a discussion on the impact of Solon's reforms: "For when the lawcourt had power, men courted the demos just as a tyrant and brought the *politeia* to its present democracy." Two chief hallmarks of the tyrant, though not exclusive to him, to be free and to rule, are implicitly reflected in the comment made by the anonymous fifth-century writer dubbed the "Old Oligarch" in his polemical treatise on the nature of Athenian democracy. He asserts that the demos "wants not to be slaves in a well-governed [or "well-ordered"] city, but to be free and to rule."[11] While this statement would apply well to the polis in its role as imperial power, the context here, significantly for our purposes, is domestic, concerned with, as Jacqueline de Romilly puts it, "home policy":[12] the author is describing the functioning of the *dēmokratia* and contrasts the phrase ἐλεύθερος εἶναι καὶ ἀρχεῖν, "to be free and to rule," with government at home (*eunomoumenēs*).

Similarly, in the context of developments that occur in the final form of democracy and that are conducive to tyranny, Aristotle comments, "For the demos wants to be *monarchos*" (*Pol.* 1313b38). Here too the context is the demos at home, and while Aristotle uses the term *monarchos,* the topic under discussion, of which the above comment is a parenthesis, is the similarities between tyranny and the extreme form of democracy. Indeed, given the intimate connection that the Greek concept of freedom has to the right to rule, tyranny and democracy, like democracy and *archē,* fit neatly together, for the demos occupies a similar position to the tyrant: the people want absolute power and are unaccountable, though they, like Aristotle's "moderate" tyrants, Peisistratus and the Orthagorids, would contend that they obeyed the laws.[13]

These passages reveal that the demos can be regarded as a tyrant at home, as Jeffrey Henderson also emphasizes in his essay. Yet Raaflaub has posed a crucial question in considering the *dēmos tyrannos,* namely, over whom would it rule within a domestic context? Defined as the collective, all-inclusive citizenry, the objection underlying his question is valid. The sources mentioned above, however, as well as Aristophanes (as Henderson also notes), can and do represent the demos as an interest group in the polis as distinct from an elite minority. Thus, the demos, in this definition, would hold absolute sway over its fellow, elite citizens.

The writers just surveyed are unequivocally critical of democracy. Yet their statements do not preclude an alternative, more ambiguous, or even positive position that might emerge with a different perspective and context, especially concerning specific aspects of a tyrant's position. For example, not many Greeks of the time would find the idea of "being free and ruling" distasteful. As Plato comments in the *Laws* 661a–b, "Many other things are said to be good . . . being a tyrant and doing whatever you like." He sets this up to reject it, of course, but it presupposes a common attitude. Likewise, from an earlier period and context, when the Archaic poet Archilochus of Paros asserts, "I do not care for the possessions of Gyges, rich in gold, nor has envy ever gripped me,"[14] the rather contrarian tone suggests that other contemporaries did envy and desire the riches of that Lydian tyrant. That fragment of Archilochus' poems not only contains the earliest extant appearance of the word *tyrannos,* but also intimately links tyranny and wealth. Indeed, tyrants' wealth and specifically what they do with it are aspects in which we are most likely to find more ambiguous commentary.

TYRANNY AND WEALTH

It is a commonplace in ancient authors that the sine qua non of tyranny, and therefore an essential defining characteristic of it, is the tyrant's extraordinary wealth (usually put in terms of money).[15] That the association was made early on is clear from Archilochus' verses quoted above.[16] Thucydides

makes a causal connection between wealth and tyranny when he comments
that "when Hellas was becoming stronger and acquiring even more money
than before, tyrannies set themselves up in the cities, since revenues were increasing" (1.13). Indeed the point is often made that for those whose wealth
outstrips others', tyrannical power is almost an inevitable result. As Aristotle
(*Pol.* 1295b20) puts it, the excessively wealthy know how to govern only in
the manner of a master (ἄρχειν δὲ δεσποτικὴν ἀρχήν). Moreover, according
to Aristotle, the goal of tyranny (as that of oligarchy) is wealth (*plouton*) (*Pol.*
1311a9–10), implicitly echoed in Thucydides 1.17: tyrants did not do much
remarkable inasmuch as, among other things, they were (overly) concerned
to increase their own private wealth.

An important element of the ambiguity contained in both the tyrant
metaphor and attitudes toward tyranny was the spectacular (in a literal sense,
that is, ostentatious and meant to be seen) wealth that attended the tyrant.
The possession of such wealth (and power) was enviable and therefore something that one would desire to obtain for oneself, however morally or politically problematic it might be to critics and subjects. In ancient Greek
conceptions, how do tyrants get their wealth and what do they do with it?

TYRANTS AND TAXATION

It is a virtual topos in modern scholarship as well as in ancient literature
that tyrants, having established themselves in power, increased their wealth
through taxation.[17] According to Thucydides, the Peisistratids were moderate
in this regard, taxing Athenians only a twentieth of their produce (an *eikostē*,
6.54.5).[18] The *Ath. Pol.* reflects this tradition, though crediting Peisistratus, not
his sons, and giving a higher percentage, a tithe (*dekatē*, 16.4).[19] In the *Politics*
(1313b26), amidst a lengthy description of the stereotypical characteristics of
the tyrant, Aristotle mentions the levying of taxes (*eisphora tōn telōn*), using as
an example Dionysius the Elder, tyrant of Syracuse from the late fifth through
fourth century. The idea that one should not tax free men and that therefore
to be taxed signifies reduced status (in its extreme formulation, subjection
to a tyrant) on one level flies in the face of the reality that taxation constituted the chief means of a polis, and certainly of Athens, to raise revenue.[20]
The notion that only tyrants taxed, however, while a myth, is likely to be
explained by the distinction felt by ancients (and moderns) between direct
and indirect taxation: tyrants taxed individuals directly, a practice marking
unfree status through the loss of personal and family autonomy; by contrast,
poleis under free constitutions obtained revenue through indirect taxation

of goods and commodities. This distinction, of course, has a specious aspect, since poleis like Athens did, in times of financial strain, levy *eisphorai*, a direct tax on income; one response might have been that *eisphorai* were irregular. (Moreover, it also directly and regularly taxed its foreign residents.) Liturgies like the trierarchy and choregia were a thinly disguised form of direct taxation, but they fell on a wealthy individual only sporadically. In any case, what did tyrants do with their wealth, or rather what forms of expenditure were especially associated with them?

TYRANTS AND SPENDING

Tyrants were necessarily conspicuous, big spenders. Leslie Kurke has elucidated well the links between ostentatious spending (*megaloprepeia*) and tyranny.[21] Indeed the tyrant in an important respect was compelled to spend specifically in order to express and bolster his power as a tyrant. Moreover, he had to outspend any rivals.

On what were tyrants typically regarded as spending their wealth and demonstrating their *megaloprepeia*? In Athens, the Peisistratids were associated with a variety of expenditures that expressed their power and benefited the city, including the reorganization of the Panathenaea and rhapsodic competitions.[22] They have generally been believed to have embarked on a vigorous building program, including the temple of Olympian Zeus, which, if it had been completed, would have been the largest on the mainland. Scholars have also attributed them with buildings on the Acropolis and in the Agora, especially in the southwest corner.[23]

My concern here, however, is with perceptions of tyrants. Wolfgang Schuller, among others, sees a strong association between tyrants and building, an association disputed by Christopher Tuplin.[24] Tuplin maintains that "the phenomenon [of tyrants as builders] has no prominence amongst the characteristics which emerge from the whole range of archaic and classical comments on tyranny."[25] Yet even he concedes that Aristotle made the connection. In the midst of a lengthy passage identifying typical features of tyrants and their rule, Aristotle explicitly mentions their role as builders (*Pol.* 1313b21–24), though not in reference to the function of expressing power and accruing symbolic capital but rather in the context of public works projects aimed at keeping the populace occupied. He offers as representative examples the pyramids in Egypt, the votive offerings of the Cypselids, the building of the temple of Olympian Zeus by the Peisistratids, and Polycratean temples on Samos.

Was the perception of tyrants as builders current in the fifth century? Thucydides provides evidence that it was. Although normally reticent about facades of power (except to criticize them explicitly and implicitly as misleading reflections of *dunamis* ["power"][26]), the historian, in his digression on the Peisistratids in book 6, explicitly alludes to their building projects when he writes, "They adorned the city beautifully."[27] Moreover, Thucydides' allusion to the Peisistratids' adornment of the city casts light on a passage in Herodotus concerned with Peisistratus. Virtually all commentators on Thucydides have viewed Herodotus as one of Thucydides' sources for the Peisistratid digression,[28] though no one to my knowledge has noted the similarity in expression between 6.54.5 and Herodotus 1.59.6. In his brief but favorable assessment of Peisistratus' rule after gaining control of the city for the final time, Herodotus comments that in addition to governing according to custom and neither eliminating magistracies nor changing the existing laws, Peisistratus "adorned the city beautifully and finely" (κοσμέων καλῶς τε καὶ εὖ 1.59.6).

Commentators and translators have rendered the participle κοσμέων here as "administering," "governing," or "arranging" and the phrase κοσμέων καλῶς τε καὶ εὖ as, "he administered the city well and fairly," *vel sim.*[29] But the verb can also mean "adorn," as I have translated it above, and it is tempting to take its use by Herodotus here in this way in light of Thucydides. Moreover, there may be a slight redundancy if the verb means "administer," since Herodotus has already signaled the merits of Peisistratus' administration in his comment that he governed not as a tyrant but as a "constitutional" ruler. The brevity of his section on Peisistratid administration further lends support to this objection, for the historian hardly needs to sum up his discussion.

Herodotus, as is well known, marveled at monuments and associated tyrants with such elaborate displays of their power. It would therefore have been thoroughly in keeping with his interests to mention what he understood as Peisistratus' adornment of the city.[30] The historian was clearly impressed by the magnificence of the Polycratean monuments on Samos. In fact, he justifies his excursus on the history of the island by referring to the great works there, mentioning a tunnel, harbor and "the largest temple known" (3.60). Moreover, in his "obituary notice" of Polycrates he writes that "except for the tyrants of Syracuse, no Greek tyrant deserves to be compared with Polycrates for *megaloprepeia*" (3.125.2).[31]

It is thus likely that Thucydides is deliberately echoing Herodotus in 6.54.5 and that therefore Thucydides for one understood Herodotus (a contemporary, after all, and one with much of whose work he was demonstrably and intimately familiar) to be making a statement about the Peisistratid building program. Moreover, both passages from the historians, whatever the precise translation of Herodotus, drives home an important point: the positive assessment of the Peisistratids familiar from the *Ath. Pol.* goes back to the fifth century,[32] and it is connected to their magnificent spending on buildings as well as moderate rule before the murder of Hipparchus.[33]

There is more literary evidence, then, than Tuplin allows, but his concentration on written evidence obscures the importance of visual testimony and oral memory of the association of tyrants and buildings. In Athens, Athenians did not need to be informed by a Herodotus or Thucydides that the Peisistratids had used their wealth on ambitious building projects; considerable visual evidence lay before them, despite the Persian sack of the city in 480.[34]

This extended background has been intended to demonstrate, by a representative sampling of the body of ancient evidence, that tyranny and democracy were perceived as sharing features; that tyranny and wealth were thought to have virtually a symbiotic relationship; and that writers who were otherwise critical of tyranny could nevertheless, implicitly or explicitly, show admiration for their building projects. We are now ready to consider the idea of the demos as tyrant in its control and use of wealth.

THE DEMOS AS TYRANT AND ECONOMIC PATRON

THE REVENUES OF THE *DĒMOS TYRANNOS*

A passage from Xenophon's *Symposium* likens taxation by the demos to tyranny. Charmides is explaining to Callias why he is better off poor than wealthy: "Now I am like a tyrant, whereas before I was a slave. Then [when I was rich] I kept having to pay to the demos; now [that I am poor] the polis supports me by making payments" (4.32).[35] As Tuplin notes, "The idea of tyrants being supported by city-taxation is evidently banal enough to provide a simile for the use of public revenue to sustain the poorer classes."[36] That tyrants, like poor Athenians from hostile perspectives, were thought of as taking a free ride underlies a well-known passage in the *Wasps* (496–499). Loathecleon is complaining to the Chorus about the accusations of tyranny then endemic in Athens: If someone "asks for a free onion to spice his sardines a bit, the vegetable lady gives him the fish eye and says: 'Say, are you asking for an onion because you want to be tyrant? Or maybe you think Athens grows spices as her tribute to you?'"[37]

Significantly, in these passages, the rich are juxtaposed to the demos, and the demos in a sense is their tyrant. In this democratic context, the *dēmos tyrannos* taxed the wealthy to sustain its position and accumulate wealth to spend. These taxes took the form of liturgies and *eisphorai,* the last particularly onerous partly because of the suddenness of their imposition.[38] Burdened elites, with their financial autonomy compromised, may well have felt subject to a democratic tyranny. Of course, the demos qua the polis—and here is where the distinction between *dēmos tyrannos* and *polis tyrannos* blurs—also taxed the empire to obtain revenue, first through tribute, and then, sometime at the end of the Peace of Nicias (ca. 413), by a maritime tax that replaced tribute, the *eikostē.*[39]

The demos/polis also acquired additional, regular revenue from other sources, both imperial (e.g., from rents from sacred lands) and domestic (e.g., various taxes and silver from the mines at Laurium). The annual total may have been on the order of 1,500–2,000 talents,[40] and by the mid fifth century, close to 10,000 talents had accumulated on the Acropolis. What uses of this wealth are suggestive of tyranny?

THE ''TYRANNICAL'' EXPENDITURES OF DĒMOS TYRANNOS

Spending on display and magnificence was a symbolically loaded act in the ancient world. Aristocratic display as a measure of value and as symbolic capital to be converted into political power was a practice that in Classical Athens had been grafted fairly smoothly onto the social and political life of the polis, particularly through institutions like liturgies. Athenian elites also spent on monuments: men like Cimon in the early fifth century were known for their individual outlays on civic and religious buildings, the expectation being similarly enhanced power. This last kind of individual expenditure, however, could be far more problematic from the democratic point of view, for it arguably fell outside the institutionalized contributions expected from elites: it could suggest undemocratic ambitions.[41]

Scale and the absence of serious competition seem to be what distinguishes tyrannical from aristocratic spending: tyrants or aspirants to tyranny were de facto able to outspend all rivals, since a necessary precondition of their success was control of greater resources than those of their rivals, thereby securing their position (though this does not entirely explain their success). Aristotle's description of Cimon's "tyrant-scale property"[42] is telling in its implication of the power that could accompany such an extent of wealth. Peisistratus son of Hippias and grandson of his namesake unquestionably knew the relationship between monuments and power in his lavish dedication of the Altar of the Twelve Gods in the Agora and the Altar of Apollo in the Pythion. So did the Athenians: they later erased the inscription that would have named him as the benefactor of the Altar of the Twelve Gods (Thuc. 6.54.6–7).[43]

Beginning in the mid fifth century, an extensive monumental building program was undertaken on the Acropolis, in the Agora, and elsewhere around Athens and Attica, including most conspicuously on the Acropolis, the Parthenon and Propylaea.[44] Whatever the precise cost of the whole program,[45] the scale of expenditure was unprecedented. Later writers link Pericles directly with the overall project.[46] Extant contemporary evidence, however, explicitly connects him only with the Odeum,[47] an enormous roofed hypostyle structure abutting the Theater of Dionysus (and, significantly, likens him to a tyrant and god).[48] Such is the authority that scholars have accorded the later traditions, implied in the common label "Periclean building program," that it is easy to forget, but essential to appreciate, that the buildings were in fact fully democratic products (including the Odeum, the association of which with Pericles does not reduce its significance as a democratic monument).[49] It was the demos that heard proposals concerning them, voted in favor of them, thereby authorizing their construction, and paid for design, materials, and labor with its own moneys.[50]

This aspect of Athenian public life in roughly the second half of the fifth century is remarkable and unusual compared to its earlier (and later) history, including the fifth century before ca. 450. Indeed, while private benefactions in Greek poleis were a welcome feature of civic life (burgeoning, of course, in the Hellenistic and Roman periods), in Athens during this period there appear to have been no privately funded civic buildings.[51] That the existence of the citizens' vast public wealth at this time[52] obviated the need for private subscription or benefaction common to other periods inadequately explains this phenomenon. For there is evidence that elites did try, unsuccessfully, to continue the practice of financing buildings, and it provides an indicator that the demos *preferred* to enhance its own sense of power through expenditure and patronage rather than relinquish any to individuals.

First, Plutarch relates an anecdote (*Per.* 14) in which, responding to outrage in the assembly (provoked by Pericles' rival Thucydides son of Melesias) over the expense of (undefined) building projects, Pericles offered to pay for them himself and to put his name on the dedication. On hearing this, the people protested loudly that they would pay for them themselves. Plutarch comments that the people's response could have been prompted either by Pericles' magnanimity or by competition with him for glory. The details and wording of the story must be considered historically worthless, but if it has any claim to have originated in a contemporary debate in the Assembly, it nicely illustrates the recognition that expenditure on buildings was something that would inevitably accord the spender prestige and power and was a highly charged avenue of competition by rivals for power.

One would not want to place any weight on the anecdote by itself. It does, however, intriguingly resonate with better, contemporary evidence, to whose context it might conceivably belong. A fragmentary decree ($IG\ I^3$ 49), concerning the construction of a springhouse, contains a tantalizing reference to members of Pericles' family (with Pericles' name restored by Hiller in line 13), whom the demos was apparently praising for having offered to contribute to the building.[53] Most intriguing is that it apparently refused the offer, deciding instead to use money from (its own) public sources.[54] It provides a good illustration of the power associated with building and allows the speculation that the demos may have rejected the offer because it wanted no threats to its own power and prestige.[55] It is remarkable that the demos' refusal was inscribed on stone, itself reflecting its power.

Indeed, inscribed marble stelae pertaining to public building projects and sculpture were themselves important visual markers of the benefactions and power of the demos. Inscriptions relating details associated with a monument's construction, for example, payments of public moneys from various sources and the wages for workmen and craftsmen for monuments like the Parthenon, Propylaea, and Erechtheum, would have made clear the demos' tyrant-scale wealth and have been an expression of its sole power at home (as well as inscriptions expressing its control over Greeks abroad). Even Pericles, whose political prominence was famously dubbed "the rule (*archē*) of the first man" (Thuc. 2.65.9), was evidently unable to challenge the demos' supreme position as patron and spender, and the power and glory it conferred.[56]

The Athenians' treatment of the Altar of the Twelve Gods in the Agora neatly encapsulates the argument advanced here. Thucydides tells us that they later enlarged the Altar, the occasion on which they obliterated the inscription (6.54.7). Not only through the erasure of the dedication but especially by making the Altar even grander, the Athenian demos appropriated a monument associated with tyrants, thereby implicitly announcing that they could outdo powerful Peisistratids. Their actions deliberately blurred the line between tyrants and demos.[57]

It is perhaps significant to the argument here that the demos, like tyrants, spent largely on religious buildings, including the magnificent Propylaea,[58] the temples on the Acropolis, and, if Leslie Shear is right, the Telesterion at Eleusis.[59] Disposing of accumulated reserves by spending on the city, and especially on religious monuments, would have accorded the spender moral respectability. Like tyrants who may have derived their wealth from extortions and taxation, that is, by force, but who then could mitigate the opprobrium of citizens and gods by building lavishly for the gods in the polis or at an international sanctuary like Delphi, so the Athenian demos extorted money from their subjects in the empire, enabling them to build up a reserve that could be (partly) spent on the gods.

Someone like Thucydides son of Melesias could hope for support among the people for his objections to this (mis)use of the moneys of the Greeks in the empire for domestic projects, turning it into an attack on Pericles (Plut. *Per.* 12).[60] Significantly, however, it apparently carried little weight among the demos: Thucydides, not Pericles, was ostracized (Plut. *Per.* 14). Why? I suggest that the great expenditures of their own money carried such an allure for ordinary citizens because of the expression of power, one as great as a tyrant's, if the criterion is scale of expenditure, that any objections were virtually doomed to failure. Recall the testimony of Herodotus and Thucydides on the elegant adornment of the community by tyrants like Polycrates or the Peisistratids: even one critical of tyranny per se could explicitly admire a tyrant's great works—perhaps more so in the case of a dead tyrant.

Moreover, like tyrants who were economic patrons, the demos was the economic patron par excellence. If private patronage was anathema to a democracy,[61] public patronage was alive and well. Through the funds under its control it supported a substantial labor force over some decades (cf. Aristotle's comment in the *Politics,* cited above, about the employment of labor on magnificent monuments). Local and foreign artists took advantage of the opportunities there just as under the Peisistratids, workers, artisans, and artists found ready employment.[62] Thus I am suggesting a conception of public patronage in which the demos acts in the capacity of a tyrant, dispensing tyrant-scale patronage.

By exercising economic power on an unprecedented scale, the demos strengthened its political position and advertised itself as sole ruler. Indeed, given the age-old connection between wealth and power, for the demos to be sovereign in the polis and to prevent any one individual from gaining too much power, it had to spend, and outspend any competition and to show that *it* was the source of economic opportunity for huge numbers of people. Public expenditures, that is, by the demos of its own moneys, far outstripped any private expenditures by individuals and explains why such latter outlays, notably on liturgies, could be encouraged, since they appear to have posed no threat.[63]

UNCOVERING *DĒMOS TYRANNOS*: PRESENCE BY ABSENCE IN THUCYDIDES

I want to turn now to explore whether the notion of the demos-as-tyrant as just elaborated can be teased out of our sources and, if so, what its connotations are. The first text on which we shall focus, Thucydides' version of Pericles' Funeral Oration, presents a stimulating challenge, for part of its value resides in what is not said as much as in what is. Moreover, every word, topic, and theme seemingly is designated for inclusion or omission by the historian from a calculation of how well, and how, each serves the rhetorical agenda of the speech. A decidedly polemical quality results (and is one of the aspects that makes it a strange example of epideictic oratory). As Pericles identifies characteristics of the Athenians, he often seems to be countering other views about them, some of which may originate within the polis. Indeed, packed with carefully worded, pointed assertions, the speech encourages the reader to think about what it is reacting against, what critics are being addressed, what it aims to obscure.

Both the language of and omissions from the oration suggest a deliberate resistance to, indeed denial of, the idea that the demos exercised a kind of tyranny at home, reflected in and expressed by, for example, publicly funded monumental architecture. It is precisely this strategy that helps us unpack the counter-positions lurking beneath it. Two passages in particular (2.40.1, 2.38.1), each of which has troubled scholars, are especially illuminating, one for what it says and the other for what it leaves out. Both are valuable for hinting at the existence of a linkage between the demos and tyrant, a linkage that Thucydides' Pericles aims to deny.

In 2.40.1, Pericles states, "We love the beautiful with economy, knowledge without softness; wealth we use more for action than for boasting." The words "we love the beautiful" (*philokaloumen*) and "economy" (*euteleia*) in the beginning of the first clause have especially made commentators uncomfortable. *Philokaloumen* by itself is vague: "We love the beautiful" in what realm? A. W. Gomme lists various possibilities, for example, temples, the chrys-elephantine statue of Athena, sacrifices, processions, and private buildings. Yet he and others have been at a loss to explain the meaning of *euteleia*. As he puts it, "It is difficult to be happy about this clause. Εὐτελής means either 'cheap because economical, inexpensive,' of persons 'frugal', or 'cheap, because of poor quality.'"[64] The perceived problem, for Gomme and others, lies in the suggested referents of the verb *philokaloumen*, which are neither inexpensive nor of inferior quality.

Jeffrey Rusten takes a different approach, arguing that *philokaloumen* is virtually synonymous with *philosophoumen* ("we love wisdom"), and he translates it as "we seek what is noble."[65] This is accepted by Simon Hornblower, who understands the passage as concerned with individuals, not the state.[66] There are, in my view, difficulties with understanding *philokaloumen met' euteleias* as "we love (or seek) what is noble with moderation in expense." First, it is not clear what specifically would be included in "what is noble" and in what way it would be moderate in expense; the alternative translation, without out a discussion of the context or substance, does not make *euteleia* easier to understand. Moreover, if Rusten is correct that *philakaloumen* is used synonymously with *philosophoumen*, the context and meaning are even less clear. On this view, the notion that love of wisdom might normally be regarded as entailing great expense, a notion resisted by Pericles in this passage, seems odd.[67] Second, given the impressive economy of expression in the oration, it seems rather un-Thucydidean to have two synonyms in a row, and stylistically awkward, given the trifold structure of the sentence, neatly laid out by Rusten.[68]

Finally, I find the exclusive focus on individuals and the private sphere problematic (and this is true whether the translation of *philokaloumen* is we love "what is noble" or "what is beautiful"), for the individuals referred to in that case would not be all Athenians but aristocratic Athenians, and the context one of private luxury. While Pericles in the oration nods at times to specific groups within the polis, chapter 40 makes the rhetorical point that all Athenians share the same attitude toward the pursuit of beauty and the same ideology of wealth.[69] At the same time, it is wrong rigidly to assume a single referent or interpretation, since different people in the audience would surely have understood the remark in accordance with their differing experiences (this applies to taking it as exclusively public as much as exclusively private).

The grounds for translating *philokaloumen* as "we love the beautiful" are stronger than those for the translation "we love what is noble." I suggest that it should be understood as a generalizing comment that could allow for a variety of contexts, public and private. Included in the public realm would have been the fine buildings, temples, and statues, whose beauty everyone in the polis could appreciate.[70] It is worth noting that the alternative translation arises out of the concern long expressed by scholars like Gomme over the perceived uneconomical nature of the building program and therefore the belief that the phrase "we love the beautiful with moderation in expense" taken to apply to (among other things) such monuments would make no sense or even be absurd.

Yet it is important to recognize that a more opulent reality in whatever sphere is not a cogent argument against a coexisting ideology of simplicity. As Kurke notes, "Pericles' words do not represent historical fact but democratic ideology."[71] Second, "economical," like "poor" or "rich," is a fluid term dependent on context and the perspective of the speaker. The rhetorical context will favor exaggeration, but the central issue is, with what or whom are the Athenians being implicitly compared? For example, Athenians publicly and privately may have appeared profligate compared to their neighbors because of their greater wealth, but compared to legendary Lydian and Persian (not to mention Ionian) luxury (likely targeted groups of the opposite behavior implied in this passage), they could call themselves moderate in their spending habits on beauty.[72] Moreover, the passage also invites comparison with the Spartans, whose cultivation of simplicity and lack of ostentation was an advertised national characteristic. Pericles could be saying, we lack ostentation as well, but we still can embrace and enjoy the beautiful.

A contrast to the Greek and barbarian East, or to the Spartans, then, allows the phrase "we love the beautiful with moderation in expense" to have its intended rhetorical punch. Nevertheless, if Pericles is implicitly referring, among other things, to Athens' magnificent monuments (and Athena's chryselephantine statue), the assertion could still seem paradoxical. An additional layer of nuance, however, may be present and help to explain the stress on the Athenians' moderation in their spending habits on elegance and display. As we have seen, opulence/*megaloprepeia* and tyranny were easy for Greeks to equate. As such a lavish expression of the greatness and power of the demos, the extravagant and conspicuous expenditures of the demos could be suggestive of *dēmos tyrannos* (as well as of Pericles *tyrannos*).

A function, then, of Pericles' assertion may have been implicitly to contest the impression that the excessive expenditures on the building program raised the specter of tyranny.[73] In this case, the rhetorical objective of Thucydides' Pericles, during whose political prominence the monuments were erected and in whose voice a statement on beauty and expenditure is put, would be, first, explicitly to avoid mention of the building program, and, second, implicitly to contest its extravagance by using the word *euteleia*. Certainly in the epideictic context of the oration, it would be grossly inappropriate even to hint that the Athenians (and Pericles himself by association and as speaker) could be likened to a tyrant. In other genres, by contrast, especially comedy, the linkage could and did come up, as we shall see below.

Indeed, on this reading, Pericles' claim in 2.40 reads nicely as an implicit response to the criticism explicitly lodged in Plutarch's *Pericles* 12.2–4, a passage that neatly links tyranny, wealth, and the building program (with both Pericles and the demos as the implied tyrant). In this famous anecdote, Plutarch relates a political attack on Pericles in the Assembly, the focus of which was the use of money from Athens' allies on the building program.

What brought the greatest pleasure and adornment to Athens and the greatest amazement to others . . . , namely, the construction of sacred buildings, this especially of the public measures of Pericles his enemies maligned and slandered in the assemblies. They cried out that "the people (*dēmos*) has lost its reputation having moved the common funds of the Hellenes from Delos to Athens, and Pericles has robbed them of the most plausible excuse, namely, that through fear of the barbarians it removed the common funds from that island and was now guarding them in a stronghold." And the Greeks are surely insulted by a grave dishonor and subjected to open tyranny when they see that we are gilding and ornamenting our city with their enforced contributions for the war just like a prostitute, wearing costly stones and statues and thousand-talent temples.

Plutarch continues with Pericles' response, in which the statesman insists that, provided they fulfill their military obligation, the Athenians are free to use excess funds as they please, that it is only right to enhance their reputation by beautifying the city, and that, in addition, the building program will provide work for the whole city (*Per.* 12.3–4).

Some scholars have essentially dismissed the entire passage on the grounds that it is an historically worthless, anachronistic invention by Plutarch.[74] Others, however, take the position that the "building debate" is genuine, that is, that there was opposition emanating from Thucydides son of Melesias and others to the construction of these lavish monuments with which Pericles was associated.[75] But what about the words used? Walter Ameling argues that it is impossible to tell whether the words and form of the debate as Plutarch presents it are Thucydides son of Melesias', one of the members of the "Isocratean school" in the fourth century, or Plutarch's own.[76] For those who believe that Plutarch relied on an early source and did not fabricate the anecdote, candidates have been Ion of Chios, Stesimbrotus of Thasos, Ephorus, and Theopompus. Theopompus or, alternatively, Stesimbrotus has been suggested as the inventor of the image of Athens as an *alazona gunaika*, "a wanton woman."[77] Anton Powell goes furthest, arguing that the rhetoric, including the phrase *alazona gunaika*, fits well in a fifth-century context.[78]

The allusion to tyranny itself as applied to the demos could well go back to the fifth century. The metaphor, as Ameling notes, is used differently from, for example, its appearances in Thucydides. Contemporary authors, however, as we have seen above, explicitly drew connections among tyranny, monuments, and wealth, and to judge from Aristophanes, the accusation of tyranny was hurled about in every possible context at least by the 420s.[79]

To return to Pericles' comment in the Funeral Oration, the point of the clause, then, is that we are not so lavish in spending on magnificence as people claim. Or, to put it another way, Pericles is insisting that the Athenians are spending money on beauty, but they are not wasting it. There may be additional support for this approach to reading 2.40 in the final clause of the sentence: "We use wealth for action, not as an empty boast."[80] For the implicit argument as Pericles develops it seems to be that the Athenians do not draw attention to their extraordinary wealth per se; rather, they put it to good use (chiefly on power). He resists the view that it is the Athenians' wealth that will bring them fame (or lead to accusations of collective tyranny?), rather than the results of their use of wealth. As he puts it slightly farther on (2.41.1), in a section dealing precisely with the actions individually and collectively for which the Athenians should be renowned, "The power (*dunamis*) of the city provides evidence that this is no idle boast of the moment (*logōn en tōi paronti kompos*) rather than the truth of deeds (*ergōn alētheia*)."

A passage from Pindar's *Pythian* 1 provides an instructive counterpoint that may bring into even sharper focus the peculiar emphasis in Thucydides. In *Pythian* 1.90–94, composed in 470, addressed to Hieron, tyrant of Syracuse, Pindar holds up as a model Croesus, ruler of Lydia:

> If you are fond of always hearing sweet things spoken of
> you, do not be overly distressed by expenditures;

but just as a pilot, let your sail go to the wind. Do not be
deceived by false gains;
the loud acclaim of men to come, consisting of glory,
reveals the way of life of departed men
by storytellers and poets alike. The kindly generosity
of Croesus does not perish.

Pindar urges Hieron not to worry over expenditures but, rather, "to sail
boldly for the ends of the earth in expenditure,"[81] precisely because his acts of
expenditure will bring glory, literally, a "boast of glory" (auchēma doxas) for
posterity. By contrast, Pericles urges expenditures (implicit in kairōi ergou), but
they are for action, for power. In other words, it is not the expenditure-act—
or the wealth itself—that should serve as the object of a boast. Indeed, by
contrast to Hieron, for whom the goal is a "boast of glory" about his wealth,
Pericles devalues its equivalent, the "boast of the moment."[82]

Let us now turn to an earlier passage in the Funeral Oration (the second
one alluded to at the outset of this discussion) in which an even more glaring omission of reference to the achievements on the Acropolis occurs. Their
absence here may add further support to the argument that it was not part of
Thucydides' agenda in composing the speech, precisely in order to muffle the
subject of tyranny, to have Pericles draw attention to, much less celebrate, the
imposing architectural and artistic displays of the Athenians.

In this passage, the statesman turns briefly to the enjoyments available
to the Athenians at home through, in essence, display: "Further, we provide plenty of means for the mind to refresh itself from business. We celebrate games and sacrifices all the year round, and the elegance of our private
(idiois) buildings forms a daily source of pleasure and helps to drive away
pain" (2.38.1). The lack of any mention of the Parthenon and the rest of the
splendid public, religious monuments has occasioned more than one com-
mentator to propose an emendation for idiois like hierois or dēmosiois[83] or to
explain it away on the grounds that such buildings are irrelevant to a context
of recreation.[84] Neither of these attempts to deal with the passage is satisfying. There are no good grounds for emending the text, and splendid public
and religious buildings would have given abundant pleasure and driven away
pain. Two other explanations suggest themselves, first, that Thucydides is
downplaying deliberately something that within his own historiographical
framework is insignificant or even specious as a sign of what matters to him,
namely, power.[85] Most relevant here, however, is the possibility that Thu-

cydides/Pericles purposely wants to keep from this oration, of all orations, reference to anything that might evoke the idea of tyranny, as applied either to Pericles or to the demos.[86]

For apart from issues of genre (mentioned above), we must consider questions of political nuance. The overarching theme of the Funeral Oration, besides that of Athens' *dunamis,* is the aristocratic, not tyrannical, nature of Athenian democracy. By the end of the oration, Pericles has brilliantly reshaped and remolded all Athenians so that they are all potentially *aristoi,* within a *dēmokratia* that is in a sense really an *aristokratia.*[87] In this schema, to evoke the lavishness of the demos' *megaloprepeia* would not only be inappropriate but also unwanted, because its excessiveness carries it beyond an aristocratic to a tyrant-scale level.

We can read the Funeral Oration in part as countering a current strand in Athens that saw the possession and lavish spending of wealth by the demos as evocative of tyranny. The competing view may be discernable in Plutarch's *Pericles* 12, but contemporary testimony may be found in Aristophanes, in which the linkage among the demos, its wealth, and tyranny comes out clearly and, intriguingly, is not entirely negative in connotation. Indeed, the comic stage is precisely the site in which ambiguous or positive representations of the demos as tyrant could be constructed. Not only is the genre often "democratic" in terms of topic and attitudes, but it also can safely flirt with democratically risky—from the official point of view—notions precisely because it simultaneously pokes fun at them.[88]

DĒMOS TYRANNOS IN ARISTOPHANES

In Aristophanes' *Knights,* performed in 424, shortly after Paphlagon and the Sausage-Seller relate their rival dreams—Paphlagon's, in which Athena pours "health and wealth" (*plouthugieian*) over the demos, and the Sausage-Seller's, in which Athena pours a libation of ambrosia over Demos' head (and garlic-brine over Paphlagon's)—the Chorus sings to Demos, "Demos, you have a fine sway, since all mankind fears you like a man with tyrannical power."[89]

Gomme noted the similarities between this passage and that from Pericles' last speech in Thucydides (2.63.2), mentioned above. He commented that, unlike references to Athens-the-tyrant put in the mouths of non-Athenians, in these two passages the perspective is Athenian.[90] An important distinction, however, is that Pericles' concern lies explicitly with the Athenians' role as an imperial power (it is their *archē* that is like a tyranny), while the context in Aristophanes seems chiefly to apply to the domestic realm, since the Chorus continues by alluding to Demos' gullibility in the Assembly.[91] Moreover, the larger narrative context in leading up to this passage is the role of Demos and his relationship to Paphlagon and the Sausage-Seller in Athens.

What are the connotations and nuances of the passage in the *Knights* and the significance of the Athenian perspective? Given that in the play to this point Demos has been presented much as a doddering old fool, capable of being manipulated by shameless political profiteers like Paphlagon and Sausage-Seller, the lines quoted above might almost seem sarcastic. Yet the following lines tell against such an interpretation, for the Chorus goes on to sing, "*But* you're easily led astray: you enjoy being flattered and thoroughly deceived, and every speechmaker has you gaping. You've a mind, but it's out to lunch" (1115–1120, my emphasis). In other words, the Chorus concedes that the *archē* that Demos holds is fine (*kalēn*), inasmuch as he is feared just like a "tyrant man," and charges him with gullibility and susceptibility to flattery—a standard topos of the tyrant. Thus, the underlying assumption is that it is a fine thing to be a tyrant. Given the troubling presentation of Demos throughout most of this play, the passage certainly contains ambiguity, but it needs to be appreciated that it is not a negative comment about the notion of the demos-as-tyrant.

At the end of the play, Demos has been magically transformed (lit. "boiled down") by Sausage-Seller, in an Athens of old, that is, the Persian War period, a "Golden Age" in Aristophanic plays.[92] The Chorus Leader invokes, "Oh Athens the gleaming, the violet-crowned, the envy of all, show us the monarch of Greece and of this land!"[93] Out comes Demos, described by the Sausage-Seller as "wearing a golden cricket, resplendent in his old-time costume, smelling not of ballot shells but peace accords, and anointed with myrrh" (1331–1332). The description evokes a magnificent, old-style opulence,[94] and indeed the clothing here is clearly meant to signify the style in which the Athenian elite used to dress, to which Thucydides explicitly alludes in his Archaeology (1.6);[95] but, significantly, that style is and was understood to be imitative of eastern, specifically Lydian luxury.[96]

The refashioning of Demos as an explicitly Athenian old-style aristocrat removes the character far from the symbolic demos in the *Wasps,* the chorus of old, poor jury-goers, or the simple farmer Dicaeopolis in the *Acharnians,* characters who likewise hark back to the great old days when men like themselves fought at Marathon but who are portrayed as coming from well below the elite. That the right-thinking, straightened-out Demos, as he is revealed in his new state, is aristocratic is on the face of it rather startling. Equally so is that at the same time he is still regarded, and explicitly so, as a monarch: the Chorus hails him as "king of the Greeks."[97]

The figure of the transformed Demos functions on several coexisting levels. His dress recalls the fancier attire worn by Athenians in the old days, and Ionians more generally, making him aristocratic. At the same time, such luxurious attire emphatically advertised itself as "Eastern Style," as it did in reality both when worn by earlier Athenians and again when its popularity resurfaced during the later fifth century. In turn, if we add a further layer to that aristocratic power and eastern luxury, namely, Demos' explicit identity as a sovereign ruler, a *monarchos,* it is but a small stepping stone to *dēmos tyrannos.* I suggest that in this representation as a quasi-eastern potentate, Demos would have had a broad and immediate appeal to the ordinary Athenian citizen.

Two years later, in 422, the *Wasps* was produced. In one section of this play, Lovecleon sets out to prove to his son Loathecleon that his and other jurors' power is not inferior to that of a king. Lovecleon asks, "Isn't this high authority, and derision of wealth?"[98] Here the context is clearly domestic: Lovecleon and his cronies (i.e., the demos) have power at home so great because of their capacity as jurors that they can be completely unimpressed by the riches of their social superiors. Why? The answer is clearly because of their own perceived wealth and power, which allows them to exert it unimpeded. As they claim, they cannot be called to account (587).

Like Demos in the *Knights,* a transformation in dress is used to mark a fundamental conversion of a character, in this case, Lovecleon. In a later scene near the end of the play, Loathecleon, earlier called a "lover of monarchy" (and "demos-hater," 474), brings out a new cloak and boots for his father to put on (1122–1164) to symbolize his rehabilitation. The cloak is explicitly labeled a Persian garment, *Persis,* or *kaunakēs,* "woven in Ecbatana."[99] A. G. Geddes argues that the Persian costume would have suggested "arrogance and tyranny," given that Persia evoked authoritarianism to Greeks since the early fifth century, and he downplays the association of luxury with the cloak.[100] But this deprives the passage of a crucial layer of nuance,[101] since as Loathecleon makes clear, the change of attire is effected to allow Lovecleon to "step out opulently . . . with a sort of luxurious swagger" (1168–1169). As Margaret Miller points out, Loathecleon "tries to 'elegantise' his father Philokleon (1131–1147, esp. 1137)."[102]

Like Demos in the *Knights,* the new attire elevates him to the status of an Athenian elite. Yet it also emphatically, while humorously, makes a statement that the wearer is like an eastern potentate who demonstrates his power by showing off his wealth to an excessive degree. Moreover, as in Demos' case, Lovecleon's conversion is located within the domestic realm of the polis (although as noted above, Demos is also acknowledged "sovereign of Greece" as well).

THE COMPLEXITIES OF TYRANNY AND
DĒMOS TYRANNOS

Some of the texts I have explored have represented or allowed an implication of tyrantlike demos in negative terms, others more ambiguously. Some passages, however, allow an appealing construction to be placed on the figure of *dēmos tyrannos,* a construction that complements the positive nuances that I have suggested would have accompanied the notion of *dēmos tyrannos* in its capacity as builder of great monuments and patron of the arts and crafts. The demos figures in Aristophanes, through both descriptive and visual presentation, reflect this appeal (though it is by no means unqualified throughout). After initial resistance, Lovecleon in the *Knights,* for example, in donning thick, luxurious garb from the East, literally warms up to the enviable role of eastern potentate. His position of *monarchos/tyrannos* per se is uncontested as something desirable. As the Chorus sings, "Tyranny is a fine thing." Its qualification, that the tyrant is feared, might suggest ambiguity; on the other hand, in Greek thought, a marker of one's power is the fear it instills in one's subjects.

Yet, if we return to the discussion at the outset of this essay, specifically the negative presence of tyranny in the fifth-century democratic fabric, then the question arises, how did such representations as we have seen become possible? The complex historical context of the fifth century, first, the Persian Wars, then the rise of the Athenian *archē,* the evolution of democracy, and finally the Peloponnesian War carried with it inevitable shifts in attitudes and behavior as historical experience changed, specifically, toward Persia and the idea of tyranny from the tyrant's perspective.

This background is vital to appreciate as we assess the representations of tyranny and *dēmos tyrannos* in texts like Thucydides and Aristophanes. In the Archaic period, as Leslie Kurke has elegantly shown, elites embraced excessive, eastern-style luxury, *habrosunē.* It became, however, a casualty (from the aristocratic perspective) of the Persian Wars and the egalitarian tendencies in the polis to which Thucydides alludes (1.6).[103] To be sure, both the experience of the later years of the Peisistratids' reign and the Persian Wars made tyranny a charged and potent, indeed, the ultimate negative symbol, crucial to the shaping of Athenian democracy.

Yet a blanket statement that the positive associations of eastern luxury and the power it accorded its devotees disappeared completely in the fifth century obscures the changes and modifications in perceptions and attitudes as the fifth century progressed. By its midpoint at the latest, the combination of *archē* and the vast (from a Greek perspective) monetary resources possessed by the sovereign demos (in this context, "the people" as a whole), effectively complicated, if not diminished, the negative potency of the symbol of tyranny. The conspicuous expenditures of the demos expressed its power in a vivid and transparent way. Moreover, competition for leadership in the polis between elite rivals, and in turn contestations over leadership and sovereignty between politically prominent individuals and demos (in this context, the "common people"), are also important to take into account, since such questions as "who is in charge?" reveal a desire on the part of each to be on top. Finally, the shift away from Persia to Sparta by the late 460s into the 450s as the focus of hostilities, culminating in the Peloponnesian War, likewise would have played a significant role in changing perceptions.

The Peloponnesian War, the backdrop of the narrative texts explored here, is likewise essential for appreciating the complexity of the idea of tyranny and of attitudes toward eastern tyranny. If nothing else, the Athenians' overtures to Persia for help against the Spartans (Thuc. 4.50; cf. Ar. *Ach.*) is a nice barometer of the windshift. So too is the popularity of eastern-style dress, which, as Miller has shown, filtered down below the elite in the last part of the fifth century.[104] Whether this is to be understood as reflecting the appeal of Persia, or the appropriation of the (somewhat erstwhile) enemy's cultural trappings as a way of signaling superiority over him, it suggests a more complex historical picture than that, as far as can be known, in the period immediately following the Persian Wars.

These historical developments, like those at any time, inevitably affect the conceptual realm. If, as I have suggested, the demos in its control of wealth and its expressions of power through expenditure and public patronage developed a self-definition as a tyrantlike authority before the Peloponnesian War, and if the notion of the tyrant city over an empire was appealing as well, then the war arguably necessitated the maintenance and the reinforcement of such self-conceptions.

Here the blurred boundary between *polis tyrannos* and *dēmos tyrannos* is important. If Athenians were desperate to hold onto their *archē*—and these undeniably would have included the common citizenry, who stood to gain materially from it as a group as much as if not more than elites collectively—then we should expect to discern rhetorical, conceptual expressions of that position. I have suggested that one realm in which such expressions are reflected is the comic stage, and one form it takes is an embracing of the power of the demos, at home, as well as abroad. There, an aristocratic lifestyle, but also tyrantlike power, is offered not to elite characters but to the common man in a political role. Far from being stigmatized, it is elevated to the status of an empowering way to appear and live.

Like a tyrant in his city, the demos is all-powerful and without checks on that power. Its power was perceived as being connected to its wealth. Thus when Loathecleon pokes holes in what he sees as an illusion of power, his argument is that Lovecleon—and the demos by extension—is not as wealthy and therefore not as powerful as he thinks; and by implication, he is not a tyrant. But the important point is that tyranny is expressed—from the standpoint of the speaker—as a great thing. The rub is not that tyranny is not a great thing, if you have it, but that Demos and Lovecleon erroneously think they have it. In other words, "Let us grant that tyranny is a great thing; I'm afraid you don't have it like you think you do."

Equally important to appreciate is resistance to the notion of the power of the demos-as-tyrant. As we have seen above, the Funeral Oration provides an intriguing text from this perspective. It is in part the different generic contexts that allow Aristophanes and Thucydides/Pericles to represent divergent conceptions and ideologies. They both share an elevation of the aristocratic, but they unequivocally part ways over the uses of wealth and its implicit associations not just with aristocratic lifestyle but with a tyrantlike power. While the demos or demos representatives in Aristophanes see conspicuous consumption as an important demonstration of their wealth, manifest, among other ways, by their dress, Thucydides' Pericles rejects that mode of behavior. Like Xenophanes (DK 21B3), he implicitly views *habrosunē* of the type cultivated by the Aristophanic characters as useless. If we set these passages in context, they suggest a vigorous contemporary debate over the appropriate uses of wealth as well as over the connotations of lavish display.

CONCLUSION

I have attempted in this essay to discern from diverse kinds of contemporary Athenian evidence reflections, glimpses, and even striking expressions of the conception of the demos-as-tyrant, focusing specifically on the sovereign people's expenditures and patronage in conspicuous arenas like the building projects and more generally on positive flirtations with the notion in comedy and on an implied, though ambiguous referent of *dēmos tyrannos* in Pericles' Funeral Oration. I have had a starting assumption, to be sure: that an ordinary male citizen would find it exciting and appealing to think that he, as a part of the collective demos, had the wealth and power of a tyrant and, moreover, could point to, for example, the buildings on the Acropolis and the patronage he exercised as unambiguous testimony to that wealth and power.

Both ordinary citizen and collective demos would have been aware of and not averse to the comparisons that could be drawn between themselves and the Peisistratids and other tyrants. Within the framework of wealth, expenditure, and display, they will have thought most about the similarities, not the differences. Like its tyrannical predecessors and contemporaries, the demos enhanced its power by spending lavishly on religious buildings from riches appropriated from those around it, including the Athenian elite and the subjects in the empire. Moreover, by virtue of its ability to outspend everyone around it, its position was secure by being strengthened in this way at home. Individuals who might attempt, or be regarded as attempting, to threaten the power of the demos, would have to express their power in ways other than the "normal" avenues of potential or actual tyrants, that is, through expenditure on magnificent monuments.

This notion was not the only available or advertised one in the polis, which was a wonderfully fertile site for competing images, ideas, and expressions of who the Athenians were. It was, I have suggested, a powerfully compelling one, but it was one of many: for example, the demos as bewitched by the rhetorical spell of Pericles, the demos as slaves to demagogues like Cleon, the idea of the imperial tyrant (as either a good thing, as morally problematic), and the Athenian identification with freedom grounded in fundamental opposition to Persia, and to tyranny generally. At the same time, however, this impression of another democratic self-fashioning does not in all respects contradict the official antityranny stance, for there is a significant distinction and appreciable distance between the conception of the demos (or polis) as tyrant and the abhorrence of subjection to a tyrant. In short, it is great to be a tyrant; no one would want to live subject to one.

Such a strand of thinking about *dēmos tyrannos* is necessarily mostly implicit in our sources—hence the fundamentally speculative nature of my argument. It was, as I suggested at the outset, *a* kind of democratic ideology, but not one that perhaps could be spoken about overtly in a community whose "official" identity was so firmly rooted in the "Antityrant." Thus, we find reflection of it in "safe" fora like the comic stage. On the other hand, if one appreciates the variety of milieux in which the notion of *dēmos tyrannos* surfaces implicitly—the comic stage, the monuments, inscriptions, or explicitly in the demos' role as imperial tyrant—it takes a place in Athenian democratic life that could be submerged or be on the surface, hinted at, rejected, or embraced, but never far away.[105]

[1] Οὐδὲν τυράννου δυσμενέστερον πόλει, 429. All translations are my own, unless otherwise indicated.

[2] Rosivach 1988. Kurt Raaflaub provides a good summary in his essay in this volume.

[3] See, e.g., Connor 1977; Schuller 1978; Raaflaub 1979; Tuplin 1985; Giorgini 1993: 229–233.

[4] The genesis of this chapter comes from Kallet 1998: 52–54.

[5] On the symbiosis between democracy and empire, see the recent discussions in Boedeker and Raaflaub 1998.

[6] E.g., Thuc. 2.37.1, 2.40.2, 2.42.4.

[7] Connor 1977: 102; positive examples he mentions include Soph. *OT* 380–385; Eur. *Phoen.* 506. It should be noted that while the passage from Sophocles contains heavy irony, the irony does not arise from the idea of tyranny per se.

[8] Raaflaub 1984. Cf. also de Romilly 1963: 80–81.

[9] Cf. also *Ath. Pol.* 16.8.

[10] In addition to Connor 1977, cf. also O'Neil 1986.

[11] ὁ γὰρ δῆμος βούλεται οὐκ εὐνομουμένης τῆς πόλεως αὐτὸς δουλεύειν, ἀλλ᾽ ἐλεύθερος εἶναι καὶ ἄρχειν, 1.8. Cf. also McGlew 1993: 189–190: "The city . . . was home to tyrant citizens. The freedom that was once enjoyed exclusively by tyrants was incorporated into the definition of citizenship." "Freedom" in this context usually means the license to do as one wishes; cf. also Pl. *Resp.* 360b–d (the story of the ring of Gyges), 572e.

[12] De Romilly 1963: 81.

[13] A glaring exception, in which the unaccountability of the demos was in full view, is the trial of the generals after the battle of Arginousae in 406; see Andrewes 1974; Ostwald 1986: 434–441.

[14] Fr. 19 W: Οὔ μοι τὰ Γύγεω τοῦ πολυχρύσου μέλει, οὐδ᾽ εἷλέ πώ με ζῆλος.

[15] See Seaford, this volume; also, e.g., Berve 1967: I: 111, with reference to Polycrates; O'Neil 1986: 28–29.

[16] Cf. Hdt. 1.14; Solon, Fr. 33 West (Plut. *Sol.* 14.6).

[17] The fullest study of the finance of tyrants is Andreades 1930; more accessible is Andreades 1933: 110–124.

[18] Cf. French 1975: 57, who calls the Peisistratid taxation a "desperate measure."

[19] Rhodes 1981 ad loc., following Dover, in *HCT* IV: 329–330, thinks that the term in the *Ath. Pol.* may not contradict as much as be a more generic term for the tax referred to by Thucydides. Pesely 1995 suggests the *Hellenica Oxyrhynchia* as Aristotle's source for the material in the *Ath. Pol.* not traceable directly to Herodotus or Thucydides.

[20] That the average citizen knew well how the city obtained its revenue is clear not only by inference from the business that came before the Assembly but also from sources like Aristophanes' *Wasps* 655–660 and forensic oratory involving cases concerned with taxes and trade (e.g., Lys. 22; [Dem.] 32–38, 56).

[21] Kurke 1991: 176–181.

[22] Pherekydes *FGH* I 3F2; [Pl.] *Hipparch.* 228b; Sealey 1957; Davison 1958; Berve 1967: I: 59.

[23] T. L. Shear 1978; cf. also J. S. Boersma 1970: 11–27; J. McK. Camp II 1986: 42; A. Shapiro 1989: 5–8; Camp 1994. Boersma 2000 has presented a brief but thought-provoking reconsideration of his earlier and other scholars' views about the extent of building by Peisistratus. He emphasizes the lack of evidence and rightly urges that assessments must take into account the development of the polis and evidence of collective Athenian as well as aristocratic activity. My concern here in what follows is with how fifth-century Greeks thought about the Peisistratids; see below.

[24] Schuller 1978; Tuplin 1985. See also Georges 1994: 44, with n. 154, disputing (rightly) Young 1980, who reaches a conclusion similar to Tuplin's based on archaeological evidence; cf. also Salmon 1997: 66–67.

[25] Tuplin 1985: 364.

[26] Most famously, 1.10, which is often, though perhaps erroneously, taken as an implicit attack on Herodotus. On *ergon* in Herodotus and Thucydides, see Immerwahr 1960; cf. also de Romilly 1956: 295–296; Dewald 1993; Hedrick 1993; Hedrick 1995; Kallet 2001: 56–58. I shall return to this passage below.

[27] 6.54.5: τήν τε πόλιν αὐτῶν καλῶς διεκόσμησαν.

[28] E.g., Dover, in *HCT* IV: 323. Some scholars see him as using but correcting Herodotus, e.g., Kinzl 1973.

[29] E.g., Stein 1962: ad loc.; Grene 1987; Blanco, in Blanco and Roberts 1992. Cf. also J. E. Powell 1966, s.v. κοσμέω. The exception is de Selincourt 1954.

[30] Though he may have had reasons not to dwell on them, cf. next note.

[31] Herodotus thus appreciates the achievements of these Greek tyrants. But it is undeniable that he, at the same time, chooses not to emphasize them, including the building projects, as Carolyn Dewald notes in her essay in this volume, and the question is why. Dewald argues that Herodotus sets up a dual typology of tyrants, one Greek and one eastern, but that he locates Athens (implicitly) more into the construct of the eastern, imperialistic tyrant. It is therefore tempting to speculate that Herodotus, who was likely in Athens at the very time that the spectacular monuments of that imperial city were being erected, chose not to emphasize the building projects of Greek tyrants but gave them only brief mention, because he could identify Athens more closely with eastern tyrants.

[32] As has been noted (but too easily forgotten) in Thucydides' case, most forcefully by Rawlings 1981: 106; cf. also Barceló 1990: 408.

[33] From the standpoint of actual (military) power and of the larger narrative context of his

History, however, Thucydides' comment becomes more nuanced. For, in two passages cited above, 1.10, in which he disputes physical monuments as true indicators of power, and 1.17, in which he states that tyrants did not accomplish much (i.e., in the realm of the projection of power), he makes the implicit argument that tyrants did not use their wealth in ways that brought them power on the larger Greek scene. For further discussion of these passages, see Kallet 2001: 56–58, 80.

[34] E.g., the foundations of the Peisistratid temples of Athena and Olympian Zeus; column drums of the latter were used in the Themistoclean walls; see Travlos 1971: 143, 402. Here, as above, the issue is fifth-century tradition about the Peisistratids as builders.

[35] The support referred to is likely jury duty, especially as this sentence is preceded by a picture of Charmides as a powerful jury member: "Now [that I am poor] people rise up from their seats to show respect for me, and the rich stand out of the way for me" (4.31). Cf. also [Xen.] 1.18 for a similar sentiment. See Gray 1992: 73 for a discussion of how this passage fits into the theme of the *Symposium.*

[36] Tuplin 1985: 352.

[37] All translations of Aristophanes are Henderson's (Loeb).

[38] The first ever, according to Thucydides (3.19.1), was in 428. It is unclear how often they were levied during the Peloponnesian War (cf. Dover's comment, 1950: 59), but they occurred with frequency in the fourth century. See Thomsen 1964; Brun 1983: 3–73.

[39] It is intriguing that our sole source for the imposition of this tax, Thucydides (7.28.4), mentions it in his narrative not so long after his reference to the Peisistratids' use of taxation, which he regards as moderate (6.54.5); both taxes he specifies as an *eikostē.* Does the Peisistratid *eikostē* make him think of the Athenian *eikostē* or vice versa? For discussion of the date of the imposition of the tax, see Kallet 2001: 218–222, with references.

[40] Ar. *Wasps* 656–660 provides a list. For domestic revenue, see Andreades 1933: 268–303; for imperial revenue, see Kallet-Marx 1993, index, s.v. *Prosodos*/Revenue, and for a summary, 200–202; L. J. Samons 2000.

[41] As could the kinds of expenditures on private aggrandizement to which Thucydides alludes in connection with Alcibiades, 6.15.3–4.

[42] *Ath. Pol.* 27.3: τυραννικὴ οὐσία.

[43] Its wording likely resembled that which Thucydides could still observe faint traces of on the Altar in the Pythion: "This monument of his archonship Peisistratus son of Hippias set up in the sacred precinct of Apollo Pythias." While this may have been designed to advertise his legitimate, democratic role in the community, it was evidently not enough of a departure from his family for the Athenians. See M. Arnush 1995 for a thorough discussion of the dates of the dedications. He accepts a late sixth-century date for the Altar of the Twelve Gods but pushes the Altar of Apollo in the Pythion down to the 490s.

[44] The Parthenon and Propylaea were consistently singled out, e.g., Dem. 22.13, 76;

cf. Plut. *Mor.* 349D and Demetrius of Phaleron's complaint about the expense of the Propylaea (directed against Pericles) in Cic. *Off.* 2.60. At some point, the figure of 2,000 (Diod. Sic. 12.40.2 gives a figure of 4,000 talents for both the Propylaea and the siege of Potidea; Thuc. [2.69] states that the siege of Potidea had cost the Athenians 2,000 talents), and even 2,012 talents (Heliodorus, in Harpocration s.v. *Propylaea; FGrH* 373 F1) was invented for the cost of the Propylaea. See also next note.

[45] We do not in fact have an accurate figure; the Parthenon has been reasonably estimated at around 500 talents and the entire program, including the chryselephantine statue of Athena, at around 2,000. See Zimmern 1924: 412; Stanier 1953; Miles 1989: 234 with n. 190. Burford 1965: 26 makes the important point that temples like the Parthenon were not so expensive compared to the large-scale expenditures of the polis, for example, on military power; but it would have still seemed extravagant compared to other temples.

[46] E.g., Isoc. 15.234; Lyc. Fr. 14; Cic. *Off.* 2.60; Plut. *Per.* 12; but cf. Dem. 22.76–77, who does not credit any individuals. Modern scholars have followed this tradition and have suggested lists of specific monuments associated with Pericles; see Burford 1963a: 23, n. 2; Shear 1966; Boersma 1970: 68.

[47] Some scholars have questioned its function as a music hall, despite the fact that contemporary evidence labels it such (and a much later source, Plut. *Per.* 13.11, states that it was designed for music contests at the Panathenaea), and, in my view, have made unnecessarily heavy weather over the issue (basing objections on the variety of uses of the hall attested by mostly post-fifth-century sources). See M. Miller 1997: 218–242; A. L. H. Robkin 1975. Miller's suggestion that the Odeum had a purely semiotic function, that it was "built to be rather than to do" (235), seems to me implausible. It is highly unlikely that a building of this size was intended to have not one practical function. Its primary function as a hall for music contests at the Panathenaea is not compromised by its use at other times during the year for other purposes. But cf. also below, n. 57.

[48] For his association with the Odeum: Cratinus, *Thrattae* Fr. 73 PCG (= Plut. *Per.* 13.10): "Here comes the squill-headed Zeus, Pericles, wearing the Odeum on his head." For representations of him as a tyrant, cf., e.g., Cratinus, *Cheirons* Fr. 258 *PCG; Ploutoi* Fr. 171.22–23 *PCG;* see also Henderson, this volume, pp. 162–163. The lacunae in the evidence are so great, of course, that it is possible that Pericles was linked with other named buildings, but this should not be assumed; and even if so, such an association does not temper the reality of the democratic nature of these monuments, nor its implications.

[49] Kallet 1998: 48–54, in which I too fall into the trap of labeling it "Periclean."

[50] It needs to be stressed that this last point is true regardless of the original sources and locations of the funds, e.g., the treasury of Athena. For the controversy over the sources of funding of the Parthenon, see Kallet-Marx 1989, with earlier bibliography; Samons (1993); A. Giovannini (1990); Giovannini (1997); Kallet 1998: 48–49.

[51] Robkin 1975: 58–60 argues that the Odeum was put up at Pericles' private expense, because a reference to it in Strabo (9.1.17) lies in the context of privately financed buildings. Her argument depends on uncritical and selective reading of the passage (e.g.,

there are publicly financed monuments [i.e. temples] to which he refers) and acceptance of highly uncertain views (e.g., that Peisianax paid for the Stoa Poikile).

[52] Of course the Peloponnesian War put a considerable dent in its size. But it is important to remember that even during the war, publicly funded monumental construction continued, e.g., the Erechtheum and the temple of Athena Nike on the Acropolis, as well as building in the Agora.

[53] Davies 1971: 459, n. 1, suggested the connection between Plut. *Per.* 14 and the "Springhouse Decree." (Note, however, that Plutarch does not, as Davies implies, mention the Parthenon and Propylaea as the buildings for which Pericles offered to pay.) Cf. also Stadter 1989: 181–182, for discussion and bibliography; Podlecki 1998: 86–87.

[54] Specifically, tribute: "to spend from the moneys which are paid for the tribute of the Athenians after the god has received the customary due" ([ἀπαναλίσκεν δὲ ἀπὸ τὸν χρεμάτον] *hόσα ἐς τὸν φόρον τὸν Ἀθεναίον τελ[ἐται,* 14–15).

[55] This interpretation holds even if Pericles' name is correctly restored in the inscription, since the demos is in any case politely refusing an offer of a benefaction from private individuals.

[56] As Henderson notes in his essay, this volume, p. 162, "Pericles was not a tyrant because all power remained vested in the people." Later on, following the destruction of the empire, the ostentatious displays of the fifth century could be regarded with great discomfort; e.g., Isoc. 8.82–83. But note that in different rhetorical contexts the same speaker could cite great monuments and power approvingly: Isoc. 7.66, 15.234.

[57] The objections raised above to Miller's view of the function of the Odeum do not invalidate or in any way weaken the idea that the building was intended to express power, nor, more specifically, Miller's strong and suggestive argument that it was intended to evoke the East, specifically, Persia. If she and others are correct that the building was based on Achaemenid architectural precedents, specifically, the Apadana at Persepolis, then there are intriguing implications for the notion of *dēmos tyrannos* suggested here. For in this case, not only are the monumental displays and the patronage involved in their construction reflective of tyrantlike power but also some would have been intended to reflect the demos' collective identity as a power to be compared to the Persian King. Besides the case of the Odeum, a number of scholars have argued for specific Persian precedents in the Parthenon frieze or even the whole Acropolis program, e.g., Lawrence 1951; Pemberton 1976; Root 1985. Some of this is fairly fanciful; cf. Kroll 1979, who disputes the idea that the Parthenon frieze had eastern models.

[58] I disagree strongly with Podlecki's view (1998: 86) that it was "a totally secular structure."

[59] T. L. Shear 1982; Plut. *Per.* 13.7.

[60] If this is an anecdote to be taken seriously. See below.

[61] Millett 1989.

[62] See Burford 1963 for a discussion of the labor force for the Parthenon; also Morgan 1963: 102–108.

[63] Kallet 1998: 55–56, and above. Indeed, extravagant liturgical expenditures could be cited as proof of being a good, democratic citizen, e.g., Lys. 21. Conversely, expenditures by someone like Alcibiades aroused great public unease, surely largely because they were in "unsafe" areas like horse races that were not channeled into the institutional structure of the democratic polis and thus brought excessive power to an individual. For the narrative linkages between Alcibiades' tyrannical behavior and that of the demos, see Kallet 2001: 80–81.

[64] *HCT* II: ad loc.

[65] Rusten 1985, 1989 ad loc.; following Burkert 1960: 174.

[66] Hornblower 1991 ad loc.; see also Lattimore 1998: 93, who, however, disputes the translation "we love what is noble."

[67] A possible implied context, the expense of a sophistic education, seems unlikely. In that case, Pericles would be saying, "We Athenians do not, like others—or like some might think about us—spend extravagantly on sophistic training," a statement that would in any case apply to so few Athenians as not to have much rhetorical force.

[68] Rusten 1985, against Kakrides 1961. This obviously raises the problem of the composition of the speeches: would Thucydides' or Pericles' use of language be at issue? As we do not possess any speeches of Pericles, it is impossible to say, but in any case, redundancy in this oration still seems out of place.

[69] This is not to deny that the oration projects aristocratic values appropriated as civic values in the democracy, for which see Bliss 1964; Loraux 1986; for the tendency generally, see Will 1975: 239–241.

[70] For an explicit recognition of beauty in architecture, cf. Pl. *Resp.* 400e.

[71] Kurke 1992: 106, n. 60.

[72] Cf. Thuc. 1.6 on the increasing simplicity of the Greeks (especially the Spartans) compared to the East. Moreover, Athenians could point to the simplicity of their attire and private housing; for the former, cf. Thuc. 1.6; on domestic architecture, cf. Wycherly 1962: 175–180. The general simplicity of houses does not of course mean that there was no distinction between those of rich and poorer; cf. Wycherly 1978: 237–245.

[73] Bliss (1964: 6) in a similar vein, argues that Pericles uses the phrase to "rebut the charge usually directed at a materialist civilization, that its love of beauty was based on principles of conspicuous waste," and that "extensive public works, and private too, fall into the class of extravagant and god-tempting acts of tyrannical Hybris."

[74] E.g., Andrewes 1978; cf. Ameling 1985, who, while he thinks the account reflects a genuine fifth-century debate, comments that Plutarch need not have had a particularly good knowledge of the period to write this part of the account. It is important to keep in mind that isolating untrue statements (e.g., that the allies supply neither a ship nor a horse, only money) as an argument against the historicity of the passage completely sidesteps the nature of rhetorical invective, in which gross exaggeration is a key strategy.

75 E.g., Meiggs 1977: 139–140; Ameling 1985: 52; Stadter 1989: 146; A. Powell 1995; Podlecki 1998: 86–87.

76 Ameling 1985: 52–53.

77 Ion: Sauppe 1896: 502; Powell 1995: 262–263; Stesimbrots: Meyer 690, n. 1; Theopomps: Raubitschek 1960 [1991]; Ruschenbusch 1979: 179–180; Ephorus: Fowler 1901: 213–214. For general discussion, see Meiggs 1977: 139–140; Ameling 1985: 48–55; cf. also Frost 1964: 389–392. Ameling dryly makes the point that these authors are so different from one another that none is likely to be the source for this section.

78 Powell 1995, who also links Plut. *Per.* 12 with the absence of any mention of the Parthenon in the Funeral Oration but with a different interpretation from the one I am suggesting here.

79 E.g., *Wasps* 488–489 and MacDowell 1971 on line 345. Ameling 1985 discusses the difficulty of anchoring the debate chronologically, since parts of the extended passage *Per.* 12–14 seem to belong to the beginning stages of the building program, while others presume that the buildings are standing for all to see.

80 πλούτῳ τε ἔργου μᾶλλον καιρῷ ἢ λόγου κόμπῳ χρώμεθα.

81 Kurke 1991: 47.

82 Note that this clause is thoroughly Thucydidean, with its deliberate if not contrived *logos/ergon* contrast. Here *logos* is clearly, as in the preceding parts of the oration, the inferior member of the dichotomy.

83 Schmid 1888: 629: *hierois;* Classen-Steup 1963; ad loc.: *dēmosiois.*

84 Flashar 1969.

85 See 1.10, mentioned above, on the relationship between buildings and power. This possibility applies even though the immediate context of the passage is escape from troubles if we appreciate the extent to which he vigorously, explicitly and implicitly, objects to spending on beauty. See Kallet 2001: 48–66.

86 By contrast, Thucydides later on artfully implicates the demos as a tyrant in a thoroughly negative construction; see Kallet 2001: 79–82.

87 Note how the oration ends, with the words ἄνδρες ἄριστοι πολιτεύουσιν, "the best men are citizens." The paradoxically aristocratic nature of parts of the oration has been noted by, e.g., Kakrides 1961: 24–27; Gomme in *HCT* II: 108–109; Parry 1981: 165; Loraux 1986.

88 The composition of the audience at dramatic performances, but even more so its size, is of obvious importance here. It is usually assumed that the audience reflected a cross-section of male society (so, e.g., Henderson, this volume), while scholars disagree over whether women could attend: cf. Goldhill 1994 (no); Podlecki 1990 (yes); Henderson 1991 (yes). The comedies to be explored here, the *Knights* and the *Wasps,* were both produced at the Lenaea. There is some doubt as to whether the dramatic productions at the festival were held in the Theater of Dionysus in the fifth century or elsewhere, most likely the Agora. Both the evidence and probability lean toward the Theater of Diony-

sus, especially by the 420s, when these plays were performed. See Pickard-Cambridge 1988: 39–40; Csapo and Slater 1995: 123. Estimates of the seating capacity of the Theater of Dionysus range between 14,000–20,000 in the fifth and fourth centuries (Pickard-Cambridge 1988: 263; Csapo and Slater 1995: 286). But cf. S. Dawson 1997, who argues, unconvincingly, for an estimate of only ca. 3,700–4,500. Difficulties with his approach and argument include acceptance of Travlos' hypothetical reconstruction of the theater at its height as a fact, an assumption that wooden seats would take up more room than marble ones and also that the poor would not have been able to afford an admission fee before the *theorikon* was introduced. On the last point, even if the payment was as high as one drachma in the fifth century (it was only two obols in the fourth century, according to Dem. 18.28), it would not have been difficult for the majority of ordinary citizens to save up such an amount for a once- or twice-yearly festival, and the incentive, especially for comic performances, would have been great.

[89] Ὦ Δῆμε, καλήν γ᾽ ἔχεις / ἀρχήν, ὅτε πάντες ἄν / θρωποι δεδίασί σ᾽ ὥς / περ ἄνδρα τύραννον, 1111–1114. Cf. also *Knights* 40–45, where the despot, Demos, buys a slave, Paphlagon.

[90] Gomme, in *HCT* II: ad loc.

[91] At the end of the play, Demos is described as ruler "of Greece and of our land," i.e., both foreign and domestic realms.

[92] For my purposes, it does not matter whether Demos is now also young or simply cured from his disease. For earlier bibliography and a recent argument in favor of the former, see S. D. Olson 1990; for the latter, Edmunds 1987a: 256; Edmunds 1987b: 43. For a discussion of costume changes and transformations in Aristophanes, see Stone 1981: 399–407.

[93] ὦ ταὶ λιπαραὶ καὶ ἰοστέφανοι καὶ ἀριζήλωτοι Ἀθῆναι, δείξατε τὸν τῆς Ἑλλάδος ἡμῖν καὶ τῆς γῆς τῆσδε μόναρχον, 1329–1330.

[94] Note the Pindaric tag, ὦ ταὶ λιπαραὶ καὶ ἰοστέφανοι (dithyramb Fr. 76 Maehler; cf. schol. on Ar. *Ach.* 637), which makes even more potent, in a clearly positive sense, the element of luxury.

[95] Cf. also Neil's lengthy note, 1901: ad loc.

[96] E.g., Xenophanes DK 21B3; Asius Fr. 13 (Kinkel) (= Athen. 12.525e–f); see Donlan 1980: 53; Geddes 1987; Kurke 1992.

[97] βασιλεὺς τῶν Ἑλλήνων, 1333. Landfester 1967: 97–98 discusses the various titles and terms used to refer to Demos.

[98] 575: ἆρ᾽ οὐ μεγάλη τοῦτ᾽ ἔστ᾽ ἀρχὴ καὶ τοῦ πλούτου καταχήνη.

[99] 1137; 1143. See MacDowell 1971: ad loc. The boots are described as Laconian (1158).

[100] Geddes 1987: 321.

[101] Even Geddes concedes (321, n. 136), "It is true that Philokleon was too hot in the warm cloak and that suggests that it was excessively luxurious."

[102] Miller 1997: 154. As she notes, "The humour of the scene presupposes recognition of the

kaunakēs as an imported garment by the audience and a belief that it was Persian. . . .
The *kaunakēs* was evidently visually distinctive. . . . Aristophanes presumably chose
it from the possible range of foreign garments because its distinctive qualities best
suited his dramatic purpose. Garments that assimilated more easily into the Athenian
repertoire, or that showed their exotic qualities only on close inspection of design,
decoration, and fabric, were less useful." The joke lies partly in Lovecleon's unawareness
of the origins of the garment. MacDowell 1971: 279, comments that "Philokleon's ignorance of it must be laughable, yet credible; so the passage shows that such cloaks were
worn by some Athenians, but only rarely."

[103] Kurke 1992; cf. also Johnstone 1994: 222–223.

[104] Miller 1997. She amply demonstrates the overall receptivity to things Persian, especially
in the later fifth century.

[105] I am grateful to Kathryn Morgan, for organizing a stimulating conference and for offering valuable comments on drafts, and to the participants at the conference for making it
so productive an experience. I also thank Jack Kroll, for comments and suggestions, and
Nancy Moore, the copyeditor for the University of Texas Press.

JEFFREY HENDERSON

DEMOS, DEMAGOGUE, TYRANT
IN ATTIC OLD COMEDY

It is generally agreed that in imperial Athens, the people's perception of tyranny was entirely negative and that their fear that tyranny still threatened the democracy was unrealistic. After all, the actual threat ended with the Persian invasions and the ostracisms of the 480s,[1] and the perennial threat to democracy thereafter was not tyranny but oligarchy. Tuplin's 1985 survey of explicit references to tyranny in contemporary sources finds them in fact to be relatively scarce and more ideologically than historically informed, suggesting that the very concept of tyranny was largely a historical myth.[2] It would seem, then, that in fifth-century Athens, tyranny and the threat of a new tyrant were chimerical notions, effective perhaps as metaphors or rhetorical tropes but in practical terms not real determinants of political life.

It is too early to adopt this conclusion, however, for some of the evidence has not been fully assessed, in particular the evidence to be found in Old Comedy. Here references to tyranny both explicit and implicit, together with the assumptions underlying them, often reveal popular attitudes that supplement and can help us control the other evidence. We will find that in Old Comedy the notions of collective tyranny and an imperial tyrant-polis were not merely "elite and dissident" criticisms applied to the demos[3] but fair characterizations of popular ideology. Moreover, while the threat of individual tyranny may seem to us in long retrospect to be unrealistic, the contemporary Athenian demos, having developed its own definition of the tyrant, did not see it that way. The democratic majority, as portrayed by the comic poets, viewed tyranny, even if unhistorically remembered, as important in both conceptualizing their own collective prerogatives and identifying potential usurpers. Indeed the "history of tyranny" is itself essentially a creation of democratic Athens and reflects the Athenians' own problems of self-identity.

The comic evidence helps us trace how a peculiarly Athenian, and quite elastic, concept of tyranny took shape in the crucible of fifth-century politics and played a significant role in creating the ideology, and enforcing the regime, of radical democracy and imperialism.

Certainly the image of the individual tyrant was carefully nurtured in democratic law, ideology, and popular art and became the central negative model of personal and civic behavior. Story and song told, if rather fancifully, how Harmodius and Aristogeiton had liberated their fellow Athenians from enslavement to the tyrant,[4] so that citizens could enjoy freedom and equality under the law. Their statues in the Agora, and the honors enjoyed by their descendants, kept a tyrannicidal founding moment of democracy ever in view. The bouleutic oath inaugurated in 501 contained a curse against anyone who would again aspire to tyranny; so did the announcements that opened meetings of the Assembly[5] and the City Dionysia.[6] The Draco-Solonian laws against tyranny were remembered and periodically reinforced.[7] We also find legislation against tyranny as a threat to democracy applied in the allied cities, as in the Erythrae Decree of the late 450s (*IG* I[3] 14.32–37 = ML no. 40). The tyrannical citizen could be punished by outlawry, ostracism, or death, and during the Peloponnesian War, as we will see, populist leaders could brand as tyrannical any behavior that could be popularly construed as unegalitarian.

But this resolutely negative concept of tyranny as applied to the individual citizen assumes a more ambiguous complexion when applied to the corporate demos. During the ascendancy of Pericles, both external enemies and internal detractors began to charge Athens with being a tyrant city: the now-sovereign Athenian demos had arrogated to itself collectively the freedoms and power once enjoyed by the tyrannical individual and had begun to assert the right to rule others as far as its sheer might allowed.[8] This was certainly meant as a negative charge, and yet the tyrant metaphor was not wholly rejected by democratic leaders. Both Pericles and Cleon exploited it in the Assembly to characterize the demos' rule. This encouraged Connor to look for "ambiguity" in the use of tyranny thus applied, allowing for a positive connotation.[9] But the word tyranny, except when applied to a god, turns out never to lack at least some pejorative connotations so that Tuplin could object that "Athenians might logically exult in their tyranny. But there is no evidence that they did."[10] Still, we are left wondering just what Pericles and Cleon were up to when they addressed the demos as a collective tyranny.

It is true that the Athenian demos is never described as calling itself a tyranny; people preferred the more flattering terminology of monarchy to characterize their absolute rule. But it does not necessarily follow that the demos rejected the ideology of collective tyranny along with the word itself. The use of the metaphor by Pericles and Cleon suggests that the acquisition of arguably tyrannical powers was considered by the majority of the Athenian demos to be a justifiable, indeed a legitimate ambition, even if appeals to that ambition had to be couched for the most part in other terms. The comic evidence will confirm this impression.

If that is so, the concept of tyranny not only served as a negative model of individual behavior but was also involved in the fundamental questions of fifth-century democracy: the freedom of the individual, the justice of popular sovereignty, and the proper role of leaders under its regime. In short, the new idea of a democratic state or system that would define the individual and the collective under abstract laws and principles required the generation of an ideology. Domestically, the operative ideology was, in the words of Huey Long's ditty, "Every man a king, but no one wears a crown." As for external policy, the fruits of a subject empire were an entitlement that the Athenians had won in the Persian Wars. It was mainly the controversy generated on the political level by these ideological positions that sustained the vitality of the tyrant image, despite its unreality. The central issue was, Whether and how was the absolute power of the demos to be constrained?

In default of actual political oratory from the imperial period, Old Attic Comedy, with its topical focus and uniquely large and inclusive audience,[11] provides our best view of how the tyrant metaphor was popularly understood and politically deployed. Since comedies are datable to particular years, they can often help us trace the evolution of ongoing political themes and issues in response to events. In the case of the tyranny theme, the comic evidence takes us from the heyday of Pericles through the aftermath of the oligarchic coup of 411. Comedy is thus a valuable supplement to, and check on, the historical and epigraphic record.

But comic evidence is seldom straightforward. The inherent ambiguity of humor aside, the comic poets often had their own political axes to grind, as recent research has (in my view, at least) satisfactorily established. That is, political comedy did not merely reflect Athenian politics but could also participate: the comic festival, as a privileged extension of political debate, could serve as a forum for experimental politics, raising issues that could not be raised, or raised in the same way, in forensic venues.[12] In Aristophanes' case we must reckon with the presence of a consistent and systematic pattern of bias. There is hostility toward populist leaders in the mold of Pericles and Cleon and any of their policies that threatened the wealth and power of the elite classes. Men like Nicias, Laches, Alcibiades, those implicated in the scandals of 415, and the oligarchs disenfranchised after the coup d'état of 411—potential targets at least as obvious as Pericles and Cleon—are entirely spared and occasionally even defended.[13] There is criticism of the way the Council, the Assembly, and the courts exercised their authority but mainly when private wealth in Athens and the empire was thereby threatened; there is doubt that the demos as a whole could exercise power intelligently and justly on its own; there is a neo-Cimonian attitude toward imperialism, including calls for joint hegemony with Sparta; and there is disapproval of the Peloponnesian War but mainly when it threatened the interests of Attic landowners. Aristophanes' comic rivals seem largely to have shared these rightist biases.

Our evaluation of Aristophanes' plays must therefore be conditioned by his own political agenda, but their value is hardly diminished for being partisan. In using the theme of tyranny to enhance his own overtly tendentious portrayals, Aristophanes exemplifies its multivalent potency in both positive and negative constructions of democratic ideology. A serious complicating factor is our current uncertainty about the size and social complexion of comic audiences: how could comedies that ran counter to the prevailing political mood win prizes in demos-sponsored competitions? Was the audience unrepresentative of the demos as a whole, as has recently been argued by Sommerstein (1997a)? Perhaps so, but I am unconvinced.

It seems implausible that at the dramatic festivals, the city's most spectacular and expensive annual events, members of the host demos were significantly outnumbered by elite minorities; nor in arguing their political agenda do the comic poets seem to be preaching to the converted. So I work from the assumption that comic audiences were representative and consequently that the comic poets' political agenda still had some persuasive power, as indeed was still the case in actual politics. In other words, comic portraits of the demos were intended to play to the actual demos and did not represent a different, elite perspective.[14]

This paper will take more a chronological than a thematic approach, because the deployment of the tyranny theme both in Athenian politics and in comedy changed in step with events. But one constant and central theme of the comic take on tyranny is this: the Athenian demos held and deserved to hold arguably tyrannical power at home and abroad, but the beneficiary of that power was not the demos but dishonest demagogues; and it was the demagogues, not the demos, who deserved blame for misuse of that power. In short, the comic poets involved themselves in the political battle between populist leaders and their elite opponents that was being waged before the sovereign demos. It was a battle about leadership, and the ambivalent ideology of tyranny was one of the weapons.

That under Pericles Athens had become a tyrant city was a salient element of anti-Athenian propaganda:[15] Athens had replaced the Persians,[16] and her subject allies had become slaves,[17] while Sparta was the liberator and the enemy of tyrants.[18] But Pericles accepted the tyrant metaphor for Athens:[19] by his ideological lights, absolute rule enjoyed collectively by a free people was the perfection of the tyrant's freedom.[20] It was of course also like a tyrant's rule in being resented and therefore dangerous to let go of, lest the subjects revolt for their own freedom, so that vigilance and, if necessary, violence was required of the master. Nor was all this merely a Periclean or Thucydidean conceit: the Athenians' claim to rule over their allies was expressed in both documentary and literary sources in brutally frank terms[21] and thereby asserted a status that contradicted not only the normative and ideal relationship between allied poleis but also the Athenians' own domestic principles of freedom and autonomy. Pericles acknowledged that the attainment of such an *archē* (rule) could involve what is *adikon* (unjust).[22] Pericles' embrace of the tyrant metaphor may have been intended to startle the Athenians out of any notion that their rule was more like a monarchy, implying the devotion of its subjects,[23] but his successor Cleon's reuse of the tyrant metaphor in the debate on Mytilene shows its lasting persuasive power.[24] In the course of the war the metaphor hardened into principle, as the Melian dialogue illustrates.[25]

Old Comedy confirms that the status of absolute and unaccountable ruler was one that most Athenians were happy to apply to themselves, and though the distinction drawn by Lisa Kallet[26] between tyrant demos (domestically) and tyrant polis (abroad) is real, it seems more a distinction drawn by outsiders and theoreticians than by the comic poets, for whom the demos' tyrannical power is all of a piece. Indeed power, according to democratic ideology, was always a good thing, so long as it belonged only to the people collectively.[27] That is why comic criticism of the demos' exercise of power was always directed at bad leaders rather than at the demos itself.

In *Wasps*, power both at home and abroad is the chief source of pride for Philocleon, who represents the views of the demos generally and who compares his power to a king's, even to Zeus (546–547, 619):[28]

PHILOCLEON: Right out of the gate I'll demonstrate that our sovereignty is as strong as any king's. . . . So then, don't I wield great authority, as great as Zeus'?[29]

Similarly the rejuvenated Demos in the *Knights* (1329–1330):

CHORUS: O Athens, the gleaming, the violet-crowned, the envy of all, show us the monarch of Greece and of this land!

It is noteworthy that in comedy this rulership is typically characterized as "rule" (*archē*), "monarchy" or the like rather than as "tyranny," but in one passage in *Knights,* to which I will return, the chorus means to flatter Demos by comparing him to a tyrant (1111–1120):

CHORUS: Demos, you have a fine sway, since all mankind fears you like a man with tyrannical power. But you're easily led astray: you enjoy being flattered and thoroughly deceived, and every speechmaker has you gaping. You've a mind, but it's out to lunch.

The formulation in this passage typifies Aristophanes' consistent attitude: the demos' collective right to absolute rule both at home and abroad—for that is the meaning of "all mankind"—is nowhere questioned or criticized, and the Athenian role in repelling the Persians is constantly kept in view as the justification for empire.[30] All Aristophanes' demotic characters and choruses are associated with the victory at Marathon.

Now it is true that Aristophanes' lost play *Babylonians,* produced at the Dionysia of 426, did somehow criticize Athenian imperial rule. It may even be, as many have thought, that its chorus of branded mill slaves represented the Athenian allies.[31] But even if that is so, I doubt that any sympathy for the allies was expressed in terms of a protest against their subjection to Athenian rule per se. After the performance, Cleon tried to prosecute Aristophanes for attacking the demos and its officers in the presence of the allies, but Aristophanes' actual target was probably the self-serving behavior of men like Cleon. The charge was usurpation by the individual demagogue of the prerogatives rightly belonging to the demos, as in *Knights.* This was certainly the rationale offered by Aristophanes in his own defense, recapitulated in *Acharnians* the following year, and it is consistent with the passage cited from *Knights:* Aristophanes emphatically dissociates criticism of the demagogues from criticism of the polis (514–517):

Why do we blame the Spartans for this? For it was men of ours—I do not say the city, remember that, I do not say the city—but some trouble-making excuses for men.

It is significant that in *Acharnians* the allies are mentioned only for their deceptive flattery of the Athenian Assembly (642–651). Allied flattery, incidentally, no doubt helped to create the sort of complacency that Pericles and Cleon meant to puncture by embracing the tyrant metaphor.[32]

It is also true that the demos as domestic sovereign is routinely ridiculed in comedy for all manner of foolishness and misgovernance, including implicitly tyrannical behavior in the negative sense. In *Acharnians,* for example, the demos is bellicose abroad, high-handed and harshly punitive at home; consorts with and admires barbarians; is paranoid enough to believe the most outrageous claims of the "sycophants"; and easily falls for the most obvious flattery. In *Knights* and *Wasps,* the demos' readiness to see conspiracy everywhere is yet another hallmark of the insecure tyrant. One could mention other such behavior from lost plays, for example, manipulation of the state religion by tampering with the calendar[33] or introducing alien gods like Bendis and Cotyto to please the allied Thracians.[34] But in all these cases, the demos is ultimately absolved from blame. Again, it is demagogic leaders who are held responsible for the demos' mistakes, as in this exchange from the final scene in *Knights* (1335–1337):

DEMOS: It's that I'm ashamed of my former mistakes.
SAUSAGE SELLER: But you aren't to blame for them, never think it! The blame's with those who deceived you this way.

Comic satire of the tyrant demos thus tends to follow democratic ideology: the demos should hold the power—tyranny and monarchy after all are winner-take-all games—and leaders should not interfere with or usurp any of it. But the comic poets differed from the majority view in identifying those leaders who posed a threat to the demos' rule. The demos tended to view with suspicion those whom the comic poets favored: elite citizens who opposed the policies of Pericles and his successors and whom popular leaders branded as potential tyrants. This was a natural suspicion, since one point of similarity between democrats and tyrants was opposition to the aristocracy.

For the comic poets, on the other hand, the danger came not from the threat of an elite tyrant but from crooked demagogues. For the comic poets, as for the Old Oligarch, the answer to the question, Over whom does the tyrant demos tyrannize? was, The allies abroad, at home the elite. Men like Philocleon would be happy to agree. But people like Philocleon would not tend to agree with the comic poets that the real beneficiaries were the demagogues, nor with comic defense of the motives of the elite as being in the best interests of the demos and therefore as untyrannical.

In the process of advancing their case, from the 430s until the end of the war, the comic poets tried to undermine the claims of popular leaders to be servants and watchdogs of the demos and attacked the popular conception of tyranny and its history by arguing that fear of the tyrant's return was merely a scare tactic used to discredit the city's best people. The effort was not solely defensive: in *Birds* Aristophanes presented an ideal scenario, in which the tyranny of an elite leader best assured the sovereignty of the demos.

The long ascendancy of Pericles raised the paradox of the democratic strongman and with it the whiff of tyranny. The idea of Athens as a tyrant city could not have been entertained in isolation from the policies of its *prostatēs* (leading citizen), since his will was equated with the will of the polis as a whole.[35] Thucydides, in his famous postmortem of Pericles in 2.65, tried to resolve this paradox, and thus bypass the tyrant issue, by attributing Pericles' supremacy to sheer leadership: only a sovereign people could achieve what Athens had achieved, but to do it they needed a wise and selfless leader. That is, Pericles was not a tyrant because all power remained vested in the people; after all, the demos could and did punish even Pericles.

But this was not the view of Pericles' opponents among the traditional elite, whose influence over the people he had eclipsed. Their view is preserved in comedies by Cratinus, Hermippus, and other comic poets during the 430s,[36] in which Pericles was portrayed as a tyrant with Zeuslike powers, as in this song from Cratinus' *Cheirons* (Fr. 258):

> CHORUS: Stasis (Discord) and eldest-born Time commingled and begat the greatest tyrant, the one whom the gods call Head-Compeller [punning on epic "Cloud-Compeller" (of Zeus)].

The specifics were that Pericles used allied tribute to outspend his rivals in garnering popular support, an effort of which the building program was Exhibit A. He bullied the allies to serve his own ends, most notoriously in the war against Samos, which he allegedly undertook to please his Milesian mistress, Aspasia (an allegation later recycled by Aristophanes to fit the Peloponnesian War). He threw the Greek world into turmoil by provoking the Peloponnesians. He nourished a following of young supporters dubbed "the new Peisistratids." He did all this with the tyrannical aim of gaining personal power and unique privileges at the people's expense. When in Cratinus' *Thracian Women* he came onstage wearing the Odeum as a crown (Fr. 73), the point was that the building program was for the greater glory of Pericles, not the people. Aristophanes would continue to level such criticisms against Pericles even after his death, and he expressed sympathy with Thucydides son of Melesias, who had led the opposition to Pericles.[37]

Pericles' death in 429 precipitated a profound change in Athenian politics, which Thucydides accurately summarizes in 2.65 but which he does not treat in any detail. For the role played by the tyranny metaphor, we rely mainly on comedy. Without Pericles to restrain it, the sovereignty of the demos was truly unleashed, as Cratinus put it in *Ploutoi* (Fr. 171.22–23):

The rule of tyranny ⟨has been lifted⟩ and the demos has the power.

Into this vacuum stepped the "new politicians," men without traditional family or political alliances, who competed for political ascendancy on the strength of their individual prowess in assembly and court and who took a new populist line.[38] Meanwhile, men from the traditional ruling families abruptly lost, and to a certain extent intentionally ceded, their authority over the demos. This political redirection was accelerated by the stubbornness of the war, increasing financial pressures,[39] and the growing threat of allied rebellion. As a result, the Athenian demos became even more tyrannical. Assemblies and courts became more willful and high-handed, and imperial rule, harsher and more exacting. The burden of financing the war fell especially hard on wealthy Athenians, who began to be hit with special levies in 428, and on the allies, whose tribute was sharply increased in 425—both tyrannical moves, in the view of their targets.

The 420s, especially under the ascendancy of Cleon, were also marked by a fiercely divisive politics of class warfare, in which the charge of individual tyranny took a new direction. The sort of attack on an aspiring tyrant that in the days of the Olympian Pericles might have been handled by the open means of partisan politics or by ostracism was redirected at alleged conspirators among the elite, now the political outs, whom the demagogues succeeded in portraying as hostile to popular sovereignty.[40] The threat of tyranny was now both a rallying point for the demotic majority and a weapon against the elite minority. The picture painted by Aristophanes in *Knights* and *Wasps* shows that populist charges of tyrannical conspiracies were a novelty. They were also leveled so frequently, were so broadly construed, and directed at

such unlikely targets as to be arguably absurd, as in this passage from *Wasps*
(484–502):

> BDELYCLEON: Heavens above, I do wish you'd get off my back! Or is it
> now decreed that we're to spend the whole day skinning each other alive?
> CHORUS: No, never, not while there's any breath left in my body: a man
> who plans to be our tyrant!
> BDELYCLEON: How you [*var.* we] see tyranny and conspirators every-
> where, as soon as anyone voices a criticism large or small! I hadn't even
> heard of that word being used for at least fifty years, but nowadays it's
> cheaper than sardines. Look how it's bandied about in the marketplace.
> If someone buys perch but doesn't want sprats, the sprat seller next door
> pipes right up and says, "This guy buys fish like a would-be tyrant." And if
> he asks for a free onion to spice his sardines a bit, the vegetable lady gives
> him the fish eye and says, "Say, are you asking for an onion because you
> want to be tyrant? Or maybe you think Athens grows spices as her tribute
> to you?"
> XANTHIAS: My slut got sharp-tempered with me too, when I went
> to her place yesterday noon. I told her to ride me, and she asked if I was
> jockeying for a tyranny à la Hippias!
> BDELYCLEON: Yes, these people enjoy hearing talk like that, if my
> present case is any indication. Just because I want my father to quit his
> dawn-wandering, nuisance-suing, jury-serving, trouble-seeking habits
> and live a genteel life like Morychus, for my efforts I get called a conspira-
> tor with tyranny in mind.

The very frequency of this charge shows its effectiveness as a weapon of in-
timidation.[41] An earlier passage underlines the class-antagonism that was so
central an element in this new deployment of the tyranny metaphor (463–
476):

> CHORUS: Don't the poor folk see it plainly, how tyranny has sneaked up
> on me from behind and tried to jump me, now that you, you troublesome
> troublemaker, you long-haired Amynias, debar us from our country's
> established legal rights, without making any excuse or dextrous argument
> but autocratically?
> BDELYCLEON: Might we enter into discussion and compromise with-
> out this fighting and shrill screaming?
> CHORUS: Discussion with you, you enemy of the people, you lover
> of monarchy, you buddy of Brasidas, with the woollen fringes on your
> clothes and the untrimmed beard on your face?

Incidentally, if Kallet is correct that Pericles had tried to counter the image of the tyrant demos by constructing Athens rather as a collective aristocracy,[42] it was an idea that was apparently (and understandably) not embraced by the elite in the subsequent class warfare. The comic poets portray the power of the demos solely in monarchic or tyrannical terms, and its culture as ludicrously alien to all the norms of the aristocracy. The paradigmatic juryman, Philocleon of *Wasps,* detests all things aristocratic and prides himself on his "contempt for wealth" (575). In *Knights* it is laid down at the start that no aspirant to political ascendancy can any longer afford to betray the slightest trace of noble background (180–194). This is by contrast with the demos in its glory days, before Pericles. The appearance and character of the rejuvenated Demos at the end of *Knights* suggest that the demos used to be more aristocratic and ought to be so again.

Now, there is no evidence that anyone was actually prosecuted on a tyranny-related charge in the 420s or that any target of the demagogues' accusations was really an antidemocratic conspirator. Taken together, however, these accusations did prepare the ground for the political convergence of tyranny and oligarchy (from the demotic standpoint) that would be precipitated by the events of 415–411, when popular sovereignty was actually threatened by elite conspirators. The comic evidence thus calls into question the impression given by Thucydides that serious concerns about tyranny began only in 415. Take, for example, the charge made by the dicast-chorus in *Wasps* 376–378:

CHORUS: [We'll put a stop to Bdelycleon] so that he'll know better than to trample on the Two Goddesses' legislation (*tain theain psēphismata*).

To accuse Bdelycleon of undermining the Eleusinian Mysteries sounds paranoid, since we have seen him do nothing of the sort. Aristophanes clearly meant the charge itself to sound overwrought, and so it might have been in 422. Even so, it was not a fantastic charge, since it anticipates the later prosecution of Alcibiades and his friends on accusations fueled by popular fears of tyranny. This passage, incidentally, has gone unnoticed in treatments of the events of 415 because of editorial preference for the banalized reading in R (*tōn theōn*), rightly rejected in recent editions.[43]

Aristophanes tried to discredit Cleon's charges by painting them as baseless and hysterical, as in the *Wasps* passages already mentioned. At the same time, he tried to make the people's choice of leaders the issue, by portraying Cleon as the real threat to their sovereignty. His scathing portrait of the demagogue in *Knights* inaugurated a whole subgenre of comic satire.[44] Cleon in fact styled himself the successor of Pericles and Themistocles, not as an Olympian leader but as the selfless watchdog of the people's interests. As Philocleon says of jurors, "We're the only ones Cleon doesn't badger" (*Wasps* 596–598). Apparently, Cleon also compared himself to Harmodius, perhaps even claimed him as an ancestor.[45] Not so, according to Aristophanes: in reality, Cleon and his friends were stealing the lion's, or the tyrant's, share of what the people had won at Marathon and amassed from their empire, a claim most succinctly put in this passage in *Wasps* (698–712):

> BDELYCLEON: Then consider this: you could be rich, and everyone else too, but somehow or other these populists have got you boxed in. You, master of a multitude of cities from the Black Sea to Sardinia, enjoy absolutely no reward, except for this jury pay, and they drip that into you like droplets of oil from a tuft of wool, always a little at a time, just enough to keep you alive—because they want to keep you poor, and I'll tell you the reason: so you'll recognize your trainer, and whenever he whistles at you to attack one of his enemies, you'll leap on that man like a savage. If they wanted to provide a living for the people, it would be easy. A thousand cities there are that now pay us tribute. If someone ordered each one to support twenty men, then twenty thousand loyal proles would be rolling in hare meat, every kind of garland, bee stings, and eggnog, living it up as befits their country and their trophy at Marathon. As it is, you traipse around for your employer like olive pickers!

The scenario of *Knights* is similar. Demos has grown old and mindless, so that his newly imported Paphlagonian slave has been able to seize control of his grand estate by flattering him and intimidating the honest slaves, all the while living like a king and feeding Demos only scraps.

In these "demagogue comedies," Aristophanes portrays popular leaders as all-powerful not in their own right but by having usurped the demos' power, for example, in the knights' promise to the Sausage Seller, if he succeeds in replacing Cleon (838–842):

> O paramount benefactor of all mankind revealed, I envy you your ready tongue! Keep thrusting forward this way, and you'll be the greatest man in Greece, hold sole power in the city, and rule over the allies, in your hand a trident for shaking them and quaking them and making lots of money.

Thus the demagogues were not tyrants in the familiar sense, and Aristophanes never explicitly calls them tyrants. But this was a politically strategic maneuver. After all, an important element of the comic demagogue was his essential lowness: he was a liar, a thief, and a slanderer who concealed his ill-gotten power, not an impressive figure in the mold of Pericles or for that matter an elite gentleman like Bdelycleon, for whom the tyrant label was not obviously disproportionate.[46] Then, too, Aristophanes could not very well debunk the charge of tyranny as a chimera and at the same time try to affix it explicitly to Cleon.

Nevertheless, as usurpers of the people's sovereignty, the demagogues did enjoy implicit tyrannical power, on their own conspiratorial definition of that term, and so the hallmarks of the Classical tyrant are not hard to find in their comic caricature. Cleon uses public and imperial funds for his own pleasures, especially sexual excess, gluttony, and heavy drinking; violently suppresses opposition; lords it over the people's administrative and military officers and over the allies; intrigues secretly with enemy states; harasses the elite classes, including homosexuals;[47] is paranoid about conspiracies; maintains a circle of toadies and a gang of young toughs as bodyguards; pursues Demos as an *erastēs* (lover);[48] and controls the Agora, the financial and public center of the polis.[49] There are a few direct suggestions of tyranny too: Cleon is compared to the tyrants Antileon of Chalcis and to Pittacus of Mytilene. The latter comparison is especially pointed, since in context it counters Cleon's singing of the Harmodius song and his claim to be a descendent of Harmodius. Here there is a suggestion that he was a descendent rather of the bodyguards of Hippias' wife (445–449):[50]

> PAPHLAGON: I say that you're descended from the polluters of our Goddess! [i.e., the followers of Cylon]
> SAUSAGE SELLER: And I say your grandfather was among the body-guards—
> PAPHLAGON: What bodyguards? Go on.
> SAUSAGE SELLER:—of Hippias' wife, Pursine! [punning on her actual name, Myrsine, for a joke about tanning, Cleon's trade]

This passage neatly encapsulates the fluidity of the ideological dispute over where to direct the people's fears of tyranny: toward the elite or toward the demogogues.

A salient component of the Aristophanic portrayal of the demos is its tyrantlike gullibility in the face of demagogic flattery and deception. In *Knights* Aristophanes enacts a hopeful scenario of the people's salvation from a threat they did not seem to acknowledge. Under the sponsorship of the elite, represented by the knights, the vulgar, but in the end honest, Sausage Seller rescues the House of Demos from the evil overseer Cleon, restores to Demos the youthful power that was his in the days of Miltiades and Aristides, and returns to favor the loyal servants whom Cleon had alienated from their master. The duet between Demos and Knights expresses Aristophanes' wishful thinking about the demos' attitude toward its false leaders and its ability to use its own powers wisely (1111–1150):

> CHORUS: Demos, you have a fine sway, since all mankind fears you like a man with tyrannical power. But you're easily led astray: you enjoy being flattered and thoroughly deceived, and every speechmaker has you gaping. You've a mind, but it's out to lunch.
> DEMOS: There's no mind under your long hair, since you consider me stupid; but there's purpose in this foolishness of mine. I relish my daily pap, and I pick one thieving political leader to fatten. I raise him up, and when he's full, I swat him down.
> CHORUS: In that case you'll do well; and[51] your character really does contain, as you claim, very deep cunning, if you deliberately fatten these men, like public victims, on the Pnyx, and then when you chance to lack dinner, you sacrifice one who's bloated, and have yourself a meal.
> DEMOS: Just watch me and see if I don't ingeniously trick them, those who think they're smart and that I'm their dupe. I monitor them all the time, pretending I don't even see them, as they steal; and then I force them to regurgitate whatever they've stolen from me, using a verdict tube as a probe.

The Sausage Seller differs from Cleon only in being a true servant of Demos and an ally of Demos' true friends, the elite.

In *Wasps* two years later, the picture has become more pessimistic. The demos' would-be redeemer this time is not a vulgar sausage seller but a cultivated *apragmōn* (political quietist). Bdelycleon tries to reform Philocleon by breaking his allegiance to the demagogues, removing him from his demotic environment and remaking him in the image of the elite. Aristophanes exploits the parallelism between Philocleon's position in the city (enthrallment by the vulgar Cleon) and his status in his own household (dependence on his elite son) to consider what might happen if men like Bdelycleon were to win the allegiance of Cleon's followers. Bdelycleon invites his father to an elegant symposium—an environment assumed to be unfamiliar to the rank-and-file—and coaches him in the appropriate etiquette. But the symposium is a disaster: misunderstanding the freedom from legal constraints that his son had assured him is an elite prerogative, Philocleon becomes drunk and disorderly, insults the guests, abducts the piper girl, and assaults the ordinary citizens he meets on his way home. Bdelycleon can only look on helplessly. Clearly Philocleon's vulgarity, arrogance, and aggression have not been tempered but rather let loose on society at large even more virulently than before. The implication is that the demos is incorrigible, its ability to handle freedom an illusion. Apparent too is the impotence of the elite to change the demos: perhaps a self-referential comment by Aristophanes on his own inability to reeducate the demos about Cleon, who by 422 had scuttled the truce of 423 and regained his ascendancy.[52]

The Peace of Nicias was a period of political realignment that favored the fortunes of the elite, especially Alcibiades, who together with Nicias in 417 engineered the ostracism of Hyperbolus, Cleon's successor as chief demagogue and comic butt.[53] When war resumed with the launching of the Sicilian Expedition in 415, the initiative came no longer from the demagogues but from Alcibiades and his friends. Their ascendancy, however, was short-lived: the demagogues removed them from leadership of the initiative by prosecuting them on charges of *asebeia* (impiety: a traditional hallmark of the tyrant)[54] in the affairs of the Mysteries and the Herms. In doing so, they played on the people's fear of tyranny, as Thucydides says:

> The many, growing alarmed at the immensity both of the licentiousness of his own appetites and private life and of the attitude he took on every occasion toward whatever he undertook, became hostile to him as one aiming at tyranny. . . . (6.15) The demos, knowing by report that the tyranny of Peisistratus and his sons had become harsh in its last period, and further that it had been overthrown not by themselves and Harmodius but by the Spartans, were in constant fear and took everything suspiciously. . . . (6.53.3) Reflecting on these events, and recalling whatever they knew by report, the Athenian demos grew harsh and suspicious toward those persons charged in the affair of the Mysteries, and concluded that it was all the work of an oligarchic and tyrannical conspiracy. . . . (6.60.1) As for Alcibiades, the Athenians were harshly disposed toward him, being urged on by the same enemies who had attacked him before he sailed out. Now that they thought they understood the affair of the Herms, they were more convinced than ever that the affair of the Mysteries too, in which he was implicated, had been perpetrated by him with the same plan, a conspiracy against the demos. (6.61.1)

A deliberate irony of Thucydides' account, underlined by his repetition of the word *chalepos* (harsh), is that the demos, fearing the harshness of tyranny, itself behaved as harshly as a tyrant.[55] I will return to Thucydides' emphasis on the people's historical knowledge of their tyranny, which would seem an apparent novelty in the political use of the tyrant theme. For now, two features of his analysis deserve comment.

First, that he mentions tyranny in the context of internal politics for the first time here might mislead us into thinking that this was a new development in 415. But the comic evidence of the 420s shows that in 415, Alcibiades was a figure who brought to life a tyrant-image already well established by the demagogues and their conspiracy theories and whose behavior seemed to justify them. It also confirms the impression given by comedy that at least by the 420s, tyranny was, in the popular mind, the opposite of democracy. If Alcibiades' conduct suggested a lack of devotion to democratic values, especially equality and obedience to the laws, it was tyranny that came first to mind as a motive for his parody of the Mysteries. Recall the Wasps' identical accusation against Bdelycleon in 422.

Second, Thucydides' phrase "oligarchic and tyrannical conspiracy" suggests a formal broadening of the definition of tyranny to include all forms of antidemocratic activity. This is confirmed in the wording of the decree of Demophantus (Andoc. 1.97):

> And all Athenians shall swear over perfect victims, by tribes and demes, to kill the one who does this. And this shall be the oath: "I will kill by word, by deed, by vote, and by hand, so far as lay in my power, whosoever shall overthrow the democracy at Athens, whosoever shall hold any public office after the democracy is overthrown, and whosoever shall attempt to become tyrant or help another to do so. . . .

This decree, enacted in 410 just after the fall of the oligarchy, put "overthrow of the democracy" on a par with the older Draco-Solonian tyranny laws and by its universal loyalty oath, put every Athenian under potential suspicion as a tyrant or an abettor of a tyrant.[56] Again, however, the ideological ground had been prepared in the 420s. In each case, the bogey of tyranny was invoked "to breathe new ideological life into democratic regimes that were enervated by military failures and internal conflict."[57]

The response of the comic poets to the events of 415 is difficult to establish, because in all the comedies produced between 415 and 411, there is virtually no explicit mention of Alcibiades or any of the dozens of others implicated in the scandals. This silence may or may not be the result of the mysterious decree of Syracosius of 415, which somehow abridged comic freedom of attack.[58] In any case, comic silence is consistent with the political bias of the comic poets.[59] If there was any comic response to 415, we would expect it to be sympathetic to Alcibiades, along the lines of Aristophanes' earlier expressions of sympathy for Pericles' victim Thucydides son of Melesias or Cleon's victim Laches.[60] As I have recently argued, I think we find just such a sympathetic response, albeit in fantastic guise, in the *Birds* of 414.[61]

The topicality of *Birds* is notoriously difficult to interpret. Its plot is too close to contemporary reality to justify reading it as merely a detached escapist fantasy, but at the same time not close enough to reward an allegorical interpretation of the kind invited by *Knights* or *Wasps*. Nevertheless, it is perverse to deny that *Birds* does embody contemporary Athenian fantasies of renewed imperial conquest on a grand scale and that it recapitulates, however fancifully, the events of 415. But what is its ideological spin?

Sick of Athens, the hero Peisetaerus goes to the birds in search of a *topos apragmōn*, a place without political and legal botheration. Discovering that Tereus is the ineffectual leader of the weak but potentially strong race of birds, Peisetaerus becomes his advisor. He shows Tereus how the birds, if they could be persuaded to follow a bold plan, might win an empire and so become masters of the universe. Since men are the great oppressors of birds, the birds are initially hostile to Peisetaerus. But in a series of sophistic speeches, Peisetaerus lives up to his name by persuading the birds to adopt his plan. The birds then naturalize him and invite him to lead them in carrying out the plan. It is a complete success: the birds become a master race, supplanting even the gods, and Peisetaerus becomes its absolute sovereign—indeed, explicitly its tyrant (1708). Popular fears about tyrants, exemplified in the traditional theatrical announcement of their outlawry, are laughed away by the chorus leader. There follows a series of spoof-proclamations specially created for Cloudcuckooland (1072–1076):

> CHORUS LEADER (*to the spectators*): As you know, on this particular day the proclamation is repeated that any of you who kills Diagoras the Melian will receive a talent, and anyone who kills one of the tyrants—the deceased ones—will receive a talent. So now we want to make our own proclamation in this place. . . .[62]

The similarities between Peisetaerus and Alcibiades could not have failed to strike every spectator. Like Alcibiades, who faced initial hostility from a demos ever wary of elite tyranny, Peisetaerus must face initial hostility from the birds, the traditional victims of human tyranny who, in the play, bear a distinct resemblance to the Athenian demos. Like Alcibiades, who challenged Nicias, architect of the peace of 421 and current leader of a quiet Athens, Peisetaerus challenges the quietist Tereus. On their side, the Athenians, who had not added to their empire during the war and who had lost military momentum since 421, are reminded, like the birds, of their former imperial glory and recalled to activism. Just as the Athenians had accepted Alcibiades' plan and his leadership, so the birds accept Peisetaerus and his plan. Alcibiades had argued that this unity would depend on the demos' willingness once again to accept leadership by those, like himself, who were naturally fit to lead. So too Peisetaerus, who proposes to the birds, adapting a sophistic phrase, I will be your brains (*gnōmē*), you will be my brawn (*rhōmē*), and together we will all have what we truly want: power and happiness.[63]

Thus Peisetaerus realizes the dream of every sophist and his elite pupils since the days of Pericles: he actually persuades the demos to acknowledge his superiority and grant him power. And Peisetaerus is a beneficent master, sharing the benefits of his plan in common and deriving power from the consent of the birds. He is thus an ideal tyrant, whose sovereignty derives from, and in turn protects, the ultimate sovereignty of the bird-demos. Indeed, he recreates the Thucydidean Pericles without his selfish and politically divisive ambitions and foreshadows the good tyrant of later philosophical speculation, thus neatly eliminating the problem of the tyrant demos in need of a strong leader.

Now the spectators could easily see where the play and reality part company, for the plot of *Birds* differs from actuality principally by ignoring the democratic attack on the elite and the fall of Alcibiades. In the play, the birds grant Peisetaerus' dream of personal rulership and thus realize their own dream of imperial rulership; in actuality, the Athenian demos pursued its own dream while smashing that of Alcibiades and rejecting the elite culture that had produced him. Unless we choose to read the play as entirely ironic—a mode for which the text gives no signals and that is unparalleled in Aristophanes—it is hard to avoid the conclusion that in *Birds,* Aristophanes presented a fantasy of what might have happened had the demos in fact united behind Alcibiades, if it had in fact accepted not merely his plan but his culture as well. What Aristophanes shows us is a fantasy of success and happiness for all, a dream that all Athenians could share but have not yet realized because they keep choosing the wrong leaders. If the Athenians feared that elite rule must mean loss of their power to a tyrant, as the demagogues constantly warned, *Birds* seems to allay this fear by portraying Peisetaerus' hegemony over polis and empire as beneficial and in such a way as to imply that the Athenians' fears had been misplaced.

In the event, lack of strong leadership did doom the Sicilian expedition to a defeat that seriously jeopardized Athenian security, destabilized the empire, and discredited the demagogues, so that the demos voluntarily surrendered some of its sovereignty to a board of ten Probuli and soon proved vulnerable to an oligarchic coup d'état in 411. That the old fears of tyrannical conspiracy now became even stronger in the popular mind is clear from the emphasis the tyranny theme receives in Aristophanes' *Lysistrata,* produced early in 411, some months before the coup.[64] Aristophanes' emphasis on the tyranny theme is a gauge of its current prominence in the rhetoric of democratic leaders seeking to bolster their shaken regime.[65]

Lysistrata, which imagines a secret conspiracy of women to force a nego-tiated settlement of the war, well captures the contemporary atmosphere of popular paranoia and elite machination. The women's conspiracy is distinctly elite: it is Panhellenic; its insistence on a negotiated peace was current oligar-chic policy (Thuc. 8.70–71); and its leaders, Lysistrata and her older helpers on the Acropolis, are explicitly characterized as members of the wealthy and cul-tivated class,[66] while their warmongering opponents are rank-and-file jurors and assemblymen enthralled, as ever, by self-serving demagogues. Among the women's agenda is the correction of false majority views, with particu-lar emphasis on the demagogues' use of the tyranny threat to smear their elite opponents, exemplified in this play by the women, as in the parabasis (617–635):

MEN'S CHORUS: I think I smell much bigger trouble in this, a definite whiff of Hippias' tyranny! I'm terrified that certain men from Sparta have gathered at the house of Cleisthenes and scheme to stir up our godfor-saken women to seize the Treasury and my jury pay, my very livelihood. MEN'S LEADER: It's shocking, you know, that they're lecturing the citizens now and running their mouths—mere women!—about brazen shields. And to top it all off, they're trying to make peace between us and the men of Sparta, who are no more trustworthy than a starving wolf. Actually, this plot they weave against us, gentlemen, does aim at tyranny! Well, they'll never tyrannize over me: from now on I'll be on my guard, I'll "carry my sword in a myrtle branch" and go to market fully armed right up there beside Aristogeiton. I'll stand beside him like this: that way I'll be ready to smack this godforsaken old hag right in the jaw!

Among the novel features of Lysistrata is its unusually frequent reference to Athenian history in the past hundred years, especially the end of the tyranny. Thucydides' account of the events of 415 contains a similar emphasis, confirming that historical recollection was indeed a salient feature of the politics of this period. The details, however, are problematic. Thucydides gives inconsistent reports about what the Athenians believed about the end of their tyranny. He twice says that "most" Athenians mistakenly thought that Hipparchus was the tyrant and that Harmodius and Aristogeiton had ended the tyranny by killing him (1.20.2, 6.54.2), but he also says that in 415 the Athenians "knew by report" about the harshness of the tyranny "in its last period" and that the Spartans and the exiled Alcmeonidae, not the Athenians, had ended it.[67] Since this latter account, according to Thucydides, helped to inflame the people against Alcibiades, presumably his enemies had used it to stress the harshness of a tyrant and the difficulty of getting rid of him.[68] This information, even though it was the truth, nevertheless seems out of place in demagogic rhetoric: it challenges the founding myth of democracy; accepts a key claim of enemy propaganda, that the Spartans were the traditional foes of tyranny;[69] and acknowledges the charge of Athenian passivity in the face of tyranny that the Harmodius myth had always served to answer.[70]

We get a different impression from the characterization of the men's chorus in Lysistrata, which assumes that the traditional tyranny myth was still very much alive among the rank-and-file. The Spartans are still associated with tyranny, an article of faith among the demos as early as the 420s, for example, in the Farmers of ca. 424 (Fr. 110):

I grow everything except the Spartan fig, because that fig's hateful and tyrannical. It wouldn't be small if it weren't very hostile to the demos!

Harmodius and Aristogeiton are still the liberators of the people and role models for all citizens vigilant against a new tyranny. The demagogic equation of antidemotic conspiracy with tyranny is still in force. Later in the play Lysistrata corrects the men by emphasizing the enslavement of the Athenians under Hippias and by reminding them that it was the Spartans alone who had freed them (1149–1156):

Do you Athenians think I'm going to let you off? Don't you remember the time when you were dressed in slaves' rags and the Spartans came in force and wiped out many Thessalian fighters, many friends and allies of Hippias? That day when they were the only ones helping you to drive him out? How they liberated you and replaced your slaves' rags with a warm cloak, as suits a free people?

It is worth noting that Lysistrata felt no need to correct the false belief mentioned by Thucydides as to who was tyrant, Hippias or Hipparchus. As we have seen, comedy at least since 424 (*Knights* 449) presupposes that the Athenians knew Hippias was the tyrant. Also interesting is the historical specificity of Lysistrata's account—indeed the "other allies" of Hippias in line 1153 is unattested in any other source.[71] This confirms Thucydides' emphasis on renewed interest in the history of tyranny in this period, but the comic details suggest that the historical refutation of popular beliefs was a weapon not of the demagogues but rather of their elite opponents.

In any case, *Lysistrata* is notable for being more hopeful about the demos' ability to govern than *Birds*. Like the Sausage Seller of *Knights,* the heroine returns authority to the people after discrediting its bad leaders. Perhaps this confidence was dictated by the play's generally upbeat themes of peace and reconciliation at home and abroad. On the other hand, it could be that in an atmosphere of such extreme political instability, Aristophanes did not want to voice too much warmth for the notion that the people could no longer govern themselves.

Yet *Frogs* of 405, produced in a similar political atmosphere, is notable for its unabashedly elite sympathies. The play explicitly supports Alcibiades, who is aligned with Achilles and Aeschylus and held up as the last hope for Athenian salvation.[72] It appeals for reenfranchisement of the oligarchs of 411, for which Aristophanes was decreed a commendation, a crown, and the unprecedented honor of a reperformance of the play. It attacks the last of the demagogues, Cleophon, who shortly after the second performance was arrested on trumped-up charges, tried in a kangaroo court, and summarily executed, all at the direction of men who would soon be participants in the rule of the so-called Thirty Tyrants.[73] Sommerstein has recently asked whether the crown and the reperformance were moved by these men as an element of their campaign to discredit Cleophon. If they were, was Aristophanes the unwitting dupe of these men or their collaborator in a quid pro quo deal?[74] What we have seen of Aristophanes' attitude over the years toward both popular and individual tyranny makes our choice of answer far from simple.[75]

Notes

[1] Hippias fought with Darius at Marathon, and the Peisistratids with Xerxes in the invasion of 480: Hdt. 6.102–108, 7.6, 8.52.

[2] In general, see Cobet 1988; Raaflaub 1988a; and V. Parker 1998.

[3] Raaflaub, this volume, p. 59 above.

[4] The concept of citizens under a tyrant as slaves goes back to Solon and remained central in the ideology of tyranny; cf. Raaflaub 1985: 65–70, 108–125.

[5] Cf. Ar. *Thesm.* 338–339, Ostwald 1986: 357–358.

[6] Ar. *Birds* 1072–1074. McGlew 1993: 186 is wrong to think that this announcement merely refers to a comic provision of Cloudcuckooland; see Dunbar 1995: ad loc.

[7] Ostwald 1955.

[8] On "imperial tyranny," see Hunter 1973–1974; Connor 1977; Lanza 1977: 236–239; Schuller 1978; Raaflaub 1979, 1984, and this volume; Tuplin 1985; Scanlon 1987; Barceló 1990.

[9] Connor 1977: 102, Raaflaub (1984: 76) accepted this in connection with the idea of the absolute freedom of the demos, but he has now changed his mind (this volume).

[10] Tuplin 1985: 362. The use of "tyrant" in a neutral or favorable sense was never normal (as maintained by, e.g., Andrewes 1956: 20–30; so too Parker 1998, who further argues that the negative connotation was exclusively Attic) and very rare (Tuplin 1985: 374; O'Neil 1986).

[11] On the supracivic nature of the dramatic festivals, see Henderson 1991 and 1996: 4–14.

[12] Henderson 1990.

[13] For political bias in the choice of people ridiculed in comedy, see Sommerstein 1996b.

[14] For a fuller defense of this view, see Henderson 1998b: 12–22, and cf. Edmunds 1987: 32–33, 36–37.

[15] Cf. Thuc. 1.22.3, 1.124.3, 2.63.3, 3.37.2, 6.85.1; n. 8 above.

[16] Cf. Thuc. 1.69, 6.76–77, 82.

[17] Cf. Thuc. 1.98.4 (of Naxos); [Xen.] *Ath. Pol.* 1.18.

[18] A fifth-century development, based on Sparta's antityrannical policy in the previous century, that took shape in response to Athenian imperialism: see Bernhardt 1987, and below.

[19] Thuc. 2.63.2; cf. Smarczyk 1990: 2–16.

[20] See esp. Raaflaub 1984, and note Pl. *Resp.* 562, where the freedoms of the democratic citizen and the tyrant are aligned.

[21] See, e.g., Thuc. 5.18.7, 5.47.1–2; Ar. *Wasps* 700: *poleōn archōn;* Smarczyk 1990: 15, n. 45.

[22] Thuc. 2.63.2.

[23] See Tuplin 1985: 374.

²⁴ Thuc. 3.37.2, and Andrews 2000: 56–62 on the transgressive implications of Cleon's appeals.

²⁵ Thuc. 5.84–113.

²⁶ This volume, p. 118.

²⁷ Cf. Seager 1967: 7 and n. 14.

²⁸ Tyranny when applied to gods could of course have a positive connotation.

²⁹ The translations in this paper are my own; those of Aristophanes are from my Loeb edition (Harvard University, 1998–2002).

³⁰ For this justification as standard, see Thuc. 5.89.

³¹ As suggested by Fr. 71; for discussion, see Welsh 1983.

³² Storey (1990: 17–18) suggests that Eupolis' *Golden Age,* which also portrays Cleon as master of the allied cities (cf. Fr. 311, cf. *Knights* 75, 159), predates *Babylonians.*

³³ E.g., *Clouds* 607–626.

³⁴ See in general R. Parker 1996: 188–198.

³⁵ So Smarczyk 1990: 11 and n. 4.

³⁶ Cf. Plut. *Per.* 16, *PCG* on Telecl. Fr. 45; for a general survey, see Schwarze 1971. The similarities between Pericles (or Periclean Athens) and Sophocles' Oedipus, the only tragic protagonist characterized as a tyrant, have often been noted and thus may be another response to the same political conundrum.

³⁷ Pericles: *Ach.* 530–534, *Peace* 604–614; Thucydides: *Ach.* 703–712, with Ostwald 1986: 185–187.

³⁸ Connor 1971 remains the classic treatment.

³⁹ See now Samons 2000: 254–275.

⁴⁰ For ostracism versus the charge of conspiracy, cf. McGlew 1993: 187–190.

⁴¹ The claim of Tuplin 1985: 374 that the tyrant metaphor was rare in public speech (not extant for this period and so not included in his survey) does not jibe with the picture drawn in *Knights* and *Wasps.*

⁴² This volume, p. 137.

⁴³ Sommerstein 1983; Henderson 1998b. The reason given by MacDowell 1972 for rejecting the reading of the other MSS, the obvious *lectio difficilior,* is that "accusations of profanation of the Eleusinian Mysteries did not become fashionable until 415." But this is of course circular, because the *Wasps* passage can itself be such evidence.

⁴⁴ Lind 1990; Sommerstein 1997b and 2000.

⁴⁵ Cf. *Knights* 786–787. His wife was probably a sister-in-law of Harmodius of Aphidna; cf. Davies 1971: 145, 320, 476–477.

⁴⁶ For "tyrant" reserved for exceptional political opponents, see Tuplin 1985: 375.

[47] For tyrannical hostility toward homosexuals as an aspect of the legend of Harmodius and Aristogeiton, cf. Pausanias' speech in Pl. *Symp.* 182.

[48] Literalizing Pericles' striking metaphor in Thuc. 2.43.1; see McGlew 1993: 183, 188–190. To contest Cleon's dominance, the Sausage Seller must assume the role of Cleon's *anterastēs* (rival lover).

[49] For the conceptual dynamics of *oikos* (household) and *agora* (marketplace) in terms of the people's money, see Crane 1998.

[50] *Knights* 445–449 (Hippias), 1044 (Antileon); *Wasps* 1232–1233 (Pittacus).

[51] With Bergler's *kai* (*ei* MSS, "if").

[52] Aristophanes explicitly admits this failure in *Clouds* 581–594, composed between 423 and ca. 417.

[53] See Lehmann 1987: 41–43; *Nub.* 551–559, *PCG* on Eupolis *Maricas* and Plato Com. *Hyperbolus*.

[54] Lanza 1977: 84–94, who also points out (180) that the stage tyrant inevitably refuses the authority of Delphi or its representative; Sophocles' Oedipus (cf. n. 36 above) is paradigmatic (Lanza 145).

[55] See Connor 1984: 179–180.

[56] See Ostwald 1955, esp. 113–114; Gagarin 1981.

[57] McGlew 1996: 186.

[58] Phrynichus Fr. 27 = Schol. Ar. *Birds* 1297. For a recent discussion, see Atkinson 1992.

[59] The theory that Alcibiades was attacked in Eupolis' *Baptae* (?418/17) is based only on a late anecdotal tradition unverified by the fragments of the play; see Storey 1990: 20–22.

[60] *Wasps* 891–994.

[61] Henderson 1998a, 2000: 5–8.

[62] ". . . so now . . . in this place" marks the contrast between actual practice (in Athens) and the new provisions for Cloudcuckooland (in the play).

[63] *Birds* 636–637; cf. Gorgias, *Epit.* DK 82B6; Agathon Fr. 27 Snell.

[64] For the date, see Henderson 1987: xv–xxv and 2000: 254–256, 444–446.

[65] For hatred of tyranny also in contemporary tragedy, esp. Sophocles' *Philoctetes* and Euripides' *Phoenician Women,* see Ostwald 1986: 413–414.

[66] Note especially the women's chorus at 638–647 and the assimilation of the heroine to the Polias priestess, Lysimache (Henderson 1987: xxxvii–xl).

[67] 6.53.3, 6.59.4–60.1; cf. also Hdt. 5.55, 5.62–65, 6.123, emphasizing the role of the Alcmeonidae. It is possible, though not demonstrable, that the publication of Herodotus' history influenced public perceptions in this period.

[68] So Dover, *HCT* iv: 329.

[69] See n. 18 above.

[70] For this charge, see Hdt. 6.121–123, [Arist.] *Ath. Pol.* 16.8–9.

[71] See Sommerstein 1990; ad loc.

[72] See Sommerstein 1996a: 12–20.

[73] For discussion, see Sommerstein 1996a: 21–23.

[74] See Sommerstein 1993.

[75] For suggestions and criticism I am grateful to the conference participants, to Lowell Edmunds and Loren J. Samons, and to the 2000–2001 Fellows of the Center for Hellenic Studies in Washington, D.C.

KATHRYN A. MORGAN

THE TYRANNY OF THE AUDIENCE
IN PLATO AND ISOCRATES

As other essays in this volume show, the Athenians found the figure of the tyrant compelling. As a democracy, Athens celebrated its resistance to tyranny, although it was also fascinated by the more questionable aspects of autocratic power. My contribution examines how Plato and Isocrates, two writers in Athens' "dissident" literary tradition,[1] appropriated and transformed their cultural heritage of fascination with tyranny. The concept of tyranny and kingship resonates for Plato and Isocrates in a number of ways. They address themselves to multiple audiences that include kings and tyrants (both historical and psychic). They deprecate the "tyrannical" attitudes of their Athenian audience, the fruit of a rhetorical culture that privileges pleasure over rational calculation of appropriate ends. They seek to establish their own discursive authority over the reception of their texts, a legitimate rule established over the audience and accompanied by its reasoned consent. The problem of the tyrant is thus intimately connected to the problem of reception. Plato and Isocrates create an analogy between the "literary" author and his audience, and the politician and his, so that reception is a political act each author tries to control.

These concerns about problematic and "tyrannical" reception are explored by Plato and Isocrates in two ways, which I shall call "the move out" and "the move in." The move out (explicit in Isocrates and implicit in Plato) expands the horizon of reception beyond that of their individual polis (Athens) to multiple audiences in many constitutional situations.[2] This intellectual Panhellenism is facilitated by overt ethical interests. Isocrates' Panhellenism has often been the focus of scholarly attention but is seldom examined, as here, in terms of the problematics of power relationships between author and audience and their "tyrannical" potential. In the case of Plato, concentration on decontextualized argument has sometimes obscured the political implications of reception. The move in occurs when Plato (famously) and Isocrates conceive the soul as a polity. This means that individual behavior (including reception of literary/political texts) can be viewed in political terms.

Plato and Isocrates systematically confound the ethical and the political. Such confusion was not strange in the world of Athenian politics, where those active in civic life could regularly expect scrutiny of their characters.[3] This process is, however, taken to a new level by blurring political, constitutional, and ethical distinctions. We are not dealing merely with the old equations of the rule of the demos with the rule of the "base," or aristocracy with the rule of the "fine," but with the transference of political terminology to the world of the soul.[4] Taken together, these two moves, the psychic and the Panhellenic, result in a dehistoricizing approach to politics in which constitutional terminology loses historical specificity. Once they have established an overriding ethical agenda, Plato and Isocrates can advance their own conservative approach to the reception of discourse.

My discussion has three parts. In "The Move Out," I describe the conditions in the first part of the fourth century B.C. conducive to the development of constitutional relativism and a literary practice that spoke to multiple audiences.[5] I examine the blurring of constitutional boundaries in the rhetoric of Isocrates and Isocrates' attempts to ingratiate himself with his multiple audiences. Finally, I briefly consider the Panhellenic implications of Plato's authorial silence and his use of the dialogue form. "The Move In" traces the continuum between civic and psychic politics in Plato's *Gorgias* and *Republic* and in Isocrates' *To Nicocles*. The third section explores Plato's and Isocrates' attempt to reconfigure their audiences as a reaction to the corruption of political discourse. The underlying question in each section is, What is the tyrannical potential of the audience, and how can that tyranny be resisted?

THE MOVE OUT

What conditions encouraged Plato and Isocrates to adopt a Panhellenic perspective allowing for constitutional relativism? Athens was, of course, part of a larger community of Greek-speaking peoples, with differing types of political constitutions. Democracy, oligarchy, and monarchy existed in close proximity, which doubtless increased the (justified) anxiety of any given political community about being engulfed by another.[6] Athens had long prided itself on its opposition to tyranny and monarchy, and at the beginning of the fourth century, oligarchy had been discredited in the wake of the disastrous rule of the Thirty. The century was to see the resurgence of monarchic rule in

Sicily and elsewhere, as well as a more positive approach to the idea of monarchy.[7] Yet the excesses of the preceding century had shown that no form of government had a monopoly on civic and international virtue or vice. Simplistic equations of the many with the base, the few with the fine, or even of monarchy with tyranny were ineffective.

Nevertheless, the tradition of ethical implication gave political theorists a powerful tool, particularly when combined with an ability to think in terms of collective entities. Thus the concept of the people, the demos, had been anthropomorphized during the late fifth century.[8] As other essays in this volume show, this anthropomorphism allowed the demos to be associated with a tyrant both positively and negatively. So, too, the oligarchic junta of the Thirty was soon seen as a collective tyrannical entity, the "Thirty Tyrants," despite the contradiction of a plurality of ruling tyrants.[9] Mere numerical plurality, therefore, could no longer be decisive in evaluating forms of government, and the ethical could come to the fore.

Whether the object of analysis is a city, a soul, or a ruling system, it can be described as both a unity and a plurality. This makes it easier to describe one thing in terms of another: the demos as a tyrant, for example. The combination of these developments allows Plato and Isocrates to view constitutions and citizen groups as locally and chronologically complex and variable entities and to aim their philosophical rhetoric at the widest audience. They can direct their messages at cities beyond Athens because they intend ethics to win out over constitutional specificity. This is itself a political and antidemocratic move.

In the case of monarchy, the range of ethical resonance was particularly large. Terms such as king (*basileus*), tyrant, and dynast are not only technical descriptions. The contrast between good and bad kings was a commonplace as far back as Hesiod, but the strong distinction between ancestral rule by legitimate kings and the usurpation of power by an illegitimate "tyrant" seems to be a product of political circumstances in Athens.[10] Pindar, by contrast, calls Hieron of Syracuse a king, yet he can also by gnomic implication call him a tyrant (*Pyth.* 3.85).

We should assess Isocrates' monarchic vocabulary against this background. Isocrates follows both Athenian and Pindaric practice.[11] On the one hand, he uses the word *tyrannos* and its cognates as if their resonance were ethically neutral, as in the case of Evagoras in Cyprus (a rule he also calls a *basileia*). Ethical/terminological distinctions are more carefully watched in Plato, who establishes criteria for the moral and immoral use of political power and thus between king and tyrant.[12] On the other hand, Isocrates can equate tyranny with evil kingship. Thus, at the end of his *Philip,* Isocrates can exhort Philip to rule the Macedonians in a "kingly" rather than a "tyrannical" fashion (154: *basilikōs* versus *tyrannikōs*). In *On the Peace* Isocrates insists that the Athenians should detest tyrannical rule over their allies and emulate instead the situation of the Lacedaimonian kings (142).

The laxity in Isocrates' terminology has been recognized previously, but its ramifications have not, perhaps, received enough attention. In an Athenian context, giving tyranny ethical neutrality is unusual. The explanation lies in Isocrates' intention to write for multiple audiences. I mean by this not only that different orations have different purported addressees but that there are multiple addressees for any given oration. One might argue that in a monarchical context, tyranny/kingship can be approved, whereas in a democratic one, the orator will adopt democratic, antityrannical sentiment. This option is unattractive, however, since Isocrates expects both potential audiences to be aware of what he has written to the other. He is an advocate of situational ethics, but he also attempts to convince his audiences that he offers consistent advice.[13] If the language of Isocratean tyranny is neutral, it is aggressively neutral and designed to make a political point.[14]

How does Isocrates construct his relationship with multiple audiences? One noticeable characteristic is his concentration on his own status as writer and advisor. Lack of self-confidence and a weak voice, he says, made him avoid a political career. He makes up for this by casting a wider net: his discourses are Hellenic, political, suitable for festivals (*Antid.* 46). A favorite topic was the necessity of a unified Greece making war upon Persia. At first he casts Athens as leader of this crusade, but later he turns to Philip of Macedon. Not all his orations are Panhellenic, however. He was also a composer of eulogy and advice to kings such as Philip and Nicocles of Cyprus. None of this is problematic. Matters become complicated when we realize that even orations to Philip and Nicocles seem intended not just for their addressees but for a wider audience.[15] So, for example, chapters 17–22 of the *Philip* (where Isocrates' story of his promise that he would publish the "letter" to no one else in the city but his associates, so that they could vet it) imply that normally such a "speech" would have been shown to others in the city, as well as to its formal addressee.

Isocrates' oration *To Nicocles* is even more instructive. In itself, the oration is a collection of commonplaces on good kingship. More interesting is how Isocrates talks about it at the beginning of the *Antidosis.* His remarks show, first, that he expected the piece to be known in Athens and, second, that he felt the need to defend the oration to a democratic audience.

> I have decided to show [this discourse] to you now for the same reason, not because it is the best written of my works but so that, as a result of it, I shall make it clear in what way I am accustomed to associate with both private citizens and dynasts. It will be clear that I spoke to him freely and worthily of the city, not paying court (*therapeuōn*) to his wealth or power but coming to the aid of his subjects and, as much as I was able, making their form of government be as gentle as possible. And if I talked on behalf of the demos to a king, I certainly suppose that I would urgently exhort those active under a democratic constitution (*tois en dēmokratiai politeuomenois*) to pay court to (*therapeuein*) the demos (*Antid.* 69–70).

The apologetic intent is clear. Isocrates is defending himself from an imagined charge that like Socrates, he corrupts the youth of Athens.[16] His students, say his accusers, are not just private citizens but "orators, generals, kings, and tyrants." Moreover, nobody is his equal for writing speeches that give pain to the people of Athens (35). Isocrates must show that the range of his audience is not in itself an affront to the demos. He claims, predictably, that no citizen has been harmed by his writing. This is, however, an insufficient defense in the face of widespread suspicion that he was training people to disempower the demos. His injury consists in a conservative agenda expressed in speeches critical of Athenian foreign policy and in supportive speeches to monarchs. *To Nicocles* is evidently felt to exemplify the kind of injurious speech with which his accusers tax him. In the passage cited, Isocrates sets up parallel situations to defend himself. He shows how he associates with both "private citizens and dynasts" and thus implies a consistent oratorical practice in both instances. He does not pay court to the tyrant but helps his subjects. Equally, then, he would pay attention to the demos in a democracy.

This defense presumes multiple audiences and turns the tables on the demos. When Isocrates introduces the quotations from his writings, he expects that they will be known to at least some of the audience. He also says that the speech to Nicocles, far from being the injurious rhetoric it has been presumed to be, makes known his egalitarian principles. *To Nicocles,* then, as well as other orations, was known in Athens. Thus a speech for a monarch was published simultaneously for an Athenian audience, and Isocrates affects dismay that the latter could have found it threatening. His self-justification turns on a double use of the verb *therapeuein,* which means "to flatter, pay court to" as well as "to take care of, heal" (used of medical activity).[17] Isocrates did not flatter Nicocles but spoke to him freely and worthily of Athens. He can even pretend that he came (democratically) to the aid of Nicocles' subjects. Far from paying court to the tyrant, he implies, he pays court to the demos. The same verb is used of what he did not do with Nicocles, and what he advises people to do with the demos. He rejects the unpleasant activity of flattery when he deals with his own relationship to the king but implies that one must engage in precisely this activity with the demos. The king-advisor relationship is marked by freedom, whereas the orator-demos relationship is marked by flattery (unless one interprets *therapeia* of the demos as the attempt to heal it by the excellence of Isocratean oratory). Two political systems move towards each other as the traditional virtue and vice of democracy and tyranny are inverted.

The three passages from his own orations that Isocrates cites in the *Antidosis* form an interesting progression. He starts with the *Panegyricus,* praising Athens and exhorting it to take up *hēgemonia* ("hegemony," or "command"). He then cites *On the Peace,* which condemns an Athenian naval empire he calls a monarchy (64). Finally, the quote from *To Nicocles* establishes his bona fides as a democrat on good terms with monarchs. All three speeches are presented as a defense of his oratory in an imagined democratic court, yet all three address monarchical or quasi-monarchical leadership. We start with Athens as *hēgemōn,* move on to Athens as monarch, and end with a real monarch who can be treated with democratic freedom. An underlying message is that there are no constitutional absolutes. We have merely the wise orator trying to make his way and the implication that it is not necessarily a democracy in which one has the most freedom of speech.

Isocrates' defense in the *Antidosis* works by problematizing the democratic audience and redescribing it in almost tyrannical terms. His treatment of this audience is indirect, but twice he reports second-order conversations that make his presuppositions explicit. The first instance concerns Timotheus. Timotheus, says Isocrates, was not a "hater of the people" (*misodēmos*) but was unpopular because he was no good at *therapeia,* paying court to them (131). Isocrates urges Timotheus to practice this *therapeia,* since the multitude is susceptible to flattery and prefers smiling cheats to honest servants. Timotheus, however, was not the kind of man who could fit himself to those who hate their natural superiors (138) and thus came to a bad end. The context makes it clear that Timotheus is an analogue for Isocrates himself, who in his actual antidosis trial was confounded, he says, by the same jealousy of inferior toward superior.

Similarly, Isocrates reports that an associate tried to dissuade him from reciting his benefactions, since he would give pain to the majority of his listeners (141). Envy and deprivation, we are told, make the many hate the noble and side with criminals. Envy on the part of those less fortunate is exactly one of the dangers that threatens the tyrant. From this point of view, the superiority of Timotheus and Isocrates might seem to place them in the tyrant's role, particularly since they can be cast as "haters of the people." Yet their portrayal as servants and advisors thwarts this move. In fact, the person who prefers flattering cheats to self-respecting servants is the tyrant, who characteristically cannot endure those who do not lie and pay court to him.[18] These discussions of appropriate rhetorical strategy in a democracy illustrate how, like a tyrant, democracies prefer flattery to honesty and are unable to tolerate natural superiors. Isocrates attempts to manipulate an Athenian audience into allowing the claims of superior politicians (and thus potential tyrants and "demos haters") in order not to be thought of as a tyrant itself. He cleverly turns democratic ideology against itself.[19] This renders the oration congenial to those at odds with the democratic system.[20] The orator speaks to multiple audiences simultaneously and creates a situation where not to agree with him is to behave like a tyrant.

The famous passage on Isocrates' *logoi amphiboloi* (ambiguous discourse) in the *Panathenaicus* (234–261) reinforces the need to be aware of potential multiple audiences. Isocrates' Spartan ex-student is said to accuse him of writing discourses that can be interpreted in many ways, such that the same speech may, depending on the audience, be conceived to be a praise of Sparta or a praise of Athens.[21] Thus Isocrates is said to include "discourses of double meaning, which belong no more to those who praise than to those who blame," and this procedure is called "noble and philosophical" (240). In fact, he asserts, Isocrates' attempt to gratify (*charisēi*) the mass (*plēthos*) of Athenian citizens is really a form of political moderation (*sōphronōn*) (237)—an interesting inversion of Isocrates' purported rhetorical ethics. The pupil concludes that Isocrates praised Athens "in accordance with the opinion of the many" but Sparta "according to the calculation of those who try to aim at truth" (261). Isocrates neither endorses nor rejects this view, but by including it as another second-order conversation, he stresses its possibility (*Panath.* 265, cf. 247).

It is significant that the Isocratean rhetoric discussed here concerns evaluation of opposed constitutional forms. Isocrates creates rhetoric that installs itself in the political mindset of its immediate audience, as his student realizes. The student also distinguishes between the large audiences at national festivals where speakers malign Isocrates' works and the smaller cultivated audiences who appreciate them, although even those who criticize Isocrates are represented as secret admirers (263). We see that types of reception can be feigned (for political purposes?) and that Isocrates creates a world in which his orations are a central concern to others both in public and in private. A fruitful tension thus underlies Isocrates' choice to produce faux public discourses aimed for circulation among an intellectual elite. Because Isocrates' discourses are not really for public performance, he can generate comment and discussion;[22] Panhellenic aspirations favor ambiguity and *amphibolia*.[23] It is clear enough that Isocrates' agenda is generally conservative and aristocratic: the naturally superior should command the inferior. This basic agenda, however, emerges primarily as an ethical statement, which then guides his reaction to specific situations.[24]

By assigning free speech to monarchy and flattery to democracy, Isocrates creates a political no-man's land where he is free to speak to democrats, oligarchs, and monarchists. The previous passages I have examined have focused on Isocrates' self-justification in the face of an Athenian audience to whom he has transferred the vices of monarchy. Such blurring of political boundaries is not, however, confined to his portrayal of the Athenian demos. It also characterizes his portrayal of a monarch, further flattening out historical specificity. In his encomium of the Cypriot monarch Evagoras, Isocrates tells his audience that Evagoras

> subjected his friends to himself through his good deeds and enslaved the rest by his great-heartedness. He inspired fear not through being angry at many but by far surpassing the nature of others. He led his pleasures and was not led by them. By small toil he acquired great leisure but did not leave incomplete great works because of a little laziness. All in all, he omitted none of the qualities appropriate to kings but chose the best part from each form of constitution: he was like a friend of the people (*dēmotikos*) in his service (*therapeia*) to the multitude, a statesman (*politikos*) in his management of the city as a whole, a general (*stratēgikos*) through his good counsel in the face of danger, and a tyrant (*tyrannikos*) in his preeminence in all these respects (*Evag.* 45–46).

We note first the cultivated paradox of "enslavement" and "subjection" through benefaction. Whereas a tyrant rules through terror, Evagoras rules through magnanimity. Second, we observe that in Isocrates' rhetorical world, Evagoras mixes constitutional forms: he is democrat (*dēmotikos*), statesman, general, and tyrant, and what makes him "tyrannical" is that he surpasses everybody in good qualities.[25] Kingship expresses itself as ethical preeminence rather than as a defined constitutional form. The adjectives describing Evagoras create a metaphorical climate: it was not a democracy, but Evagoras was like a man of the people, or a general, or a tyrant. Thus we are encouraged to believe in the relativity of constitutions: that a form of government is called a monarchy does not mean it is despotic or unfriendly to the people. Conversely, a democracy does not necessarily serve the best interests of the demos.

Ideological slippage happens not just synchronically but diachronically, since constitutions vary through time as well as by locality. Isocrates often affects to praise Athenian democracy, with the caveat that he means not the current depraved democracy but rather the "constitution of the ancestors."[26] Thus even the term "democracy" can be emptied of the connotations that most fourth-century Athenians would have applied to it and reduced to a version of "aristocracy," as we see in the *Areopagiticus*. Recalling government by the Areopagus Council in the good old days, Isocrates remarks that election is more "democratic" than assigning offices by allotment, since it is easier for oligarchs to be allotted to office than elected (23). The allotment of most Athenian state offices was a hallmark of the developed democracy, while election was generally seen as allowing the accumulation of improper influence. Isocrates defines as democratic the practice that many Athenians would have seen as a relic of a political past oriented towards the interests of the elite. Similarly, Isocrates' plan for a reformed Athenian democracy in the *Areopagiticus* envisions an aristocratic democracy where the demos will have powers "like a tyrant," and the elite will be "like servants" (26).[27]

A similar strategy animates the *Panathenaicus*. At 119–133 Isocrates constructs the framework that allows his political elisions. There was a time when all government was monarchy, but even then, monarchy in Athens ruled for the good of the people, whereas monarchies elsewhere were characterized by tyrannical perversions (121–122). The truth is that aristocracy is not a separate kind of constitution but an option contained within democracy, oligarchy, and monarchy (131–132). Thus we can have good and bad versions of each constitution, but all good versions share aristocratic characteristics. Once again the ethical approach to politics elides constitutional differences. A little later Isocrates speaks of the ancestral constitution as an aristocracy mixed with democracy, where office was awarded by election (153). This was real democracy, he declares, and so excellent that the (oligarchic/royalist) Spartans emulated it when forming their own constitution. The audacity of this claim is breathtaking, and doubtless any Spartan would have found the claim laughable. Nor would any Athenian democrat have recognized the Spartan system as democratic. Isocrates labels as democracy his own constitutional preferences, but more as a propagandistic rhetorical coup than as a historical claim.

In sum, we can conclude that a king can be like a democrat, and the demos like a king (whether as the recipient of royal pleasures or as the wielder of tyrannical power). Spartan oligarchy is a derivative form of Athenian democracy, whereas the proto-oligarchical rule of the Areopagites is the truest form of democracy. Aristocracy is an ethical option in all constitutions. The implication is that we must go beyond the definitional and cut to the heart of the matter: is power exercised by the good or the bad? Simple polar ideology replaces a more historicized approach.

This blurring of constitutional boundaries and redefinition of constitutional forms are part of a larger conservative project. By the middle of the fourth century it was a commonplace of the "dissident" Athenian intellectual tradition that democracy corrupts the meaning of words.[28] Thucydides' account of the perversion of language during the *stasis* in Corcyra was taken up both by Plato in the *Republic* (560c–e) and by Isocrates (*Areopag.* 20). By implication, his democratic audience should not trust its own rhetoric (although Isocrates himself establishes his position by cavalier redefinition of political terms). Isocrates sets himself above the verbal niceties of the constitutional fray, speaking freely to all.

Isocrates' rhetorical strategies are determined by his intellectual choices. He is committed to the position that one cannot obtain precise knowledge (*epistēmē*). The best one can do is use conjecture (*doxa; Antid.* 270–271), and try to arrive at the best course. If the best is situational, there will be no absolute standard of constitution against which one can measure excellence. If one is committed to what is best, but wants audiences in Cyprus, Athens, and Macedonia, one must encourage each audience to find at least the potential for the best in itself. Isocrates must mediate between the two possible activities associated with *therapeia:* he must heal the wounds of the body politic and keep his own integrity as wise advisor, while also paying court to his addressees. This is a delicate dance, in which Isocrates must simultaneously flatter and stand up to a potentially tyrannical audience.

The lack of an explicit voice for the implied author of the Platonic dialogue means that we have only indirect evidence for Plato's intended reception and the audience he envisioned. Letters to dynasts are preserved in the Platonic corpus, but their authenticity is doubtful. Nevertheless, if we are to believe the biographical tradition at all, Plato was involved in an attempt to establish a philosopher king in Syracuse, in the person of Dionysius II.[29] These attempts leave no definitive trace in his corpus. Yet although there is a gap between historical specifics and literary content, the figure of the tyrant or monarch was important for Plato. This importance is amply attested by large portions of the *Republic,* the *Statesman,* and the *Laws,* and we can make fairly reliable inferences about his attitudes to tyrants and other audiences from his metaphysics and ethics, as well as from the way he presents philosophical discussion. In all these areas, Plato contrasts the Isocratean approach. Whereas Isocrates constantly meditates on his relationship with his audience, Plato is silent and refuses to engage in formal oration. Isocrates struggles to control reception; Plato seems not to try. These contrasting approaches reflect the differing metaphysical commitments of the two authors. Isocrates relies on *doxa* and on situational ethics and attempts obtrusive direction of his audiences to ensure that each audience receives him properly. Plato believes in accurate knowledge and an absolute truth that depends neither on the situation of the reader nor on his mediating authorial lens. Any overt courting of his audience would be immoral, since the truth must be sought for its own sake. Ideally, an argument should ensure its own reception.[30]

Plato's absence from his text and indeed, his practice of writing dialogues, carry political implications. When Socrates says, "I know how to provide one witness to the things I say: the man with whom I am having my discussion, but I say farewell to the many" (*Grg.* 474a5–7), he rejects a mass audience and hence speech to the demos qua demos.[31] The same is true of the Platonic dialogue; it speaks to anyone who is interested but not to the demos as a whole. The emphasis is on personal, rather than mass, reception. The dialogue form, whether narrated or dramatic, creates an intimate relationship with the reader.

Consider the informality of the famous opening of the *Republic:* "I went down to the Piraeus yesterday with Glaucon, the son of Ariston." Socrates is talking to someone, to us, and yet the "us" is unspecified. This abrupt beginning tells us immediately that we are not in the world of formal oration and therefore not in the world of large audiences. We are required to make an effort of imaginative identification with Socrates' unspecified conversational partner(s). We think through the argumentation as if we were there, but with enough distance to ensure critical evaluation. Since, moreover, Plato uses Socrates (or philosophical strangers) as chief speakers, he refuses to let his own personality influence the audience.

Like Isocrates, Plato aims at Panhellenic reception.[32] Since Plato does not embed his dialogues in any formal structure, the reader in any city can provide his own rhetorical context. The opening of the *Symposium,* for example, is a series of nested narratives that make us intensely aware that we are dealing with a discourse that circulates widely.[33] The situation at the beginning of the *Theaetetus,* set in Megara, is similar. The cosmopolitan atmosphere of the Platonic dialogue aims, then, at a Panhellenic audience. As with Isocrates, this may include private citizens, orators, generals, kings and tyrants, and students. We should not, like Ryle, suggest that Plato wrote specifically for contemporary tyrants.[34] Nevertheless, like Isocrates, Plato must face the possibility of addressing a tyrannical reader, whether in the person of an actual monarch or the Athenian demos.

The measures I have mentioned above help create the proper climate for correct reception. Even more important is the system of performance and reception ethics elaborated in the *Republic* and the *Gorgias.* In both, Plato focuses on the individual soul as audience and, as we shall see, stresses the need to control the soul's desires: the discerning reader must refrain from acting the tyrant by privileging her own political and literary desires. The universalizing implications of this ethic are particularly clear in the *Republic,* where the audience is encouraged to reject a corrupt democracy for an idealized city that will transcend Athens or any other earthly city. The description of the utopia of the *Republic* as a paradigm set up in the heavens, of which anyone who wishes may be a citizen (592b), underlines a movement outwards from narrow parochial interests.[35] This decontextualizing and dehistoricizing slant in Platonic treatments of civic and psychic tyranny will be examined in the next section.

I end this section with a response to a possible objection to the picture of "the move out" I have presented here. It might be suggested that the creation of multiple audiences by Plato and Isocrates is a trivial byproduct of the fact that the dialogues and orations were aimed at readers. This position does not, however, explain why Plato and Isocrates thematize the problem of reception, both explicitly and implicitly. The circulation of the work of Plato and Isocrates as a written text is indeed an important aspect in our understanding of the Panhellenic reception of both authors. The community of readers is a political community and is instructed in the proper attitude to bring to the text. Both Plato (*Phd.* 107b4–9; *Grg.* 513c7–d1) and Isocrates (*Panath.* 136; *Philip* 29) envisage a situation where lines of argument are examined repeatedly.[36] Circulating a written text provides an opportunity for such examination and creates a politics of reception: careful reading and consideration over an extended period of time, free from emotional outbursts, rhetorical manipulation, and the pressures brought to bear by political context.[37]

Aiming one's work at a reading audience and simultaneously capitalizing on and thematizing the associated possibilities of reception is no trivial achievement. The Platonic dialogue and the Isocratean oration are simulacra of dialogue and oration, evoking immediacy but distancing reaction. This tension between immediacy and distance encourages the audience to think through problems of reception, but it also insulates the writer from immediate response and thus provides a forum for free speech. Both Plato's personal silence and Isocrates' *amphibolia* challenge the reader to work through multiple levels of authorial intention and foreground the hard work of interpretation. The variable world of reception offered by Panhellenic audiences enables and demands this interpretative project.

THE MOVE IN

In this section, I examine the converse of Plato and Isocrates' Panhellenic move: their construction of a continuum between civic and psychic politics. My discussion of psychic politics in Plato will focus on the *Gorgias* and *Republic.* In both the figure of the tyrant looms large, and in both, Plato constructs a continuum between city and psychic politics. The *Gorgias* presents an analogy between the political orator and the tyrant and meditates upon a complex of interrelated themes that are important for my consideration of a politicized audience: the role of pleasure in attaining and enjoying power, the use of rhetorical expertise as a means to power, and the relationship of power and pleasure to tyranny. It focuses on the operation of power and pleasure in the individual soul as a crucial aspect of the operation of power and pleasure in the larger body politic.

Socrates contests grand claims for the power of rhetoric, suggesting it is merely a species of flattery, a "knack" that aims at *charis* (gratification) and *hēdonē* (pleasure) (462c–463a). He makes the key claim that the political art is concerned with the soul, a notion fundamental to the development of the analogy between city and soul. When Socrates' opponent Polus exalts rhetoric, he asks, "Don't orators, like tyrants, kill whomever they like and take away their possessions, and don't they throw out of the city whomever they decide to?" (466b–c). Socrates counters that orators and tyrants are in fact powerless, since they act in ignorance. Both Socrates and Polus, then, agree that the orator is like a tyrant, but they disagree about whether this is a good thing. The basis of the analogy between tyrant and orator is power, since in fourth-century Athenian democracy, rhetorical power bestows political influence.[38] Indeed, in the *Republic* the demagogue can develop into a tyrant. Yet even as the power of the rhetorician is assimilated to that of the tyrant, the significance of that power is diminished. Socrates says that he could threaten someone with a knife and claim this to be a tyranny (*tyrannis*) and power (*dynamis*), because he could kill whomever he liked (469c–e), yet this power is meaningless. Socrates defuses its force by using an illustration that strips tyranny of its specificity through exaggeration. Power is given significance only by ethical application.

For Socrates, then, tyrannical power conceived as the power to do evil is not really power at all. His next move is even more significant. Gorgias' hangers-on in the dialogue assimilate the power of the orator to that of the tyrant. This seems a logical move: the power of the individual speaker is mapped onto the power of the individual monarch. Gorgias' followers are, moreover, following good Gorgianic precedent. In his *Encomium of Helen,* Gorgias stated that speech (*logos*) is a mighty dynast (*dynastēs,* 8).[39] In this vision, the orator controls what the crowd wants to hear, and this control might be conceived as threatening to subvert the democracy.[40] Socrates, however, thinks this a crude oversimplification. He argues that the orator can succeed only by saying what the audience wants to hear. He must flatter his audience, speak with a view to their gratification (502d–e). It is the audience, therefore, that is the *tyrannos,* the one with the power.[41]

The dialogue moves from the identification of the tyrant with an individual, the orator, to identifying him with a corporate body, the audience, whose subordinate the orator is.[42] This happens because there is a complicity between political actors and those who are acted upon in badly ordered states. Whether one is living in a democracy or a tyranny, one must imitate the type of government under which one lives (512e). Thus, to protect oneself, one must rule (*archein*), be a tyrant (*tyrannein*), or be on friendly terms with the system of government (a *hetairos* of the *politeia*) (510a). In a tyranny, the only safe person is one who shares the likes and dislikes of the tyrant. Similarly, for Callicles to be successful in Athens, he must imitate the demos as closely as possible (513a–c). At this point, tyranny is less a historically specific monarchy than a pact of mutual imitation entered into by the base elements in the soul and in society.

Thus far we are dealing with the same system of metaphor as in Isocrates: the Athenian demos is assimilated to the tyrant whom the orator must court.[43] This picture is nuanced, however, by a more complex approach to the rule of the tyrant and the nature of his power. Callicles thinks that the naturally superior individual should rule in the city. Socrates' first countermove is to argue that since the many are more powerful in Athens and frame their laws to restrain the extraordinary individual, they are the naturally superior. Note that for Socrates' argument to have force, the many must be conceived as a collective; what Callicles meant to apply to the individual is transferred to the group. Callicles will have none of this:

> CALLICLES: But *I* said that those who are thoughtful about the affairs of the city and who are courageous [are the better and the more powerful]. It is fitting that these rule the city, and this is justice, that these have more than the rest—I mean the rulers (*archontas*) than the ruled (*archomenous*).
> SOCRATES: Well, my friend, what about themselves? Are they the rulers (*archontas*) or the ruled (*archomenous*)?
> CALLICLES: What do you mean?
> SOCRATES: I mean that each individual rules himself. Or is this not necessary, that someone rule himself but only others?
> CALLICLES: What do you mean "rule himself"?
> SOCRATES: Nothing subtle—just what the many say. I mean being temperate and in command of oneself, ruling the pleasures and desires that are in one (491c6–e1).

Here the concept of rule is extended from the realm of the city to the individual soul. The ruler rules not only the city but himself.[44] By implication, only the person who rules himself properly could possibly be qualified to rule others. Callicles thinks that the best life is the one in which one gratifies one's appetites to the greatest possible extent. Conventional wisdom deprecates these excesses, but those who have attained a tyranny acknowledge no master and know that intemperance brings happiness (491e5–492c8). This approach equates happiness with lack of mastery, whereas Socrates advances the claims of a popular notion of self-control. Lack of control and the unrestrained pursuit of pleasure assimilate one not to the tyrant but to the pathic homosexual who experiences a compulsive need to scratch a sexual itch (494e).

Socrates' strategy is double-edged. He appeals to a popular notion of self-control, but the implications of this move are conservative. It had long been clear that the success of a polis depended on self-restraint (*sōphrosynē*); this virtue was linked with freedom (*eleutheria*) in an Attic *scolion* of the first half of the fifth century.[45] Closer to Plato's time, *sōphrosynē* had tended to be associated with oligarchy, but Antiphon had connected it with the ability to rule (*kratein*) and conquer (*nikan*) oneself.[46] In the context of a discussion of tyranny, and especially when the analogy between tyranny and democracy is close to the surface, the idea of self-rule takes on political resonance. The depravity of power exercised without restraint by a tyrant is acknowledged by democratic ideology, but if the tyrant is metaphorical, say, the demos, the idea becomes an indictment. "The many" say that ruling oneself is a good thing. Socrates wishes to unpack this notion and concludes that one should govern one's passions with a view to overall goodness (507a–e). Yet this must be so for the city as for the individual,[47] as Socrates makes clear when he remarks that discipline must be applied when needed, whether the recipient is a private individual or a city (*idiōtēs ē polis*, 507d4–5). One should pursue self-control when conducting one's own affairs (*ta hautou*) and those of the city (*ta tēs poleōs*) (507d7–8). The point of the analogy between soul and city is to use a popular idea about self-control to argue against a democratic political process wherein orators are free to pander to democratic desires. In Socrates' opinion, even renowned politicians such as Pericles are guilty of this crime (503a–d).

The *Gorgias* is a dialogue much concerned with the proper reception of philosophic argument. At one point, Callicles accuses Socrates of being a popular orator (*dēmēgoros*, 494d1), and each accuses the other of deceitful argumentative moves (489b, 499b–c). Each is eager to accuse the other of capitalizing on "childishness,"[48] and this childishness extends beyond the philosophical into the political arena. In particular, Socrates declares that orators treat the people (*dēmois*) like children because they flatter and gratify their audiences, telling them what they think they want to hear (502e2–503a1). This can be the case even in philosophic discussion (487a–488a); one of the reasons that the debate between Callicles and Socrates ends unsatisfactorily is that Callicles agrees with Socrates "so that I may gratify Gorgias" (501c7–8). The dialogue thus creates a parallel between the political and philosophical audience, but precisely this parallelism prevents any useful conclusion. Callicles' rhetorical priorities infect the argumentative structure. To progress, one must rethink rhetorical politics and abandon the pursuit of victory and pleasure. One must not answer with a view to gratification (as though one were addressing a tyrant), nor must one ride roughshod over one's audience for one's own gratification (like a tyrant) without awakening their better judgment.

Like the *Gorgias,* the *Republic* uses power relationships in the individual soul as a model for such relationships in the body politic. The continuum between civic and psychic politics is fundamental, since the dialogue uses the analogy between city and soul to isolate the meaning of justice (435). It would be otiose to recapitulate the function of the city/soul analogy throughout the dialogue. I shall focus here on the discussion of *sōphrosynē* at 430, since it parallels *Gorgias* 491c6–e1, discussed above. Both civic and psychic concord are attained by the virtue of *sōphrosynē,* as Socrates says to Glaucon:

"I suppose," I said, "that temperance is a certain order, and mastery of certain pleasure and desires, *as they say, being stronger than oneself,* (*hōs phasi kreittō de hautou*) rendering it I don't know how. And people say other such things, which are like traces of it."
"Absolutely," he said.
"So then, isn't the phrase 'stronger than oneself' laughable? For someone who is stronger than himself would also be weaker than himself, I suppose, and the weaker would be stronger, since the same person is spoken of in all of these locutions."
"Of course."
"But," I said, "this phrase seems to me to mean that in man himself one part of his soul is better and one part worse, and whenever the better part masters the worse part, this is being 'stronger than oneself'—it's a term of praise, of course—but whenever the better part, which is smaller, *is mastered by the mass of the worse* (*kratēthē hypo plēthous tou cheironos*) because of evil upbringing or some association, this is a matter of reproach, and people call someone who is so disposed undisciplined and un-self controlled, and blame him."
"So it seems," he said.
"Look now," I said, "at our new city, and you will find one of these two options in it. You will say that one can justly call it master of itself, if indeed we must call temperate and stronger than itself something whose better part rules the worse" (430e6–431b7).

As in the *Gorgias,* Socrates has taken a popular locution about self-mastery (*hōs phasi, "as they say"*) and turned it inside out. Moreover, the saying is an archetype of other similar sayings, which are "traces" of it. The problem, however, is that people do not realize its implications. The phrase seems laughable to Socrates and makes sense only on the assumption that the soul has parts. Socrates' puzzlement and solution bring to our attention the problem that has run through this essay of the collective and the individual. We have been investigating how a group, the demos, may be a collective individual, but here we come at the problem from the other end: how can we understand the individual as a collective? Socrates' discussion of the functioning of the soul is explicitly political. Lack of self-control occurs when the smaller and better part of the soul "is mastered by the mass of the worse." The word used to describe this psychic mass, *plēthos*, also denotes the mass of citizens in Athenian democracy. The move from the psychic to the civic realm is thus made even before the focus on the ideal city at the end of the passage quoted. The self-controlled realm is the one in which the many and licentious are ruled by the few and best (431c–d). Socrates' reading turns a popular saying into an indictment of Athenian democracy. His analysis mocks the intellectual and verbal capacity of the many and makes the argument that at one level, the people do indeed endorse aristocracy: since they endorse the rule of the best part in the self, they should endorse it also at the civic level.

The notion of self-control as self-rule we met in the *Gorgias* has been rendered intelligible by positing parts of the soul. The intelligibility of the exposition, however, depends on the application of a political model where the political and the ethical interpenetrate each other. The best city, like the best soul, is ruled by its best elements. This rule is kingship, or perhaps aristocracy. In the case of the city (445d3–6), the line between kingship and aristocracy is blurred, since it is assumed that the best all desire the same things. At this point, however, the metaphor of king/tyrant has been so widely applied that it loses specificity. Virtuous kingship is not really distinguished from aristocracy; tyranny reminds us of democracy (and the reverse); self-rule is the same as civic rule. How can one support the rule of the many when one does not know how many are included in the term and whether it applies to one's neighbors or one's appetites? Moreover, as in the *Gorgias*, democratic freedom is argued out of existence, since it produces its opposite (563–564). Democracy is characterized by the possibility of doing whatever one wants (*exousia . . . poiein hoti tis bouletai,* 557b). Such a constitution "praises and honors rulers who are like the ruled and the ruled who are like rulers, both in public and in private" (562d7–9). Historical, political, and social distinctions are discarded, and this anarchy produces the tyrant and the tyrannical city, where (for the tyrant) there is the illusion of freedom and the uncontrolled satisfaction of desire. Democratic anarchy leads to the production of a demagogue and proto-tyrant.

Plato does not, however, simply conflate democracy and tyranny. His discussion of the decline of constitutions shows that he is aware of how tyranny functions as the democratic "other." Any excess, he says, gives rise to a change towards the opposite (563e), and therefore excessive freedom gives rise to uttermost slavery, both for the individual and for the city (564a). Tyranny arises from democracy and no other constitution (a historical perversity that is often remarked).[49] Democracy exists in complicity with tyranny, and both constitutions bestow illusory mastery. Both make the rulers the slaves of their pleasures and dispose them to associate with flatterers.

The extremity of Plato's language is striking: tyranny arises from democracy and no other constitution. Yet the account of constitutional decline in books 8 and 9 strikes modern readers as antihistorical. For the sake of presenting a smooth political process, Plato ignores the historical evidence that, for example, made it clear that the Peisistratid tyranny resulted in (not from) Athenian democracy. What is one to make of this? One approach is that of Julia Annas, who stresses the unreality of Plato's account of tyranny to de-emphasize its political implications. She argues that the tyrant as depicted in the *Republic* is unreal and that Plato does not examine what makes a successful dictator. The material concerning tyranny is merely tacked on for the sake of argumentative completeness.[50] More recently, she has maintained that it is anachronistic to read the dialogue as Plato's answer to the problem of Athenian democracy, since there is no evidence for situating the *Republic* in the context of Plato's supposed attitude to politics. Nor do Athenian politics of the fifth and fourth centuries shed any light on the *Republic*. Plato's oligarchy and democracy bear no resemblance to actual historical entities. Since his political suggestions are absurd, it should be clear that the discussion of the state is present only to illuminate the discussion of the soul. Socrates himself remarks that it is unimportant whether the ideal state actually exists or not.[51]

It is beyond the scope of this essay fully to engage with this challenging reading. Annas and I draw opposite conclusions from Plato's ahistoricity. For Annas, Plato's cavalier treatment of historical constitutions makes the *Republic* apolitical. For me, it implies a programmatic reinterpretation that empties constitutions of their history. Annas' stress on the importance of ethics reflects a crucial aspect of the dialogue but does not take into account the degree to which ethics and politics interpenetrate. As my discussion suggests, political language reaches deep into the ethical realm and cannot be conceptually stripped off without impoverishing the whole. Plato's discussion of tyrannical characteristics and their relationship with the excesses of Athenian democracy fits into a broader pattern of focus on democratic and imperial ambitions and shortcomings, as the other essays in this volume show. Whether Plato's picture of tyranny is historically accurate or pragmatically feasible is almost beside the point.[52] Opinions may vary on the historical credibility of Plato's picture of tyranny, as they may on whether either he or the Athenians had any reason to fear the reestablishment of tyranny proper in the city.[53] What is important is that his sketch taps into pervasive fifth- and fourth-century political ideologies. The freedom and power of the tyrant, although illusory from a philosophical point of view, are the aspiration of the demos and the complaint of the dissident elite who saw democracy as a form of tyranny. In this context, it seems too pessimistic to say that Athenian politics of the fifth and fourth centuries do not shed any light on the *Republic*.

Perhaps ahistoricism expresses rather than disqualifies political intent. If Plato presents his readers with a series of constitutions only partly consistent with historical reality, this may show that he wishes to create a reception in which his reader will replace a set of expectations predicated upon politics as usual with a set that turns its back upon conventional politics.[54] The confounding of the ethical and the political is an important part of this strategy, since the establishment of an "aristocratic" ethical agenda for the soul carries immediate political consequences, unhappy ones for advocates of fourth-century Athenian democracy. Yet the shift to a focus on internal constitutions distracts us, if only temporarily, from such political implications. Socrates' city is not, after all, a real city; it is introduced as an analogy.[55] In the end, however, the derivation of tyranny from democracy, the conflation of aristocracy with kingship, the mingling of the ethical and the political, and the questionable historicism of the presentation are all ideological moves. These moves may not be philosophically satisfactory political theory, but they are extremely effective political practice.[56]

Let us return to Plato's presentation of the harmonious soul and city to complete this discussion of psychic politics. Plato's picture reminds us of Isocrates' ideal in the *Panathenaicus* and *Areopagiticus*. In Isocrates' version of "real" democracy, the best rule by the consent of the rest. So too in the *Republic* the rulers and the ruled have the same opinion (= *homonoia, symphonia*, 432a6–9) about who should be in charge of the city (431d9–e2), and the two inferior parts of the soul agree (*homodoxōsi*) that the rational part should run the soul

(442c–d).[57] The rule of the best is not tyranny because of this agreement and because the aim of the psychic or civic polity is not gratification but a rational conception of the best. The nature of this rule corresponds to a rehabilitated conception of monarchy in the fourth century.[58]

Political developments, then, as well as philosophical analysis, suggest that the model of psychic *homonoia* is the correct one to apply to the *Republic*. Gill has recently distinguished two ways of interpreting the statements of the *Republic* on the rule of reason in the soul. Some passages, like those above, suggest that the virtuous soul is characterized by harmonious agreement between the different parts. Others suggest that the rational part rules by coercion and that virtue necessarily involves internal struggle. Gill concludes that the balance of the argumentation favors a harmonious agreement in the soul.[59] It is striking, however, that even this enlightened scenario leaves traces of a less positive conception. This ambivalence suggests that the shadow of earlier negative Greek conceptions of monarchy still lingers. The coercive model tends towards the starkly monarchic, while the model of psychic harmony conforms to the model of aristocratic "democracy" in Isocrates and philosopher king(s) in the *Republic,* where the inferior parts agree to be ruled by the superior. Here too the juxtaposition of a historicist and nonhistoricist model proves useful. Historically and ideologically from the standpoint of Classical Athenian culture, monarchic and/or oligarchic culture is coercive and tyrannical. By abandoning a historicist perspective, Plato can suggest a more benign aristocratic system.

Isocrates too perceives an analogy between the civic and psychic realms. In his case, the comparison is between the soul and the form of government. Thus at *Areopagiticus* 14 he declares that "the *politeia* is the soul of a state and has as much power as the mind has over the body. This is what deliberates on all matters, preserving what is good and warding off misfortunes. Both laws and orators and private citizens must assimilate themselves to it."[60] The state is the person, the constitution, its soul. Clearly, a rational and ethically good constitution will produce a good state, just as a good soul will produce a good person when it is allowed to direct affairs. The soul is not divided into parts, but Isocrates' rhetoric makes it clear that he conceives the polis as a collective entity comparable to a person.

Like Plato, Isocrates makes "the move in" to internal constitutions. We saw earlier how Isocrates' ahistorical approach blurred political distinctions and resulted in constitutional relativism. My examination of *Evagoras* 46 showed how a ruler might be portrayed both as a "man of the people" (*dēmotikos*) and as "tyrannical" (*tyrannikos*). In his oration for Evagoras' son, *To Nicocles,* Isocrates replays this move and then continues into the psychic realm. At the external political level we see the conflation of monarchic and democratic constitutions.

> Exercise concern for the multitude and think it important to rule with a view to their gratification (*kecharismenōs*). Recognize that whether the constitution is an oligarchy or something else, it lasts longest when it best serves/pays court to (*therapeuein*) the multitude. You will be a good leader of the people (*dēmagōgēseis*) if you neither allow the mob to commit outrages nor suffer them (*To Nic.* 15–16).

The word used for "lead the masses" specifies that by ruling with a view to the gratification of his citizens, Nicocles will be a "demagogue." This is an interesting choice of words, since "demagogue" is a term that can express the most extreme disapproval of democratic politicians. Isocrates' vision of benevolent despotism rehabilitates the demagogue as monarch and the monarch as demagogue: monarchy does not rule out gratifying the people or being a "popular" leader.[61] Note, moreover, the affected indifference to constitutional form expressed in the words "whether the constitution is an oligarchy or something else." Monarchy, democracy, and even oligarchy begin to merge. The "move inside" comes in chapter 29: "Govern yourself no less than others, and consider this to be most kingly (*basilikōtaton*), if you are enslaved to no pleasure but rule your desires more than your citizens." Nicocles is to progress from external to internal kingship, and the latter is privileged over the former. Psychic rule becomes a model for civic rule and creates an argument for monarchy, read as enlightened control.

To sum up: both Plato and Isocrates stress the king/tyrant as metaphor rather than reality. The force of the political office is internalized and de-historicized. This move parallels the move to the outside I talked about in the first part of this paper. There, I argued that Plato's and Isocrates' Panhellenic aspirations created a rhetorical strategy aimed at multiple potential audiences corresponding to a multitude of potential constitutions. Political vocabulary becomes multifunctional and is based (in the case of Isocrates) on an implicit relativism that slides back and forth between internal and external, between kingship, tyranny, aristocracy, and democracy. Plato maintains the absolute integrity of positive kingship (conflated with aristocracy), portrays democracy in terms of tyranny, and presents us with a positive model that assimilates psychic and civic harmony to aristocracy where the best rule by consent. The model of psychic monarchy, for both Isocrates and Plato, is developed from a popular notion of self-control subsequently problematized.

THE TYRANNY OF THE AUDIENCE

The notion of control returns us to the question of audiences, both the Panhellenic and Athenian external audience, and the internal psychic audience. All of them suffer the same potential weaknesses: the pursuit of gratification rather than of what is best. Conservative thinkers hold in common the idea that a democracy constitutes a particular kind of audience. It is fickle, liable to be impressed by splash and emotional appeal. It is therefore corruptible. Because it wants to be entertained, there is the danger that someone will speak *pros hēdonēn* or *pros charin* (with a view to pleasure or gratification), making people look to their immediate pleasure rather than their long-term good. The orator thus becomes a parasite on their vast appetite for self-indulgence.

Claims that success in a democracy depends on paying court to the audience, flattering it, seducing it with pleasure, create an analogy between the democratic and the tyrannical audience. Both pursue irresponsible pleasures and force those who address them to conform and say only what they want to hear.[62] Plato and Isocrates are key players in this construction of a democratic audience. We have seen how Isocrates uses the *Antidosis* to create a model of Athenian rhetorical culture in which a speaker is forced to gratify the pleasures of a tyrannical audience and how Plato describes a similar relationship obtaining between speaker and demos in the *Gorgias*. My examination of the "move in" has shown that the possibility of such a corrupt relationship exists inside the soul, where the realms of ethics and politics interpenetrate. Because ethics cannot be separated from politics, the reception of speech is always political.

Plato presents a fundamental connection between "musical" and political reception. In the *Republic,* Socrates describes how the democracy inculcates its values by praise and blame and names four locales for this activity: the Assembly, the lawcourts, the army camp, and, notably, the theater (492b–c). The *Gorgias* again prefigures this connection when Socrates' discussion of the preeminence of audience pleasure as opposed to the pursuit of what is best moves from flute playing to choral poetry to tragedy and concludes that poetry is a form of public speaking (*dēmēgoria*) and is rhetoric (501d7–502d3). Socrates then compares this rhetoric to that directed at the demos (502d10–e2). In all instances, it is the mass nature of the audience that causes problems.

Drawing upon these passages and others, Wallace has explored the idea of Athens as a theatocracy.[63] This position had been anticipated by Cleon in Thucydides' Mytilenean debate (3.37–38), when he complained that the Athenians viewed debate in the Assembly as a kind of rhetorical contest.[64] They were, to quote Crawley's translation, "slaves to the pleasure of the ear, and more like the audience of a rhetorician than the council of a city." One of the most telling passages adduced by Wallace is *Laws* 700a–701b, where the undisciplined applause of an ignorant audience bent on pleasure leads to a breakdown in musical law. *Aristokratia*, the rule of the best, gave way to *theatokratia*, the rule of the audience (701a). If this "democracy" had been confined to the sphere of music, no terrible damage would have been done, but in fact, musical lawlessness and the conceit of wisdom led to universal lawlessness and ignorance. The point could not be more clearly made that reception has political implications. Corruption of political and literary forms goes hand in hand, encouraged by the spatial isomorphism of theater and *ekklesia* (in the fourth century, the Theater of Dionysus was used for meetings of the Assembly).

The corruption and tyrannical potential of the mass audience (conceived as consumer both of musical and of political discourse) causes Plato and Isocrates to choose forms of writing and publication in which they can create and manipulate multiple audiences. If the audience is a tyrant, Plato and Isocrates are wise advisors who speak without fear. Their attempt to master audience corruption expresses their conservative agenda. Both turn away from public performance. Thus Isocrates defines himself by refusing to accept the role of public speaker, instead privileging the written over the oral, his own small voice over that of the ranting demagogue.[65] Plato too seems to turn away from normal politics, speaking and writing instead for an elite.[66] Their audience is not the citizen body in assembly but multiple individuals or small groups. They deprive mob oratory of its occasion and opportunities, helped in their efforts by their ethical focus on the individual soul.

Isocratean treatises either (a) mimic public occasions while being designed for reading or (b) are purportedly designed for individuals while also being aimed at a wider publication audience. In either case, they block the possibility of en masse reaction. Individual readers or small groups of listeners must read and think independently. If they do not understand Isocrates' point, or if they tire, they are to stop and start again later (*Antid.* 12). The Platonic dialogue does not situate itself in a context of public speech. It presents individual interactions and asks to be read in such a context, although designed for public circulation. Thus the beginning of the *Timaeus* sets up the philosophical conversation as the private counterpart of a Panathenaic oration.[67] The *Theaetetus* draws an elaborate comparison between the speaker in a law-court and the philosopher. The speaker in court is constrained by a time limit on his speech (172e1). He is a slave himself and talks to his master (the demos) about a fellow slave, learning how to "flatter his master (*despotēn*) in word and fawn upon him in deed" (172e4–173a3). By contrast, the philosophical interlocutors have "no jury or audience member" (*dikastēs ē theatēs*) standing over them to censure or rule (*arxōn*) them (173c4–6). They can take their time (this stress on the leisure necessary for a successful discussion is a frequent theme in Plato's dialogues).[68] The contrast here between slavery and mastery/freedom is politically resonant: the public arena is one of slavery and flattery, while nonpublic discussion retains freedom.

This move away from mass audience is analogous to and justified by the move from civic constitutions to internal psychic rationality. Platonic and Isocratean texts speak with the interior voice of reason. Since reason is the best part of us and should rule us, their relationship with the reader is that of enlightened rule by consent. Isocrates constructs his rule by refusing to pander to the audience—an ostentatious statement of his own rhetorical authority. Isocrates is aware that he is attempting to create a new type of discourse. His conversations with Timotheus and the Spartan pupil parade anxieties about the capacities of the democratic audience and sketch the possibility of a different reaction. His concentration on the small or individual reading audience (even when mimicking public oration) is an important change in literary focus. This emerges clearly in *To Nicocles,* where he configures the king as his perfect audience, a single person who can make a decision, and contrasts this audience with the audience of tragedy and other poetry (*To Nic.* 46–51), which is admonished ineffectively.[69] Audience ideology is reversed. The democratic audience is unified in its servility to passion and pleasure. The good king, however, can be effectively admonished, can be, as Gill puts it, the personality unified by reason's rule (the ideal of Plato's *Republic*).[70]

We should not overstate the similarities between Platonic and Isocratean audience construction. Plato is more aware than Isocrates that in the end, the reception of the text is uncontrollable. As he puts it in the *Phaedrus,* once a discourse is published, it is read both by those who understand and by those who have no business with it and "is not capable of defending or helping itself" (275e1–5). All that Plato can do is attempt to indicate what sort of reading we should give his text and insist that we are self-conscious about our intellectual method. We must, above all, say what we really think and refuse to pander to our intellectual and political desires. At the same time, his interlocutors in the dialogues create a powerful argument for an aristocracy of reason that has inescapable political consequences. It is impossible for the reader to proceed without engaging with this critique and acknowledging the political nature of reading. Plato's indirect presentation of his authorial self reinforces this necessity. For all his attractions, "Socrates" is not a mere cipher for "Plato." By nesting Socratic speech inside his own silence, Plato creates an oblique relationship with his audience and forces us to question our own relationship with the text and its author. In comparison with Isocrates, then, Plato constructs a more problematic reception, precisely because his dialogues are meant to be the beginning, rather than the end, of philosophical engagement with the issues presented.

Like Isocrates, Plato's Socrates does not tailor his remarks with a view to audience approval. His opponents are sophists and those with an eye to political domination: proto-tyrants and their teachers. Constraints of space forbid detailed discussion of the role of literary pleasure in the construction of reception. It would be remiss, however, not to note that although both Plato and Isocrates condemn speech that aims at pleasure, they both employ effectively the varied weapons of the literary arsenal. In *Against the Sophists* (18), Isocrates claims that good teachers will produce speakers who imitate his rhetorical grace and charm.[71] Plato's notorious literary charm, greater than Isocrates' for being less obtrusive, certainly plays its part in ensuring a continuing readership. The distinction (which deserves further exploration) must be that our literary pleasure is not intended to deceive us into abandoning the claims of reason but to enhance the experience of intellection. Reason and pleasure are to unite in the complete personality. The latter's role must always be subordinate, however. Thus we see that Plato has the Eleatic Stranger state that the intellectual usefulness of a discussion is more important than praise or blame directed at features like length or digressiveness (*Plt.* 285d5–287a7), while Isocrates too maintains his freedom to digress even when it spoils the literary balance of his work.[72]

I began this paper with the idea of multiple audiences, suggesting that both Plato and Isocrates aim their work beyond Athens. They expect a Panhellenic readership that will transcend individual poleis and speak to an individual who is encouraged to rule himself, although this individual may be king or commoner. This rule is not to be one of tyrannical self-abandonment to pleasure (since this is in fact no rule at all) but benevolent kingship over the self. In some situations this kingship may be realized, and the audience may indeed be a tyrant or king, but his internal rule will render his external rule rational and beneficial. Athens, the city that concerns them most nearly, is to transform the tyrannical sovereignty of the demos into a self-regulating aristocracy. Civic virtue is to begin with the individual and work its way out into the wider city.[73] It follows, then, that in a world where the individual is, in a sense, the state, prior constitutional distinctions will cease to have force. By concentrating its ideological energies on literal tyranny, Athens has missed the point. Democracy, glossed as rule in the interests of the people, need not conflict with aristocracy or even monarchy.

The aim is a collective entity (city or soul) ruled by reason and aiming at the best. The *logoi* of Plato and Isocrates act as paradigms of rational discourse. They both argue for a conservative political program (although the nature of this program differs) and provide methodological guidance on constructing a rational intellectual community whose goal is the avoidance of tyranny in all its guises. At the same time as advocating a particular political and ethical relationship between governor and governed, they must, because of the political and ethical ramifications of literary reception, instantiate that relationship in their own with the reader. They must guide us, but only with our reasoned consent, by presenting a model of psychic monarchy that we can accept and internalize. If we accept their discourse as the voice of reason, then we acquiesce in their "kingship" over us, the readers. Paradoxically, the audience is most truly master of itself when it is ruled, but not tyrannized, by these authors.[74]

Notes

[1] Ober 1998.

[2] For further comments on Isocratean cosmopolitanism, see Ober 1998: 254–256.

[3] Wallace 1994; Ober 1998: 148.

[4] See Osborne 2000: 23–28 for the contested language of class and evaluation in the fifth century B.C.

[5] By "constitutional relativism" I mean the blurring of boundaries between different constitutional types.

[6] Giorgini 1993: 30.

[7] Frolov 1974b: 401–402 and passim; Frolov 1974a: 398–399; Rosivach 1988: 56–57; Barceló 1993: 251–253, 256–258. Giorgini (1993: 270) associates the rehabilitation of the monarch with the multiplicity of possible political positions in the fourth century. But see also Eder 1995.

[8] Schubert 1993: 69–71.

[9] Frolov 1974a: 255–259.

[10] V. Parker 1998: 168–171.

[11] On Isocrates and Pindar, see Race 1987.

[12] Eucken (1983: 220) notes that Isocrates generally uses "tyrant" and "tyranny" in the same sense as "monarch," "monarchy," "king," and "kingship" and contrasts this (as does V. Parker 1998: 165–166) with a Platonic practice that draws careful distinctions between good and bad monarchy. In note 31 Eucken refutes Kehl's contention that Isocrates modified the meaning of tyrant vocabulary according to the nature of his audience, stressing, as I do, that Isocrates' audience should always be conceived as Panhellenic and multiple.

[13] On the problems of Isocratean consistency, see K. Morgan forthcoming 2003.

[14] I am grateful to John Henderson for emphasizing this point.

[15] See Usener 1994: 31–38 for further discussion of double audiences.

[16] On the intertextuality between the *Antidosis* and Plato's *Apology*, see Nightingale 1995: 28–29, 40–43; Ober 1998: 260–263.

[17] On the analogy between politics and medicine, see *On the Peace* 39–40, and Jouanna 1978 (cf. Yunis 1996: 123). Jouanna's analysis of the figure of the doctor as model for the lawgiver concentrates on Plato's *Gorgias* and *Laws*. His exposition of the interactive relationship between the free patient and free doctor in the *Laws* draws on passages from the Hippocratic corpus that stress the importance of catering (somewhat) to the pleasure of the patient (90). The importance of rhetoric in the Hippocratic relationship provides a suggestive model for Isocrates' politico-rhetorical aims.

[18] Tyrannical hatred of the upright and preference for the vicious: Hdt. 3.80; Xen. *Hier.*

5.1–2; Pl. *Resp.* 567b–d. Prevalence of and necessity for flattery in tyrannical courts: Hdt. 3.80; Xen. *Hier.* 1.14–15; Pl. *Resp.* 575e–576a, 579d–e.

[19] Ober (1998: 272) suggests that in the Timotheus digression, Isocrates does not speak as a "rejectionist critic" but as "a concerned member of both the democratic and the critical communities." One's interpretation of Isocrates' advice to Timotheus turns on how ironic one thinks his criticism of Timotheus for not pandering to the masses. I think that Isocrates' perception of the similarity between his own and his pupil's problems requires an antidemocratic interpretation.

[20] Cf. Ober 1998: 258.

[21] Eucken (1983: 3–4) sees this passage as programmatic for interpreting Isocrates. So also Too 1995: 70–73.

[22] Cf. *Panath.* 271: Isocrates claims to write discourses that are more philosophical and serious than those written for display. They aim at the truth rather than seeking to overwhelm the audience; they admonish, rather than being composed with a view to pleasure (*hēdonēn*) and gratification (*charin*) (cf. *Panath.* 135).

[23] On the connections between Isocratean *amphibolia* and the later *logos eschēmatismenos*, see Bons 1993: 166–168. Cf. also Wardy 1996: 130–131.

[24] The dichotomy between Isocrates as "a political propagandist or a moralizing sophist" (Harding 1973: 142) is overdrawn (cf. Morgan 1998: 116). As Harding points out, Isocrates couches his "so-called propaganda" in moral terms. Harding pushes the notion that as moralizing sophist, Isocrates used moral terminology without strong political resonance. I find it difficult to believe, however, that he or his audiences were so innocent. It is exactly the merging of the moral with the political that is significant. Isocrates himself is sensitive that he may seem to speak only for the moment and may suggest (through the comments of the Spartan pupil) that this is not the case (*Panath.* 239). Too's (1995: 61–67) thoughtful analysis of the problem of Isocratean contradiction extends Harding's hypothesis of antilogical composition and argues that antilogies "are to be approached as oppositions that one cannot and should not attempt to explain away" (67). Inconsistencies in Isocrates there are, but there is a consistent conservative ideology behind his ambiguous political presentation.

[25] The text here is uncertain. Θ and Λ read τυραννικός, while Γ reads μεγαλόφρων. It is easy to see how the unexpected capping adjective *tyrannikos* could have confused later readers who were unused to positive descriptions of tyrants. Forster 1912: 96 (ad loc.) remarks that it "is hardly conceivable that Isocrates wrote . . . μεγαλόφρων" and compares *To Nic.* 53, where a good advisor is said to be the "most tyrannical" of possessions. Both passages cultivate the paradox wherein the wise behavior of a king is called tyrannical, and the point is precisely in the paradox, which forces a redefinition of "tyranny." I cannot agree, therefore, with the comments of Mathieu and Brémond (1956: 158, n. 2 ad loc.), who read μεγαλόφρων. *Tyrannikos*, they say, introduces a different idea to the passage, but this is only true if we interpret "tyrannical" negatively.

[26] Thus *Panath.* 114–118. Cf. *Peace* 75–78; *Areopag.* 14–18; Too 1995: 103.

[27] Ober (1998: 279–280) brings out how illusory these "tyrannical" powers were to be.

[28] Schubert 1993: 178–179; Ober 1998: 273–276.

[29] Even the study of Riginos 1976, which concludes (199) that the anecdotal tradition is unreliable as a source of information about Plato's life, concedes that Plato did make multiple trips to Syracuse (70). She wisely warns that "the majority of the anecdotes dealing with Plato's relations with the two tyrants are markedly influenced by the stock motif of the philosopher versus the tyrant and seem far removed from factual reports" (74). It is interesting, however, that most of these anecdotes deal with Plato's outspokenness in the face of the tyrant (75–83). This motif fits well with the contrasts between outspokenness and flattery that emerge from the texts under consideration here.

[30] As we learn from *Phaedrus* (275d4–e5), it is impossible for any piece of writing to do this effectively. We would need, then, to draw the difficult distinction between an argument and its literary formulation. The latter is contextualized and *ad hominem;* the former might claim analytical independence.

[31] Cf. Wardy 1996: 76.

[32] See Usener 1994: 195 for anecdotal evidence of circulation of Platonic dialogues outside Athens in the first half of the fourth century.

[33] On the narrative framework of the opening of the dialogue, see Bury 1973: xv–xix; Halperin 1992: 97–98.

[34] As when he proposes that Plato composed a proto-*Republic* for delivery to Dionysius I in 367–366 B.C. (Ryle 1966: 61).

[35] It is evident, however, from 469b–471b that Socrates' universalizing aspirations do not stretch beyond Panhellenism.

[36] Cf. Blank 1986; K. Morgan 2000: 196.

[37] Usener 1994: 65–67, 80–92, 218–222. Usener concludes correctly that for both authors, reception by a small (elite) group is a preferred option. She further differentiates between an Isocratean ideology of solitary reading (viewed positively as an opportunity for study) and a Platonic one (viewed negatively as forestalling the opportunity for critical discussion).

[38] Cf. Rocco 1997: 77–78, who notes the analogy and points out that the power of the orator is mirrored and opposed by the power of the Socratic elenchus.

[39] On the connection between persuasion, force, and tyranny (and Gorgias' *Helen*), see Yunis 1996: 120. MacDowell 1982: 36 (ad loc.) rightly cites as comparandum for the Gorgias passage Eur. *Hec.* 814–819. Hecuba laments that although persuasion (*peithō*) is the only real *tyrannos* for mortals, we do not pay to learn it. The link between rhetoric and tyranny here is strong, if oblique. It is interesting, given the association between tyranny and money described by Kallet and Seaford in this volume, that Hecuba refers to the economic expenditure that enables one to acquire rhetorical tyranny. The primary reference, as MacDowell points out, is to the money paid for lessons in rhetoric.

[40] Wardy 1996: 38–39.

[41] Cf. Ober 1998: 208. Aristotle, too, draws the analogy between tyranny and a democracy where the masses act like a capricious monarch (*Pol.* 1292a15–21). For discussion and further instances of the analogy in Aristotle, see Giorgini 1993: 346–347; also Ober 1998: 293–294.

[42] The move from one soul to many is made at 501d.

[43] In the *Gorgias*, the analogy between political and medical practice is explicit: 479a–c, 504a–505b. Cf. Wardy 1996: 75, 78–79.

[44] Cf. Kahn 1983: 103: "The shift from political rule to self-rule reminds us that the fundamental issue of the dialogue is moral rather than political . . . how one should live one's life (492d5); and it suggests that the answer to this question will also determine one's position on matters of natural justice and political rule." Clearly, I would want to shift the balance of this perceptive formulation and stress that the moral implies the political.

[45] North 1966: 12, 34.

[46] Fragment 58; North 1966: 89, 116.

[47] Cf. Rocco 1997: 82–83.

[48] Callicles on the childishness of philosophy: 484c5–485d6; on Socrates' argumentative childishness: 499b4–6; Socrates on Callicles' argumentative childishness: 499b9–c2. For discussion of the philosophical significance of childishness, see K. Morgan 2000: 171–173, 175–177.

[49] Opinions differ on the extent of this perversity. Adam (note ad loc.) notes that Arist. *Pol.* 5.1305a7–17 says that in early times, democracies used to give birth to tyrannies. Thus in ancient times, when the same man was a *dēmagōgos* and *stratēgos,* he could become a tyrant, for most early tyrants came into being *ek dēmagōgōn.* Clearly, however, there were other origins for tyranny. Giorgini (1993: 320–321) follows Adam's lead in adducing the fourth-century parallel of Dionysius I, whose chronological proximity to Plato may have been influential. For Giorgini, this proximity is decisive: Plato simply distorts the historical situation. Some distortion is surely present. Robin Osborne, however, points out to me that it would not be unreasonable for an Athenian to draw conclusions from the fact that the tyranny of Peisistratus succeeded the establishment of Solonian democracy. Plato's account is not, then, an obvious travesty of Athenian history. Nevertheless, the quasi-mythological significance of the tyrannicides as (re)founders of Athenian freedom and democracy must have ensured that the emergence of democracy from tyranny (rather than the reverse) was at the forefront of Athenian ideological consciousness. Adam is surely right to say that "Plato deliberately selects that particular origin which accords with his psychological standpoint."

[50] Annas 1981: 302–305.

[51] Annas 1999: 72, 77–82. Brunt 1993 makes similar points. He suggests (1) that there is not enough evidence to sustain the thesis that it was a chief aim of Plato's academy to prepare its students for statecraft (330); (2) that the Academy (in contrast to Socrates) was left in peace by the Athenians because "its concern in politics appeared entirely theoretical" (301); (3) that Plato's suggestions for improving the government of the polis were

impractical (302–303), and thus, given "the futility of framing codes on a set of principles that would not win acceptance," we should conclude that the primary aim of Platonic studies was not political (312–313). Yet even if we accept that the Academy was not a training ground for politicians, it surely underestimates the role and power of Platonic ideology to conclude that because it was theoretical, it was not perceived as challenging democratic structures. As for the impracticality of Platonic codes and utopias, their very lack of connection with current practice is, as this paper suggests, a political statement.

[52] But see the valuable remarks of Schofield 1999 (35): "The *Republic*, then, points us to a reading of its political proposals which both is and is not utopian. It implies that the ideal Socrates has described is—as ideal—an unrealisable paradigm. But at the same time it stresses that the point of a paradigm is just that—to be something we can aim at and approximate to." See also Ober, this volume, p. 233.

[53] Contrast the comments of Raaflaub, this volume, with the statements of Frolov 1974a: 231–232, 398–399, and in particular that of Adam (ad 564a4): "Granted that Plato thought Athens was still degenerating, he must certainly have expected her, unless the process of decay should be arrested, to end in a tyranny."

[54] This is, for example, his aim in his Atlantis narrative (K. Morgan 1998).

[55] Schofield (1999: 69–70) underlines the disjunction between the real and the formal basis for the introduction of political theory into the dialogue: "Formally speaking, the entire discussion of the *polis* is introduced . . . to illuminate by analogy a question in personal ethics," but the elaboration of the model "show[s] that his preoccupation with questions of political theory goes much deeper and further in the *Republic* than the formal role of the city-soul analogy would require."

[56] I thank Catherine Atherton for calling my attention to this distinction.

[57] For the importance of *homonoia* in the political world of the fourth century, see Ober 1989: 297.

[58] See note 7 above. The transformation of monarchy into a benevolent rule is evident also in Xen. *Cyr., Ages.,* and *Hier.* (Frolov 1974b: 420–427; Barceló 1993: 248–252).

[59] Gill 1996: 245–246, 259–260.

[60] Cf. *Grg.* 510d4–9, 512e4–513b8, and the discussion on pp. 197–198 above.

[61] We may contrast here Plato's picture at *Resp.* 565c9–566a4, where the extremes of democracy conjure forth a man to protect the demos, one who becomes a tyrant.

[62] Cf. *Grg.* 510a6–e2 on success under a tyranny with 512e5–513c3 on success in Athens. For the rule of desires in the democratic man, see *Resp.* 559c and 561c–d; for tyrannical appetites, see *Resp.* 573a–d.

[63] Wallace 1997a: 97–99 and n. 3.

[64] Cf. Yunis 1996: 90–91.

[65] Too 1995: 84–102.

[66] Cf. Brunt 1993.

[67] K. Morgan 1998: 104–105.

[68] On the importance of leisure for Platonic philosophy, see K. Morgan 2000: 176–177 with n. 43.

[69] Cf. the same strategy at *Philip* 12–15 and *Letter to Dionysius* 5–7.

[70] Gill 1999: 240 ff.

[71] For Isocrates' charm and technical polish, see also *Panath.* 2, *Paneg.* 10–12, and *C. soph.* 16–18.

[72] *Panath.* 74–75, 84–86 (note the privileging of justice over expediency at 86). See also K. Morgan (forthcoming 2003).

[73] On the collapse of the distinction between public and private, see D. Cohen 1991: 230–236; Yunis 1996: 154–155 (on Socrates in the *Apology*); Ober 1998: 110 (on Alcibiades in Thucydides). Cohen gathers together a number of passages that document how the critics of democracy wanted to break down the separation between public and private. Thus Isocrates, Plato, and Aristotle argue that the state must regulate the private sphere.

[74] I would like to acknowledge the contributions of the following to the improvement of this essay: Carolyn Dewald, Vincent Farenga, Andrea Nightingale, Stephen Todd, and audiences in Los Angeles, Cambridge, Oxford, and Keele.

J O S I A H   O B E R

TYRANT KILLING AS THERAPEUTIC *STASIS:*
A POLITICAL DEBATE IN IMAGES AND TEXTS

My starting point is the evolving relationship between Athenian democratic ideology and the arguments developed by politically dissident Athenians, that is, those who were not willing to accept that democracy was the best of all political worlds or even the best that could reasonably be hoped for.[1] I have argued elsewhere that democratic ideology, with its quasi-hegemonic tendencies, was challenged in texts produced by members of an informal yet self-consciously critical "community of interpretation."[2] Here, I hope to show that the contest between democratic ideology and a dissident sensibility that sought political alternatives informs some notable moments in the long and intellectually fertile Greek engagement with the concept of tyranny.

As other essays in this volume have demonstrated, the general issue of the tyrant, his nature, and what to do about him was conceptually very important within Athenian democratic ideology and equally important within what I am calling the "dissident sensibility." But the tyrant issue was also important for debates between democrats and their critics from the early fifth century B.C. through the late fourth. Both democrats and dissidents agreed in general terms on why tyranny is at once morally and politically unacceptable: the tyrant is wicked because he uses illegitimately acquired public power systematically to alienate from "us" that which is most dear to us.[3] Tyranny, by embodying a negative political extreme, the intolerable *politeia* (or non-*politeia*), in turn helps to define what "we" require "our own" *politeia* (present or hoped-for) to secure and ensure for us. It also helped dissident Greek intellectuals to explore the positive political extreme—the ideal or best-possible *politeia,* and it helped them to think more deeply about "moderate" political alternatives.[4]

In the context of debate, certain questions arise: Who is the (actual or potential) tyrant? Who are "we"? What should we do about tyrants? The answers to these questions will help to establish some conceptual similarities between democrats and their opponents but also to distinguish democratic ideology from critical challenges. In brief summary: For Classical Greek democrats, the tyrant can be defined as *anyone* who would seek to overthrow "we the demos." This demotic definition equates oligarchic revolutionaries with tyrants. An obvious example of conflation is Thucydides' reference to Athenian demotic fears of an "oligarchico-tyrannical conspiracy" (ἐπὶ ξυνωμοσίᾳ ὀλιγαρχικῇ καὶ τυραννικῇ, 6.60.1). The democratic association of oligarchs with tyrants is one reason that tyranny remained such a lively issue for the Athenian for so long after the threat of "actual" tyranny (of the Archaic Greek sort) was past.[5]

Defense of the democracy tended to be equated with resistance to tyrants. That resistance might culminate in tyrannicide and therefore murderous violence by citizens against fellow citizens. Tyrant slaying thus becomes, in democratic ideology, a rare example of therapeutic civil conflict. Dissidents, in seeking alternatives to democratic ideology, sought to complicate this simple scenario. They argued that the demos was the real tyrant. They posited a spectrum of regimes as an alternative to the binary "democracy/tyranny" political universe. They offered alternative narratives about the actions and motives of tyrannicides and about when *stasis* in the polis was and was not therapeutic.

THE DEMOCRATIC IDEOLOGY OF TYRANNY IN ICONOGRAPHY AND TEXT

Among the arresting features of the ideological debate over tyranny is that it can be traced in both textual and iconographic registers. Moreover, the texts and iconography of tyrant killing are mutually implicated and in a variety of ways: texts referring to tyrannicide pay explicit and implicit homage to artistic monuments, and the iconography of tyrannicide is often transparently narrative. My discussion of the iconography of "democracy and tyranny" is necessarily selective. I begin with two very familiar monuments (Figs. 8.1, 8.2, 8.4) from early and late in the history of the independent Athenian democracy. They are perhaps, for students of Athenian democracy, even overly familiar in that their repeated photographic reiteration may have evacuated for us some of their evocative power.

Fig. 8.1. Critius and
Nesiotes group. Photo by
permission of Museo
Nazionale, Naples (Inv.
no. 6009).

CRITIUS AND NESIOTES' TYRANNICIDE STATUE GROUP

This group was erected in the Athenian Agora in ca. 477 B.C. (Figs. 8.1,
8.2). The group, which survives in a Roman copy, depicts Harmodius and
Aristogeiton in the act of assassinating Hipparchus. This monument replaced
an earlier tyrannicide group sculpted by Antenor, erected in the Agora in
the very late sixth or very early fifth century and taken as war booty by the
Persians in 480/79. The exact date and ideological force (aristocratic? democratic?) of the Antenor group are debatable. By contrast, the Critius and
Nesiotes group seems quite transparent. Following a general scholarly consensus, elaborated by Burkhard Fehr, Michael Taylor, and others, I take the
Critius and Nesiotes statue group as a self-consciously democratic monu-

Fig. 8.2. Critius and Nesiotes group (restored cast). Photo by
permission of Museo dei Gessi dell' Università, Rome.

ment, put up by the Athenians immediately after the Persian Wars to celebrate democratic Athenian unity and boldness in action.[6]

As Vincent Farenga has astutely noted, the expressed ethos of the composition is not one of conflicted values; it suggests no disjunction between inner
qualities of being and the external signs of appearing and doing. The monument exists within what Farenga (drawing from Bakhtin) has called a "citizen
chronotope."[7] Yet the Critius and Nesiotes group, with its dramatic and kinetic composition, is also very much an image of "becoming": the killers,
acting as a cooperative team, boldly advancing upon their foe, are caught by
the sculptors at the moment just before the death blow was struck; the viewer

is drawn into the action and invited to complete the narrative for himself.[8] As we know from the critical comments of Thucydides and other writers, the canonical Athenian way of completing the story was with the establishment of the democracy: the kinetic energy of the tyrant slayers carrying through to the creation of a new identity in which Athenian citizens would not be passive subjects but active participants in the history-making business of public life.[9]

One element missing in the preserved Roman copy of the tyrant-slayers monument (Fig. 8.1) is weaponry. Presumably this is a mere accident of preservation, but the broken swords draw our attention to the weapons employed by the tyrant-killer. The swords are clearly illustrated on a depiction of the moment of the assassination on a red-figure stamnos by the Copenhagen Painter, dating to about 470 B.C. (Fig. 8.3).[10] The standard way for a Greek tyrant to "take the point" of his own illegitimacy is literal death by sword (*xiphos*) or dagger (*encheiridion*).[11] The implicit argument of the Athenians' act of reerecting the statue group and of the sustained democratic Athenian

Fig. 8.3. Stamnos by the Copenhagen Painter, showing tyrannicide, ca. 470 B.C. Beazley, *ARFVP* 257, no. 5. Photo by permission of Martin von Wagner Museum, Universität Würzburg. Photo: K Oehrlein.

reverence for the tyrannicides, is that Harmodius and Aristogeiton killed a tyrant, and after the death of the tyrant came democracy.

As several essays have noted, the tacit popular assumption that "tyrannicide ergo democracy" became a hot topic in Athenian critical-historical literature by the later fifth century. It was explicitly challenged by Thucydides, who goes so far (6.53.3) as to claim that at least by 415 B.C., the Athenian citizenry actually "knew by hearsay" (ἐπιστάμενος γὰρ ὁ δῆμος ἀκοῇ) that the tyranny was not overthrown "by themselves and Harmodius" (i.e., in 514) but by the Spartans (i.e., in 510). But, whatever the complexities of the Athenians' historical memory of how tyranny was ended in Athens, by the later fifth century, solidarity with the tyrannicides was clearly regarded, by democrats and their critics, as the essence of traditional democratic patriotism.[12]

The Critius and Nesiotes group thus came to express the "democratically correct" response of Athenian citizens to threats to the democratic order. The Athenian quickness to associate subversion with tyranny and the tyrannicide group with active citizen-centered defense of democracy against subversion are illustrated by a comic passage. In Aristophanes' *Lysistrata* (631–634), produced in 411, the chorus of old Athenian men staunchly declare, "These women won't set up a tyranny over me, for I'll stand on guard, and I'll carry my sword in a myrtle bough; I'll stand to arms in the Agora beside Aristogeiton: Like this! I'll stand beside him" (ἐν τοῖς ὅπλοις ἑξῆς Ἀριστογείτονι, / ὧδέ θ᾽ ἑστήξω παρ᾽ αὐτόν, trans. Sommerstein 1990). The old men of the chorus, quoting the evidently well known *scolion,* imagine themselves taking up arms in the public space of the Agora, next to the statue group. In taking their stand "beside Aristogeiton," Aristophanes' old men explicitly take on the role of Harmodius. We must imagine the dancers of the chorus, as they sing "Like this!" mimicking the form of the Harmodius statue, assuming for a moment the "Harmodius stance": right (sword) arm cocked behind the head, preparatory to dealing what B. B. Shefton has called the "Harmodius blow" (Fig. 8.2).[13] To be a defender of democracy against subversion, then, is to "become" Harmodius—and explicitly to become Harmodius as he is depicted in the Critius and Nesiotes group.

The Copenhagen Painter, presumably working within a few years of the erection of the Critius and Nesiotes monument, is not captive to the statue-group iconography. He depicts (Fig. 8.3) the tyrannicide figures as draped and thus represents the historical moment rather than, as vase painters around 400 B.C. would (see below), the statue group itself. Moreover, the Copenhagen painter depicts Aristogeiton's position (thrusting home his sword) quite differently from the way he is depicted in the restored Critius and Nesiotes statue (draped left arm forward, right [sword] arm behind). Harmodius' position, however, is identical in both vase painting and statue. Likewise, on a badly damaged but roughly contemporary skyphos from the Villa Giulia, the one clearly recognizable iconographic element is Harmodius' raised sword-arm.[14]

Although the iconographic sample is small, it appears that the "Harmodius stance" quickly achieved canonical status as the single most stable visual element in Athenian tyrannicide iconography. The Harmodius stance might, therefore, serve as synecdoche for the monument, the event, and its (imagined) narrative continuation. This supposition is strengthened by the Aristophanes passage, which suggests that by the late fifth century, not only the tyrannicides but the tyrannicide *statue group* itself, and especially the *stance* of the Harmodius figure, were closely associated with the defense of the existing democratic regime against "tyranny." The passage strongly implies that to "stand as Harmodius" was to declare oneself an enemy of tyranny and a defender of the existing democratic regime. So we might guess that in the context of a debate between democrats and dissidents, the Harmodius stance would become a contested visual icon, just as the story of the act of tyrannicide and its meaning was contested in historical narrative.

If the democrats modeled themselves on the tyrannicides, dissident intellectuals like Thucydides challenged the tyrannicides' motives and character. In Farenga's terms, they sought to complicate the straightforward ethos expressed by the monument by drawing a distinction between the act (assassination) and the inner motives of the actors. That story is treated in other essays in this volume; there is no need to recapitulate it in detail here.[15] Suffice it to say that in the late fourth century, debates centering on the character of the tyrannicides were still being rehearsed. According to the Aristotelian *Ath. Pol.* (18.5), "democratic writers" (*hoi dēmotikoi*) claimed that Aristogeiton, when captured after the assassination, fooled his captors into destroying their own supporters, whereas "others" (i.e., dissidents) say that he betrayed his comrades.[16]

Some elements of the population were, moreover, suspected by the Athenian democrats of disrespecting the national heroes. As Kurt Raaflaub points out, at some unknown time in the fifth or early fourth century, the democratic state passed legislation forbidding slander of the tyrannicides and prohibiting the use of their names for slaves.[17] Whatever the truth of Thucydides' claim about what the Athenians "actually knew" of their own history, there can be no doubt that from the late fifth century at least, and through the late fourth, the relationship between the assassination of Hipparchus, the overthrow of the tyranny, and the origins of democracy were at the center of the debate between democratic ideology and critical discourse on various levels. The dissident side of the debate is preserved in historical narratives that seek to refute the demotic narrative linking tyrannicide with the origins of democracy. Public iconography shows that the democratic ideology of tyrannicide was asserted at the visual level. Moreover, the *Lysistrata* passage suggests that "official" democratic visual icons were recapitulated at the level of gesture (and thus subject to comic attention). We will return below to the question of whether it is possible to detect a critical response to the democratic iconography of tyrannicide.

EUCRATES' NOMOS

The second well-known image crowns the stele publishing an antityranny law, passed on the proposal of Eucrates in 337/36 B.C. The document relief depicts personified Demos, seated, being crowned by personified Demokratia, standing (Fig. 8.4). As with the Critius and Nesiotes statue group, the document relief consists of two figures. But the composition of the relief offers a marked contrast to the drama and suspense of the tyrannicide group. On the relief, Demokratia is "crowning," but Demos is not "doing" much of anything at all. His right arm rests comfortably on his left leg; his left hand would have rested on a staff. He seems completely at peace on his throne, sure of himself, a quietly self-confident Demos, "being" personified. Yet this peaceful image graces an inscription, a *nomos* enacted by the Athenian state in 337/36 B.C. that concerns the possibility of antidemocratic revolution and encourages the violently patriotic act of tyrant killing. It explicitly exonerates any potential tyrant killer from prosecution (ὅς . . . ἀποκτείνῃ, ὅσιος ἔστω: 10–11) and threatens with disenfranchisement (*atimia*) and property confiscation any member of the Council of the Areopagus who fulfills his official function while the *dēmos* or the *dēmokratia* is overthrown.[18]

The implicit argument made by this monument—its text and its iconography—is striking: what is remarkable is not that it implies that to challenge democracy is to embrace tyranny—this was, as Aristophanes' *Wasps* and *Knights* demonstrate, already a familiar enough claim in the late fifth century (see Henderson, this volume). What *is* striking is that it suggests that the overthrow of the *dēmokratia* and the *dēmos* and the establishment of a tyranny would not terminate the legitimate authority of Demos or the instrumental

Fig. 8.4. Eucrates *nomos,* documentary relief, 337/36 B.C. Demos
Crowned by Demokratia. Athenian Agora. Photo by permission
of the American School of Classical Studies, Agora Excavations.

capacity of the Athenian demos to reward and punish the political behavior
of individual Athenians.

In 410/09, in the context of the extended *stasis* of the late fifth century,
the Athenians had passed a decree on a motion by Demophantus, mandating
the use of a "loyalty oath" to compel a prodemocracy, antityrant response
on the part of the citizens, if and when "the demos is overthrown."[19] The
Eucrates *nomos* echoes some of the language of the late fifth-century decree.
But by the later fourth century, there is no longer any perceived need for an
oath to be sworn by each citizen. Now, in the place of the oath-bound individual, democratic governmental authority and the authority of democratically enacted law are imagined as continuous *through* a tyrannical interlude.
Under late fourth-century conditions, a coup d'état is indeed imaginable, but
the democratic restoration that will follow the collapse of the tyranny (presumably via assassination) is simply taken for granted. Democracy has become
an "ordinary" condition, a "state of being" that may perhaps be in some sense
interrupted by tyrannical interludes but that remains "the once and future"
politeia, the legitimate form of authority that somehow continues despite any

lapse in the actual power of the actual demos. And so, personified Demos (and the political order he represents) will still sit on his metaphorical throne even if "the demos" is (momentarily) overthrown.

We seem to have come a long way from Thucydides' paranoid Athenians of 415, who feared the establishment of a tyranny because they "knew from hearsay" that it was "not they themselves and Harmodius" who had overthrown the tyrants, but the Spartans. Thucydides' imagined Athenians suppose that, since they cannot expect Spartan benevolence to recur, a tyrannical coup d'état would permanently end the democracy. Five years later, and following an oligarchical interlude, the Athenians who voted for the Demophantus decree hoped that a sacred oath might bind each citizen to a democratic code of behavior in the absence of democratic governmental authority and so allow for the restoration of democracy. After another seventy-five years, and another coup d'état, the Athenians who voted for the Eucrates *nomos* seem much more sure of themselves, even while the dichotomy of tyranny/democracy remains at the center of their conception of the political universe.[20]

Tyranny and democracy were regarded in "official" Athenian ideology as antithetical from the early fifth through late fourth centuries. The antithesis is underlined by the positive democratic valuation of tyrant slaying. The model tyrant slayers were Harmodius and Aristogeiton: remembered as heroes in the popular folk tradition, challenged as immoral and selfishly motivated in critical political literature, and so familiarly and so powerfully realized in the statue group in the Agora that "standing like Harmodius" could be employed as synecdoche for prodemocratic resistance to tyranny. By the late fourth century, because individual democrats are assumed to be ready to take up the Harmodius stance and strike the Harmodius blow when threatened by a tyrant, "old man Demos" can sit comfortably, unarmed, on his throne, accepting his crown from Demokratia.

We may sum up the Athenian demotic agenda (as consolidated by the restoration of 403 B.C.) as follows: Tyrants are bad, because the tyrant uses illegitimately acquired power to alienate from the *politai* (citizens) that which is "theirs," especially citizen dignity, that is, the freedom, equality, and security of the citizen.[21] Those who seek to replace the democracy with any other form of government are tyrannical. Democracy and tyranny thus define a bipolar political universe. There is no legitimate "third way" between the rule of the demos and the rule of the tyrant as there was, for example, in the Persian Constitutional Debate in Herodotus book 3 (on which see Dewald, this volume) or in the multi-*politeia* schemata of Plato and Aristotle (on which see Osborne, this volume). Oligarchs, as nondemocrats, are by democratic ideological definition, tyrants. Killers of tyrants are defenders of democracy and therefore deserve immunity, honors, and celebration. This ideology was reinforced by the events of 411–403 B.C. Obvious examples include the public decree of honors for the killer of Phrynichus, a leader of the "Four Hundred," and the heroizing of the "men of Phyle" for having overthrown the "Thirty Tyrants."[22] The Eucrates *nomos* points to the continued salience of the dichotomy through the fourth century.

Why, we may ask, does "tyrant-killing" remain such a vital notion, given that (with the possible and highly contested exception of Hipparchus) no actual tyrant was ever killed by a patriotic assassin in Athens? As I briefly suggested above, a notable feature of the democratic tyrant-killer ideology is that it offers a rare Classical Greek example of *therapeutic* civil conflict (*stasis*) in the polis: a moment in which it is (at least in retrospect) regarded as having been healthy and right for one citizen to run at another with sword drawn and to shed blood in a public place. At Athens, in the difficult years after 403 B.C., the familiar tyrant-killing imagery, which (to judge by preserved vases; see below) seems to have enjoyed a floruit around 400 B.C., allowed a highly troublesome period of *stasis,* which lasted for months and exposed divisions within the citizenry (rural/urban, *dēmos/dunatoi,* cavalry/foot-soldiers), to be reimagined by (albeit imperfect) analogy with the democratic interpretation of the events of 514 B.C. and their aftermath. That is, the *stasis* of 404 could be "misremembered" as having been ended by a single moment of legitimate violence. Reenvisioning the *stasis* of the late fifth century via the satisfying image of the demos' heroes confronting and dispatching the aberrant, illegitimate power holder was among the mechanisms that encouraged forgetfulness regarding the frightening divisions that had emerged among the citizens.[23]

The late fifth-century *stasis* situation was formally ended in Athens at the end of the fifth century not by actual tyrant slaying but by the Amnesty Decree and its attendant rituals, including an oath and a parade to the Acropolis.[24] Through those rituals, the *stasis* became a distinct interlude with a beginning and a formalized ending; the ceremony proclaims that before and after the stasis, *dēmokratia* was the norm. This leads organically to the peaceful image of Demos on the Eucrates *nomos* document relief. In the fourth century, many democrats and some of their critics (e.g., Isocrates) favored an elaborate pseudohistory that imagined the Peisistratid tyranny as a usurpation, an interruption in a continuous democratic tradition extending from Solon (or even Theseus) onwards. But the tyrant-killer ideology was not forgotten, as shown by the provisions of the Eucrates *nomos* itself. Indeed, the years around 403 saw a flourishing of public reverence for Harmodius and Aristogeiton. New honors were voted for their descendants.[25] Iconographic citations of the Critius and Nesiotes group on red-figured vases, unknown since ca. 460–450, suddenly reappear in ca. 400 B.C., most notably in the shield emblem of the Athena Promachus figure on three Panathenaic amphorae.[26] The appearance of the tyrannicides on the Panathenaic vases is especially significant in that (unlike most vases) Panathenaic amphorae were commissioned by the democratic state.

TYRANNICIDE IDEOLOGY OUTSIDE ATHENS

The persuasive power of the democratic Athenian association of tyrant killers with democrats and tyrants with antidemocrats is elucidated by evidence for tyrant-slayer ideology in democratic poleis outside Athens. Even the briefest glance at the broader Greek geographic and chronological context serves to reinforce Sarah Morris' and Kathryn Morgan's point (this volume) that neither the Classical Athenian ideology of tyranny nor the critical intellectual engagement with that ideology existed in an "Athenocentric" cultural vacuum. In the world outside Athens, the Greek experience with full-scale tyranny was not uniquely a phenomenon of the Late Archaic period. In Syracuse, Pontic Heraclea, and Achaea—to cite just the most obvious examples—tyranny was a serious issue in, respectively, the fifth, fourth, and third centuries. A public inscription (*OGIS* 218) offers detailed information on exactly what tyrant killing was deemed to be worth in Hellenistic Ilion. Both material goods and special honors were offered; the extent of these depended on the status (citizen, metic, or slave) of the killer.[27] In the case of a citizen tyrant-slayer, the killer was to receive the following (lines 21–28):

- one talent (of silver) immediately upon committing the act
- a bronze statue of himself, to be erected by the demos
- free meals for life in the *prytaneion*
- a front seat at the public contests, along with public proclamation of his name
- a stipend of two drachmas a day, for life.

The Iliotes' almost obsessive concern with the danger of tyranny recalls Athenian legislation against tyranny, including the Eucrates *nomos*. A tyrant-killing citizen of Ilion could, however, expect to receive much more than Eucrates' bare assurance of freedom from the risk of prosecution for his act. There are no doubt good contextual reasons (largely irrecoverable, given how little we know of the internal history of Hellenistic Ilion) both for the similarity of the concern with tyranny and for the differential reward system. The Athenian situation, while distinctive in many ways, was still part of a broader Greek cultural pattern. Athenian citizens, writers, and artists were well aware of the Hellenic world beyond Attica, a world where political relations were sometimes interestingly similar to those pertaining in Athens, even if at other times they were quite different. By the same token, Athenian history and public iconography might sometimes influence the representation and imagination of tyranny elsewhere in the Greek world.

A public inscription from the polis of Erythrae in Asia Minor, probably roughly contemporary with the Eucrates *nomos* at Athens, brings us back to the question of how politicized debates over tyrant killing might be carried on at the visual level of public iconography.[28] A decree of "the *boulē* and the *dēmos*" of Erythrae mandates repairs to and honors for a statue of a tyrannicide. Evidently the statue took the form of a standing male figure (*andrias:* line 5) holding a sword (*xiphos*). Sometime after the statue was put up (presumably by a prior democratic government), Erythrae experienced a period of oligarchy. According to the decree, the Erythraean oligarchs (οἱ ἐν τῇ ὀλιγαρχίᾳ) had removed the sword from the tyrannicide statue (ἐξεῖλον τὸ ξίφος). Moreover, and most interestingly, the democratic government that erected the inscription attributes a motive to the oligarchs: they removed the sword "thinking that the [statue's] stance was entirely aimed at them" (νομίζοντες καθόλου τὴν στάσιν καθ᾽ αὐτῶν εἶναι, 5–6).[29] The ideological force of this political ascription of motive is clarified by our prior consideration of the Critius and Nesiotes group in Athens and the line from Aristophanes' *Lysistrata:* it seems a fair guess that the Erythraean tyrannicide figure was depicted in the Harmodius stance or some Erythraean gestural analogue thereof.[30]

According to the democrats' implicit argument, this "stance" was identified by all Erythraeans, oligarchs and democrats alike, with the defense of democracy. The democrats' claim that the Erythraean oligarchs had believed that the position taken by the statue, and especially its menacing sword, was "entirely aimed at them" as opponents of democracy. And so, according to the democratic narrative, by removing the sword, the oligarchs had compromised: they left the statue standing and thereby acknowledged the importance of an established public icon. Yet by removing the sword, supposedly aimed at themselves, the oligarchs accepted a bipolar political taxonomy that associated oligarchs, as antidemocrats, with tyrants. The new democratic government of Erythrae, in a series of pointedly ideological moves that underline the power of public images, publicly decreed the restoration of the sword, ordered that the monument be cleaned up, and mandated that the statue be crowned at appropriate times in the ritual calendar. Moreover, the democrats erected the inscription as a record of their own and their opponent's motives and actions. For any viewer potentially confused by iconographic subtleties, the inscription clarified the political point of the statue's stance and suggested that the tyrannicide's sword was indeed forever aimed at oligarchs.

The democrats of Erythrae claimed, in effect, that oligarchs and democrats were in full agreement about the association of tyrant killing with democracy, tyrants with oligarchs. Would the Erythraean oligarchs actually have agreed? Let us assume for the sake of the argument that the oligarchs really did remove the sword from the monument. What might they have meant by doing so? Perhaps, rather than symbolically removing a threat to themselves, the oligarchs were symbolically proclaiming an end to an era of citizen-on-citizen violence, the end of *stasis*. Perhaps they were seeking to make an iconographic statement with a historical point: "Tyrant killing was once a legitimate part of our political life, but it is no longer necessary for any citizen to threaten another with a weapon, because, with the institution of the moderate ('third way') regime of oligarchy, we Erythraeans have put *stasis* behind us. Thus tyranny is no longer a threat." Of course this is just a guess; we have no way of knowing what the Erythraean oligarchs actually meant by the act of disarming the tyrannicide statue. It is nevertheless possible to suppose that rather than accepting the democrats' democracy/tyranny antithesis with its associated assertion that tyrannicide was therapeutic *stasis,* the Erythraean oligarchs might have sought to change the discursive playing field.

"Changing the discourse" (in Osborne's terms, this volume) is, in any event, what dissident Athenian writers sought to do. A self-conscious recognition of the profound symbolic power of the democratic "tyranny ideology" and a consequent recognition of the importance of challenging that ideology are among the factors that led fourth-century Athenian dissidents to depict the demos itself as the "true" tyrant, to refine and develop the idea of a spectrum of regimes, and to rethink the place of *stasis* in political life.

REWRITING THE DEMOCRATIC IDEOLOGY OF TYRANNY: PLATO

By the last years of the fifth century, Athenian intellectuals critical of democracy were confronted with an increasingly coherent and pervasive democratic account of tyranny. Moreover, Plato, at least, was convinced that Greek intellectuals, along with oligarchic activists, had explicitly or implicitly internalized the bipolar conception that equated democracy's opponents with tyrants. This is the context of Plato's *Gorgias* and *Republic* (especially books 1 and 2). Socrates' interlocutors (Polus, Callicles, Thrasymachus) argue that the tyrant, the individual who enjoys the greatest capacity to do whatever he wishes, without social restraint and without fear of punishment, lives the happiest possible life. Both Callicles and Thrasymachus posit that democratic sociopolitical conventions were devised by "the many and the weak" to protect themselves against the naturally superior individual who would, if he could, make himself the master of his fellows. For Plato, only philosophers—people like Socrates, Glaucon, and Adeimantus—were capable of resisting the alluring dream of seeking to become a happy tyrant. He saw that for as long as antidemocratic elites remained seduced by the superficial attractions of the life of the happy tyrant, the bipolar democratic account of tyranny would stand uncontested, and celebration of resistance to tyranny would remain a stable mainstay of democratic culture. Thus the democrats would retain their monopoly on an antityrannical strand in Greek thought that stretched back through Herodotus, to the lyric poetry of Solon, and perhaps ultimately to Homer's negative depiction of Agamemnon in the *Iliad*.[31]

As several other essays in this volume rightly emphasize, Plato was not the first Athenian writer to challenge the political taxonomy that associated opponents of democracy with tyranny. In the fifth century, as Jeffrey Henderson discusses in detail, Aristophanic comedy explicitly linked the demos with tyranny. In a similar vein, Pseudo-Xenophon (*Ath. Pol.*) implicitly resorted to the imagery of tyranny when he suggested that the demos (qua lower classes) was wicked because it alienates from society's true shareholders that which is theirs, especially their private property. Moreover, he claimed, the demos alienates from shareholders their proper social and political positions and their ideological authority. In the current (democratic) *politeia*, it is the demos that levies taxes, distributes offices (via lottery to the "unworthy"), and sets the ideological agenda. By this definition, the demos itself, rather than the antidemocrat, could be construed as holding tyrannical authority, and democracy might be reenvisioned as a form of tyranny. According to this line of argument, legitimate (i.e., nontyrannical) government can arise only when the demos has been deposed from its tyrannical position and political authority returned to those few who actually deserve it and are capable of its appropriate exercise.[32]

The force of pre-Platonic attempts to show that "demos-tyrant" was, however, limited in that the "demos-tyrant," unlike a single individual, cannot literally be assassinated. The argument of Ps.-Xenophon's antidemocratic tract collapses into *aporia* (reaches a dead end) at the point of asking the question, What is to be done?[33] Likewise, the regime of the Thirty, whatever initial constitutional plans may have been harbored by its "moderates," collapsed into an orgy of violence and greed when faced with the task of actually building a legitimate nondemocratic political order.[34] In the aftermath of 404, Plato saw clearly that a new (nondemocratic) political order would have to be focused on education rather than assassination. Comprehensive political change would have to involve reeducation of both the intellectual elite and the mass of ordinary citizens. The elite must be taught to understand and resist their own enslavement by the tyrant-demos, and the people must be "tamed"—taught to relinquish their tyrannical authority over property, offices, and ideology.

The argument of Plato's *Gorgias* concerns what "we should want for ourselves," and his point is that most people are incapable of wishing for what is actually good for them. Gorgias' two students, Polus and Callicles, actively embrace the "happy tyrant" ideal. They are students of Gorgias precisely because they suppose that mastery of rhetoric is the royal road to tyrannical bliss. As we have seen, the standard ideology of tyranny emphasized the tyrant's propensity to alienate from others their goods. Polus at one point adduces the wicked ruler, Archelaus of Macedon, as witness to the happiness of tyrants, emphasizing that they can take whatever they pleased (470d–471d). But Socrates rejects the argument from witnesses, responding: "You keep trying to refute me rhetorically, as those in lawcourts do," by providing a great number of highly esteemed witnesses. Although Polus could no doubt get almost all Athenians, and foreigners too, to agree to his position, this will still not budge Socrates from his "own possession" (*ousia:* i.e., philosophy) or from the truth (471e–472b). The point is that although the tyrant can certainly use his power to seize the material possessions of others, the philosopher remains secure in that no one can deprive him of his "true possession," even if one were to deprive him of his life. Thus Socrates is able to assert that he cannot be harmed in any meaningful way by a tyrant. This means that the philosopher can commit his life to a new sort of therapeutic *stasis*. As we have seen, the demos imagined tyrant killing as a uniquely therapeutic form of *stasis*. Plato's Socrates employs some of the vocabulary of *stasis* to describe his own behavior. Socrates, however, does not seek to kill tyrants but rather to exterminate, through elenctic education, his interlocutor's unhealthy desire for tyrannical authority.

Callicles aspires to become a sort of tyrant in Athens through manipulative leadership of the demos. Socrates proceeds to show him that it is the demos that is the real tyrant in Athens, by playing upon the theme of Callicles' role as a "lover of demos." At *Gorgias* 491d–492c Callicles predicates the happy-tyrant argument on the natural rightness of maximizing his own pleasure, which in turn means maximizing desire so as to maximize satisfaction of desire. But Socrates shows him that the impulse to maximize desire and pleasure logically results in the lifestyle of the penetration-loving homosexual (*kinaidos*) whose "itches" are, in Callicles' case, "scratched" by the demos (494e).[35] Rather than achieving the unrestrained position of the tyrant who can do whatever he pleases, the aspiring political leader ends up as the willing sexual victim of the tyrant-demos. The *kinaidos* metaphor graphically asserts Callicles' inferior relationship relative to the demos. The position Callicles takes up is not that of the bold warrior advancing on his foe but rather that of a submissive inferior. With Socrates' rude image of Callicles, the would-be tyrant, being penetrated by his demos-lover, sword becomes phallus. The familiar political image of "demos-as-tyrant-killer" is reconfigured in the comic imagery of "demos-as-sexual-aggressor."[36] As long as Callicles remains possessed by the dream of the happy tyrant, he will remain enslaved by the dominant democratic ideology.

The point is reinforced later in the dialogue, this time explicitly in the language of tyranny: Socrates initially posits, and Callicles avidly agrees, that if a man does not wish to suffer injustice he must arm himself with powerful resources. The craft (*technē*) of provisioning oneself with security is to rule over the polis by being either an actual tyrant or (Callicles' approach) a loyal comrade (*hetairos*) of the tyrannical *politeia* (510a). Yet security, as it turns out, comes at a great cost: the only way to be safe under the rule of a tyrant is to submit to him, agree with everything he says, be ruled by him, and indeed become as much like him as possible (510b–e); that is to say, to give up one's individual identity and sense of self. Given that the discussion has been centered on politics in democratic Athens, the "tyrant" in question is once again the Athenian demos, and those who submit to the tyrant-demos by becoming just like it are the public speakers, men like Callicles himself.

The distinction Plato draws between "Socratic politics" and the sort of "tyrannical" leadership in the democratic state sought by Callicles is underlined by Callicles' eventual admission (521a–c) that his own political practice, unlike that of Socrates, does not constitute "going to battle with the Athenians" (διαμάχεσθαι Ἀθηναίοις) to improve them like a medical doctor, but rather it is a form of "menial service" aimed at gaining gratitude (charis) and avoiding punishment. Socrates of the Gorgias establishes a key distinction between democratic politics as a form of flattery aimed at pleasure and Socratic politics as a technique of education, by repeatedly employing the language of battles fought within the polis and/or within an individual soul: Socrates' approach to politics is "not via gratification but by battling it through" (μὴ καταχαριζόμενον ἀλλὰ διαμαχόμενον, 513d). The root contrast drawn here is between charis-seeking and battle, which we soon recognize as an analogy to the contrast between charis-seeking and medical treatment (therapeia: e.g., 513e).[37] Paralleling the democratic ideology of tyrant killing as a moment of "therapeutic stasis," Socrates of the Gorgias correlates therapy and education with "doing battle" with one's fellow citizens, and so politics becomes a way of "curing" them. Socrates teaches active resistance to ideological mystification, which is therapeutic for the individual citizen and for the polis. But although Socratic politikē technē is imagined via the metaphor of stasis, a Socratic "battle within the polis" does not result in the death either of the tyrant-demos or of the tyrant-demos' orator-servants. Rather, the desired outcome is a new disposition, an elimination of the tyrannical impulse. Therapeutic stasis becomes a metaphor for Socrates' educative mission. We are, in a sense, invited to replace the central democratic image of the tyrant killer's healing and death-dealing sword with the Apology's image of the gadfly's tonic "sting."

The issue of stasis and tyrannicide recurs in the Republic. At a pivotal moment in the dialogue, Socrates posits that for a truly excellent polis to come into being, either philosophers must be kings or kings and rulers must truly philosophize (473c–e). But this bold vision will not be realized without at least metaphorical violence. Glaucon warns Socrates that his proposal will be attacked by many distinguished people (ἐπὶ σὲ πάνυ πολλούς τε καὶ οὐ φαύλους). They will immediately pull off their cloaks, and, stripped naked, grab up whatever weapons lie to hand, "rushing forward avidly as if undertaking noteworthy deeds."[38] So Socrates had better be able to "defend himself by logos" (473e–474a).

This vivid passage adopts the familiar imagery of the canonical Athenian iconography of tyrannicide: the many distinguished folk will strip, take up arms, and rush forward avidly, imitating the kinetic energy and the heroic nudity of the sword-bearing tyrannicides of the Critius and Nesiotes group. The armed and naked men, anticipated by Glaucon as opponents of a new and quasi-monarchical element in the polis, are counterparts of democratic "tyrant killers." Their hostile response to Socrates' revolutionary proposal accords with the oath sworn by the Athenians in 410/09 to oppose the overthrow of democracy by whatever means necessary. Notably, however, it is not just ordinary citizens that Glaucon imagines as rushing at Socrates—although many (*polloi*), they are "not undistinguished" (*ou phauloi*). The would-be assassins who misrecognize Socrates as a would-be tyrant are members of the elite, but they have internalized the democratic account of "the tyrant and what we should do about him." We might say that in opposing Socrates' proposal for philosopher-rulers, they join Aristophanes' chorus of old Athenians, taking up their stand in the Agora next to Aristogeiton, determined that no one will ever set up a tyranny over them. The *Republic* passage underlines, through the familiar topoi of the tyrannicide ideology, the extent of reeducation that will be necessary before philosopher-rule could be welcomed, even as an ideal and even among the elite.

Yet later in the dialogue, the optimistic reader is offered reason to hope that something like the ideal of the philosopher-ruled city Plato called Callipolis might be attained. Socrates suggests that while difficult to achieve, the rule of the philosopher-king was not impossible in practice (οὐ γὰρ ἀδύνατος γενέσθαι, οὐδ᾽ ἡμεῖς ἀδύνατα λέγομεν, 499d). The gentlemen who Glaucon had imagined rushing at Socrates with weapons drawn will be forced to admit the logical force of the argument for philosophical rule (501c). Even the masses could come to accept such a regime, if they could just be taught what a philosopher really was (499d–500b). The potential depth of popular trust in true philosopher-leaders is suggested at the end of book 7 (540e–541a), where *stasis* imagery once again recurs, although in a very different form. For the transition from the old, corrupt regime to a new philosopher-led regime to be accomplished most easily and quickly within an existing polis, the philosopher-rulers will banish all citizens over age 10 to outlying agricultural districts; the banished evidently are expected to concur and head off gracefully, leaving their children behind.

The situation Plato envisions here recalls a common pattern of Greek civil strife, well known from (e.g.) Thucydides' depiction of the *stasis* at Corcyra

(3.70–82): when a faction takes over the main town of a polis, the opposing faction retreats to strongholds in the countryside. That pattern had recently been played out in Athens, when in 404 the Thirty held the city, and the democrats held the rural stronghold of Phyle. Yet in this part of the *Republic* the terrors of *stasis* have been thoroughly domesticated. The demos gives up its urban possessions and progeny without a struggle, evidently seeing that these sacrifices are preconditions to the therapeutic extermination of its own corrupted beliefs and practices. To realize Callipolis, the demos is, in effect, alienated from every attribute that a greedy human tyrant might desire: goods, homes, children, hope for the future. Yet the division of the city into alienated rural population and privileged city dwellers is imagined as voluntary. Moreover, the change, once accomplished, is permanent and irrevocable.

In Plato's text, realizing Callipolis requires first that its founders survive a metaphoric tyrannicide and then that most of the polis' adult population accepts—once and for all—living conditions ordinarily associated with tyranny and *stasis*. Yet once in place, the society of the *Republic*'s Callipolis, predicated on the strict education of the Guard class and a set of "noble lies," eliminates all possible sources of conflict within the state and within the souls of its individual members. Callipolis' Guards could not be alienated from that which was "their own," since ownership (of family and goods) was either nonexistent or communal. The education of Guards ensures that they treat the lower orders strictly in accordance with justice. The censorship of literature in the ideal city ensures that Callipolis' residents never learn about the existence of *stasis*. Thus, Socrates' attempt to exterminate the tyrannical impulse in the souls of his interlocutors through reasoned argument reaches its end point in Callipolis, with the elimination of any possible motive or means for *stasis*. By the end of the *Republic*, Plato has led his reader to a position that is significantly different from that of Socrates as he is presented in the *Apology* and *Gorgias* (with his imagery of stings and battle) and, a fortiori, from the citizens of Athens itself, who kept the possibility of "therapeutic *stasis* within the polis" before themselves through public iconography and patriotic tyrant-killer tales of the sort objected to by Thucydides.

Plato's conception of politics is obviously very different from that of Athenian democrats. Here I underline two differences particularly salient in terms of the ideology of tyranny. First, contrary to the attempt of Athenian democrats to define a bipolar (democratic/tyrannical) political universe, Plato (like Aristotle and other fourth-century political thinkers) describes a wide spectrum of political options. In the *Republic's* hierarchical taxonomy of regimes (Callipolis, timocracy, oligarchy, democracy, tyranny) Callipolis defines the best-possible state, tyranny, the worst. But timocracy, oligarchy, and democracy are distinct (if, after the perfection of Callipolis, unsavory) political alternatives. Second, and equally important, is the imagination of change. In Plato's scheme, Callipolis, once achieved, remains static, existing in a steady state of excellence. The rules are fixed, and change is regarded as not only undesirable but disastrous. As soon as a mistake is made, as soon as change is introduced, the conditions of justice are destroyed, Callipolis is irretrievably lost, and the society is condemned to degenerate through a cycle of ever-worsening political regimes, ending in the horrors of tyranny (*Republic* books 8–9).

The democratic vision of political change was, as we have seen, quite different from Plato's, at once more pessimistic about the likelihood and frequency of serious political mishap and more optimistic about the capacity of existing political values and practices to survive mishaps. Tyrants are imagined as likely to arise, but they are also capable of being resisted and eventually overcome. For the Athenian, Iliote, and Erythraean *dēmoi* alike, the figure of the tyrant killer was thought to be salutary. *Stasis,* at least in fourth-century Athenian democratic political thought, is simply an interval, an interruption in a continuous democratic narrative. As the Eucrates law of 337/36 demonstrates, the moral authority of the demos is imagined as extending through periods of oligarchic or tyrannical rule; the demos is regarded as capable of restoring itself in the aftermath of a healthy moment of tyrant-slaying violence. This robust democratic optimism may go a ways toward explaining the resilience of democracy in Hellenistic Athens and in the poleis of Asia Minor, in the face of overwhelming Macedonian royal power.[39]

REENVISIONING THE DEMOCRATIC IDEOLOGY OF TYRANNY: DEXILEOS

If the argument I have developed above is along the right lines, we might hope to find iconographic evidence for the debate about the relationship between democracy, *stasis,* tyrants, and tyrant killers. Linking Classical works of art to specific political positions or even to general political sensibilities is fraught with difficulty, but it is not an inherently absurd undertaking. We have no material traces of the tombstone of Critias, the leader of the Thirty at Athens who died fighting the democrats at the decisive battle of Mounichia. But according to a scholion to Aeschines, *Against Timarchus* (DK 88A13), his tombstone featured a relief depicting personified Oligarchia, brandishing a torch and setting fire to Demokratia. The monument also reportedly featured an epigram: "This is the memorial (*mnēma*) of good men (*andres agathoi*) who, for a short while, restrained the hubris of the accursed demos."[40] It is tempting to speculate about the artistic sources of this monument's iconography: might it have drawn on the imagery of Dike (Justice) assaulting Adikia (Injustice)? an Amazonomachy? a city siege? It is equally tempting to seek significance in the apparent dissonance between the murderous violence depicted in the relief and the language of restraint employed in the epigram — perhaps a reflection of two phases, quasi-constitutional and openly savage,[41] of Critias' brief career as ruler?

Finally, it is surely significant that on the gravestone of the leader of the gang Athenian democrats called the Thirty Tyrants, it is Oligarchia and not Tyrannia who is igniting Demokratia. Critias' tombstone, as described by the scholiast, rejects the bipolar democratic reading of democracy's enemies as tyrants. Unfortunately, there is no way to establish that the monument described by the scholiast was ever in fact erected. But the (undatable) story of Critias' memorial, whatever its imagined iconography, points to Athenian tombstones as possible iconographic sites of ideological contestation. Moreover, it points to the aftermath of the rule of the Thirty as a particularly "hot" ideological era. As we have seen, this same era saw a recrudescence of tyrannicide iconography in Athenian vase painting. Accepting that we should not expect to discover anything nearly so explicit as an oligarch's tombstone depicting Demokratia in flames, we might, following the scholiast's pointers, find it worthwhile to look for more subtle responses to the democratic ideology of tyranny in the iconography of Attic tombstones of the decades around 404 B.C.

I have suggested that the memory and imagery of Athens' "tyrant slayers" were especially in the forefront at the turn of the fifth and fourth centuries. Moreover, on the basis of the passage in Aristophanes' *Lysistrata,* I posited that the "Harmodius stance" — warrior moving right to left (rather than the usual, heroic, left to right), with right sword-arm cocked behind the head preparatory to delivering the "Harmodius blow" — came to serve as a shorthand visual cue to the democratic tyrant-killer ideology. There is some danger of finding a tyrannicide lurking behind every raised right arm. But the demonstrable Athenian concern with tyranny and tyrannicides in the late fifth and fourth centuries renders it more plausible that visual citations of the

Harmodius stance during that era were read by contemporary viewers as something more than politically innocent artistic conventions.

Athenian artists did in fact quote Critius and Nesiotes' Harmodius in designing late fifth- and fourth-century funerary sculpture. A nice example is the fourth-century funeral relief of Stratocles son of Procles (Fig. 8.5; Clairmont 1993: 2.217), portraying a hoplite (presumably Stratocles himself) assuming Harmodius' stance while preparing to strike a fallen foe. As Christoph Clairmont suggests, "The [Harmodios] motif is well known from the group of tyrant-slayers which is no doubt reminisced here."[42] In the Stratocles Relief, a figure (presumably Stratocles himself) whose face and dress offer some similarities to Demos of Eucrates' *nomos* (mature, bearded, drapery over left shoulder, chest exposed) takes on the active role of Harmodius. It is perhaps not too much to guess that an Athenian looking at this monument was invited to read Stratocles' military service as having served the same role in preserving democratic Athens as Harmodius' assassination of the tyrant, although how explicit that claim was meant to be, on the part of artist or commissioner of the tombstone, necessarily remains obscure.

Perhaps the most remarkable visual citation of Harmodius in later Athenian art is the Albani Relief (Fig. 8.6; Clairmont 1993: 2.131). Certainly funerary in nature, it remains a matter of debate whether it is a public or a private monument, and it has been variously dated from ca. 430 through the 390s.[43] Here, a young (unbearded), lightly draped cavalryman has just dismounted from his horse and prepares to dispatch a fallen, mostly nude youth with the Harmodius blow.[44] The metamorphosis of Harmodius into an Athenian cavalryman introduces an interesting wrinkle, in light of the strongly aristocratic associations of the Athenian cavalry. The relationship between cavalry and democracy became that much more fraught after 404, due to the active cooperation by the Athenian cavalrymen with the reign of the Thirty.[45] Whatever its exact date, it seems likely that the monument's citation of tyrannicide iconography sought to associate potentially politically suspect elite cavalrymen with the defense of democracy.

In an admittedly speculative reconstruction, Clairmont suggests that the Albani Relief supported a surviving inscribed frieze listing the Athenian cavalry casualties of 394/93 B.C.: ten horsemen and a phylarch lost at the Battles of Corinth and Coroneia (National Museum of Greece inv. 754 = *GHI* II.104). Since the inscription was authorized by the Athenian state, Clairmont's reconstruction would make the Albani Relief part of a public monument of

Fig. 8.5. Stratocles relief. Clairmont, *CAT* 2.217. John H. and Earnestine A.
Payne Fund, courtesy of Museum of Fine Arts, Boston. Reproduced with
permission. ©2000 Museum of Fine Arts, Boston. All rights reserved.

the mid 390s, honoring the horsemen who died in defense of the democratic
polity. In conformity to the established practices of democratic Athenian
public burial, the deceased cavalrymen of the 390s were listed individually
on the monument frieze, but the individuality of the fallen warriors was subsumed to the value of community, as emphasized in their common burial and
by their common grave monument.

One of the ten dead horsemen listed on the inscribed frieze of 394/93 is Dexileos son of Lysanias of the deme Thoricus. Dexileos' family evidently decided that the state's communal commemoration was not enough. Shortly after his death and public burial, Dexileos' family erected a large and splendid cenotaph monument in his honor in the Ceramicus cemetery, complete with a sculptural relief and an inscription (Fig. 8.7).[46] The popularity of the tyrant-killer iconography in the 390s is confirmed by an early fourth-century red-figure oinochoe found by excavators in Dexileos' cenotaph precinct (Fig. 8.8).[47] The vase fragment depicts the Critius and Nesiotes monument itself, with Harmodius to the front in his distinctive stance, although, as Emily Vermeule pointed out in her original publication of the fragment, his sword looks more like a limp rag than a real weapon. Aristogeiton's sword is hidden behind his own right hip. This vase, along with four others of the same early fourth-century date but featuring conventional scenes recalling the Anthesteria "coming of age" festival, was apparently deposited by the family of Dexileos in his cenotaph at the time the monument was consecrated.

What, if any, ideological significance ought we to attach to this cluster of

Fig. 8.6. Albani relief. Clairmont, *CAT* 2.131. By permission of Villa Albani Torlonia, Rome (Inv. 985).

Fig. 8.7. Dexileos relief (394/93 B.C.). By permission of Deutsches Archaeologische
Institut, Athens (Inv. P 1130).

Fig. 8.8. Oinochoe fragment depicting tyrannicide monument, ca. 390 B.C.
Henry Lillie Pierce Fund, courtesy of Museum of Fine Arts, Boston.
Reproduced with permission. ©2001 Museum of Fine Arts, Boston.
All rights reserved.

artifacts? A possible pointer is offered by Dexileos' peculiar cenotaph inscription (*IG* II² 6217 = *GHI* II.105), which, surprisingly, lists both his birth and death dates: 414/13 (archon Teisander) and 394/93 (archon Euboulides). It is the only known Attic funerary inscription to do so. Glenn Bugh, following a conjecture originally made by Colin Edmonson, plausibly argues that the birth date was added to exculpate the horseman Dexileos from the possible charge of prooligarchic activities during the reign of the Thirty. The prominent birthdate proclaims that Dexileos was simply too young to have ridden against the democrats at Phyle.[48]

Dexileos' relatives might well have been especially concerned to make some sort of ideological disclaimer because they chose to erect a remarkable, highly visible, and iconographically striking monument to decorate the new cenotaph enclosure. This sort of ostentatious private commemoration had been out of fashion in democratic Athens—and elsewhere in Greece—for a century or more. It might well (and might rightly) be seen as offering a private response, even a covert challenge by a wealthy family to the democratic practices of commemorating fallen warriors as equals, via funeral oration, common burial, laconic casualty lists, and communal sculptural reliefs.[49]

The challenge would be especially stark if we follow Clairmont in imagining the Albani Relief as a public monument of 394/93: the iconography of the Albani and Dexileos reliefs is clearly interrelated (whether directly or via a common source). I suggested above that the visual quotation of the Harmodius stance in the Albani Relief should be read as asserting that the cavalry defended democracy. The Dexileos inscription, with its implicit claim that "I was too young to be an oligarch, and I died defending democratic Athens at Corinth," might be seen in a similar light, as an attempt to deflect demotic jealousy and ire at ostentatious private self-advertisement by the family of an aristocrat. This would be an acknowledgment, at the level of the inscribed text, of democratic ideological authority. The oinochoe dedication, with its portrayal of the tyrannicide monument might be (and has been) read in the same general light, as making a philodemocratic statement of some sort.[50]

Yet the relief's iconography adds another level of complexity. As Brunilde Ridgway has noted, the Dexileos Relief is distinctive (although not unparalleled; cf. again, the Albani Relief) in depicting the "heroic" horseman (presumably Dexileos himself) who prepares to skewer his fallen foe as draped, and his defeated enemy as nude. Ridgway suggests that this may be an example of a reversal of the ordinary association of nudity: here, rather than heroism, nudity may reflect the helpless position of the defeated warrior.[51] Yet for our purposes, it is even more remarkable that the nude fallen soldier quite faithfully maintains the familiar Harmodius stance of swordarm overhead, even in collapse, although this time the Harmodius blow is offered by a dying man as a futile response to the mounted enemy who is spearing him.[52] The nude fallen warrior clutches a shield (rather than a scabbard) in his left hand, but his shield arm (like that of Stratocles, Fig. 8.5) is draped with a chlamys and thereby recalls the draped arm of the otherwise nude Aristogeiton figure of the Critius and Nesiotes group. If the Albani Relief (whatever its exact date) presents to its viewer "Harmodius as victorious Athenian cavalryman," thus celebrating the defense of democracy by the Athenian horsemen, then it is tempting to see in the private Dexileos Relief a metaphoric overthrow by the aristocratic cavalryman of the democratic tyrannicide heroes and so, one might suppose, the overthrow of democracy itself.

The Dexileos Relief's visual quotation of the Critius and Nesiotes group stretches the canonical representation almost to the breaking point. Indeed, if we did not know about the dedication at the cenotaph of an oinochoe depicting the tyrannicide monument, the association of the Dexileos Relief with the Critius and Nesiotes group would be harder to defend. But the oinochoe was deposited at the cenotaph, strong evidence that the people who commissioned the monument were acutely aware of tyrant-killer iconography. Given the oinochoe dedication, and given the similarity of the iconography of the Dexileos monument to other near-contemporary sculptural citations of the tyrannicide monument, the Dexileos citation may be taken as intentional. If intentional, in the atmosphere of the 390s, it could hardly be innocent of political meaning.

Assuming, as I suppose we must, that those who commissioned the Dexileos cenotaph were sensitive to tyrannicide iconography, we may guess that they anticipated that similarly sensitive viewers would respond, one way or another, to it. So how might an early fourth-century Athenian witness read the Dexileos monument, taken as a whole? Might he or she see a visual narrative of an alternative, counterfactual, "aristocratic-utopian" Athenian history, one in which the *stasis* of 404 had resulted not in democratic restoration following the humiliating rout of the pro-Thirty cavalry in a snowstorm but rather in the aristocratic cavalry's therapeutic destruction of the democratic aspirations of the "men of Phyle"?

Yet the Dexileos inscription militates against such a straightforward antidemocratic reading. The juxtaposition of the ostentatious private monument, its subtly subversive iconography, and its subtly defensive inscription, with their potentially clashing ideological messages, suggests that reading the Dexileos monument, even for a contemporary Athenian, was no simple matter. Should we then regard the Dexileos monument as so semiotically overdetermined as to be ideologically illegible — to us or to its contemporaries? Perhaps not, if we regard it in light of Isocrates' highly self-conscious "double-pointed speeches" (*logoi amphiboloi*).[53] Kathryn Morgan (this volume) emphasizes the multiplicity of Isocrates' implied audiences. Isocrates' carefully crafted, deliberately ambiguous texts explicitly offered at least two readings, depending on the reader's sophistication and political tastes (in the case of the *Panathenaicus,* a pro- or an anti-Spartan reading). Unlike an Isocratean didactic text, the sculptural monument does not teach us how to read by offering a convenient meta-rhetoric. But with Isocrates' "lesson" in mind, we might view the Dexileos monument as "amphibolic." In common with political texts of the same period, the monument can be read as hovering in the field of tension created by the powerful democratic ideology and a powerful elite impulse to dissent from that ideology. Like an Isocratean *amphibolos logos*, the monument seems to be an artifact specifically designed to be read differently by different audiences. Like an Isocratean text (and unlike the Erythrae tyrannicide monument with its clarifying inscription), it resists simple appropriation by any particular political tendency. But that resistance to interpretive appropriation does not render it innocent of political meaning.

MIXED MEDIA

The "amphibolic" reading I have suggested for Dexileos' monument is a far cry from the straightforward, oligarchic reading the scholiast offered of Critias' tombstone, and deliberately so. Thinking in terms of Isocrates' craftsmanly and self-conscious ambiguity might provide an entrée into a way of viewing some Greek works of art that would take into account the sort of ideological negotiations that scholars have traced in Greek texts.[54] There are other Attic tombstones in which a defeated soldier struggles to respond to his attacker with the Harmodius blow: for example, the very beautiful although fragmentary Clairmont 1993: 2.230, which is very close iconographically to the Dexileos Relief; the cruder, and perhaps later Clairmont 1993: 2.251; or a recently published relief fragment tentatively identified as a public monument of ca. 338 B.C.[55] A better understanding of these reliefs might help us to read more into other Attic reliefs depicting triumphant draped horsemen and fallen nude infantrymen who do not offer the Harmodius blow: for example, National Museum of Greece inv. 2744, a public monument again commemorating the fallen of 394/3, or a striking square base found near the Academy depicting three perspectives of the same general battle scene (Clairmont 1993: 2.213).

The tyrant-slayer motif encourages us to explore the close interaction of ideology and dissent and of text and image. Tracing the complicated and criss-crossing system of cultural references, a task this paper has only begun, requires moving across a variety of media and between various genres: monumental sculpture and vase painting; comic poetry, history and philosophy; inscribed public decrees; public and private funerary and documentary reliefs; erudite marginalia reporting monuments that may or may not have existed. It leads us to traverse long periods of history and to move outside Athens. The point of seeking to trace the web of references across media, genres, time, and space is the chance to glimpse the growing density of associations that elite and ordinary Athenians (and other Greeks, as suggested by extra-Attic epigraphic traces) brought to the problem of "thinking the tyrant." As the political and cultural resonances grew richer, the skilled interlocutor—whether artist or writer or (with Aristophanes' chorus) gesturer—could say more, in different registers and potentially to various audiences, with increasingly subtle allusions. Such circumstances demand both imagination and interpretive modesty on the part of the modern reader. At best we will catch only some references, and we should certainly never hope to fix the "full and final" political meaning of any given citation of the visual or literary canons.

The evolving democratic discourse on tyrannicide depended on both stability and change, on both "being" and "becoming." It required the continuity over time of a core ideological association of tyrant killing with salutary defense of the democratic regime. But (absent serious challenges by genuine tyrants) the democratic discourse on tyranny risked ossification. It gained the capacity to extend its imaginative scope only when faced by substantial dissident responses. That dissident response might be at the level of text, of iconographic representation, or of political action, or, sometimes, all three at once. If the oligarchs of Erythrae had never sought to change the discourse by taking away a tyrannicide's sword, then the restored democrats would have had no chance to counter-claim that those who removed the sword had revealed that it was pointed at themselves. Although we should never forget how nasty Greek politics could become in practice, it is in such high-stakes ideological debates that Greek political life reveals its semiotic versatility and intellectual vitality.

Notes

[1] On Athenian dissidents, cf. Ober 1998. I received helpful responses to earlier versions of this chapter from audiences at UCLA, the University of Toronto, University of Tel Aviv, Johns Hopkins University, and Cornell University. Special thanks are due to W. A. P. Childs and Ralf von den Hoff for help with iconographic questions; to Vincent Farenga for his thoughtful commentary; and to Richard Neer for sharing an advance draft of parts of his dissertation (now Neer 2002) and for his insightful comments on an earlier draft of this chapter. Unless otherwise noted, all translations are by the author.

[2] The argument for "democratic hegemony" is made in Ober 1989: 332–339 and the essays collected in Ober 1996. I suggest in Ober 1998 that democratic ideology is best regarded as "quasi-hegemonic" in light of the extent of opportunities for public and private dissent of various sorts. The term "community of interpretation" is borrowed from Fish 1980.

[3] Because proponents of what I call "democratic ideology" and the "dissident sensibility" agreed that tyrants are wicked does not, of course, imply that all Athenians thought so. The Athenian demos (as depicted in, e.g., Aristophanes, Thucydides book 6, and the Eucrates *nomos* discussed below) and Plato (in *Gorgias* and *Republic*) agreed that there were in fact men in Athens who regarded the tyrant's life as the pinnacle of human happiness, desired tyranny for themselves, and would seek to seize it if given a chance. It is important to avoid supposing that the "democratic/dissident" debate adequately maps the political terrain of classical Athens. It is a debate joined by those who accept that justice is something like "the common good" and so leaves out self-interested and self-aggrandizing types who sincerely regard their individual and personal advantage as the only good worth pursuing. It is worth noting that Socrates of the *Gorgias* contrasts Callicles' moral beliefs to certain moral convictions (488e–89b: it is preferable to suffer than to do wrong; 491d–e: *enkrateia* [self-control] is a virtue) held commonly by Socrates and "the many."

[4] Osborne (this volume) rightly emphasizes that after 412 both oligarchy and "moderate" variants of democracy were granted more serious analytic attention as "third ways" between "radical" democracy and tyranny. But he seems to me to overstate the "sea change" and "transformation" of Athenian political ideology and practice in the era 412–403 and to underestimate the continued salience of tyranny as defining "the worst case" in both the democratic and dissident political imagination in the fourth century. Tyranny continued to hold an undisputed position (e.g., for Plato, *Republic,* for whom it is the final point in the degeneration of regimes and for Aristotle, *Politics,* for whom it is the worst of the "incorrect" regimes) as the undoubted bottom of the political barrel. Consequently, the label "tyrant" retained its bite, even as oligarchy and "moderate" democracy gained (among intellectuals) greater conceptual clarity.

[5] This peculiarity is addressed by several other essays in this volume: Raaflaub, Kallet, Seaford, Henderson, and Osborne. Henderson notes the tendency to equate tyranny and all forms of antidemocratic activity, citing Andoc. 1.96–98, as well as the evidence of comedy.

[6] The Critius and Nesiotes group: Taylor 1991; Fehr 1984; Brunnsåker 1971; Castriota 1997; further bibliography: Neer 2002. I leave aside the unanswerable question of the motives of those who erected the original group sculpted by Antenor, whoever they were, whatever the Antenor group's pre-480 date, and whatever its precise form. For further discussion and bibliography on the Antenor group, see Raaflaub (this volume), who also cites the evidence for the formal honors offered by the state to the tyrannicides and their descendents.

[7] Vincent Farenga, formal comments on an earlier draft of this paper, March 28, 1998.

[8] Fehr 1984: 35–38, on the active unity of purpose and its democratic associations.

[9] On history making: Spinosa, Flores, and Dreyfus 1997.

[10] The Copenhagen Painter has now been associated with the Syriscus Painter: Neer 2002. The three (or perhaps four) vase paintings depicting the tyrannicide from the years 475–450 and the five from around 400 B.C. were originally studied as a group in Beazley 1948; their connection with democratic and elitist sensibilities is sensitively examined by Neer 2002.

[11] Cf. Thuc. 6.58.2: Hippias searches Panathenaic marchers for *encheiridia* after the assassination of Hipparchus and holds those with daggers guilty, since it was the tradition to march in the procession only with shield and spear. Thucydides' account was challenged by [Arist.] *Ath. Pol.* 18.4, as anachronistic.

[12] Hdt. 5.55–57.1 (noting that Hippias was the tyrant, that Hipparchus was his brother, and that the tyranny lasted for another four years, and became harsher, after the assassination); Thuc. 1.20.2, 6.53.3–6.60.1; [Arist.] *Ath. Pol.* 18. For further discussion of these passages, see Raaflaub, this volume.

[13] Harmodius blow: Shefton 1960. Cf. the stage directions added to the translation, in Sommerstein 1990: ad loc. *"Striking attitude, right leg thrust forward, right arm raised as if swinging back sword."* I am tempted to add *"with cloak thrown off"* on the strength of Pl. *Resp.* 473e–474a; see below. On the importance of tyrant language and examples from history in this play, see Henderson, this volume.

[14] Villa Giulia vase: Beazley 1948: 26 with fig. 1.

[15] The relevant texts (cited in n. 12, above) are conveniently collected in Stanton 1990.

[16] For further discussion of this passage, see Ober 1998: 359–360.

[17] Raaflaub, this volume.

[18] Meritt 1952: 355–359 = *SEG* 12.87. For a detailed discussion of the relief, its artistic sources, and bibliography, see Lawton 1995: 99–100 (no. 38, with pl. 20).

[19] The Demophantus Decree: Andoc. 1.96–98, with Raaflaub and Osborne, this volume.

[20] And so, with Osborne, this volume, something very substantial has indeed changed within discourse and practice, but I would contend that those changes must be read in the context of some very substantial ideological continuities.

[21] On freedom, equality, security as the core triad of Athenian democratic values, see Ober 1996: 86–88.

[22] Honors for the killer of Phrynicus: ML no. 85. The assassin is not actually described as a "tyrant killer" but is rewarded for having "done what was necessary." Krentz 1982: 16, n. 2 on the early association of the terminology of "tyranny" with the Thirty. Osborne, this volume, (1) points to efforts on the part of late fifth- and fourth-century Athenian intellectuals to define a "third way" and (2) suggests that those efforts found expression in constitutional reforms. The first point is certainly true, and the second is, I believe, very likely (see, further, Ober 1998: 369–373). But I do not see that there is any evidence that Athenian "official ideology" ever gave up on the "primacy of tyranny" as democracy's antithesis, or that Athenian intellectuals ever abandoned the "primacy of tyranny" as the worst-case *politeia*. So, once again, I resist Osborne's argument for a "sea change" comparable to the revolutionary era of the late sixth century.

[23] On the role of forgetting in the Athenian response to *stasis,* see Loraux 1997. For a detailed discussion of the ideological response to the *stasis,* see Wolpert 2002.

[24] Rituals ending the stasis of 404: B. S. Strauss 1985: 69–72.

[25] See, further, Taylor 1991: 1–5.

[26] Brunnsåker 1971: 104–105, no. 6, pl. 23.6. Simon and Hirmer 1981: 157, color pl. LI. Further discussion in Neer 2002.

[27] *OGIS* no. 218. My thanks to John Ma for bringing inscriptions from Troy and Erythrae to my attention.

[28] Dittenberger in *SIG* 284 with Gauthier 1982. Date: ca. 334 B.C., according to Dittenberger ad loc., on the grounds that Alexander in that year mandated that all the poleis of Asia Minor would be democracies (Arr. *Anab.* 1.18.1–2; *GHI* II no. 192, lines 3–4). One might legitimately say that oligarchy at Erythrae did not fail but was overthrown. But we still need an answer for why Alexander reversed Philip's general policy of promoting oligarchy in allied cities. The easiest answer would seem to be that Alexander put in place the government he supposed would be most stable (ergo, least troublesome to him) because it was most in tune with what the Greeks of Asia Minor wanted. N.B. the similarity of formulaic language between this inscription (ἀγαθῆ τύχη δεδόχθαι τῆ βουλῆ καὶ τῷ δήμῳ [with good fortune, be it resolved by the Council and the demos]) and the Eucrates *nomos* (ἀγαθῆ τύχη τοῦ δήμου τοῦ Ἀθηναίων· δεδόχθαι τοῖς νομοθέταις [with good fortune of the demos of the Athenians, be it resolved by the *nomothetai*]).

[29] ἐπειδὴ οἱ ἐν τῆ ὀλιγαρχίᾳ τῆς εἰκόνος τῆς Φιλίτου, τοῦ ἀποκτείναντος τὸν τύραννον, τοῦ ἀνδριάντος ἐξεῖλον τὸ ξίφος, νομίζοντες καθόλου τὴν στάσιν καθ᾽ αὐτῶν εἶναι.

[30] On the Harmodius and Aristogeiton imagery on coins and statuary outside Athens, see Fehr 1984: 7–8 with ills. 2–3.

[31] The pro- and antityrannical strands in earlier Greek thought: see Seaford, this volume. Cf. Raaflaub and Kallet, both this volume and responding to Connor 1977. On Herodotus' very complex depiction of tyranny and tyrants, see Dewald, this volume.

[32] On demos as tyrant in Aristophanes, see Henderson, this volume. As Raaflaub (this volume) points out, "Demos-tyrannos" appears in fifth-century literature explicitly in comedy, implicitly in literature critical of democracy. Kallet (this volume) discusses

some of the implicit fifth-century and explicit (critical) fourth-century associations of demos with tyrant. On Ps.-Xenophon as a critic of democracy, see Ober 1998: 14–23.

[33] Ps.-Xenophon's *aporia:* Ober 1998: 23–27.

[34] Possible constitutional-reform plans of the Thirty: Krentz 1982; Osborne, this volume.

[35] The *kinaidos* as an Athenian social type: Winkler 1990. Kahn 1983: 105–107 and Wardy 1996: 81–82 discuss the social, political, and personal ramifications for Callicles of assimilation to the *kinaidos.*

[36] Image of demos as passive/active lover: Aristoph. *Knights,* with comments of Nightingale 1995: 187–190, who suggests that in this passage Plato is "harnessing comedy's 'voice of criticism'" (190). Cf. Pericles' injunction in the Funeral Oration to Athenian citizens to "become the lover" (*erastēs*) of the polis, with discussion of Monoson 1994.

[37] Cf. Morgan, this volume, pp. 185–186 with n. 17.

[38] οἶον ῥίψαντας τὰ ἱμάτια, γυμνοὺς λαβόντας ὅτι ἑκάστῳ παρέτυχεν ὅπλον, θεῖν διατεταμένους ὡς θαυμάσια ἐργασομένους.

[39] Hellenistic democracy: Gauthier 1993; Habicht 1997; Ma 1999.

[40] μνῆμα τόδ᾿ ἐστ᾿ ἀνδρῶν ἀγαθῶν, οἳ τὸν κατάρατον δῆμον Ἀθηναίων ὀλίγον χρόνον ὕβριος ἔσχον.

[41] See Osborne, this volume.

[42] Stratocles son of Procles relief = Clairmont 1993: 2.217. Quote: Clairmont 1993: 2.157.

[43] Albani Relief: Clairmont 1993: 2.131, with discussion of date and speculative reconstruction as a public monument of 394/3; Hölscher 1973: 109–110 with n. 529.

[44] Cf. Stupperich 1994: 99: "The victor in the Albani Relief and the victorious Stratocles . . . who are both shown contrary to the usual direction of the victor as moving from right to left, adopt the stance of Harmodios."

[45] Cavalry and the Thirty: Bugh 1988: 120–153.

[46] The Dexileos monument: I. Morris 1992: 143–144; Ridgway 1997: 3–7, 162; Hölscher 1973: 102–103, 108.

[47] The vase: Fig. 8.8 (see Ober and Hedrick 1993: 57 for color photograph). Its excavation context and date: Vermeule 1970. Further discussion and bibliography: Ajootian 1998.

[48] Bugh 1988: 139.

[49] I. Morris 1992: 128–144 discusses the evolving size and splendor of Attic funerary monuments.

[50] Vermeule 1970: 105–106 suggests democratic associations of the (private) oinochoe dedication.

[51] Ridgway 1997: 6–7.

[52] Shefton 1960: 174 cites the Dexileos Relief as a primary example of the "defensive use" of the Harmodius blow. The earlier iconographic depictions of a fallen warrior in the

defensive Harmodius position cited by Shefton, mostly Amazonomachae, are from vase paintings.

[53] Isocratean *logoi amphiboloi:* Isoc. 12.240, with Bons 1993.

[54] Neer 2002 attempts a similar task, focusing on Attic vase painting of ca. 510–450 B.C. Texts as negotiating competing social and political ideologies: e.g., Ober 1989; I. Morris 1996; Kurke 1999.

[55] Bibliography on these Harmodius-blow reliefs: Kaempf-Dimitriadou 1986.

R O B I N   O S B O R N E

Changing the Discourse

Fifth-century Athens, as the essays in this volume have clearly shown, had an ongoing obsession with tyranny. Ostracism was probably introduced, and certainly repeatedly used, in the first quarter of the century to remove from Athens those believed to be inclined to subvert the democratic constitution for their own personal political advantage. Popular leaders in the last quarter of a century continued to throw the tyrant term around at rivals whose personal following could be made to look like the basis for a bid for extra-constitutional power for themselves.

In fourth-century Athens, as Kathryn Morgan and Josiah Ober both reveal, tyranny had almost no place in real politics. For all that Eucrates' law in 337 covers establishing tyranny as well as other forms of subverting democracy, the tyrant had become a figure sufficiently abstracted from everyday Athenian political reality to be good to think with in analyses of the strengths and weaknesses of a wide range of political constitutions.

What happened to effect such a change in the discourse of tyranny at Athens? How can we account for the paradox that the successful installation of what was recognized as a tyrannical régime at Athens (n. 17 below), the régime of the Thirty Tyrants, led not to enhanced fear of actual tyranny but to the emasculation of the term? It is commonly asserted that the horrors of the régime of the Thirty were such that no one in Athens subsequently could adopt a political position that could be identified with that of the Thirty. On this view, everyone after 403 had to claim to be some sort of democrat.[1] In this paper I will argue that the crisis in political language so clearly displayed in the "lax terminology" used by Isocrates was not so much a product of the events of 404/03 themselves but of the way in which the coups of 411 and of 404 revealed the emptiness of the earlier political discourse and political analysis.

CONSTITUTIONAL ANALYSIS IN
FIFTH-CENTURY ATHENS

When Herodotus has the Persians debate their future constitution, he characterizes Otanes and Megabyzus as urging, respectively, that power be placed "in the midst of the Persian people" (*es meson*) and that it be handed over "to an oligarchy." But the construction of the argument is such that oligarchy is never discussed.[2] Otanes devotes himself mostly to the shortcomings of a monarchy, explicitly described as the rule of a tyrant, and has a brief description of the advantages of democracy. Megabyzus agrees with the arguments against monarchy but adds arguments against democracy and then briefly concludes that oligarchy would be best since they themselves would rule. Darius devotes himself to arguing that the best monarchy has advantages over any other constitution, and he adds that monarchy had given the Persians freedom in the first place and is their ancestral constitution.

The absence of serious discussion of oligarchy in Herodotus' Constitutional Debate is exactly paralleled by the lack of discussion of oligarchy in the rest of his history. As Carolyn Dewald (this volume) shows, Herodotus conducts a subtle analysis of tyranny and monarchy, both propounding and qualifying an extremely negative "despotic template." He also, if very much less extensively, explores the working of democracy. He famously comments both on the positive effects of "liberation" (5.78) and on the way in which the many Athenians were more easy to mislead than the single ruler of Sparta (5.97.2). He shows debate at work in Athens (as over the interpretation of the "wooden walls" oracle [7.143–144]), and he brings out the ability of the Athenians to stand up to the blandishments of Persia (8.140–144). Herodotus does show the leaders of the various Greek cities attempting to arrive at decisions jointly, with rather limited success, but he shows us almost nothing of the workings of an oligarchy.

His picture of Sparta is of a city with at least three separate loci of power that are in actual or potential conflict (the two kings and the people, with a particular role for ephors). Elsewhere he shows only either monarchical figures or cities acting as a single unit. Nowhere do we have any exploration of either the virtues or the vices of oligarchy. As the pervasive tradition that early Greece was governed by kings shows, oral tradition does not seem to have found any use for accounts of aristocracy or other forms of oligarchic control, however much "small groups of elites, equals among themselves, neither showing domination by a greater power nor sharing their own with a larger franchise," to quote Sarah Morris' description, were the more common early form of government.[3]

The Herodotean polarization between democracy and monarchy is equally apparent in the other extant example of late fifth-century constitutional discussion, the debate between Theseus and the Herald in Euripides' *Suppliant Women*. Much of the argument is again negative: the Herald urges that democracy is the rule of the glib speaker over the ignorant voter. Theseus responds that monarchy denies the equality that the rule of law in democracy guarantees and that the monarch is necessarily jealous of rivals and discourages ambition. In this debate, oligarchy is not an option, even though it might seem to offer possibilities of expertise, the rule of law, and the space for the ambitious man that the Herald and Theseus put weight upon. The absence of oligarchy here parallels the absence of oligarchical government and issues arising from oligarchical government in tragedy. Alongside the frequent tragic scrutiny of tyranny, explored in this volume by Richard Seaford, tragedy devotes at least occasional attention to the workings of democracy (as in the court scene in *Eumenides,* as well as in *Suppliant Women*), but it shows no interest in oligarchy.

In commenting upon the fact that in *Suppliant Women* "the debate between constitutions, using monarchy as a foil, turns out to be nothing but a discussion of democracy," Raaflaub notes that "tyranny, it seems, remained an emotional issue and therefore a useful tool in discussing democracy. Oligarchy, on the other hand, although the real constitutional adversary of democracy, was, at least in its moderate form, too similar to (moderate) democracy to offer effective contrasts."[4] This volume has abundantly illustrated the ways in which tyranny continued to be an emotional issue in the fifth century, but was Raaflaub right to suggest that oligarchy was "the real constitutional adversary"?

CONSTITUTIONAL POLITICS IN FIFTH-CENTURY ATHENS

Tyranny was never far from the fifth-century Greek world. Tyrants dominated the cities of Sicily until after the war against Carthage in 480. Tyrants returned to Syracuse less than sixty years after the triumph of democracy there in 463. Ionia had been dominated by Persian-backed tyrants until the Ionian Revolt, and other areas dominated by Persia continued to be under such rulers. Nor was the mainland free of tyranny, though we know of few tyrannical regimes in detail. One tyrant of whom we hear is Euarchus, the aptly named ruler of Astacus in northwest Greece. We know of him because the Athenians expelled him in the first year of the Peloponnesian War. He went for help to his Corinthian backers, and they promptly restored him (Thuc. 2.30.1, 33.1–2). He must stand for perhaps dozens of such figures: that Corinth maintains him in power says something for the emptiness of Socles' principled opposition to tyranny in Herodotus 5.92.[5]

If we turn to the fourth century, evidence for such figures becomes more plentiful. The most interesting case of all is that of Euphron of Sicyon, whose story is told by Xenophon (*Hell.* 7.1.44–6, 2.11–15, 3.1–12, 4.1). Euphron, on Xenophon's account, turns himself from Sparta's greatest friend to the champion of a democracy backed by the Argives and Arcadians and then promptly subverts the new democracy, in which he is made a general, to establish himself as tyrant. Forced out by the Arcadians, who do not approve of this turn of events, he hires mercenaries from Athens and reestablishes a partial hold over the town. Hoping to persuade the Thebans also to hand over to him control of the acropolis of Sicyon, where they maintained a garrison, he visits Thebes, only to meet his death there at the hands of an assassin. This story reveals the Arcadians to be keen defenders of the democracy that was so fragile in their own cities. It also reveals how far the ability to claim a certain amount of popular support could go in enabling an individual not only to seize power but to expect democratic régimes to support him. Euphron's ability to turn himself from oligarch to democrat to tyrant recalls the ease with which Aristagoras at Miletus turned himself from tyrant to democrat.

Oligarchy was, of course, much more widespread on the Greek mainland than tyranny. But to what extent was oligarchy ever a threat to Athens? It is true that Athenian attempts to impose democracy on Boeotia had only short-lived success and that oligarchy reasserted itself there. It is true, too, that at Megara, following the failure of the pro-Athenian faction to hand the city over to Athens, a small group of oligarchs established a narrowly oligarchic constitution (Thuc. 4.74). But both these were cases of cities where the citizens were polarized over foreign policy, over whether to favor or oppose their powerful Athenian neighbors, and where constitutional preferences went with foreign policy stance (compare Thuc. 3.82.1). Athens herself was not similarly split over foreign policy. Even in the 460s, when some difference over the appropriate attitude to take to Sparta can reasonably be surmised, the Athenians faced no stark foreign-policy alternatives. If there was talk of some Athenians negotiating with the Spartans at the time of Tanagra (Thuc.

1.107.4), this only emphasizes the impossibility of any prospect of change from within Athens without active outside military intervention: "For the most part, all classes were united behind the imperial democracy for the benefits it gave them in terms of τιμή and ὠφελία, 'honor' and 'advantage'."[6]

If oligarchs looked to Sparta it was because Sparta found it convenient to exercise influence by maintaining in power groups who could not survive without their aid. The clearest examples of this come, once more, from the fourth century, in particular in the story of Spartan relations with Phlius (Xen. *Hell.* 5.2.8–10, 3.10–17, 21–25). But there is no reason to believe the fifth-century situation to have been significantly different. Sparta was not herself a model oligarchy. Indeed, her constitution was, and remains, curiously difficult to classify, with two kings, two powerful groups of magistrates, one annual (the ephors), one a lifetime occupation for select elderly (the gerousia), and an assembly that made fundamental decisions. Ancient political theorists made it the original "mixed constitution" (Arist. *Pol.* 1265b, 1294b; Polyb. 6.10). Individuals in Athens might ape the Spartan lifestyle, wearing their cloaks short and their hair long, but adopting a constitution so deeply embedded in social and political institutions that could not easily be replicated (helots, the *agōgē,* a dual kingship) was never an option.[7] It was as would-be tyrants and lovers of monarchy that those who adopted the Spartan style were identified, as *Wasps* 463–476 indicates.[8]

Dramatic as the change from oligarchy to tyranny might seem to us, there is every reason to see it, and to think that Athenians saw it, as insidious. Tyranny involved not the replacement but the overriding of the existing constitution. The stories of Peisistratus that Herodotus heard in Athens in the second half of the fifth century were about his exploitation of factionalism and his deception of the Assembly and the people. If we ask what motivated Athenian ostracism after the Persian Wars, factionalism would seem to be the most important factor. It is certainly hard for us, on the basis of surviving source material, to see Thucydides son of Melesias as individually a serious threat to anybody, but it is easier to see how Athenians might fear that his constant opposition to Pericles increased the political temperature, perhaps to a dangerous level. Cratinus' presentation of Pericles as tyrant in the 430s, discussed by Jeffrey Henderson (this volume), surely achieved its effect because it was difficult to refute rather than because it was absurd. The tradition surrounding the ostracism that finally resulted in the banishment of Hyperbolus tells us an ostracism was voted for by people who thought it necessary for the city to get rid of either Alcibiades or Nicias. This story similarly reflects a fear that the clash between charismatic leaders might cause one of them to seek extra-constitutional means to power.

The fundamental point about tyranny was that it was unprincipled. Darius in Herodotus and the Herald in Euripides' *Suppliant Women* provide a theoretical justification of sorts for monarchy, but, as the case of Euphron nicely shows, tyranny was opportunist. The many stories told of Archaic tyrants show them turning a magistracy into tyranny or seizing power unconstitutionally after being frustrated in constitutional politics. It is this sense that tyranny could be born of frustration that is the basis of the joke about "buying fish for tyranny" in Aristophanes' *Wasps* 495: as James Davidson has shown, expensive taste in fish smacked of an extravagant lifestyle in other respects, of debts and therefore of potentially subversive activities.[9] For all that Bdelycleon in the same passage claims not even to have heard the word tyranny for fifty years (he clearly had not been to Cratinus' comedies), Henderson is mistaken, I think, to say that "the actual threat ended with the Persian invasions and the ostracisms of the 480s, and the perennial threat to democracy thereafter was not tyranny but oligarchy."[10]

If my argument is correct, I clearly have a lot of explaining still to do. For if tyranny was the ever-present threat at Athens, and oligarchy not a realistic option, why is it that in 411 (and 404) Athens succumbed to oligarchy? Have I not simply replaced one paradox—that fifth-century Athens should be obsessed with tyranny even though tyranny was no threat—by another and still greater paradox, that Athenian democracy should be subverted by the oligarchy that was no threat?

THE OLIGARCHIC REVOLUTIONS AT ATHENS, THEIR CAUSES AND CONSEQUENCES

Both Thucydides and the Aristotelian *Constitution of the Athenians* have the revolution of 411 provoked by defeat in Sicily. It is indeed hard to exaggerate the extent to which the Sicilian disaster, and Athenian and other Greek perceptions of it, changed the political situation in Athens. For all the ups and downs in Athenian military fortunes during the Archidamian War, Athens never had to face the prospect of total defeat. In particular, none of Athens' failures had involved her fleet, and the worst of prospects had been having to pull in her horns as far as the empire was concerned. Now, in the words of the penultimate sentence of Thucydides 7, "Defeated in every way at every point, the suffering inflicted upon them was in no part negligible, in

the total destruction, to use the common phrase, land army and ships, absolutely everything, was destroyed, and few out of many made the journey back
home" (7.87.6).

But what Athens faced in the aftermath of the Sicilian disaster was not
just the prospect of military defeat. It was the prospect that democracy was
a failure. We do not have to believe in the detailed historicity of Thucydides' speeches to feel confident that the impression he gives is correct. The
issues involved in invading Sicily had been clearly set out in the Assembly
in advance by Alcibiades and Nicias, the expedition had been made on the
basis of an Assembly decision, and the major changes made subsequently, the
attempted recall of Alcibiades, the reinforcements with Demosthenes, had
been the Assembly's decisions in the light of information given to them.
The Athenians had heard the pros and cons, and the misjudgment was theirs.
Thucydides judges (2.65.11) that the people were to blame both in the initial
decision and in their subsequent actions; that this view was widely shared
seems confirmed by Athenian action in 413: elderly men were appointed as
probouloi, men set up to consider policy and to offer additional advice on what
to do (Thuc. 81.3).

Athenians had not previously had to contemplate the prospect that
democracy did not work. They annually looked back at their record and
applauded themselves on the occasion of the public burial of the war dead
(one cannot imagine the ironic and deconstructive treatment of the topos of
the funeral oration that is Plato's *Menexenus*[11] being written during the fifth
century). Other Greeks too, looking at Athenian history, praised Athenian
actions and attributed their success to democracy (so Hdt. 5.78, 7.139.5). Those
who disapproved of democracy at Athens nevertheless, to judge from the
Old Oligarch, felt that they could not dispute its success. That success was, in
turn, an important part of the justification for democracy in a world where
the key question in political thought was not whether a constitution could
be matched against individual rights but whether one could find reason to
believe that a constitution would yield the right answers.

What happened in Sicily took the lid off the question of constitution. For
the previous 95 years on any reckoning (compare Thuc. 8.68), and 180 years
on the reckoning of those who took the democratic constitution to have
been founded by Solon, the practical alternatives had been either the democratic constitution or an extra-constitutional tyranny. Now, however, constitutional variation was back on the agenda, without tyranny being ruled out.
In the wake of the Spartan decarchies of the closing years of the war, and of

the events at Athens itself in 404/03, we might imagine that a Spartan-backed junta was one of the most obvious possibilities, but it may not have looked quite like that in 413. Henderson draws attention to the way in which the *Lysistrata* is unusually interested in past Athenian history and in particular in Hippias' tyranny and tyrannicide.[12] When the men's chorus and its leader associate the women's desire for peace with Sparta with tyranny (616–635), this association arises in part from the Spartan attempts to install Isagoras/restore Hippias to power (compare the earlier reference to Cleomenes at 274–282). If it has some contemporary resonance, this resonance must be weak enough not to undermine entirely Lysistrata's later praise of Spartans for getting rid of Hippias in the first place (1150–1156). Although critics have claimed that the *Thesmophoriazusae* displays a strikingly different attitude to tyranny,[13] this is hard to justify. The first reference in that play to tyrants comes in a mock curse and is exactly parallel to that in the *Birds* 1072–1075; only the second, identifying Athena as tyrant hater in a very distinctive meter, might demand special explanation, and there too parody seems a more likely determinant than politics.

Continuing fear of tyranny certainly played some part in the events of 412/11, but it was tyranny of a traditional sort, the manipulation of democratic politics by a charismatic individual, to which Athenians were alert. We see shadows of that in the murder of Androcles (Thuc. 8.65.2) and in what Thucydides says about Antiphon and the suspicion in which the people held him (8.68.1). But the most telling incident is that involving Alcibiades and Phrynichus. Both Phrynichus' own perception of Alcibiades as self-interested, and his ability to trick the generals into believing Alcibiades to be motivated by personal pique, feed upon that tyrant model. In the end, of course, it is Phrynichus himself who falls victim to that same model, assassinated in the Agora (Thuc. 8.92).

What played a much larger part in the events of 411 is oligarchic constitutional theory. I make that claim baldly, but it is a claim many would question. They would question it since genuine constitutional debate plays no part in Thucydides' account of the Four Hundred. His account is of an elaborate pretense that oligarchy was necessary to secure support from Persia, of secret and underhand maneuvers, of covert violence breeding an atmosphere of terror, and of talk of a hoplite democracy as a cover for permanent rule by a small group of self-chosen cronies. A trace of constitutional debate emerges in Thucydides only when the Four Hundred are overthrown, the régime of the Five Thousand instituted, and a "moderate mixture" of rule by the few and rule by the many established (Thuc. 8.97.2). The belief that Thucydides misrepresents what went on in 412–411 rests in part on this "intermediate régime": such a régime was not, cannot have been, created without fore-thought in the wake of the naval defeat off Eretria. The decision to adopt a citizen body of 5,000 was not arbitrary but built on the same discussions that had led the Four Hundred to pretend to be playing to and for such a citizen body. But the claim rests even more strongly on the account in the Aristotelian *Constitution of the Athenians* 29–33.

At the center of the Aristotelian account of the Four Hundred are two constitutional descriptions. The author presents chapter 30 as what a consti-tutional committee of one hundred, set up by the Five Thousand following the initial constitutional proposals of the committee of thirty (itself set up by the Assembly that abolished democracy) drew up. Only at the beginning of chapter 31 does [Aristotle] describe what he has outlined in chapter 30 as the "constitution for the future" (i.e., the constitution under which the Five Thousand ruled). What follows in chapter 31 is presented as the "constitution for the present" (i.e., the constitution under which the Four Hundred ruled). It is implausible that either constitution is what it is claimed to be: chapter 31 does not accord with Thucydides, and chapter 30 is incoherent and cannot be the description of a constitution that actually ran.

Because of this and because we cannot tell where the Aristotelian re-searcher got the information from, scholars tend to ignore the constitutions outlined in these chapters. This seems to me to be an overreaction. The two constitutions are neither well integrated into the Aristotelian text nor them-selves well formulated. The latter makes it unlikely that they came from any propagandist document written to justify the Four Hundred after the event. Suggestions that they come from Antiphon's defense speech seem to me in-compatible with Thucydides' praise of that speech. But they must surely have come in some way out of the events of 411, just as it is plausible too that Draco's constitution in chapter 4 of the *Constitution of the Athenians* comes out of those events.[14] Their interest, and in particular the interest of the constitu-tion outlined in chapter 30, lies in the appetite for constitutional debate that they presuppose.

At the heart of the constitution outlined in chapter 30 of the *Constitution of the Athenians* lie two principles (not clearly reconciled): that major magis-trates should serve on the Council and that all who have full citizen rights should serve in turn on the Council by rotation over a period of four years. For all the incoherence with which these proposals are expressed (in 30.2 the

Hellenotamiai both are included in the list of magistrates to serve *ex offi-cio* on the Council and are explicitly excluded from it), we can recognize in them a distinct political theory. That theory puts emphasis on deliberative and executive bodies being linked. In democracy, the generals seem to have had privileged access to the Council of Five Hundred, although the positive evidence for this all dates to the Peloponnesian War, and how in detail such privileged access worked is not clear. No other democratic magistrates had any place on the Council unless by chance they happened to hold both a magistracy and a place on the Council at the same time.[15] Under this constitution, it is not only the generals but all the major military officers (taxiarchs, phylarchs, hipparchs, those in charge of forts), the archons, and the major financial and religious officials who serve on the Council. All these are to be elected from an elected shortlist: everything is being done to ensure that the experts are chosen and that their expertise is available at the deliberative stage when policy is formulated.

The second thing on which the political theory embodied here places emphasis is regular high-level participation by all citizens. Rotation of membership of the deliberative Council, setting Council meetings at a reasonably realistic frequency of once in five days, and instituting fines for nonattendance all aim at getting all citizens involved. They mean, indeed, a much heavier political involvement than was possible for, let alone required of, citizens in the democracy, who could only serve on the Council of Five Hundred twice in a lifetime. Far from being a recipe for handing government over to a small group, the provisions of this constitution point to a much larger Council. If there are five thousand citizens—something not actually explicitly stated in the constitutional provisions in the chapter—and a quarter of them are to serve as the Council each year, then, even allowing that five thousand citizens over the age of 18 will yield a smaller number of citizens over the age of 30, we are dealing with a Council with close to one thousand members.

Despite the lack of clarity of its exposition, and the contradictions in its details, it is clear that the constitution outlined in chapter 30 was not dreamt up in a moment but was the result of serious thought and indeed serious research. That is made clear by the resemblances between what is proposed and what is described at *Hellenica Oxyrhynchia* 16.2 (trans. McKechnie and Kern): "At that time the situation in Boeotia was as follows. There were four councils established at that time in each of the cities. Not all the citizens were allowed to share in these, but only those with a certain level of wealth. Each of these councils in turn sat and deliberated about policy, and referred it to the other three. What seemed acceptable to all of them was approved." Similar conclusions about their serious political intent follow from close examination of chapters 4 and 31 of the *Constitution of the Athenians,* but chapter 30 is itself sufficient, I suggest, to demonstrate that there were Athenians in 411 who were looking for a workable alternative to the existing democratic constitution. It is sufficient, too, to show that the chief concern of such Athenians was for efficient and effective government, not for the promotion of their individual or class interests. The failure of the Four Hundred to bring into practice what some, at least, were preaching should not blind us to oligarchy becoming in 412/11 for the first time in the fifth century, a realistic alternative to democracy and to tyranny.

As the very fact of an intermediate regime makes clear, what the Athenians got rid of after the naval defeat off Eretria was not oligarchy but prospective group tyranny. The concentration on the vilification of individuals through the honors passed for the assassins of Phrynichus, the condemnation of Archeptolemus and Antiphon as traitors ([Plut.] *X orat.* 833d–834b), and the ongoing series of further trials of individuals turned the political changes of 411 into the products of a self-interested personal agenda. The decree of Demophantus (Andoc. 1.96–8) legitimated the killing of "anyone who overthrows the democracy at Athens, and anyone who, when the democracy has been overthrown, holds any office thereafter" as well as of anyone who sets himself up as tyrant. Nevertheless this decree envisages only action against individuals and not the situation where the democratic constitution is amended to give a greater say to some citizens than to others. The reenactment (or at least reinscription) of the statute of limitations on the Council of Five Hundred may have been particularly addressed to moves to enhance the role of the Council over that of the Assembly.[16] But in general, oligarchy seems to have been driven off the Athenian political agenda almost as quickly as it had been put on it. Cynically, we might observe that democratic politicians (and some who had been oligarchs in 411) saw more capital in conducting witch-hunts than in continuing the constitutional discussion with a view to serious political reform. Only the threat of imminent defeat by Sparta made the Athenians heed appeals like those in the *parabasis* of Aristophanes' *Frogs* (especially 687–694) and pass Patrocleides' decree making it possible for members of the Four Hundred, along with other exiles, to return to Athens (Andoc. 1.77–79).

The way in which Athens returned after the events of 411 to radical democratic business as usual is quite remarkable. It is true that new projects were instituted that had constitutional implications—notably the republication of the law code—but none of the issues to which some Athenians, at least, had given serious thought since 413 were tackled. This is revealed most graphically in the treatment of the generals after the sea battle at Arginousae. The way in which the Assembly turned itself into a court, and the insistence on the people's right to do what they wanted to do regardless of normal procedures (and common justice), was not so much a return to old ways of doing things as a travesty of them. Two factors best explain this: one is the focus immediately after 411 on reprisals against individuals; the second is the extent to which the immediate military crisis that led to the downfall of the Four Hundred was successfully negotiated and Athenian fortunes turned round. Right up until the sea battle at Aegospotami, defeat was not staring Athenians in the face.

What happened in Athens following her surrender is presented even more unanimously and explicitly by our ancient sources as the installation of tyranny than is the case for 411. Xenophon makes Critias ridicule the naïveté of anyone who thinks that because there are thirty of them they are not a tyranny, has Theramenes state his opposition both to extreme democracy and to those who think the only oligarchy is the one in which a few hold tyrannical sway, and remarks that the death of Theramenes allowed the Thirty to rule tyrannically without fear (*Hell.* 2.3.16, 48; compare 2.3.49, 2.4.1).[17] The Aristotelian *Ath. Pol.* claims that the Thirty were installed after Lysander hijacked a constitutional debate involving champions of democracy and "the ancestral constitution" as well as of oligarchy. But this has been widely regarded as a result of a deliberate distortion of the truth by [Aristotle]'s sources to conceal responsibility of Theramenes, who is presented as the particular champion of the "ancestral constitution," for the establishment of the Thirty.[18] On the conventional view, a group of Athenians, Theramenes prominent among them, saw Athens' defeat at the hands of Sparta as their chance to achieve personal power as a Spartan-backed junta of the sort installed by Sparta in some other former Athenian allies: "There is no difficulty in thinking of the Thirty as a larger decarchy for a larger state."[19] Any talk of framing a new constitution or other constitutional reform was simply a way of reconciling other Athenians to their rule.

There is, however, a case to be made for the view that this orthodox view is an unhistorical retrojection from what the Thirty ended up being. Rather than claim that the Thirty were a tyranny from the beginning, the revisionist view would hold that at least some of those involved had a genuinely oligarchic and nontyrannical program. The case for this revisionism rests on the attitude of the Thirty to law. Xenophon attests that devising a new constitution was the task initially given to the Thirty (*Hell.* 2.3.11), that they put off doing this but did from the beginning attack those who lived off *sykophantia* (vexatious litigation). At first sight the attack on sycophants looks like a way of seeking a favorable press: in a world where anyone who brought a prosecution against you was liable to be called a sycophant, to claim to be attacking sycophants was to claim to be attacking a group to which no one would claim to belong and which few would care to defend.[20] But the account in the Aristotelian *Constitution of the Athenians* puts the attack on sycophants into a different context, one that demands closer scrutiny.

At 35.3 the *Constitution of the Athenians* reports the attack on sycophants along with the attack on those who curried favor with the people contrary to its best interests. It juxtaposes this to a report in 35.2 on the reform by the Thirty of various laws. These include those of Solon's laws that were ambiguous. The example given of an ambiguous law is Solon's law on bequeathing one's property, where the Thirty removed the qualification that such a bequest was invalid if the testator was insane, senile, or under the influence of a woman and instead made a bequest absolutely valid.[21] This was done, the *Constitution of the Athenians* says, to take away the opportunity for sycophantic prosecutions, that is, I take it, to remove the possibility of people exploiting the qualifications to undermine wills simply on the grounds that the testator was old or enjoyed the company of a woman. The effect, again explicit in the text of the *Constitution of the Athenians,* was to undermine the power of the dicasts: from now on, the only issue for the court was whether there was or was not a genuine will.

Solon's law on wills appears to have become the stock example of a Solonian law that promoted rather than ended discussion. It is the law referred to in the discussion in the *Constitution of the Athenians* 9.2 of the democratic features of Solon's legislation, which counters the view that Solon deliberately made his laws ambiguous to increase the power of the courts.[22] Just what the lawgiver should define, and what not, clearly continued to be a subject of considerable discussion. Aristotle opens his *Rhetoric* (1254a18–b22) with a discussion of what sorts of issues it is appropriate for the plaintiff or defendant in court to address, what the law should cover, and what the dicast needs to have an independent and settled view about. Aristotle is there insistent that well-made laws should define as many issues as possible and leave as few decisions as possible to the dicasts.

The way in which Solon's law on wills is discussed in the context of Solon as legislator, along with the general discussion of the issue in Aristotle's *Rhetoric*, makes it clear that what the Thirty are alleged to have done in 404 was not something isolated. Rather it was the enactment of a particular line on how the court system should work. That line has a direct bearing, as the *Constitution of the Athenians* stresses, on the issue of sycophancy, and it offers a rather different slant on the attack on sycophants from that offered by Xenophon. Rather than sycophants simply being a suitable object for attack because they were generally hated, sycophants are a suitable object for attack because they are the people who have exploited precisely those features of the existing law code that the new régime considers unsatisfactory. The attack on sycophants is to be seen as the outward and visible sign of the cleaning up of the court system, of which the invisible counterpart is the repeal of clauses from Solon's laws that were open to interpretation. Where the attack on such clauses differs from the attack on sycophants is that there is no alternative, pragmatic explanation available to account for it: any group prepared to engage in detailed legal revision of the sort involved in changing the law on wills must have been serious about altering the working of the constitution. Contrary to Xenophon's implication, the Thirty do seem to have taken their role in constitutional reform seriously.

Once we allow that the Thirty did seriously engage in legal and constitutional reform, then it becomes much more difficult to dismiss, as mere post-eventum propaganda, the further claim of *Constitution of the Athenians* 35.2 that the Thirty repealed the laws of Ephialtes and Archestratus about the Areopagites.[23] The repeal of the reforms that had stripped the Areopagus of many of its judicial powers makes excellent sense in the context of the wider review of court proceedings to which the amendment of Solon's laws and attack on sycophants attests. We can see the Thirty as engaged in a program of political reform that began with the courts, unlike the program in 411, which focused on the Council and Assembly. This makes some sense in terms of the background of members of the Thirty: several of them had been exiled by the democratic courts. It also makes sense in terms of the moments of tension in the years since 411: the "trial" of the generals after Arginousae was only the worst excess in more than five years of continuous use of the courts to persecute political enemies.

But if we accept that there are good independent reasons for believing the claim that the Thirty undid the Ephialtic reforms of the Areopagus, then it is hard to imagine that they would have done so without once more bandying about the slogan "ancestral constitution." The *Constitution of the Athenians* tells of the repeal of the Areopagus reforms in the same sentence in which it also claims that the Thirty claimed to be pursuing the ancestral constitution.[24] The Ephialtic reforms were the last major constitutional change before the 411 coup (see *Constitution of the Athenians* 41.2) and were the chief barrier between radical and Cleisthenic democracy.[25]

All this has implications for what we make of the account of the setting up of the Thirty in the *Constitution of the Athenians*. If the case is accepted, it becomes hard to dismiss its claim that there was a faction pursuing the ancestral constitution at the time that the Thirty was set up. Rather than thinking that the "ancestral constitution party" was invented later, as a way of suggesting that the Thirty was not all bad, we must rather credit to later invention the claim that the ancestral constitution "party" lost out to the extremist oligarchs in the debate because of Lysander's support for the latter. The list of supporters of the ancestral constitution in 404 at *Constitution of the Athenians* 34.3 looks to be a "dream team" for those who would claim Theramenes to have been a hero rather than a villain, but it is nevertheless seriously possible that it is not an invention.[26] It is true Theramenes is the only one of those listed who became a member of the Thirty, but that does not exclude the possibility that all those mentioned were initially happy with the appointment of the Thirty and hopeful that they would deliver the ancestral constitution.

More importantly, all this has consequences for what we believe about serious discussion of constitutional reform at Athens. If the revisionist case is accepted, then the background to the appointment of the Thirty has to include not merely bullying tactics by Lysander and an Athens reduced to desperation by the length of time it had taken Theramenes to come to an agreement over the terms of surrender. It has also to include discussion of what was wrong with democracy and how to deal with its faults. The big domestic issues of the period after 411 had not been to do with the threat of tyranny, but, as the Demophantus and Patrocleides Decrees in their different ways show, about the way in which democracy disciplined its own members. If the Thirty spent any time at all planning for reform of the courts, then some at least of their number must have expected the institutions of constitutional government to continue. Further support for that claim can perhaps also be gathered from Xenophon's account (*Hell.* 2.3.11) of their appointment of a Council and magistrates (albeit at their own whim).

Whatever we take to be the mind of (a significant proportion of) the Thirty at its appointment, there is no disputing that the Thirty turned into a collective tyranny that did little more than play with constitutional rules (as in the new laws under which Theramenes was condemned). The *Constitution of the Athenians* 35.4 reckons at fifteen hundred the number of Athenians who were killed and whose property was taken by the Thirty.[27] As after 411, so also after the Thirty it was the prominent individuals, and above all others Critias and Theramenes, who were remembered. It was with the blackening, or whitening, of the memory of Theramenes that those most concerned to ensure that the Thirty left, or did not leave, a scrap of positive reputation mainly concerned themselves. So much is most obviously clear from the way the Theramenes papyrus answers the allegations made in Lysias 12.[28] This tendency to remember what happened as the doings of particular individuals, rather than as the promotion of certain political ideas, was reinforced, rather than countered, by the agreement not to mention past ills, which created the presumption that what had happened had been a series of unconnected events.

Yet politics after the downfall of the Thirty was not like politics after the restoration of democracy in 410, let alone like the politics of democracy before the Sicilian disaster. The year 403 saw some fundamental constitutional changes carried, above all the formulation of a distinction between laws and decrees. It also saw other proposals for constitutional change brought and defeated. The issues of the nature of the democratic constitution, of the makeup of the citizen body, and of the powers of the Assembly were discussed and decided upon. Shortly afterwards, the issue of effective access to, and participation in, the Assembly was brought up over the question of Assembly pay. The Athenians did not systematically review every organ of government— it is notable that the courts seem to have been left untouched despite, or perhaps because of, the Thirty's interest in them—but they did rethink some of the fundamentals of the working of democracy.

How are we to explain this willingness for constitutional reform in 403? One possible story concerns the Spartans. In 403, as not in 411, the end of the oligarchy was possible only because a foreign army decided to withdraw its support. Xenophon's account makes Pausanias responsible for the amnesty and for setting up Eleusis as a safe haven for oligarchs (*Hell.* 2.4.38). It has plausibly been suggested that it was fear that Sparta would intervene to enforce the agreement that made the Athenians relatively faithful in keeping the amnesty, at least until Sparta became preoccupied with other matters in 400–399.[29] But while Sparta clearly did have an interest in Athens not being ridden with civil strife, it is hard to think that Pausanias or anyone else at Sparta had much interest in constitutional niceties.

A second possible story concerns Archinus. Archinus' interest not just in reconciliation but in constitutional arrangements is revealed in the actions singled out for praise by the *Constitution of the Athenians* 40.1–2, in particular the opposition to enfranchising slaves who had a part in the return from Phyle. Archinus is known to have been interested in a wide range of constitutional matters. In or before 405 he had combined with Agyrrhius to reduce the payments to comic poets at the Dionysia and Lenaea (Schol. Ar. *Frogs* 367), and in 400 he introduced the new procedure of *paragraphē* (the entering of a plea that a prosecution was inadmissible).[30] The *Constitution of the Athenians* presents Archinus as loosely associated with Theramenes before the creation of the Thirty, that is, as someone keen to turn the clock back and reestablish a less radical form of democracy. If this is correct, then we might see him as taking advantage of Spartan presence to ensure that some of that same program got enacted once democracy was restored. What we would love to know is what hand, if any, Archinus had in framing the fundamental division between laws and decrees.

What happened in 403, however, can hardly have been the doing of one man. It was the Athenian Assembly as a whole that agreed to the constitutional changes, and it is much more important historically to understand why the Assembly agreed to them than to know who in particular promoted the reforms. I suggest that what was crucial in 403 was the widespread awareness that the analysis of political conflict that had been current through virtually the whole fifth century was bankrupt. That analysis emphasized the danger from particular individuals and focused on what might happen if a charismatic individual used his personal following to monopolize power not simply informally, as Pericles might be thought to have done, but in some formal ways. After 411 the Athenians insisted on reasserting that model, ill though it fitted the sequence of events. After 404 the tyrannical template continued to have some uses, primarily in court and in theoretical discussions, but in terms of the working of everyday politics, all the signs are that it was dead. In 404, as in 411, individual charm certainly played some part in softening up the Athenians for the coup: in 411 it was the persuasion of Peisander, in 404 that, primarily, of Theramenes. But in both cases, what had been held out as attractive was not a world in which one individual would fix everything, but a world in which constitutional change would iron out the glitches that had brought the problems the democracy was facing. In both cases, constitutional change, not the joy of following a charismatic leader, was the carrot that caused the Athenians to lower their guard.

An alternative way of stating the position in 403 is to take up the terms that Kurt Raaflaub uses in his analysis in this volume. If in the earlier fifth century, tyranny had been what played the crucial role in defining, by contrast, what it was to be a democrat, in 403 it was apparent that the quality of "not being tyranny" did not define being a democrat anything like closely enough. There was just too much that would turn out to be not democracy even though it was not on the face of it tyranny. At the same time, the rhetorical use of the term *dēmos tyrannos,* however specialized in its contexts, and the possibility it raised of thinking of democracy as itself tyrannical, can have only further broken down the absoluteness of the opposition between democracy and tyranny.

CONCLUSION

We are now in a position to understand why the discourse of tyranny changes between the fifth and fourth centuries. The killing of Phrynichus catalyzed opposition to the Four Hundred, but that did not mean that his charisma had been responsible for the successful coup, any more than the killing of Hipparchus said anything about how Athens came to have tyranny in the sixth century. Stories of the role of deceit in tyrannical coups were no protection against the sort of widespread uncertainty upon which Thucydides puts so much stress in 411 and that plays a clear, if less celebrated, role also in 404.[31] Treating tyranny as the bogey-man had done nothing to protect democracy: if democracy was indeed to be safeguarded, new defenses needed to be erected. Against Ober, I suggest that the "Athenian demotic agenda" of the fifth century was not consolidated but fundamentally changed by the events of 403.[32] Heroic acts against individuals were eclipsed by the united attack on the régime of the Thirty: that the Athenians both made moves to honor all those who had taken part in the return from Phyle and also passed an amnesty for those who opposed the democratic restoration served to stress the strength of the people as a whole as the only guarantee of democratic security. As Ober himself suggests, it was those who had reservations about democracy who now advertised single deeds of valor, as with the monument to Dexileos.[33] What needs to be stressed about Eucrates' Tyranny Law of 337/36 is not its repetition of conventional antityrant clauses from previous laws but its insistence on disabling the Areopagus;[34] once more, with Ober, we need to note the very different iconography of its relief.

The blurring of constitutional boundaries that Kathryn Morgan traces in Isocrates' work can be seen as a reflection of the sea change in Athenian perceptions following the events of 412–403. All the play with "the ancestral constitution" and what "really" constituted democracy, all the canvassing of what different observers might call either moderate democracy or broad-based oligarchy, all the various manifestations of tyranny from the tyranny of the demos in the Arginousae trial to the tyranny of the Thirty (or was it just of Critias?), all these rendered fragile not only the dichotomous democracy:tyranny model but all attempts to classify constitutions neatly. While Morgan is no doubt right to connect Isocrates' endowment of tyranny with ethical neutrality with his aim at multiple audiences, we can nevertheless see how the events of the last decade and a half of the fifth century at Athens would make even an Athenian audience receptive to this move: democracy's antityrannical stance had been shown void.

The strongest defense of democracy in the fifth century had been that it worked. The events of the end of the century revealed to Athenians that democracy did not necessarily work. Some Athenians doubtless went on believing blindly in the necessary virtues of democracy, and they are roundly mocked for it by Plato in *Menexenus*. But the constitutional changes made when democracy was restored, and those that continued to be made subsequently, reveal the death of doctrinaire radical democracy. Democratic commitment to selection of officials by lot not only is questioned by Isocrates, it was repeatedly compromised by decisions to select newly created magistrates by election (one notes, for example, the elected committee of ten whose creation has been revealed by the discovery of Agyrrhius' grain-tax law of 374/73).[35]

The death of doctrinaire democracy not only changed the discourse of practical politics, it also changed the discourse of political theory. In the fifth century, political theory either concentrated on explaining how fiendishly clever democracy was in protecting its own interests, as in the Old Oligarch, or working out a philosophical, and in particular an epistemological, basis for democracy.[36] In the fourth century, Plato and Aristotle, and also Isocrates in his own way, engaged in far more wide-ranging and far more open-minded investigation of the varieties of constitution and their various strengths. Attempts to label Plato or Aristotle as pro- or antidemocrat endeavor to pigeonhole them in a way that might have been appropriate in the fifth century but was no longer appropriate in the changed discourse of the fourth century.

What this volume has done is reveal very sharply the contours of fifth-century political discourse at Athens and the central place of tyranny in that discourse. It has also pointed forward to the changed world of the fourth century. What this essay has tried to do is to point to the importance of the actual political events at Athens in 412–403 in changing that discourse and to the magnitude of the transformation that occurred in Athens at the end of the fifth century.[37]

Notes

[1] Cf. Ober 1998: 280–282 (on Isocrates).

[2] Raaflaub 1989: 43.

[3] Morris, p. 7 above.

[4] Raaflaub 1989: 46.

[5] Note also Thuc. 6.59.3 for tyranny at Lampsacus.

[6] Hornblower 1991: 171.

[7] Cf. Davidson 1997: 61–63 on Critias' exegesis of Spartan lifestyle. Against Whitehead 1982–1983, I do not believe that the Thirty were attempting to transpose a Spartan constitution to Athens.

[8] Henderson, pp. 164–165 above.

[9] Davidson 1993.

[10] Henderson, p. 155 above; cf. Raaflaub, p. 71 above: "at a time when tyranny was extremely rare in the core areas of Greek world"; Raaflaub's own account at pp. 69–71 seems to me not to support that claim.

[11] Monoson 2000: 181–205.

[12] Henderson, p. 174 above.

[13] Sommerstein 1977: 122; cf. Henderson 1987: 151.

[14] Cf. Rhodes 1981: 385–389 (who is prepared to see the two chapters as condensed from proposals actually brought during the rule of the Four Hundred) and, on Draco's constitution, 86–87.

[15] See Allen 2000: 306–307.

[16] *IG* I³ 105 with Lewis 1967: 132. On the original date of this inscription, note Ryan 1994.

[17] For explicit reference to the Thirty as a tyranny, see Diod. Sic. 14.3.7; schol. Aesch. 1.39.

[18] Rhodes 1981: 434 and cf. 420, 422, 440.

[19] Lewis 1994: 30.

[20] Osborne 1990; Christ 1992, 1998.

[21] The full Solonian law seems to have been reinstated in 403 and is cited by Dem. 46.14, including clauses about being drugged, ill, or in chains.

[22] Cf. the discussion of the law on wills in Plut. *Solon* 21, and of ambiguity in his laws in Plut. *Solon* 18.4.

[23] For discussion and a defense of the historicity of this claim, see Wallace 1989: 140–143.

[24] For the text at this point, see Rhodes 1981: 439–440.

[25] For Cleisthenic democracy as the ideal to go back to, cf. Cleitophon's rider in 411: *Constitution of the Athenians* 29.3.

[26] A dream team because Cleitophon's one claim to fame was to have proposed looking into the constitution of Cleisthenes in 411, because Anytus and Archinus were with Thrasybulus and involved in the return from Phyle, because Archinus was prominent in the restored democracy standing against the extremes of democratic radicalism, and because Phormisius was the man who proposed in 403 that the franchise be limited to those who owned land. On all these, see Rhodes 1981: 431–432.

[27] This figure is also found in other sources; see Rhodes 1981: 447.

[28] See Merkelback and Youtie 1968: 161–169; Hennins 1968: 101–108; Andrewes 1970: 35–38; and Luppe 1978: 14–16.

[29] Todd 1984.

[30] He was also responsible for bringing the Ionic alphabet into official use; see D'Angour 1999.

[31] The role in 404 is brought out the more once we acknowledge the plausibility of the *Constitution of the Athenians'* analysis of the different groups debating what should be done in 404.

[32] Ober, pp. 224–225 above.

[33] Ober, pp. 239–242 above.

[34] Wallace 1989: 180–184.

[35] Stroud 1998.

[36] For the latter, see Farrar 1988; Kraut 1984.

[37] Some of the ideas explored here were aired at a conference at Northwestern University organized by Robert Wallace. I am grateful to participants on that occasion and to Professor P. J. Rhodes and the editor for comments and criticism.

K A T H R Y N   A .   M O R G A N

AFTERWORD

This collection of essays has explored the variety of ways in which tyranny
was a "popular" concept. Much has been achieved. We have surveyed a historical development in what it meant to think tyranny and monarchy. Far
from describing something uniform, the words "tyrant," "tyranny," "monarchy," and related vocabulary are used to characterize a wide range of political phenomena, ranging from figures such as Peisistratus and Xerxes to the
Athenian demos itself. It is no easy task to decide on the precise valence and
purpose of each term in individual instances. The essays here have presented
real disagreements about how tyranny was to be evaluated in an Athenian
context. Yet this heterogeneity is a strength. Although no final consensus
has emerged (and indeed, individual positions have become more distinct
during the editing process as dialogue has clarified the issues), the essays
have mapped out a series of distinctive positions that may serve as a basis for
further research.

The convergence of literary and political/historical analysis in these essays
demonstrates the merits of an interdisciplinary approach. Tyranny was a
central topic in Greek political culture and imagination, and any cultural
history of tyranny must spread a wide methodological net. Yet as I noted
in the introduction, this volume has made no attempt to cover exhaustively
(even within Athens) all genres and areas where tyranny was an issue. One
might profitably investigate the extent to which attitudes to tyranny and
sovereignty were conditioned by genre and modified by individual authors,
as well as varying chronologically. Lyric and elegiac poetry would provide
a particularly rich mine for this type of analysis.[1] It is clear that kings and
tyrants continued to be central to Greek politics and imagination in the centuries that followed the Persian Wars and led up to the establishment of the
Hellenistic monarchies.

The final impression that emerges from the analyses here is one of variety. The Greeks used "tyrant" to describe tyrants proper, but they also used it metonymically for individuals and for the city. The tyrant, as Simonides and Hieron discuss in Xenophon's *Hieron,* embodies the Greeks' deepest desires for wealth and the power it brings to maximize power and pleasure (in food, drink, praise, sex, and honor). If an individual pursues those desires, he becomes a danger to the larger community; he must, therefore, be restrained. Yet the image remains seductive. Everyone (bar the philosophers) would like to be a tyrant, and if one cannot be an individual monarch, the next best thing is to be a member of a hegemonic society that pursues power, prestige, and pleasure. Each society must decide for itself how far these pursuits must be restrained. The contradictions that emerge when we consider the problem of tyranny (in Athens and elsewhere) indicate how delicate a matter this is.

NOTE

1 My own current research focuses on Pindaric odes written for Sicilian tyrants and their henchmen.

.

Bibliography

CAH   *Cambridge Ancient History* 2nd ed. Cambridge University, 1970–.
DK   H. Diels and W. Kranz. *Die Fragmente der Vorsokratiker.* 10th ed. Berlin: Weidmannsche Verlagsbuchhandlung, 1960.
FGrh   F. Jacoby. *Fragmente der griechischen Historiker.* Leiden: Brill, 1923–.
GHI   M. N. Tod. *A Selection of Greek Historical Inscriptions. Vol. II from 403 to 323 B.C.* Oxford: Clarendon, 1948.
HCT   A. W. Gomme, A. Andrewes, and K. J. Dover, eds. *A Historical Commentary on Thucydides.* Oxford: Clarendon, 1945–1981.
IG   *Inscriptiones Graecae.* Berlin: De Gruyter, 1873–.
ML   R. Meiggs and D. M. Lewis, eds. *A Selection of Greek Historical Inscriptions.* 2nd ed. Oxford: Clarendon, 1988.
OCD   *The Oxford Classical Dictionary.* 3rd ed. Oxford: Clarendon, 1996.
OGIS   W. Dittenberger. *Orientis Graeci Inscriptiones Selectae.* Hildesheim: G. Olms, 1986.
PCG   R. Kassel and C. Austin, eds. *Poetae Comici Graeci.* Berlin: de Gruyter, 1983–.
SEG   *Supplementum Epigraphicum Graecum.* Alphen aan den Rijn: Sijthhoff & Nordhoff, 1923–.
SIG   W. Dittenberger. *Sylloge Inscriptionum Graecarum.* 3rd ed. Hildesheim: G. Olms, 1982.

* * * * *

Where possible, periodical abbreviations are those in *L'Année Philologique* (Paris: Les Belles Lettres).

* * * * *

Adam, J. 1902. *The Republic of Plato.* 2 vols. Cambridge: Cambridge University.
Adkins, Arthur W. H. 1960. *Merit and Responsibility: A Study in Greek Values.* Oxford: Clarendon. Reprint 1975. Chicago: University of Chicago.
Ajootian, A. 1998. "A Day at the Races." In *Stephanos: Studies in Honor of B. S. Ridgway,* eds. M. Sturgeon and K. Hartswick: 1–13. Philadelphia: University Museum, University of Pennsylvania for Bryn Mawr College.
Allen, D. S. 2000. *The World of Prometheus: The Politics of Punishing in Democratic Athens.* Princeton: Princeton University.
Allison, J. 1989. *Power and Preparedness in Thucydides.* Baltimore: Johns Hopkins University.

Ameling, W. 1985. "Plutarch, Perikles 12–14." *Historia* 34: 47–63.

Anderson, G. Forthcoming. *The Athenian Experiment: Building an Imagined Political Community in Ancient Attica, 508–490 B.C.*

Anderson, P. 1998. *The Origins of Postmodernity.* London: Verso.

Andreades, A. 1930. "The Finance of Tyrant Governments in Ancient Greece." *Economic History.* Supplement to *Economic Journal* II: 1–18.

————. 1933. *A History of Greek Public Finance,* trans. C. N. Brown. Cambridge, MA: Harvard University.

Andrewes, A. 1956. *The Greek Tyrants.* London: Hutchinson. [Reprinted. New York: Harper and Row, 1963.]

————. 1970. "Lysias and the Theramenes Papyrus." *ZPE* 6: 35–38.

————. 1974. "The Arginousai Trial." *Phoenix* 28: 112–122.

————. 1978. "The Opposition to Perikles." *JHS* 98: 1–8.

————. 1982. "The Tyranny of Pisistratus." *CAH* 3.3: 392–416.

Andrews, J. A. 2000. "Cleon's Hidden Appeals (Thucydides 3.37–40)." *CQ* 50: 45–62.

Annas, J. 1981. *An Introduction to Plato's Republic.* Oxford: Oxford University.

————. 1999. *Platonic Ethics, Old and New.* Ithaca, NY: Cornell University.

Arnush, M. 1995. "The Career of Peisistratos Son of Hippias." *Hesperia* 64: 135–162.

Arrowsmith, W. 1973. "Aristophanes' *Birds:* The Fantasy Politics of Eros." *Arion* n.s. 2, vol. 1.1: 119–167.

Asheri, D. 1988a. "Carthaginians and Greeks." *CAH* IV: 739–780.

————. 1988b. *Erodoto, Le storie libro I: La Lidia e la Persia. Introduzione, testo e commento.* Milan: Arnaldo Mondadori.

Atchity, K., and E. Barber. 1987. "Greek Princes and Aegean Princesses: The Role of Women in the Homeric Poems." In *Critical Essays on Homer,* ed. K. Atchity: 15–36. Boston: G. Hall.

Atkinson, J. E. 1992. "Curbing the Comedians: Cleon versus Aristophanes and Syracosius' Decree." *CQ* 42: 56–64.

Austin, M. M. 1990. "Greek Tyrants and the Persians, 546–479 B.C." *CQ* 40: 289–306.

Bakewell, G. 1997. "Μετοικία in the *Supplices* of Aeschylus." *ClAnt* 16.2: 209–228.

Barceló, P. 1990. "Thukydides und die Tyrannis." *Historia* 39: 401–425.

————. 1993. *Basileia, Monarchia, Tyrannis: Untersuchungen zu Entwicklung und Beurteilung von Alleinherrschaft im vorhellenistischen Griechenland. Historia* Einzelschriften 79. Stuttgart: Steiner.

Beazley, J. D. 1948. "Death of Hipparchus." *JHS* 68: 26–28.

————. 1951. *The Development of Attic Black-Figure.* Berkeley: University of California. Repr. 1986.

————. 1956. *Attic Black-Figure Vase-Painters.* Oxford: Clarendon.

————. 1957. "ΕΛΕΝΗΣ ΑΠΑΙΤΗΣΙΣ." *PBA* 43: 233–244.

————. 1963. *Attic Red-Figure Vase-Painters.* Oxford: Clarendon.

Belfiore, E., 2000. *Murder among Friends.* Oxford: Oxford University.

Benardete, S. 1969. *Herodotean Inquiries.* The Hague: Martinus Nijhoff.

Bernhardt, R. 1987. "Die Entstehung der Legende von der tyrannenfeindlichen Aussenpolitik Spartas im sechsten und fünften Jahrhundert v. Chr." *Historia* 36: 257–289.

Berve, H. 1954. "Wesenszüge der griechischen Tyrannis." *HZ* 177: 1–20. [Reprinted in Kinzl 1979b: 161–183.]

―――. 1967. *Die Tyrannis bei den Griechen.* 2 Vols. Munich: C. H. Beck.

Blanco, W., and J. Roberts, eds. 1992. *Herodotus: The Histories.* Trans. W. Blanco. New York: W. W. Norton.

Blank, D. L. 1986. "Socrates' Instructions to Cebes: Plato, 'Phaedo' 101d–e." *Hermes* 114: 146–163.

Bleicken, J. 1979. "Zur Entstehung der Verfassungstypologie im 5. Jh. v. Chr. (Monarchie, Aristokratie, Demokratie)." *Historia* 28: 148–172.

―――. 1994. *Die athenische Demokratie.* 2nd ed. Paderborn: Schöningh.

Bliss, F. R. 1964. "Ἡδὺ ἐν Σικελίαι—Democracy and Pleasure." In *Laudatores Temporis Acti: Studies in Memory of Wallace Everett Caldwell.* The James Sprunt Studies in History and Political Science. Vol. 46, eds. M. F. Gyles and E. W. Davis: 3–14. Chapel Hill: University of North Carolina.

Blok, Josine. 2000. "Phye's Procession: Culture, Politics and Peisistratid Rule." In Sancisi-Weerdenburg 2000: 17–48.

Boardman, J. 1974. *Athenian Black Figure Vases.* London: Thames and Hudson.

―――. 1999. *The Greeks Overseas: Their Early Colonies and Trade.* 4th ed. London: Thames and Hudson.

Boedeker, D. 1998. "Presenting the Past in Fifth-Century Athens." In Boedeker and Raaflaub 1998: 185–202.

―――. 2001. "Paths to Heroization at Plataea." In Boedeker and Sider 2001: 148–163.

Boedeker, D., and J. Peradotto, eds. 1987. *Herodotus and the Invention of History.* Arethusa 20.

Boedeker, D., and K. Raaflaub, eds. 1998. *Democracy, Empire, and the Arts in Fifth-Century Athens.* Cambridge, MA: Harvard University.

Boedeker, D., and David Sider, eds. 2001. *The New Simonides: Contexts of Praise and Desire.* Oxford: Oxford University.

Boersma, J. S. 1970. *Athenian Building Policy from 561/0 to 405/4 B.C.* Groningen: Wolters-Noordhoff.

―――. 2000. "Peisistratos' Building Activity Reconsidered." In Sancisi-Weerdenburg 2000: 49–56.

Bons, J. A. E. 1993. "ΑΜΦΙΒΟΛΙΑ: Isocrates and Written Composition." *Mnemosyne* 46: 160–171.

Bowra, C. M. 1961. *Greek Lyric Poetry from Alkman to Simonides.* 2nd ed. Oxford: Clarendon.

―――. 1964. *Pindar.* Oxford: Clarendon.

Brandt, H. 1998. "Pythia, Apollon und die älteren griechischen Tyrannen." *Chiron* 28: 193–212.

Briant, P. 1996. *Histoire de l'empire perse: De Cyrus à Alexandre.* Paris: Fayard.

Briant, P., and P. Lévêque, eds. 1995. *Le Monde grec aux temps classiques,* Vol. 1, *Le Ve siècle.* Nouvelle Clio. Paris: Presses Universitaires de France.

Brun, P. 1983. *Eisphora-Syntaxis-Stratiotika: Recherches sur les finances militaires d'Athènes au IVe siècle av. J.-C.* Paris: Belles Lettres.

Brunnsåker, S. 1971. *The Tyrant-Slayers of Kritios and Nesiotes.* 2nd ed. Stockholm: Svenska Institutet i Athen.

Brunt, P. A. 1993. "Plato's Academy and Politics." In *Studies in Greek History and Thought:* 282–342. Oxford: Clarendon.

Bryce, T. 1998. *The Kingdom of the Hittites.* Oxford: Oxford University.

Bugh, G. R. 1988. *Horsemen of Athens.* Princeton: Princeton University.

Buitron-Oliver, D., and E. Herscher, eds. 1997. *The City-Kingdoms of Early Iron Age Cyprus in Their Eastern Mediterranean Context.* BASOR 308.

Burford, A. 1963. "The Builders of the Parthenon." *G&R* 10, Supplement: 23–35.

———. 1965. "The Economics of Greek Temple Building." *PCPhS* n.s. 11: 21–34.

Burkert, W. 1960. "Platon oder Pythagoras? Zum Ursprung des Wortes 'Philosophie.'" *Hermes* 88: 159–177.

———. 1995. "Lydia between East and West, or How to Date the Trojan War: A Study in Herodotus." In Carter and Morris 1995: 139–158.

Bury, R. G. 1932. *Plato: The Symposium.* 2nd ed. Cambridge: Heffer.

Cambitoglou, A., and J. Papadopoulos. 1993. "The Earliest Mycenaeans in Macedonia." In *Wace and Blegen: Pottery as Evidence for Trade in the Aegean Bronze Age 1939–1989.* eds. C. Zerner, P. Zerner, and J. Winder: 289–302. Amsterdam: Gieben.

Camerer, L. 1965. "Praktische Klugheit bei Herodot: Untersuchungen zu den Begriffen mechane, techne, sophie." Doctoral dissertation, Universität Tübingen.

Camp, J. McK. II. 1986. *The Athenian Agora: Excavations in the Heart of Classical Athens.* London: Thames and Hudson.

———. 1994. "Before Democracy: The Alkmaionidai and Peisistratidai." In *The Archaeology of Athens and Attica under the Democracy,* eds. W. D. E. Coulson, O. Palagia, T. L. Shear, Jr., H. A. Shapiro, and F. J. Frost: 7–12. Oxbow Monograph 37. Oxford: Oxbow.

Carlier, P. 1984. *La Royauté en Grèce avant Alexandre.* Etudes et Travaux 6. Strasbourg: AECR.

———. 1995. "Qa-si-re-u et Qa-si-re-wi-ja." In *Politeia: Society and State in the Aegean Bronze Age,* eds. R. Laffineur and W.-D. Neimeier, 355–364. Aegeum 12. Liège and Austin, TX: Annales d'archéologie égéene de l'Université de Liège et UT-PASP.

Carter, J. 1995. "Ancestor Cult and the Occasion of Homeric Performance." In Carter and Morris 1995, 285–312.

Carter, J., and S. Morris, eds. 1995. *The Ages of Homer: A Tribute to Emily T. Vermeule.* Austin: University of Texas.

Cartledge, P. A., and F. D. Harvey, eds. 1985. *Crux: Essays in Greek History Presented to G. E. M. De Ste. Croix on His 75th Birthday.* London: Duckworth.

Cartledge, P. A., P. C. Millett, and S. C. Todd, eds. 1990. *Nomos: Essays in Athenian Law, Politics and Society.* Cambridge: Cambridge University.

Castriota, D. 1997. "Democracy and Art in Late Sixth- and Fifth-Century Athens." In Morris and Raaflaub 1997: 197–216.

Cerri, G. 1975. *Il linguaggio politico nel Prometeo di Eschilo: saggio di semantica.* Rome: Edizioni dell'Ateneo.

———. 1982. "Antigone, Creonte, e l'idea della tirannide nell'Atene del v Secolo (Alcuni tesi di V. di Benedetto)." *QUCC* 39: 137–155.

Christ, M. 1992. "Ostracism, Sycophancy, and the Deception of the Demos [Arist.] *Ath. Pol.* 43.5." *CQ* 42: 336–346.

———. 1994. "Herodotean Kings and Historical Inquiry." *ClAnt* 13: 167–202.

———. 1998. *The Litigious Athenian*. Baltimore: Johns Hopkins University.

Clairmont, C. W. 1983. *Patrios Nomos: Public Burial in Athens during the Fifth and Fourth Centuries B.C.: The Archaeological, Epigraphic-Literary and Historical Evidence*. BAR International Series 161. 2 vols. Oxford: British Archaeological Reports.

———. 1993. *Classical Attic Tombstones*. 8 vols. Kilchberg: Akanthus.

Classen, J. 1963. *Thukydides*. Revised by Julius Steup. Berlin: Weidmann.

Cobet, J. 1977. "Wann wurde Herodots Darstellung der Perserkriege publiziert?" *Hermes* 105: 2–27.

———. 1981. "König, Anführer, Herr; Monarch, Tyrann." In *Soziale Typenbegriffe im alten Griechenland und ihr Fortleben in den Sprachen der Welt*, ed. E. Welskopf 3: 11–66. Berlin: Akademie-Verlag.

———. 1988. "Herodot und mündliche Überlieferung." In Ungern-Sternberg and Reinau 1988: 226–233.

Cohen, B., ed. 2000. *Not the Classical Ideal: Athens and the Construction of the Other in Greek Art*. Leiden: Brill.

Cohen, D. 1991. *Law, Sexuality and Society: The Enforcement of Morals in Classical Athens*. Cambridge: Cambridge University.

Connor, W. R. 1971. *The New Politicians of Fifth-Century Athens*. Princeton: Princeton University.

———. 1977. "Tyrannis Polis." In *Ancient and Modern: Essays in Honor of Gerald F. Else*, eds. J. H. D'Arms and J. W. Eadie: 95–109. Ann Arbor: University of Michigan.

———. 1984. *Thucydides*. Princeton: Princeton University.

———. 1987. "Tribes, Festivals, and Processions: Civic Ceremonial and Political Manipulation in Archaic Greece." *JHS* 107: 40–50.

———. 1989. "City Dionysia and Athenian Democracy." *C&M* 40: 7–32.

Coulomb, J. 1979. "Le prince aux lis de Knossos reconsideré." *BCH* 103: 29–50.

Crane, G. 1998. "Oikos and Agora: Mapping the Polis in Aristophanes' *Wasps*." In Dobrov 1998: 198–229.

Csapo, E. and W. J. Slater, eds. 1995. *The Context of Ancient Drama*. Ann Arbor: University of Michigan.

D'Angour, A. 1999. "Archinus, Eucleides and the Reform of the Athenian Alphabet." *BICS* 43: 109–130.

Davidson, J. N. 1993. "Fish, Sex and Revolution at Athens." *CQ* 43: 53–66.

———. 1997. *Courtesans and Fishcakes*. London: Harper Collins.

Davies, J. K. 1971. *Athenian Propertied Families: 600–300 B.C.* Oxford: Clarendon.

———. 1993. *Democracy and Classical Greece*. 2nd ed. Cambridge, MA: Harvard University.

———. 1997. "The 'Origins of the Greek *Polis*': Where Should We Be Looking?" In Mitchell and Rhodes 1997: 25–38.

Davis, E. 1995. "Art and Politics in the Aegean: The Missing Ruler." In Rehak 1995: 11–20.

Davison, J. A. 1958. "Notes on the Panathenaea." *JHS* 78: 23–42.

Dawson, S. 1997. "The Theatrical Audience in Fifth-Century Athens." *Prudentia* 29: 1–14.

Day, Joseph. 1985. "Epigrams and History: The Athenian Tyrannicides, A Case in Point." In *The Greek Historians: Literature and History, Papers Presented to A. E. Raubitschek*, 25–46. Saratoga, CA: ANMA Libri (Department of Classics, Stanford University).

de Graaf, F. 1989. "Midas Wanax Lawagetas." In *Thracians and Mycenaeans.* Proceedings of the Fourth International Congress of Thracology, Rotterdam, 24–26 September 1984, eds. J. Best and N. De Vries: 153–155. Leiden: E. J. Brill.

Deger-Jalkotzy, S. 1995. "Mykenische Herrschaftsformen ohne Paläste und die griechische Polis." In *Politeia: Society and State in the Aegean Bronze Age*, Aegaeum 12, eds. R. Laffineur and W.-D. Niemeier: 367–377.

Demand, N. 1997. "The Origins of the *Polis:* The View from Cyprus." In *Res Maritimae: Cyprus and the Eastern Mediterranean from Prehistory to Late Antiquity.* CAARI Monograph Series, Volume 1, eds. S. Swiny, R. L. Hohlfelder, and H. W. Swiny: 99–105. Atlanta, GA: Scholars.

Dewald, C. 1998. "Introduction" and notes. In Waterfield 1998: ix–xli, 594–735.

———. 1999. "The Figured Stage: Focalizing the Initial Narratives of Herodotus and Thucydides." In *Contextualizing Classics: Ideology, Performance, Dialogue: Essays in Honor of John J. Peradotto*, eds. T. Falkner, N. Felson, and D. Konstan: 221–252. Lanham, MD: Rowman and Littlefield.

Dewald, C., and J. Marincola. 1987. "A Selective Introduction to Herodotean Studies." In Boedeker and Peradotto 1987: 9–40.

Diehl, E., ed. 1925. *Anthologia Lyrica Graeca*, II. 2nd ed. Leipzig: Teubner.

Dobrov, G. W., ed. 1998. *The City as Comedy: Society and Representation in Athenian Drama.* Chapel Hill: University of North Carolina.

Donlan, W. 1970. "Changes and Shifts in the Meaning of *demos* in the Literature of the Archaic Period." *PP* 135: 381–395.

———. 1980. *The Aristocratic Ideal in Ancient Greece.* Lawrence, KS: Coronado.

———. 1985. "Pistos Philos Hetairos." In Figueira and Nagy 1985: 223–244.

———. 1989. "The Pre-State Community in Greece." *SO* 44: 5–29.

———. 1992. "Review of E. Stein-Hölkeskamp." *AJPh* 113: 137–140.

———. 1997. "The Relations of Power in the Pre-State and Early State Polities." In Mitchell and Rhodes 1997: 39–48.

———. 1998. "Political Reciprocity in Dark Age Greece: Odysseus and His *Hetairoi.*" In Gill, Postlethwaite, and Seaford 1998: 51–71.

Dover, K. J. 1950. "The Chronology of Antiphon's Speeches." *CQ* 44: 44–60.

———. 1978. *Greek Homosexuality.* New York: Vintage Books.

Dreher, Martin. 2000. "Der Ostrakismos." In *Grosse Prozesse im antiken Athen*, eds. L. Burckhardt and J. von Ungern-Sternberg: 66–77 with 262–264. Munich: Beck.

Drews, R. 1972. "The First Tyrants in Greece." *Historia* 21: 129–144. [German translation in Kinzl 1979b: 256–280.]

———. 1983. *Basileus: The Evidence for Kingship in Geometric Greece.* New Haven: Yale University.

Dunbar, N. 1995. *Aristophanes*, Birds: *Edited with Introduction and Commentary.* Oxford: Clarendon.

Eadie, J. W., and J. H. D'Arms, eds. 1978. *Ancient and Modern* [Festschrift G. F. Else]. Ann Arbor: University of Michigan.

Earle, T. 1997. *How Chiefs Come to Power: The Political Economy in Prehistory.* Stanford: Stanford University.

Eder, W. 1988. "Political Self-Confidence and Resistance: The Role of *Demos* and *Plebs* after the Expulsion of the Tyrant in Athens and the King in Rome." In *Forms of Control and Subordination in Antiquity*, eds. T. Yuge and M. Doi: 465–475. Leiden: Brill.

———. 1992. "Polis und Politai: Die Auflösung des Adelsstaates und die Entwicklung des Polisbürgers." In *Euphronios und seine Zeit*, eds. W.-D. Heilmeyer and I. Wehgartner: 24–38. Berlin: Staatliche Museen.

———. 1995. "Monarchie und Demokratie im 4. Jahrhundert v. Chr.: Die Rolle des Fürstenspiegels in der athenischen Demokratie." In *Die athenische Demokratie im 4. Jahrhundert v. Chr.: Vollendung oder Verfall einer Verfassungsform?*, ed. W. Eder: 153–173. Stuttgart: Steiner.

Edmunds, L. 1987a. "The Aristophanic Cleon's 'Disturbance' of Athens." *AJPh* 108: 233–263.

——— 1987b. *Cleon, Knights, and Aristophanes' Politics.* Lanham, MD: University Press of America.

Ehrenberg, V. 1950. "Origins of Democracy." *Historia* 1: 515–548. [Reprinted in Ehrenberg 1965: 264–296.]

———. 1954. *Sophocles and Pericles.* Oxford: Blackwell.

———. 1956. "Das Harmodioslied." *WS* 69: 57–69. [Reprinted in Ehrenberg 1965: 253–264.]

———. 1965. *Polis und Imperium: Beiträge zur Alten Geschichte*, eds. K. F. Stroheker and A. J. Graham. Zurich: Artemis.

Erbse, H. 1992. *Studien zur Verständnis Herodots.* Berlin: Walter de Gruyter.

Euben, J. P., ed. 1986. *Greek Tragedy and Political Theory.* Berkeley: University of California.

Euben, J. P., J. R. Wallach, and J. Ober, eds. 1994. *Athenian Political Thought and the Reconstruction of American Democracy.* Ithaca: Cornell University.

Eucken, C. 1983. *Isokrates: Seine Position in der Auseinandersetzung mit den zeitgenössischen Philosophen.* Berlin: de Gruyter.

Evans, A. 1921–1935. *The Palace of Minos at Knossos*, I–IV. London. Reprinted 1964.

Evans, J. A. S. 1979. "Herodotus' Publication Date." *Athenaeum* 57: 145–149.

———. 1981. "Notes on the Debate of the Persian Grandees in Herodotus, 3.80–82." *QUCC* 7: 79–84.

———. 1987. "Herodotus 9.73.3 and the Publication Date of the *Histories*." *CPh* 82: 226–228.

———. 1991. *Herodotus, Explorer of the Past.* Princeton: Princeton University.

Fadinger, V. 1993. "Griechische Tyrannis und Alter Orient." In *Anfänge politischen Denkens in der Antike: Die nahöstlichen Kulturen und die Griechen*, eds. K. Raaflaub and E. Müller-Luckner: 263–316. Munich: Oldenbourg.

———. 2000. "Peisistratos und Phye." In Pircher and Treml 2000: 9–70.

Farenga, V. 1981. "The Paradigmatic Tyrant: Greek Tyranny and the Ideology of the Proper." *Helios* 8: 1–31.

Farrar, C. 1988. *The Origins of Democratic Thinking: The Invention of Politics in Classical Athens.* Cambridge: Cambridge University.

Fehling, D. 1985. *Die sieben Weisen und die frühgriechische Chronologie: Eine traditionsgeschichtliche Studie.* Bern: Peter Lang.

Fehr, B. 1984. *Die Tyrannentöter: Oder: Kann man der Demokratie ein Denkmal setzen?* Frankfurt am Main: Fischer.

Ferrill, A. 1978. "Herodotus on Tyranny." *Historia* 27: 385–398.

Figes, E. 1976. *Tragedy and Social Evolution.* London: J. Calder.

Figueira, T., and G. Nagy, eds. 1985. *Theognis of Megara: Poetry and the Polis.* Baltimore: Johns Hopkins University.

Finkelberg, M. 1991. "Royal Succession in Heroic Greece." *CQ* 41: 303–316.

Finley, M. 1957. "Homer and Mycenae: Property and Tenure." *Historia* 6: 133–159.

Fish, S. 1980. *Is There a Text in This Class?: The Authority of Interpretive Communities.* Cambridge, MA.: Harvard University.

Fitton, J. L. 1995. *The Discovery of the Greek Bronze Age.* London: British Museum.

Flashar, H. 1969. *Der Epitaphios des Perikles: Seine Funktion im Geschichtswerk des Thukydides.* Heidelberg: C. Winter.

Flory, S. 1987. *The Archaic Smile of Herodotus.* Detroit: Wayne State University.

Fol, A., and N. G. L. Hammond. 1988. "Persia in Europe, apart from Greece." In *CAH* 4: 234–253.

Fornara, C. W. 1967. "Two Notes on Thucydides." *Philologus* 111: 291–295.

———. 1968a. "Hellanicus and an Alcmaeonid Tradition." *Historia* 17: 381–383.

———. 1968b. "The 'Tradition' about the Murder of Hipparchus." *Historia* 17: 400–424.

———. 1970. "The Cult of Harmodius and Aristogeiton." *Philologus* 114: 155–180.

———. 1971a. "Evidence for the Date of Herodotus' Publication." *JHS* 91: 25–34.

———. 1971b. *Herodotus: An Interpretative Essay.* Oxford: Clarendon.

———. 1981. "Herodotus' Knowledge of the Archidamian War." *Hermes* 109: 149–156.

———, ed. 1983. *Archaic Times to the End of the Peloponnesian War.* Translated Documents of Greece and Rome, Vol. 1. 2nd ed. Cambridge: Cambridge University.

Fornara, C. W., and Samons, L. J. II. 1991. *Athens from Cleisthenes to Pericles.* Berkeley: University of California.

Forrest, W. G. 1966. *The Emergence of Greek Democracy, 800–400 BC.* New York: McGraw-Hill.

———. 1975. "An Athenian Generation Gap." *YClS* 24: 37–52.

Forsdyke, S. 1999. "From Aristocratic to Democratic Ideology and Back Again: The Thrasybulus Anecdote in Herodotus' *Histories* and Aristotle's *Politics.*" *CPh* 94: 361–372.

———. 2000. "Exile, Ostracism, and the Athenian Democracy." *ClAnt* 19: 232–263.

Forster, E. 1912. *Isocrates: Cyprian Orations.* Oxford: Clarendon.

Fowler, H. N. 1901. "The Origin of the Statements Contained in Plutarch's Life of Pericles, Chapter XIII." *HSPh* 12: 211–220.

French, A. 1975. *The Growth of the Athenian Economy.* Westport, CT: Greenwood.

Frolov, E. 1974a. "Die späte Tyrannis im Balkanischen Griechenland." In *Hellenische Poleis: Krise, Wandlung, Wirkung* I, ed. E. C. Welskopf: 231–400. Berlin: Akademie-Verlag.

———. 1974b. "Das Problem der Monarchie und der Tyrannis in der politischen Publizistik des 4. Jahrhunderts v. u. Z." In *Hellenische Poleis: Krise, Wandlung, Wirkung* I, ed. E. C. Welskopf: 401–434. Berlin: Akademie-Verlag.

Frost, F. J. 1964. "Pericles, Thucydides, Son of Melesias, and Athenian Politics before the War." *Historia* 13: 385–399.

Fuks, A. 1972. "Isokrates and the Social-Economic Situation in Greece." *AncSoc* 3: 17–44.

Funke, H. 1966. "ΚΡΕΩΝ ΑΠΟΛΙΣ." *Antike und Abendland* 12: 29–50.

Furtwängler, A., and K. Reichhold. 1904–1932. *Griechische Vasenmalerei: Auswahl Hervorragender Vasenbilder*. Munich: Bruckmann.

Gagarin, M. 1981. "The Thesmothetai and the Earliest Athenian Tyranny Law." *TAPhA* 111: 71–77.

Gammie, J. 1986. "Herodotus on Kings and Tyrants: Objective Historiography or Conventional Portraiture?" *JNES* 45: 171–185.

Gauthier, P. 1982. "Notes sur trois décrets honorant des citoyens beinfaiteurs." *RPh* 56: 215–231.

———. 1993. "Les Cités hellénistiques." In Hansen 1993: 211–231.

Geddes, A. G. 1987. "Rags and Riches: The Costume of Athenian Men in the Fifth Century." *CQ* 37: 307–331.

Gentili, B. 1979. "Polemica Antitirannica." *QUCC* n.s. 1: 153–156.

Georges, P. 1994. *Barbarian Asia and the Greek Experience: From the Archaic Period to the Age of Xenophon*. Baltimore: Johns Hopkins University.

———. 2000. "Persian Ionia under Darius: The Revolt Reconsidered." *Historia* 49: 1–39.

Gernet, L. 1981. *The Anthropology of Ancient Greece*, trans. J. Hamilton and B. Nagy. Baltimore: Johns Hopkins University.

Geyer, F. 1925. "Leaina (3)." *Paulys Realencyclopädie der Classischen Altertumswissenschaft* 12: 1045–1046.

Gill, C. 1996. *Personality in Greek Epic, Tragedy, and Philosophy*. Oxford: Clarendon.

Gill, C., N. Postlethwaite, and R. Seaford, eds. 1988. *Reciprocity in Ancient Greece*. Oxford: Oxford University.

Gillis, D. 1979. *Collaboration with the Persians*. Historia Einzelschriften 34. Wiesbaden: Steiner.

Giorgini, G. 1993. *La città e il tiranno: Il concetto di tirannide nella Grecia del* VII–IV *secolo a.c.* Milan: Giuffrè Editore.

Giraudeau, M. 1984. *Les notions juridiques et sociales chez Hérodote: Études sur le vocabulaire.* Paris: Diffusion de Boccard.

Graf, D. 1985. "Greek Tyrants and Achaemenid Politics." In *The Craft of the Ancient Historian: Essays in Honor of Chester G. Starr*, eds. J. W. Eadie and J. Ober: 79–123. Lanham, MD: University Press of America.

Gray, V. J. 1992. "Xenophon's *Symposion:* The Display of Wisdom." *Hermes* 120: 58–75.

———. 1996. "Herodotus and Images of Tyranny: The Tyrants of Corinth." *AJPh* 117: 361–389.

Grene, D. 1987. *Herodotus: The History.* Chicago: University of Chicago.

Griffith, M. 1995. "Brilliant Dynasts." *ClAnt* 14: 62–129.

———. 1998. "The King and Eye: The Rule of the Father in Greek Tragedy." *PCPhS* 44: 20–84.

Griffiths, Alan H. 1996. "Seven Sages." *OCD* 1397.

Guépin, J.-P. 1968. *The Tragic Paradox.* Amsterdam: A. M. Hakkert.

Guthrie, W. K. C. 1962. *A History of Greek Philosophy,* Vol. 1. Cambridge: Cambridge University.

————. 1969. *A History of Greek Philosophy,* Vol. 3. Cambridge: Cambridge University. [Reprint of part I: *The Sophists.* Cambridge: Cambridge University. 1971.]

Gutmann, A. 1987. *Democratic Education.* Princeton: Princeton University.

Habicht, C. 1997. *Athens from Alexander to Antony,* trans. D. L. Schneider. Cambridge, MA: Harvard University.

Hall, E. 1989. *Inventing the Barbarian: Greek Self-Definition Through Tragedy.* Oxford: Clarendon.

————. 1996. "Is There a *Polis* in Aristotle's *Poetics*?" In Silk 1996: 295–309.

Hallager, E. 1985. *The Master Impression.* SIMA LXIX. Göteborg: Paul Åströms Verlag.

Halliwell, S. 1993. *Plato: Republic 5.* Warminster: Aris & Phillips.

Halperin, D. 1992. "Plato and the Erotics of Narrativity." In *Methods of Interpreting Plato and His Dialogues* (*OSAPh* Supplemental Volume), eds. J. C. Klagge and N. D. Smith: 93–129. Oxford: Clarendon.

Hammond, N. G. L. 1982. "The Peloponnese [in the Eighth to Sixth Centuries B.C.]." *CAH* 3.3. 2nd ed.: 321–359.

Handley, E. W. 1993. "Aristophanes and the Generation Gap." In A. H. Sommerstein et al. 1993: 417–430.

Hansen, M. H. 1991. *The Athenian Democracy in the Age of Demosthenes.* Oxford: Blackwell.

————, ed. 1993. *The Ancient Greek City-State: Symposium on the Occasion of the 250th Anniversary of the Royal Danish Academy of Sciences and Letters, July 1–4 1992.* Copenhagen: Munksgaard.

Harding, P. 1973. "The Purpose of Isokrates' *Archidamos* and *On The Peace*." *CSCA* 6: 137–149.

Hartog, F. 1988. *The Mirror of Herodotus: The Representation of the Other in the Writing of History,* trans. J. Lloyd. Berkeley: University of California.

Hawkins, J., and A. M. Davies. 1998. "Of Donkeys, Mules and Tarkondemos." In *Mír Curad: Studies in Honor of Calvert Watkins,* eds. J. Jasanoff, H. C. Melchert, and L. Oliver: 242–260. Innsbruck: Institut für Sprachwissenschaft der Universität Innsbruck.

Heath, M. 1990. "Aristophanes and His Rivals." *G&R* 37: 143–158.

Hegyi, D. 1965. "Notes on the Origin of Greek Tyrannis." *AAntHung* 13: 303–318.

Hellström, P., and B. Alroth, eds. 1996. *Religion and Power in the Ancient Greek World.* Boreas 24. Uppsala: Upsaliensis Academiae.

Henderson, J. 1987. *Aristophanes Lysistrata.* Oxford: Clarendon.

————. 1990. "The Demos and the Comic Competition." In Winkler and Zeitlin 1990: 271–313.

————. 1991. "Women and the Athenian Dramatic Festivals." *TAPhA* 121: 133–147.

————. 1996. *Three Plays by Aristophanes: Staging Women.* London: Routledge.

————. 1998a. "Mass versus Elite and the Comic Heroism of Peisetairos." In Dobrov 1998: 135–148.

————. 1998b. *Aristophanes:* Acharnians, Knights. Cambridge, MA: Harvard University/Loeb Classical Library.

————. 1998c. *Aristophanes:* Clouds, Wasps, Peace. Cambridge, MA: Harvard University/Loeb Classical Library.

————. 2000. *Aristophanes:* Birds, Lysistrata, Women at the Thesmophoria. Cambridge, MA: Harvard University/Loeb Classical Library.

Hennins, A. 1968. "Zur Interpretation des Michigan-Papyrus über Theramenes." *ZPE* 3: 101–108.

Highby, L. I. 1936. *The Erythrae Decree: Contributions to the Early History of the Delian League and the Peloponnesian Confederacy. Klio* Beiheft 36. Leipzig: Dieterich.

Hölscher, T. 1973. *Griechische Historienbilder des 5. und 4. Jahrhunderts v. Chr.* Beitr. zur Archäol. 6. Würzburg: Triltsch.

————. 1996. "Politik und Öffentlichkeit im demokratischen Athen: Räume, Denkmäler, Mythen." In Sakellariou 1996: 171–187.

————. 1998. "Image and Political Identity: The Case of Athens." In Boedeker and Raaflaub 1998: 153–183.

Homeyer, H. 1962. "Zu den Anfängen der griechischen Biographie." *Philologus* 106: 75–85.

Hood, S. 2000. "Cretan Fresco Dates." In *The Wall Paintings of Thera.* Proceedings of the First International Symposium, ed. S. Sherratt, I: 191–207. Athens: Thera Foundation.

Hooker, J. 1979. "The *wanax* in the Linear B Tablets." *Kadmos* 18: 100–111.

————. 1987. "Titles and Functions in the Pylian State." In *Studies in Mycenaean and Classical Greek Presented to John Chadwick. Minos* 20–22: 257–267.

Hornblower, S. 1991. *A Commentary on Thucydides,* Vol. I. Oxford: Clarendon.

————. 1996. *A Commentary on Thucydides,* Vol. II. Oxford: Clarendon.

Hunter, V. 1973–1974. "Athens *Tyrannis:* A New Approach to Thucydides." *CJ* 69: 120–126.

Immerwahr, H. R. 1956. "Aspects of Historical Causation." *TAPhA* 87: 241–280.

————. 1960. "*Ergon:* History as Monument in Herodotus and Thucydides." *AJPh* 91: 261–290.

————. 1966. *Form and Thought in Herodotus.* Cleveland: Scholars.

Jacoby, F. 1949. *Atthis: The Local Chronicles of Ancient Athens.* Oxford: Clarendon.

Jeffery, L. 1976. *Archaic Greece: The City-States c. 700–500 B.C.* New York: St. Martin's.

Johnstone, S. 1994. "Virtuous Toil, Vicious Work: Xenophon on Aristocratic Style." *CPh* 89: 219–240.

Jouanna, J. 1978. "Le médecin modèle du législateur dans les *Lois* de Platon." *Ktema* 3: 77–91.

Kaempf-Dimitriadou, S. 1986. "Ein attisches Staatsgrabmal des 4. Jhs. v. Chr." *Antike Kunst* 29: 23–36.

Kagan, D. 1991. *Pericles of Athens and the Birth of Democracy.* New York: Free Press.

Kahn, C. 1983. "Drama and Dialectic in Plato's *Gorgias*." *OSAPh* 1: 75–121.

Kakrides, J. T. 1961. *Der thukydidische Epitaphios: Ein stilistischer Kommentar.* Zetemata 26. Munich: Beck.

Kallet, L. 1998. "Accounting for Culture in Fifth-Century Athens." In Boedeker and Raaflaub 1998: 43–58.

————. 2001. *Money and the Corrosion of Power in Thucydides: The Sicilian Expedition and Its Aftermath.* Berkeley: University of California.

Kallet-Marx, L. 1993. *Money, Expense and Naval Power in Thucydides' History, 1–5.24.* Berkeley: University of California.

Karo, M. 1931. "Archäologische Funde von Sommer 1930 bis Juni 1931. Griechenland und Dodekanes." *AA: 211–308.*

Kearns, E. 1989. *The Heroes of Attica. Bulletin of the Institute of Classical Studies,* Supplement 57. London: Institute of Classical Studies.

Kerferd, G. B. 1981. *The Sophistic Movement.* Cambridge: Cambridge University.

Kilian, K. 1988. "The Emergence of *wanax* Ideology in the Mycenaean Palaces." *OJA* 7: 291–302.

Killen, J. T. 1994. "Thebes Sealings, Knossos Tablets and Mycenaean State Banquets." *BICS* 39: 67–84.

Kinzl, K. H. 1973. "Zu Thukydides über die Peisistratidai." *Historia* 22: 504–507.

————. 1978. "ΔHMOKPATIA: Studie zur Frühgeschichte des Begriffes." *Gymnasium* 85: 117–127, 312–326 with Tables I–II.

————. 1979a. "Betrachtungen zur älteren Tyrannis." In Kinzl 1979b: 298–325. [Rev. in *AJAH* 4, 23–45.]

————, ed. 1979b. *Die ältere Tyrannis bis zu den Perserkriegen: Beiträge zur griechischen Tyrannis.* Wege der Forschung 510. Darmstadt: Wissenschaftliche Buchgesellschaft.

Klein, R. 1979. "Die innenpolitische Gegnerschaft gegen Perikles." In *Perikles und seine Zeit,* ed. G. Wirth. Wege der Forschung 412: 494–533. Darmstadt: Wissenschaftliche Buchgesellschaft.

Knox, B. M. W. 1954. "Why Is Oedipus Called *Tyrannos?*" *CJ* 50: 97–102. [Reprinted in Knox, *Word and Action: Essays on the Ancient Theater:* 87–95. Baltimore, 1979.]

————. 1957. *Oedipus at Thebes.* New Haven: Yale University.

Koehl, R. 1995. "The Silver Stag "*bibru*" from Mycenae." In Carter and Morris 1995: 61–66.

Konstan, D. 1995. *Greek Comedy and Ideology.* New York: Oxford University.

Kraut, R. 1984. *Socrates and the State.* Princeton: Princeton University.

Krentz, P. 1982. *The Thirty at Athens.* Ithaca, NY: Cornell University.

Kroll, J. H. "The Parthenon Frieze as a Votive Relief." *AJA* 83: 349–352.

Kron, U. 1996. "Priesthoods, Dedications and Euergetism: What Part did Religion Play in the Political and Social Status of Greek Women?" In Hellström and Alroth 1996: 139–182.

Kurke, L. 1991. *The Traffic in Praise: Pindar and the Poetics of Social Economy.* Ithaca, NY: Cornell University.

————. 1992. "The Politics of ἁβροσύνη in Archaic Greece." *ClAnt* 11: 91–120.

————. 1999. *Coins, Bodies, Games, and Gold: The Politics of Meaning in Archaic Greece.* Princeton: Princeton University.

Labarbe, J. 1971. "L'Apparition de la notion de tyrannie dans la Grèce archaïque." *AC* 40: 471–504.

Lahr, S. von der. 1992. *Dichter und Tyrannen im archaischen Griechenland: Das Corpus Theognideum als zeitgenössische Quelle politischer Wertvorstellungen archaisch-griechischer Aristokraten.* Munich: Tuduv-Verlagsgesellschaft.

Landfester, M. 1967. *Die Ritter des Aristophanes: Beobachtungen zur dramatischen Handlung und zum komischen Stil des Aristophanes.* Amsterdam: B. R. Grüner.

Langdon, S. 1987. "Gift Exchange in the Geometric Sanctuaries." In Linders and Nordquist 1987: 107–113.

Lanza, D. 1977. *Il tiranno e il suo pubblico.* Turin: Einaudi.

Lasserre, F. 1976. "Hérodote et Protagoras: Le débat sur les constitutions." *MH* 33: 65–84.

Lateiner, D. 1989. *The Historical Method of Herodotus.* Toronto: University of Toronto.

Lattimore, S. 1998. *Thucydides: The Peloponnesian War.* Indianapolis: Hackett.

Lavelle, B. M. 1984. "Thucydides VI.55.1 and *Adikia.*" *ZPE* 54: 17–19.

———. 1988. "*Adikia,* the Decree of Kannonos, and the Trial of the Generals." *C&M* 39: 19–41.

———. 1993. *The Sorrow and the Pity: A Prolegomenon to a History of Athens under the Peisistratids, c. 560–510 B.C.* Stuttgart: Steiner.

———. 2002. "Herodotus and the 'Parties' of Attika." *C&M* 51:51–102.

Lawrence, A. W. 1951. "The Acropolis and Persepolis." *JHS* 71: 111–119.

Lawton, C. 1995. *Attic Document Reliefs: Art and Politics in Ancient Athens.* Oxford: Clarendon.

Lebedev, A. 1996. "A New Epigram for Harmodios and Aristogeiton." *ZPE* 112: 263–268.

Lehmann, G. A. 1987. "Überlegungen zur Krise der attischen Demokratie im Peloponnesischen Krieg: Vom Ostrakismos des Hyperbolos zum Thargelion 411 v. Chr." *ZPE* 69: 33–73.

Lejeune, M. 1965. "Le *damos* dans la société mycénienne." *REG* 78: 1–22.

———. 1969. "A Propos de la Titulaire de Midas." *Athenaeum* 47: 179–192.

Lenfant, D. 1997. "Rois et tyrans dans le théâtre d'Aristophane." *Ktema* 22: 185–200.

Lenz, J. 1993. "Kings and the Ideology of Kingship in Early Greece (c. 1200–700 B.C.): Epic, Archaeology, and History." Doctoral dissertation, Columbia University.

Lévy, E. 1976. *Athènes devant la défaite: Histoire d'une crise idéologique.* Athens: Ecole française d'Athènes/Paris: de Boccard.

Lewis, D. M. 1967. "A Note on *IG* i² 114." *JHS* 87: 132.

———. 1988. "The Tyranny of the Pisistratidae." *CAH* 4: 287–302.

———. 1994. "Sparta as Victor." *CAH* 6. Cambridge: Cambridge University: 24–44.

Libero, Loretana de. 1996. *Die archaische Tyrannis.* Stuttgart: Steiner.

Lind, H. 1990. *Der Gerber Kleon in den "Rittern" des Aristophanes. Studien zur Demagogenkomödie.* Frankfurt: Peter Lang.

Linders, T. 1987. "Gifts, Gods, Society." In Linders and Nordquist 1987: 115–122.

Linders, T., and G. Nordquist, eds. 1987. *Gifts to the Gods.* Boreas 15: Uppsala: Upsaliensis Academie.

Loening, T. 1987. *The Reconciliation Agreement of 403/402 B.C. in Athens: Its Content and Application.* Hermes Einzelschriften 53. Stuttgart: Franz Steiner Verlag Wiesbaden.

Loraux, N. 1986. *The Invention of Athens: The Funeral Oration in the Classical City,* trans. Alan Sheridan. Cambridge, MA: Harvard University. [Originally published in French under the title *L'invention d'Athènes: Histoire de l'oraison funèbre dans la "cité classique"* (Paris, 1981).]

———. 1997. *La cité divisée: L'oubli dans la mémoire d'Athènes.* Paris: Payot.

Lupack, S. 2001. "The Mycenean Wanax in the Fr Series: An Ancestral Deity? *AJA* 105: 304.

Luppe, W. 1978. "Die Lücke in der Theramenes-Rede des Michigan-Papyrus Inv. 5982." *ZPE* 32: 14–16.

Luraghi, N. 1994. *Tirannidi arcaiche in Sicilia e Magna Grecia da Panezio di Leontini alla caduta dei Dinomenidi.* Florence: Leo S. Olschki.

———. 1998. "Il Gran Re e tiranni: Per una valutazione storica della tirannide in Asia Minore durante il regno dei primi Achemenidi." *Klio* 80: 22–46.

Ma, J. 1999. *Antiochus III and the Cities of Western Asia Minor.* London: Oxford University.

MacDowell, D. M. 1962. *Andokides, On the Mysteries: Text Edited with Introduction, Commentary, and Appendices.* Oxford: Clarendon.

———, ed. 1971. *Aristophanes' Wasps.* Oxford: Clarendon.

———, ed. 1982. *Gorgias: Encomium of Helen.* Bristol: Bristol Classical.

Maddoli, G. 1970. "ΔΑΜΟΣ e ΒΑΣΙΛΗΕΣ, contributo allo studio delle origine della polis." *SMEA* xii: 7–57.

Maidment, K. J. 1968. *Minor Attic Orators* i. Loeb Classical Library 308. Cambridge, MA: Harvard University.

Mann, M. 1986. *The Sources of Social Power: A History of Power from the Beginning to A.D. 1760,* Vol. 1. Cambridge: Cambridge University.

Marinatos, N. 1988. "The Fresco from Room 31 at Mycenae: Problems of Method and Interpretation." In *Problems in Greek Prehistory: Papers Presented at the Centenary of the British School at Athens,* eds. E. French and K. Wardle: 245–251. Bristol: Bristol Classical.

Martin, R. P. 1984. "Hesiod, Odysseus, and the Instruction of Princes." *TAPhA* 114: 29–48.

Mathieu, G., and Brémond, É. 1956. *Isocrate: Discours.* Tome ii. Paris: Les Belles Lettres.

Mattingly, H. B. 1992. "Epigraphy and the Athenian Empire." *Historia* 41: 129–138.

Mazarakis-Ainian, A. 1997. *From Rulers' Dwellings to Temples: Architecture, Religion and Society in Early Iron Age Greece (1100–700 B.C.).* Jonsered: Paul Åström.

McCallum, L. 1987. "Frescoes from the Throne Room at Pylos: A New Interpretation." *AJA* 91: 296.

McKechnie, P. R., and S. J. Kern. 1988. *Hellenica Oxyrhynchia.* Warminster: Aris & Phillips.

McGlew, J. 1993. *Tyranny and Political Culture in Ancient Greece.* Ithaca, NY: Cornell University.

Meier, C. 1990. *The Greek Discovery of Politics.* Trans. David McLintock. Cambridge, MA: Harvard University.

———. 1993. *The Political Art of Greek Tragedy.* Baltimore: Johns Hopkins University.

———. 1996. "Kultur als Absicherung der attischen Demokratie: Wieso brauchten die Athener ihre Kultur?" In Sakellariou 1996: 199–222.

———. 1998. *Athens: A Portrait of the City in Its Golden Age,* trans. Robert and Rita Kimber. New York: Metropolitan.

Meiggs, R. 1972. *The Athenian Empire.* Oxford: Clarendon.

Meritt, B. D. 1936. "Greek Inscriptions." *Hesperia* 5: 355–441.

———. 1952. "Athenian Inscriptions." *Hesperia* 21: 340–380.

Merkelbach, R., and H. C. Youtie. 1968. "Ein Michigan-Papyrus über Theramenes." *ZPE* 2: 161–169.

Meyer, E. 1892. *Forschungen zur Alten Geschichte*, Vol. 1. Halle: Niemeyer.

———. 1939. *Geschichte des Altertüms*, Vol. 4. Stuttgart: J. G. Cotta.

Miles, M. M. 1989. "A Reconstruction of the Temple of Nemesis at Rhamnous." *Hesperia* 58: 131–249.

Miller, M. C. 1997. *Athens and Persia in the Fifth Century B.C.: A Study in Cultural Receptivity.* Cambridge: Cambridge University.

———. 2000. "The Myth of Bousiris: Ethnicity and Art." In B. Cohen 2000: 413–442.

Millett, P. 1989. "Patronage and Its Avoidance in Classical Athens." In *Patronage in Ancient Society*, ed. A. Wallace-Hadrill: 15–47. London: Routledge.

Mills, S. 1997. *Theseus, Tragedy and the Athenian Empire*. Oxford: Clarendon.

Mirié, S. 1979. *Das Thronraumareal des Palastes von Knossos. Versuch einer Neuinterpretation seiner Entstehung und seiner Funktion.* Saarbrücker Beiträge zur Altertumskunde 26. Bonn: Habelt.

Mitchell, L. G., and P. J. Rhodes, eds. 1997. *The Development of the Polis in Archaic Greece.* London: Routledge.

Moles, J. 1996. "Herodotus Warns the Athenians." *PLLS* 9: 259–284.

Momigliano, A. 1971. *The Development of Greek Biography*. Cambridge, MA: Harvard University.

Monoson, S. S. 1994. "Citizen as *Erastes:* Erotic Imagery and the Idea of Reciprocity in the Periclean Funeral Oration." *Political Theory* 22: 253–276.

———. 2000. *Plato's Democratic Entanglements: Athenian Politics and the Practice of Philosophy.* Princeton: Princeton University.

Montgomery, H. 1965. *Gedanke und Tat: zur Erzählungstechnik bei Herodot, Thukydides, Xenophon und Arrian.* Lund: C. W. K. Gleerup.

Moran, W. L., ed. and trans. 1992. *The Amarna Letters.* Baltimore: Johns Hopkins University.

Morgan, C. 1996. "From Palace to Polis? Religious Developments on the Greek Mainland during the Bronze Age—Iron Age Transition." In Hellström and Alroth 1996: 41–57.

Morgan, C. H. 1963. "The Sculptures of the Hephaisteion, III: The Pediments, Akroteria, and Cult Images; IV: The Building." *Hesperia* 32: 91–108.

Morgan, K. 1998. "Designer History: Plato's Atlantis Story and Fourth-Century Ideology," *JHS* 118: 101–118.

———. 2000. *Myth and Philosophy from the Presocratics to Plato.* Cambridge: Cambridge University.

———. Forthcoming 2003. "The Education of Athens: Politics and Rhetoric in Isocrates (and Plato)." In *Isocrates and Civic Education,* eds. D. Depew and T. Poulakos. Austin: University of Texas.

Morris, I. 1986. "The Use and Abuse of Homer." *ClAnt* 5: 81–138.

———. 1987. *Burial and Ancient Society: The Rise of the Greek City-State.* Cambridge: Cambridge University.

———. 1992. *Death-ritual and Social Structure in Classical Antiquity.* Cambridge: Cambridge University.

———. 1996. "The Strong Principle of Equality and the Archaic Origins of Greek Democracy." In Ober and Hedrick 1996: 19–48.

———. 1998. "Beyond Democracy and Empire: Athenian Art in Context." In Boedeker and Raaflaub 1998: 59–86.

———. 2000. *Archaeology as Cultural History: Words and Things in Iron Age Greece.* Malden, MA: Blackwell.

Morris, I., and K. Raaflaub, eds. 1997. *Democracy 2500? Questions and Challenges.* Archaeological Institute of America: Colloquia and Conference Papers 2. Dubuque, IA: Kendall/Hunt.

Morris, S. 1992. "Greece beyond East and West: Perspectives and Prospects." In *Greece between East and West, 10th–8th Centuries B.C.,* eds. G. Kopke and I. Tokumaru: xiii–xviii. Mainz: Von Zabern.

———. 1995. "The Sacrifice of Astyanax: Near Eastern Contributions to the Trojan War." In Carter and Morris 1995: 221–245.

Mossé, C. 1969. *La tyrannie dans la Grèce antique.* Paris: Presses Universitaires de France.

Muhly, J. D. 1999. "The Phoenicians in the Aegean." In *Meletemata. Studies in Aegean Archaeology Presented to Malcolm W. Wiener as He Enters His 65th Year,* Aegaeum 20, eds. P. Betancourt, V. Karageorghis, R. Laffineur, and W.-D. Niemeier: 517–526. Liège: Université de Liège Histoire de l'art et archéologie de la Grèce Antique; Austin: University of Texas Austin Program in Aegean Scripts and Prehistory.

Munn, M. 2000. *The School of History: Athens in the Age of Socrates.* Berkeley: University of California.

Munson, R. 1988. "Artemisia in Herodotus." *ClAnt* 7: 91–106.

———. 1993. "Three Aspects of Spartan Kinship in Herodotus." In *Nomodeiktes: Greek Studies in Honor of Martin Ostwald,* eds. R. M. Rosen and J. Farrell: 39–54. Ann Arbor: University of Michigan.

Murray, O. 1993. *Early Greece.* 2nd ed. Cambridge, MA: Harvard University.

Nagy, G. 1985. "Theognis and Megara: A Poet's Vision of His City." In Figueira and Nagy 1985: 22–81.

———. 1990. *Pindar's Homer: The Lyric Possession of an Epic Past.* Baltimore: Johns Hopkins University.

———. 1996. *Homeric Questions.* Austin: University of Texas.

Neer, Richard. 2002. *Style and Politics in Athenian Vase-Painting.* Cambridge: Cambridge University.

Neil, R. A. 1901. *The Knights of Aristophanes.* Cambridge: Cambridge University.

Nenci, G., ed. 1994. *Erodoto, Le storie V: La rivolta della Ionia.* Commentary by G. Nenci. Milan: Mondadori.

Nestle, Wilhelm. 1901. *Euripides: Der Dichter der griechischen Aufklärung.* Stuttgart: Kohlhammer. Repr. 1969. Aalen: Scientia.

Niemeier, W.-D. 1986. "Zur Deutung des Thronraumes im Palast von Knossos." *MDAI(A)* 101: 63–95.

———. 1988. "The 'Priest-King' Fresco from Knossos: A New Reconstruction and Interpretation." In *Problems in Greek Prehistory.* Papers Presented at the Centenary Conference of the British School at Athens, Manchester, April 1986, eds. E. B. French and K. A. Wardle, 235–244. Bristol: Bristol Classical.

Nightingale, A. 1995. *Genres in Dialogue: Plato and the Construct of Philosophy.* Cambridge: Cambridge University.

North, H. 1966. *Sophrosyne: Self-Knowledge and Self-Restraint in Greek Literature.* Ithaca, NY: Cornell University.

O'Neil, J. L. 1986. "The Semantic Usage of *tyrannos* and Related Words." *Antichthon* 20: 26–40.

Oakley, J. 1990. *The Phiale Painter.* Mainz: von Zabern.

Ober, J. 1989. *Mass and Elite in Democratic Athens: Rhetoric, Ideology, and the Power of the People.* Princeton: Princeton University.

———. 1993. "The Athenian Revolution of 508/7 B.C.E.: Violence, Authority, and the Origins of Democracy." In *Cultural Poetics in Archaic Greece,* eds. C. Dougherty and L. Kurke: 215–232. Cambridge: Cambridge University. [Reprinted as Chapter 4 of Ober 1996.]

———. 1994. "How to Criticize Democracy." In Euben, Wallace, and Ober 1994: 149–171.

———. 1996. *The Athenian Revolution: Essays on Ancient Greek Democracy and Political Theory.* Princeton: Princeton University.

———. 1997. "Revolution Matters: Democracy as Demotic Action (A Response to Kurt A. Raaflaub)." In Morris and Raaflaub 1997: 67–85.

———. 1998. *Political Dissent in Democratic Athens: Intellectual Critics of Popular Rule.* Princeton: Princeton University.

Ober, J., and C. Hedrick, eds. 1993. *Birth of Democracy.* Princeton: American School of Classical Studies.

———. 1996. *Demokratia: A Conversation on Democracies, Ancient and Modern.* Princeton: Princeton University.

Ogden, D. 1997. *The Crooked Kings of Ancient Greece.* London: Routledge.

Olson, C. 1966. "Projective Verse." In *Selected Writings of Charles Olson,* ed. Robert Creeley: 15–30. New York: New Directions.

Olson, S. D. 1990. "The New Demos of Aristophanes' *Knights.*" *Eranos* 88: 60–63.

Osborne, R. 1989. "A Crisis in Archaeological History? The Seventh Century B.C. in Attica." *ABSA* 84: 297–322.

———. 1990. "Vexatious Litigation in Classical Athens: Sykophancy and the Sykophant." In Cartledge, Millett, and Todd 1990: 83–102.

———. 1996. *Greece in the Making, 1200–479 BC.* London: Routledge.

———. 2000. "An Other View: An Essay in Political History." In B. Cohen 2000: 23–42.

Ostwald, M. 1955. "The Athenian Legislation against Tyranny and Subversion." *TAPhA* 86: 103–128.

———. 1969. *Nomos and the Beginnings of the Athenian Democracy.* Oxford: Clarendon.

———. 1986. *From Popular Sovereignty to the Sovereignty of Law: Law, Society, and Politics in Fifth-Century Athens.* Berkeley: University of California.

———. 1991. "Herodotus and Athens." *ICS* 16: 137–148.

Oudemans, T., and A. Lardinois. 1987. *Tragic Ambiguity: Anthropology, Philosophy and Sophocles' Antigone.* Leiden: Brill.

Page, D. L. 1955. *Sappho and Alcaeus.* Oxford: Clarendon.

———, ed. 1962. *Poetae melici Graeci.* Oxford: Clarendon.

———. 1981. *Further Greek Epigrams.* Cambridge: Cambridge University.

Palaima, T. 1995. "The Nature of the Mycenaean *wanax:* Non-Indo European Origins and Priestly Functions." In Rehak 1995: 119–139.

Palmer, L. 1984. "The Mycenaean Palace and the *damos.*" In *Aux origines de l'Hellénisme: La Crète et la Grèce.* Hommage à Henri van Effenterre: 151–159. Paris: Publications de la Sorbonne.

Papadopoulos, J. K. 2003. *Ceramicus Redivivus.* Hesperia Suppl. 31. American School of Classical Studies: Athens.

Parker, R. 1996. *Athenian Religion: A History.* Oxford: Clarendon.

———. 1998. "Pleasing Thighs: Reciprocity in Greek Religion." In Gill, Postlethwaite, and Seaford 1998: 105–125.

Parker, V. 1996. "Vom König zum Tyrannen: Eine Betrachtung zur Entstehung der älteren griechischen Tyrannis." *Tyche* 11: 165–186.

———. 1998. "Τύραννος: The Semantics of a Political Concept from Archilochus to Aristotle." *Hermes* 126: 145–172.

Parry, A. M. 1981. *Logos and Ergon in Thucydides.* New York: Arno.

Pelling, C. 2002. "Speech and Action: Herodotus' Debate on the Constitutions." PCPhS 48: 123–158.

Pelon, O. 1995. "Royauté et iconographie royale dans la crète minoenne." In *Politeia: Society and State in the Aegean Bronze Age,* eds. R. Laffineur and W.-D. Niemeier, 309–321. Aegaeum 12. Liège and Austin, TX: Annales d'archéologie égéenne de l'Université de Liège et UT-PASP.

Pemberton, E. G. 1976. "The Gods of the East Frieze of the Parthenon." *AJA* 80: 113–124.

Pesely, G. 1995. "Aristotle's Source for the Tyranny of Peisistratos." *Athenaeum* 83: 45–66.

Phroussou, E., ed. 1999. Η Περιφέρεια του Μυκηναϊκού Κόσμου. Α΄ Διεθνές Διεπιστημονικό Συμπόσιο, Λαμία 1994. Λαμία: Έκδόσμ ΙΔ΄ Εφορείας Προϊστορικών και Κλασσικών Αρχαιοτήτων.

Pickard-Cambridge, A. 1988. *The Dramatic Festivals of Athens.* 2nd ed. Revised by J. Gould and D. M. Lewis. Oxford: Clarendon.

Pintore, F. 1983. "Seren, Tarwanis, Tyrannos." In *Studi Orientalistici in Ricordo di Franco Pintore,* eds. O. Carruba, M. Liverani, and C. Zaccagnini: 285–322. Pavia: GJES.

Pircher, W., and M. Treml, eds. 2000. *Tyrannis und Verführung.* Vienna: Turia & Kant.

Pleket, H. W. 1969. "The Archaic Tyrannis." *Talanta* 1: 19–61.

Podlecki, A. J. 1966a. *The Political Background of Aeschylean Tragedy.* Ann Arbor: University of Michigan.

———. 1966b. "The Political Significance of the Athenian 'Tyrannicide'-Cult." *Historia* 15: 129–141.

———. 1973. "Epigraphica Simonidea." *Epigraphica* 35: 24–39.

———. 1984. *The Early Greek Poets and Their Times.* Vancouver: University of British Columbia.

———. 1986. "*Polis* and Monarch in Early Attic Tragedy." In Euben 1986: 76–100.

————. 1990. "Could Women Attend the Theater in Classical Athens? A Collection of Testimonia." *AncW* 21: 27–43.

————. 1998. *Perikles and His Circle.* London: Routledge.

Powell, A. 1995. "Athens' Pretty Face: Anti-Feminine Rhetoric and Fifth-Century Controversy over the Parthenon." In *The Greek World,* ed. A. Powell. London: Routledge.

Powell, J. E. 1966. *A Lexicon to Herodotus.* 2nd ed. Hildesheim: Georg Olms.

Price, S. 1984. *Rituals and Power: The Roman Imperial Cult in Asia Minor.* Cambridge: Cambridge University.

Raaflaub, K. A. 1979. "Polis Tyrannos. Zur Entstehung einer politischen Metapher." In *Arktouros* [Festschrift B. M. W. Knox], eds. G. Bowersock, W. Burkert, and M. C. J. Putnam: 237–252. Berlin: de Gruyter.

————. 1984. "Athens 'Ideologie der Macht' und die Freiheit des Tyrannen." In *Studien zum Attischen Seebund,* eds. J. M. Balcer, H.-J. Gehrke, K. A. Raaflaub, and W. Schuller. Xenia 8: 45–86. Konstanz: Universitäts-Verlag.

————. 1985. *Die Entdeckung der Freiheit.* Munich: Beck.

————. 1986. "The Conflict of the Orders in Archaic Rome: A Comprehensive and Comparative Approach." In *Social Struggles in Archaic Rome. New Perspectives on the Conflict of the Orders,* ed. K. Raaflaub: 1–51. Berkeley: University of California.

————. 1987. "Herodotus, Political Thought, and the Meaning of History." In Boedeker and Peradotto 1987: 221–248.

————. 1988a. "Athenische Geschichte und mündliche Überlieferung." In Ungern-Sternberg and Reinau 1988: 197–225.

————. 1988b. "Homer and the Beginning of Political Thought in Greece." *Proceedings of the Boston Area Colloquium in Ancient Philosophy,* Vol. 4: 1–25.

————. 1988c. "Politisches Denken im Zeitalter Athens." In *Pipers Handbuch der politischen Ideen* I: *Frühe Hochkulturen und europäische Antike,* eds. I. Fetscher and H. Münkler: 273–368. Munich: Piper.

————. 1989. "Contemporary Perceptions of Democracy in Fifth-Century Athens." *C&M* 40: 33–70.

————. 1993. "Homer to Solon: The Rise of the Polis. The Written Sources." In Hansen 1993: 41–105.

————. 1994. "Democracy, Power, and Imperialism in Fifth-Century Athens." In Euben, Wallach, and Ober 1994: 103–146.

————. 1996. "Equalities and Inequalities in Athenian Democracy." In Ober and Hedrick 1996: 139–174.

————. 1997a. "Greece." In *Ancient History: Recent Work and New Directions,* eds. S. Burstein, R. MacMullen, K. Raaflaub, A. Ward, and C. Thomas: 1–35. Claremont, CA: Regina.

————. 1997b. "Politics and Interstate Relations in the World of Early Greek *Poleis:* Homer and Beyond." *Antichthon* 31: 1–27.

————. 1997c. "Power in the Hands of the People: Foundations of Athenian Democracy" and "The Thetes and Democracy (A Response to Josiah Ober)." In Morris and Raaflaub 1997: 31–66, 87–103.

————. 1997d. "Soldiers, Citizens and the Evolution of the Early Greek *Polis.*" In Mitchell and Rhodes 1997: 49–59.

————. 2000. "Zeus Eleutherios, Dionysus the Liberator, and the Athenian Tyrannicides: Anachronistic Uses of Fifth-Century Political Concepts." In *Polis & Politics: Studies in Ancient Greek History, Presented to Mogens H. Hansen,* eds. P. Flensted-Jensen, T. H. Nielsen, and L. Rubinstein: 249–275. Copenhagen: Museum Tusculanum.

————. 2002. "Philosophy, Science, Politics: Herodotus and the Intellectual Trends of His Time." In *A Companion to Herodotus,* eds. E. Bakker, I. de Jong, and H. van Wees: 149–186. Leiden: Brill.

Race, W. 1987. "Pindaric Encomium and Isokrates' *Evagoras.*" *TAPhA* 117: 131–155.

Raubitschek, A. E. 1941. "The Heroes of Phyle." *Hesperia* 10: 284–295.

————. 1960. "Theopompos on Thucydides, the Son of Melesias." *Phoenix* 14: 81–95. [Reprinted in *The School of Hellas: Essays on Greek History, Archaeology, and Literature,* eds. D. Obbink and P. A. Vander Waerdt (Oxford, 1991).]

Rawlings, H. R. III. 1981. *The Structure of Thucydides' History.* Princeton: Princeton University.

Redfield, J. 1985. "Herodotus the Tourist." *CPh* 80: 97–118.

Rehak, P., ed. 1995. *The Role of the Ruler in the Prehistoric Aegean. Aegaeum* 11.

Rhodes, P. J. 1972. *The Athenian Boule.* Oxford: Clarendon.

————. 1981. *A Commentary on the Aristotelian* Athenaion Politeia. Oxford: Clarendon.

————. 1994. "The Ostracism of Hyperbolus." In *Ritual, Finance, Politics: Athenian Democratic Accounts Presented to David Lewis,* eds. R. Osborne and S. Hornblower: 85–98. Oxford: Clarendon.

Ridgway, B. S. 1997. *Fourth-Century Styles in Greek Sculpture.* Madison: University of Wisconsin.

Riginos, A. S. 1976. *Platonica: The Anecdotes Concerning the Life and Writings of Plato.* Columbia Studies in the Classical Tradition 3. Leiden: Brill.

Robinson, E. W. 1994. "Reexamining the Alcmeonid Role in the Liberation of Athens." *Historia* 43: 363–369.

————. 1997. *The First Democracies: Early Popular Government Outside Athens.* Stuttgart: Steiner.

Robkin, A. L. 1975. "The Odeion of Perikles: Some Observations on Its History, Form and Function." Doctoral dissertation, University of Washington.

Rocco, C. 1997. *Tragedy and Enlightenment: Athenian Political Thought and the Dilemmas of Modernity.* Berkeley: University of California.

Rodenwalt, G. 1939. *Korkyra II: Die Bildwerke des Artemistempels von Korkyra.* Berlin: Gebrüder Mann.

Romer, F. 1982. "The *Aisymnēteia:* A Problem in Aristotle's Historic Method." *AJPh* 103: 25–46.

Romilly, J. de. 1963. *Thucydides and Athenian Imperialism,* trans. P. Thody. Cambridge, MA: Harvard University/Oxford: Blackwell.

————. 1969. "Il pensiero di Euripide sulla tirannia." *Dioniso* 43: 175–187.

————. 1995. *Alcibiade, ou, Les dangers de l'ambition.* Paris: Editions de Fallois.

Root, M. C. 1985. "The Parthenon Frieze and the Apadana Reliefs at Persepolis." *AJA* 89: 103–120.

Rosenbloom, D. 1995. "Myth, History, and Hegemony in Aeschylus." In *History, Tragedy, Theory: Dialogues on Athenian Drama,* ed. B. Goff: 91–130. Austin: University of Texas.

Rosivach, V. 1988. "The Tyrant in Athenian Democracy." *QUCC* n.s. 30: 43–57.

Rösler, Wolfgang. 1980. *Dichter und Gruppe: Eine Untersuchung zu den Bedingungen und zur historischen Funktion früher griechischer Lyrik am Beispiel Alkaios.* Munich: W. Fink.

Ruijgh, C. 1999. "Ϝαναξ et ses dérivés dans les textes Mycéniens." In *Floreant Studia Mycenaea* (Salzburg, 1995) Vol. II, eds. S. Deger-Jalkotzy, S. Hiller and O. Panagl: 521–535. Vienna: Verlag der Österreichischen Akademie der Wissenschaften.

Rupp, D. 1988. "The 'Royal Tombs' at Salamis (Cyprus): Ideological Messages of Power and Authority." *JMA* 1: 110–139.

Ruschenbusch, E. 1978. *Untersuchungen zu Staat und Politik in Griechenland vom 7.-4. Jh. v. Chr.* Bamberg: Aku-Verlag.

———. 1979. *Athenische Innenpolitik im 5. Jh. v. Chr.: Ideologie oder Pragmatismus?* Bamberg: Fotodruck u. Verlag GmbH.

Rusten, J. 1985. "Two Lives or Three? Pericles on Athenian Character (Thucydides 2.40.1–2)." *CQ* 35: 14–19.

———. 1989. *Thucydides: The Peloponnesian War. Book II.* Cambridge: Cambridge University.

Ruzé, F. 1989. *"Basileis,* Tyrans et Magistrats." *Métis* 4: 211–231.

Ryan, F. X. 1994. "The Original Date of the δῆμος πληθύων Provisions of IG I³ 105." *JHS* 114: 120–134.

Ryle, G. 1966. *Plato's Progress.* Cambridge: Cambridge University.

Saïd, S. 1985. *Sophiste et Tyran.* Paris: Klincksieck.

Sakellariou, M. B., ed. 1996. *Colloque International: Démocratie athénienne et culture.* Athens: Athenian Academy.

Salmon, L. J. 1997. "Lopping off the Heads? Tyrants, Politics and the *Polis."* In *Archaic Greece: New Approaches and New Evidence,* eds. N. Fisher and H. van Wees: 60–73. London: Duckworth.

Samons, L. J. II. 1993. "Athenian Finance and the Treasury of Athena." *Historia* 42: 129–148.

———. 2000. *Empire of the Owl: Athenian Imperial Finance.* Historia Einzelschriften 142. Stuttgart: Steiner.

Sancisi-Weerdenburg, H., ed. 2000. *Peisistratos and the Tyranny: A Reappraisal of the Evidence.* Amsterdam: Gieben.

Sauppe, H. 1896. *Ausgewählte Schriften.* Berlin: Weidmannsche Buchhandlung.

Scanlon, Thomas. 1987. "Thucydides and Tyranny." *ClAnt* 6: 286–301.

Scheffer, C. 1990. "'Domus Regiae'—A Greek Tradition?" *Opuscula Atheniensia* 18: 185–191.

Schmid, W. 1888. "Kritisches zu Thucydides II." *RhM* 43: 628–631.

Schmitt-Pantel, P. 1979. "Histoire de tyran ou comment la cité grecque construit ses marges." In *Les Marginaux et les exclus dans l'histoire. Cahiers Jussieu* 5: 217–231. Paris: Union générale d'éditions.

Schofield, M. 1999. *Saving the City.* London: Routledge.

Schubert, C. 1993. *Die Macht des volkes und die Ohnmacht des Denkens.* Historia Einzelschriften 77. Stuttgart: Steiner.

Schuller, W. 1974. *Die Herrschaft der Athener im Ersten Attischen Seebund.* Berlin: De Gruyter.

————. 1978. *Die Stadt als Tyrann: Athens Herrschaft über seine Bundesgenossen.* Konstanzer Universitätsreden 101. Konstanz: Universitäts-Verlag.

Schwarze, J. 1971. *Die Beurteilung des Perikles durch die attische Komödie und ihre historische und historiographische Bedeutung.* Zetemata 51. Munich: C. H. Beck.

Seaford, R. 1987. "The Tragic Wedding." *JHS* 107: 106–130.

————. 1994. *Reciprocity and Ritual: Homer and Tragedy in the Developing City-State.* Oxford: Oxford University.

————. 1998. "Tragic Money." *JHS* 118: 119–139.

————. 2000. "The Dionysiac Don Responds to Don Quixote: Rainer Friedrich on the New Ritualism." *Arion* 8.2: 74–98.

Seager, R. 1967. "Alcibiades and the Charge of Aiming at Tyranny." *Historia* 16: 6–18.

Sealey, R. 1957. "From Phemios to Ion." *REG* 70: 312–355.

Segal, C. 1997. *Dionysiac Poetics and Euripides' Bacchae,* 2nd expanded ed. Princeton: Princeton University.

Sélincourt, A. de. 1954. *Herodotus: The Histories.* London: Penguin Books.

Service, E. 1962. *Primitive Social Organization: An Evolutionary Perspective.* New York: Random House.

Settis, S., ed. 1996. *I Greci: Storia, cultura, arte, società.* Turin: Einaudi.

Shapiro, H. A. 1989. *Art and Cult under the Tyrants.* Mainz on Rhein: P. von Zabern.

Shaw, M. 1999. "The 'Priest-King Fresco' from Knossos: Man, Woman, Priest, King or Someone Else?" *AJA* 104: 315.

Shear, J. 1997. "Goddess, Polis, and Heroes: The Tyrannicides and the Panathenaia." Unpublished Paper Presented at the Annual Meeting of the Archaeological Institute of America, Chicago.

Shear, T. L., Jr. 1978. "Tyrants and Buildings in Archaic Athens." In *Athens Comes of Age: From Solon to Salamis,* with foreword by W. A. P. Childs: 1–19. Princeton: Archaeological Institute of America.

————. 1982. "The Demolished Temple at Eleusis." In *Studies in Athenian Architecture, Sculpture and Topography Presented to Homer A. Thompson.* Hesperia Supplement 20: 128–140. Princeton: American School of Classical Studies at Athens.

Shefton, B. B. 1960. "Some Iconographic Remarks on the Tyrannicides." *AJA* 64: 173–179.

Shelmerdine, C. 1999. "Administration in the Mycenaean Palaces: Where's the Chief." In *Rethinking Mycenaean Palaces: New Interpretations of an Old Idea,* eds. M. L. Galaty and W. Parkinson: 19–24. UCLA: Cotsen Institute of Archaeology.

Shipley, G. 1987. *A History of Samos, 800–188 BC.* Oxford: Oxford University.

Siewert, P., ed. 2002. *Ostrakismos-Testimonien. Die Zeugnisse antiker Autoren, der Inschriften und Ostraka über das athenische Scherbengericht aus vorhellenistischer Zeit, 487–322 v. Chr.* Historia Einzelschrift 155. Stuttgart: Steiner.

Silk, M. 1996. *Tragedy and the Tragic.* Oxford: Oxford University.

Simon, E., and Hirmer, M. 1981. *Die Griechischen Vasen.* 2nd ed. Munich: Hirmer.

Sinn, U. 1996. "The Influence of Greek Sanctuaries on the Consolidation of Economic Power." In Hellström and Alroth 1996: 67–74.

Smarczyk, B. 1990. *Untersuchungen zur Religionspolitik und politischen Propaganda Athens im Delisch-Attischen Seebund.* Munich: Tuduv.

Smart, J. D. 1977. "The Athenian Empire." *Phoenix* 31: 245–257.

Snell, B. 1971. *Leben und Meinungen der Sieben Weisen*. 4th ed. Munich: Heimeran.

Snodgrass, A. 1980. *Archaic Greece: The Age of Experiment*. Berkeley: University of California.

Sommerstein, A. H. 1977. "Aristophanes and the Events of 411." *JHS* 97: 112–126.

———. 1983. *The Comedies of Aristophanes:* Vol. 4. *Wasps*. Warminster: Aris and Phillips.

———. 1987. *The Comedies of Aristophanes:* Vol. 6. *Birds*. Warminster: Aris and Phillips.

———. 1990. *The Comedies of Aristophanes:* Vol. 7. *Lysistrata*. Warminster: Aris and Phillips.

———. 1993. "Kleophon and the Restaging of Frogs." In Sommerstein et al. 1993: 461–476.

———. 1996a. *The Comedies of Aristophanes:* Vol. 9. *Frogs*. Warminster: Aris and Phillips.

———. 1996b. "How To Avoid Being a *Komodoumenos*," *CQ* 46: 327–356.

———. 1997a. "The Theatre Audience, the Demos, and the Suppliants of Aeschylus." In *Greek Tragedy and the Historian,* ed. C. Pelling: 63–79. Oxford: Clarendon.

———. 1997b. "Platón, Éupolis y la 'comedia de demagogo'" In *Sociedad, Politica y Literatura: Comedia griega antigua,* ed. A. López Eire: 183–195. Salamanca: Logo.

———. 2000. "Platon, Eupolis and the 'Demagogue-Comedy.'" In *The Rivals of Aristophanes: Studies in Athenian Old Comedy,* eds. D. Harvey and J. Wilkins: 437–451. London: Duckworth and the Classical Press of Wales.

Sommerstein, A. H., S. Halliwell, J. Henderson, and Z. Bernhard, eds. 1993. *Tragedy, Comedy and the Polis*. Bari: Levante Editori.

Spinosa, C., F. Flores, and H. Dreyfus. 1997. *Disclosing New Worlds: Entrepreneurship, Democratic Action, and the Cultivation of Solidarity*. Cambridge, MA: MIT.

Stadter, P. A. 1989. *A Commentary on Plutarch's Pericles*. Chapel Hill: University of North Carolina.

———. 1992. "Herodotus and the Athenian *Arche*." *Annali della Scuola Normale Superiore di Pisa: Classe di Lettere e Filosofia,* Ser. III, 22: 781–809.

Stahl, M. 1983. "Tyrannis und das Problem der Macht: Die Geschichten Herodots über Kypselos und Periander von Korinth." *Hermes* 111: 202–220.

———. 1987. *Aristokraten und Tyrannen im archaischen Athen*. Stuttgart: Steiner.

Stanier, R. S. 1953. "The Cost of the Parthenon." *JHS* 73: 68–76.

Stanton, G., ed. 1990. *Athenian Politics c. 800–500 BC: A Sourcebook*. London: Routledge.

Starr, C. 1986. *Individual and Community: The Rise of the Polis, 800–500 B.C.* London: Oxford University.

Stein, H. 1962. *Herodotos*. Berlin: Teubner.

Stein-Hölkeskamp, E. 1989. *Adelskultur und Polisgesellschaft: Studien zum griechischen Adel in archaischer und klassischer Zeit*. Stuttgart: Steiner.

———. 1996. "Tirannidi e ricerca dell' *eunomia*." In *I Greci: Storia, cultura, arte, Società,* II. 1, ed. S. Settis 1996: 653–679. Torino: Einaudi.

Steiner, D. 1994. *The Tyrant's Writ: Myths and Images of Writing in Ancient Greece*. Princeton: Princeton University.

Stone, L. M. 1981. *Costume in Aristophanic Poetry*. New York: Arno.

Storey, I. C. 1990. "Dating and Re-Dating Eupolis." *Phoenix* 44: 1–30.

Strasburger, H. 1955. "Herodot und das perikleische Athen." *Historia* 4: 1–25. [Reprinted in H. Strasburger, *Studien zur Alten Geschichte* 2: 592–626. Hildesheim: Olms, 1982.]

Strassler, R. B., ed. 1996. *The Landmark Thucydides: A Comprehensive Guide to the Peloponnesian War: A Newly Revised Edition of the Richard Crawley Translation with Maps, Annotations, Appendices, and Encyclopedic Index*. New York: Free Press.

Strauss, B. S. 1985. "Ritual, Social Drama and Politics in Classical Athens." *AJAH* 10: 67–83.

———. 1991. "On Aristotle's Critique of Athenian Democracy." In *Essays on the Foundations of Aristotelean Political Science*, eds. C. Lord and D. K. O'Conner: 212–233. Berkeley: University of California.

Strauss, L. 1964. *The City and Man*. Chicago: Rand McNally.

Stroheker, K. F. 1953–1954. "Zu den Anfängen der monarchischen Theorie in der Sophistik." *Historia* 2: 381–412.

Stroud, R. S. 1998. *The Athenian Grain-Tax Law of 374/3 B.C.* Hesperia Supplement 29. Princeton: American School of Classical Studies.

Stupperich, R. 1994. "The Iconography of Athenian State Burials in the Classical Period." In *The Archaeology of Athens and Attica under Democracy*, eds. W. Coulson, F. J. Frost, H. A. Shear, and T. L. Shear, Jr., 93–103. Oxford: Oxbow.

Sutton, D. 1970. "An Analytical Prosopography and Statistical Guide to the Land Tenure Tablets from Pylos." Doctoral dissertation, University of Wisconsin, Madison.

Taplin, O. 1978. *Greek Tragedy in Action*. London: Methuen.

Tartaron, T. 1996. "Bronze Age Settlement and Subsistence in Southwestern Epirus, Greece." Doctoral dissertation, Boston University.

Taylor, M. 1991. *The Tyrant Slayers*. 2nd ed. Salem, NH: Ayers.

Thalmann, W. G. 1998. *The Swineherd and the Bow: Representations of Class in the Odyssey*. Ithaca, NY: Cornell University.

Thomas, C. 1976. "The Nature of Mycenaean Kingship." *Studi Micenei ed Egeo-Anatolici* 17: 93–116.

Thomas, R. 1989. *Oral Tradition and Written Record in Classical Athens*. Cambridge: Cambridge University.

———. 1993. "Performance and Written Publication in Herodotus and the Sophistic Generation." In *Vermittlung und Tradierung von Wissen in der griechischen Kultur*, eds. W. Kullmann and J. Althoff: 225–244. ScriptOralia 61. Tübingen: Narr.

———. 2000. *Herodotus in Context: Ethnography, Science and the Art of Persuasion*. Cambridge: Cambridge University.

Thomsen, R. 1964. *Eisphora: A Study of Direct Taxation in Ancient Athens*. Copenhagen: Gyldendal.

———. 1972. *The Origin of Ostracism: A Synthesis*. Copenhagen: Gyldendal.

Thomson, G. 1929. "ΖΕΥΣ ΤΥΡΑΝΝΟΣ: A Note on the *Prometheus Vinctus*." *CR* 43: 3–5.

———. 1932. *Aeschylus, The* Prometheus Bound. Cambridge: Cambridge University.

Tod, M. N. 1948. *A Selection of Greek Historical Inscriptions. Vol. II. From 403 to 323 B.C.* Oxford: Clarendon.

Todd, S. C. 1984. "Lysias and Athens—Internal Politics, 403–395 B.C." Unpublished Doctoral dissertation, University of Cambridge.

———. 1990. "Lady Chatterley's Lover and the Athenian Orators: The Social Composition of the Athenian Jury." *JHS* 110: 146–170.

Todorov, T. 1984. *Mikhaïl Bakhtin: The Dialogical Principle*, trans. W. Godzich. Minneapolis: University of Minnesota.

Tölle-Kastenbein, R. 1994. *Das archaische Wasserleitungsnetz für Athen*. Mainz: von Zabern.

Too, Y. L. 1995. *The Rhetoric of Identity in Isocrates*. Cambridge: Cambridge University.

Travlos, I. 1971. *Pictorial Dictionary of Ancient Athens*. New York: Praeger.

Trypanis, C. A. 1960. "A New Collection of Epigrams from Chios." *Hermes* 88: 69–74.

Tuplin, C. 1985. "Imperial Tyranny: Some Reflections on a Classical Greek Political Metaphor." In *Crux: Essays in Greek History Presented to G. E. M. de Ste. Croix*, eds. P. Cartledge and F. D. Harvey: 348–375. Exeter: Imprint Academic.

Turner, J. A. 1983. "Hiereia: Acquisition of Feminine Priesthoods in Ancient Greece." Doctoral dissertation, University of California, Santa Barbara.

Ungern-Sternberg, J., and H. Reinau, eds. 1988. *Vergangenheit in mündlicher Überlieferung*. Colloquium Rauricum 1. Stuttgart: Teubner.

Usener, S. 1994. *Isokrates, Platon, und ihr Publikum*. Tübingen: Gunter Narr.

van der Veen, J. 1996. *The Significant and the Insignificant: Five Studies in Herodotus' View of History*. Amsterdam: J. C. Gieben.

van der Vliet, E. Ch. L. 1986. "'Big-Man,' Tyrant, Chief: The Anomalous Starting Point of the State in Classical Greece." In *Private Politics: A Multi-Disciplinary Approach to 'Big-Man' Systems*, eds. M. A. Bakel, R. Hagesteijn, and P. van de Velde: 117–126. Leiden: Brill.

Van Effenterre, H. 1985. *La cité grecque: Des origines à la défaite de Marathon*. Paris: Hachette Littérature.

van Wees, H. 1999. "Megara's Mafiosi." In *Alternatives to the Democratic Polis*, eds. S. Hodkinson and R. Brock, 52–67. Oxford: Oxford University.

Vansina, J. 1985. *Oral Tradition as History*. Madison: University of Wisconsin.

Veblen, T. 1899. *The Theory of the Leisure Class*. New York: Macmillan.

Vermeule, E. 1970. "Five Vases from the Grave Precinct of Dexileos." *Jahrbuch des deutschen archäologischen Instituts* 85: 94–111.

Vernant, J.-P. 1982. "From Oedipus to Periander: Lameness, Tyranny, Incest in Legend and History." *Arethusa* 15: 19–38.

Vernant, J.-P., and P. Vidal-Naquet. 1990. *Myth and Tragedy in Ancient Greece*, trans. Janet Lloyd. New York: Zone.

Vickers, M. 1997. *Pericles on Stage: Political Comedy in Aristophanes' Early Plays*. Austin: University of Texas.

Wallace, R. W. 1989. *The Areopagos Council to 307 B.C.* Baltimore: Johns Hopkins University.

———. 1994. "Private Lives and Public Enemies: Freedom of Thought in Classical Athens." In *Athenian Identity and Civic Ideology*, eds. A. L. Boegehold and A. C. Scafuro: 127–155. Baltimore: Johns Hopkins University.

———. 1997a. "Poet, Public, and 'Theatocracy': Audience Performance in Classical Athens." In *Poet, Public, and Performance in Ancient Greece*, eds. L. Edmunds and R. Wallace: 97–111. Baltimore: Johns Hopkins University.

———. 1997b. "Solonian Democracy." In Morris and Raaflaub 1997: 11–29.

Walser, G. 1984. *Hellas und Iran*. Darmstadt: Wissenschaftliche Buchgesellschaft.

Walter, U. 1993. "Herodot und die Ursachen des Ionischen Aufstandes." *Historia* 42: 257–278.

Wardy, R. 1996. *The Birth of Rhetoric: Gorgias, Plato, and Their Successors*. London: Routledge.

Warner, R. 1954. *Thucydides, History of the Peloponnesian War*. Harmondsworth: Penguin Books. [Revised ed. 1972.]

Waterfield, R. 1998. *Herodotus: The Histories*. Oxford: Oxford University.

Waters, K. H. 1971. *Herodotos on Tyrants and Despots: A Study in Objectivity*. Historia Einzelschriften 15. Wiesbaden: Steiner.

———. 1985. *Herodotos the Historian: His Problems, Methods and Originality*. Norman, OK: Oklahoma University.

Wecowski, Marek. 1996. "Ironie et histoire: Le discours de Soclès (Hérodote v 92)." *Ancient Society* 27: 205–238.

Welsh, D. 1983. "The Chorus of Aristophanes' Babylonians." *GRBS* 24: 137–150.

Welwei, K.-W. 1992. *Athen: Vom neolithischen Siedlungsplatz zur archaischen Grosspolis*. Darmstadt: Wissenschaftliche Buchgesellschaft.

Wesenberg, B. 1995. "Panathenäische Peplosdedikation und Arrephorie: Zur Thematik des Parthenonfriezes." *Jahrbuch des deutschen archäologischen Instituts* 110: 149–178.

West, M. L. 1971–1992. *Iambi et Elegi Graeci Ante Alexandrum Cantati*. 2 vols. [Vol. 2. 2nd ed. 1992]. Oxford: Clarendon.

———. 1993. *Greek Lyric Poetry: Translated with Introduction and Notes*. Oxford: Oxford University. [Paperback edition 1994.]

———. 1997. *The East Face of Helicon: West Asiatic Elements in Greek Poetry and Myth*. Oxford: Clarendon.

Whitehead, D. 1982–1983. "Sparta and the Thirty Tyrants." *Ancient Society* 13/14: 105–130.

Will, E. 1975. "Fonctions de la monnaie dans les cités grecques de l'époque classique." In *Numismatique Antique: Problèmes et Méthodes: Actes du colloque organisé à Nancy du 27 septembre au 2 octobre 1971*. Études d'Archéologie Classique IV, eds. J.-M. Dentzer, P. Gauthier, and T. Hackens: 233–246. Louvain: Éditions Peeters.

Winkler, J. J. 1990. "Laying down the Law: The Oversight of Men's Sexual Behavior in Classical Athens." In *Before Sexuality: The Construction of Erotic Experience in the Ancient Greek World*, eds. D. Halperin, J. J. Winkler, and F. Zeitlin: 171–209. Princeton: Princeton University.

Winkler, J. J., and F. Zeitlin, eds. 1990. *Nothing to Do with Dionysos? Athenian Drama in Its Social Context*. Princeton: Princeton University.

Wohl, V. 1999. "The Eros of Alcibiades." *ClAnt* 18: 349–385.

Wolpert, A. 2002. *Remembering Defeat: Civil War and Civic Memory in Ancient Athens*. Baltimore: Johns Hopkins University.

Woodard, R. 1997. *Greek Writing from Knossos to Homer: A Linguistic Interpretation of the Origin of the Greek Alphabet and the Continuity of Ancient Greek Literacy*. Oxford: Clarendon.

Woodhead, A. G. 1970. *Thucydides on the Nature of Power*. Cambridge, MA: Harvard University.

Wright, J. 1995. "From Chief to King in Mycenaean Society." In Rehak 1995: 63–80.

———. 1996. "Empty Cups and Empty Jugs: The Social Role of Wine in Minoan and

Mycenaean Societies." In *The Origins and Ancient History of Wine,* eds. P. McGovern, S. Fleming, and S. Katz: 287–309. Philadelphia: Gordon and Breach.

Wycherley, R. E. 1957. *The Athenian Agora,* III: *Literary and Epigraphical Testimonia.* Princeton: American School of Classical Studies in Athens.

———. 1967. *How the Greeks Built Cities.* London: Macmillan.

———. 1978. *The Stones of Athens.* Princeton: Princeton University.

Young, D. C. 1968. *Three Odes of Pindar.* Leiden: Brill.

Yunis, H. 1996. *Taming Democracy: Models of Political Rhetoric in Classical Athens.* Ithaca, NY: Cornell University.

Zahrnt, M. 1989. "Delphi, Sparta und die Rückführung der Alkmeoniden." *ZPE* 76: 297–307.

Zeitlin, F. 1986. "Theater of Self and Society in Athenian Drama." In Euben 1986: 101–141.

———. 1990. "Thebes: Theater of Self and Society in Athenian Drama." In Winkler and Zeitlin 1990: 130–167.

Zimmern, A. 1924. *The Greek Commonwealth: Politics and Economics in Fifth-Century Athens.* Oxford: Clarendon.

Zörner, G. 1971. "Kypselos und Pheidon von Argos: Untersuchungen zur frühen griechischen Tyrannis." Doctoral dissertation, Universität Marburg.

Zournatzi, A. 1996. "Cypriot Kingship: Perspectives in the Classical Period." Τεκμήρια 2: 154–181.

NOTES ON CONTRIBUTORS

Carolyn Dewald is Associate Professor of Classics at the University of Southern California. She works in the historiography and rhetoric of the ancient world and has written articles on ancient historiography, with special emphasis on Herodotus and Thucydides. She is, with Robin Waterfield, the co-editor of the Oxford World's Classics *Herodotus* and is an associate editor of *Classical Philology*. In 2001–2002 she was the Blegen Visiting Professor at Vassar College, and in 2002–2003 she will be a Phi Beta Kappa National Visiting Scholar. She is currently finishing a manuscript on Thucydides.

Jeffrey Henderson is Professor of Classical Studies at Boston University and Editor of the Loeb Classical Library. He is the author of *The Maculate Muse: Obscene Language in Attic Comedy* (1975) and has served as contributing editor to other volumes on ancient drama. The latest of his many contributions to the study of Old Comedy include a new Loeb edition of Aristophanes, and he is at work on a critical edition of Aristophanes' *Knights*.

Lisa Kallet is Professor of Classics at the University of Texas. Her areas of specialization are the history of Athens, with special focus on the Athenian empire, democracy, and Greek historiography. She is the author of *Money, Expense and Naval Power in Thucydides'* History, *1–5.24* (1993) and *Money and the Corrosion of Power in Thucydides: The Sicilian Expedition and Its Aftermath* (2001). She has published articles on topics concerned with Thucydides, the Athenian economy, democracy, and epigraphy.

Kathryn Morgan is Associate Professor of Classics at the University of California, Los Angeles. Her research and publications focus on fifth- and fourth-century B.C. Greek literature and intellectual history, particularly the Platonic dialogues and the poetry of Pindar. She is the author of *Myth and Philosophy from the Presocratics to Plato* (2000), which explored the appropriation of myth for philosophical purposes by the Presocratics, Sophists, and Plato. She is currently involved in a project on Platonic narratology and is working on a book about Pindar's Sicilian odes in their cultural context.

Sarah Morris is Steinmetz Professor of Classical Archaeology and Material Culture at the University of California, Los Angeles. Her training and research involve early Greek literature (Homer, Hesiod, and Herodotus), Greek religion, prehistoric and early Greek archaeology, and in particular the interaction of Greece with its eastern neighbors in art, literature, religion, and culture. Her chief book on the subject, *Daidalos and the Origins of Greek Art* (1992), won the James Wiseman Book Award from the Archaeological Institute of America for 1993. She has also edited (with Jane Carter) a volume of essays, *The Ages of Homer* (1995), on the archaeological, literary, and artistic background and responses to Greek epic poetry. A practicing field archaeologist, she has excavated in Israel, Turkey, and Greece and is currently engaged in research in the Ionian islands of Greece and in the Cyclades.

Josiah Ober is David Magie Professor of Classics at Princeton University, with a joint appointment in the University Center for Human Values. He has held grants from the National Endowment for the Humanities, the American Council of Learned Societies, and the Guggenheim Foundation. His 1989 book, *Mass and Elite in Democratic Athens*, won the Goodwin Award of Merit from the American Philological Association. His other books include *Fortress Attica* (1985), *The Athenian Revolution* (1996), and, most recently, *Political Dissent in Democratic Athens* (1998). His work currently centers on the relationship between democracy and the circulation of knowledge within Athenian society.

Robin Osborne is the Professor of Ancient History at the University of Cambridge. He was formerly a Professor of Ancient History in the University of Oxford and Fellow and Tutor of Corpus Christi College. He recently co-edited *Performance Culture and Athenian Democracy* (1999) with Simon Goldhill and has published books and articles covering a wide range of topics in Greek history and archaeology. He is currently working on the implications for Athenian social history of the changing iconography of nonmythological scenes on Athenian red-figure vases.

Kurt A. Raaflaub is currently the David Herlihy University Professor and Professor of Classics and History at Brown University. His main fields of interest include the social and political history of the Roman republic and the social, political, and intellectual history of Archaic and Classical Greece. He has published books on motivation and political strategy in Caesar's civil war (1974) and the discovery of freedom in ancient Greece (1985, forthcoming in a 2nd ed.) and edited or co-edited volumes on social struggles in Archaic Rome (1986), Augustus and his principate (1990), the beginnings of political thought in the ancient world (1993), democracy, empire, and the arts in fifth-century Athens (1998), and war and society in the ancient and medieval worlds (1999), among others.

Richard Seaford is Professor of Ancient Greek at the University of Exeter. He is the author of numerous papers on Greek religion and literature from Homer to the New Testament, of commentaries on Euripides' *Cyclops* (1984) and *Bacchae* (1996), and of *Reciprocity and Ritual: Homer and Tragedy in the Developing City-State* (1994). His next book is *Money and the Early Greek Mind* (Cambridge 2003).

General Index

Achilles, 7, 12, 65, 175
Acropolis, of Athens
  buildings on xx, 124, 128, 130
  Cylon on, 98
  parades to, 225
  revenues stored on, 127
  as shrine, 16
  stele on, 69, 73
Aeschylus, 64, 100–101, 104, 175
Agamemnon, 2, 7, 17, 21, 100–101, 229
Alcibiades, xvii, 69, 257
  attempted ostracism of, 70, 256
  and comedy, 158, 170–172, 175
  suspicion of, xxvi, 71, 165, 169–170, 174,
    258
Alcmeonids, 14, 45, 62, 67–69, 174
allies, of Athens
  tribute from, 106, 134, 166
  as victims of Athenian tyranny, 79–80,
    159, 160–163, 167, 184
amphibolia, xv, 187–188, 193, 243–244
Antiphon, 99, 196, 258–259, 261
apragmosynē, 120, 168, 171–172
Archilochus, 32, 78, 98–99, 122
Arginousae, battle of, xxiii, 262, 264, 269
Aristagoras, 32, 35, 38–40, 41, 45–47, 254
Aristides, 168
aristocracy (see also elites)
  Athens as, 137, 165, 190
  culture of, xx, 127, 142, 165
  Demos (in Aristophanes) as member of,
    138–139
  genealogical pretensions of, 10–11, 18

in Herodotus' Constitutional Debate, 29,
  75
opposition to, 25, 161
in oral tradition, 252
as virtuous rule, 182, 189–190, 198, 200–
  201, 204, 206–207
Aristogeiton (see also tyrannicides): 173, 221,
  226, 233, 239
  in Herodotus and Thucydides, 45, 174
  heroization of, 117, 224
  as liberator, 156, 174, 220
  statue of, 63–64, 217, 242
  tomb of, 65
Aristophanes, 79, 155–175 passim, 222
  and demagogues, xix, 67
  and the demos, xxii, 122, 137–140, 229
  and fear of conspiracy, 71, 135
Aristotle, 73, 95
  as constitutional theorist, 21, 225, 263–
    264, 269
  and the construction of tyranny, 25–26,
    121–122
  as dissident, xvii
  and tyrannical building programs, 124,
    130
  and tyrannical wealth, 123
Assembly, of Athens, 65, 203, 204, 255, 257,
  262
  curse at meetings of, 70, 156
  flattery of, 161
  flaws of, 138, 158
  reforms of, 261, 264, 266–267
Assembly, of Sparta, 255

Eleusinian Mysteries, profanation of, 66–
67, 104, 165, 169–170
elites (*see also* aristocracy)
as audience, 188, 204
in Bronze Age, 7, 252–253
culture of, xii, 13, 138–139
as dissidents, 59, 82, 155, 200, 244
expenditures of, xiv, 127
as faction within democracy, xxi, 122,
165, 167–169, 172–173, 189, 230
leadership of, xix, 75, 158–159, 161–163
and traditions of the Peisistratids, 67, 175
and tyranny, xi, 11, 61–62, 72, 78, 229, 233
empire, of Athens, 137, 172, 186, 256
justification for, 121–122, 157, 160
as source of benefit to Athens, xv–xvi,
140–142
taxation of allies by, 127, 130
as tyranny, xxi–xxii, 72, 77–81, 108–111,
118
envy, 29, 35, 98, 105, 122, 138, 160, 187
erastēs, 16, 41, 167, 231
erōs, 27, 49, 74
Erythrae, xv, 21, 70, 156, 227–228, 244–245
Eucrates, decree of, xvi, 70, 222–227, 235,
237, 251, 268–269
Euripides, 49, 79, 99, 104, 110–111

flattery, 191
of Athenian demos, 138, 160–161, 166–
168, 185–188, 196, 203, 205
as description of rhetoric, 193–194, 232
of speech, 31
of tyrants, xxiii, (29, 35 HDT), 187, 199
Four Hundred, 64, 225, 258–259, 261–262,
268
411 B.C., coup of, 70, 77, 251, 256, 266–268
and Aristophanes' *Lysistrata,* 173
disenfranchisement of oligarchs after, 158,
175
role of oligarchic theory in, 258–261
freedom, 67, 123, 169, 196
of Athenian demos, xix, 80, 119, 121–122,
156–157, 198–199
in Herodotus, 36, 44, 49
opposed to slavery, 81, 102, 205
opposed to tyranny, xix, 106, 224
of speech, 31, 185–186, 188, 193

of the tyrant, xx, 76, 108, 119, 159, 200
Funeral Oration (in Thucydides), xv, xvii,
119, 121, 131–137, 142

Gorgias, 194
greed, xiv, 38, 96–97, 230

Harmodius, 166–167
cult of, 65, 117, 226
role in ending tyranny at Athens, 45,
66–67, 156, 174, 220, 224
song, 63–64, 65, 167
statue of, 63, 217
stance of, 220–221, 224, 227, 236–237,
239, 242, 244
Herms, mutilation of, 66, 104, 169
Herodotus, xv–xvi, 25–49 *passim,* 72, 125–
126, 252–253
as historical source, 61, 73
and the tyrannicides, 67–69
and tyranny, 75–76, 98, 229
Hipparchus (*see also* Peisistratids)
death of, 45, 64, 67, 73, 126, 217, 222
as tyrant of Athens, 174–175
Hippias (*see also* Peisistratids)
after the death of Hipparchus, 45–46, 61,
73
in Aristophanes, 164, 167, 173–175, 258
in exile, 37, 62, 72, 75
relations with Lampsacus, 14
Histiaeus, 35–36, 38–40, 45–47
Homer, 2, 9–10, 64, 95–96, 97, 99, 229
homosexuality (see also *erastês*): 167, 196, 231

imperialism, 49, 60
Athenian, x, 79, 156, 158, 171–172, 200
Eastern, 33, 34–35, 45
impiety (*see also* ritual, abuse of): xiv,
96–98, 109, 169
individuals
as audience, 204–206
as collectives, xviii, xx–xxi, xxii, xxv, 198
danger from, 128, 267–268
in Herodotus, x, xvi, 26, 41–45
relationship with community, xii–xiii,
xxv, 5, 157, 195, 198, 207
in tragedy, xvii, 107–108
isēgoria, 62

Phyle, 64, 225, 234, 241, 243, 267, 268
Pindar, xiii, 75, 135–136, 183
Pittacus of Mytilene, 61, 74, 167
Plato, xxi–xxii, 97–98, 181–207 *passim,*
    and attitudes of, to tyranny, xx, 25–26,
        49, 76–79, 122
    as critic of democracy, xi, xiv, xvii–xviii,
        xxiv, 229–235, 269
Plutarch, 42, 128–129, 134–135
Polycrates, 96–97, 99, 124
    in Herodotus, 37–38, 44, 47–48, 96, 125,
        130

religion, xii–xiv, 3–5, 12–13, 73, 99–100
    in Athens, 70, 106, 108–109, 161
    ritual, abuse of, xiii, 96–98, 100–106,
        109–110

Scythia, 34–35, 39
Sicily
    Athenian expedition to, 66, 78, 169, 173,
        256–257
    tyranny in, xiii, 18, 60, 62, 76, 182–183,
        253
Simonides, 64, 65
Socles, 30–32, 35–36, 37, 75, 254
Solon, 226, 257
    on the desirability of tyranny, xxi, 62, 78,
        229
    in Herodotus, 18, 33, 41, 43
    laws of, 121, 263–264
    law against tyranny, 70, 156, 170
Sophists, 206
    idealization of tyranny in, 75–77, 78–80,
        172
Sophocles, 104
    Oedipus in, xxii, 72, 98, 108–110
Sparta, 83, 158, 187, 254, 266–267
    alliance with Lydia, 14
    Athenian hostility to, 141, 161, 173–174,
        258
    constitution of, 190, 252, 255
    culture of, 42, 133, 255
    as guarantor of freedom, 31, 36, 69, 76–
        77, 80, 159, 174
    as liberator of Athens, 45, 66–67, 69, 169,
        174–175, 220, 224

and the Thirty, 258, 262
stasis, 29, 75, 162, 223, 235, 243
    aristocratic, 1, 21, 83
    and Plato, 231–234
    and tyrannicide, xi, 216, 225, 228
sycophancy, 161, 263–264

taxation, 30, 66
    by Athenian demos, xiv, 126–127, 130,
        163, 229
    by tyrants, 123–124, 130
Theseus
    as democrat, 66, 75, 104, 226, 253
    opposition to tyranny of, 106, 117
Thirty Tyrants, 175, 234
    as collective tyranny, 183, 262
    overthrow of, 64, 69, 225, 243, 268
    rule of, 230, 235–237, 241, 251, 262–267,
        269
Thucydides (*see also* Funeral Oration): xxv,
        49, 79, 162
    on Archaic tyrannies, 1, 11, 73, 76, 122–
        123, 125–126, 220–221
    on Athenian tyranny, xix, xxii, 77, 137,
        159
    as dissident, 221
    on fear of tyranny at Athens, 66–68, 69,
        71, 165, 169–170, 174–175, 224, 268
    on the revolution of 411, 256–259
Thucydides, son of Melesias, 80, 128–130,
        134–135, 163, 171, 255
tragedy, x, xvii, xxii–xxiii, 15, 17, 95–111
        passim, 253
    audience of, 203, 205
    negative assessment of tyranny in, 71–72,
        75, 79
    positive assessment of tyranny in, xiii,
        xvi, xx, 75, 78
tyrannicide, xi, 258
    ideologization of, xviii, 63–69, 83, 215–
        245 *passim*
tyrannicides (*see also* Harmodius; Aristogei-
        ton): 60, 69–70
    cult of, 65
    deflation of, 45, 66–68, 73
    honors to descendents of, 66, 156, 226
    statues of, 16, 63–66, 156, 217–221

stance of (*see also* Harmodius stance) 66,
   227
tyrannis, 60, 79, 80, 194
   in Herodotus, 27–28, 29, 31, 32–33, 35–36,
      40–41
   in tragedy, 100, 104, 107, 120
tyrannos, 62, 80, 122, 183
   etymology of, 4, 25
   in Herodotus, 29, 31, 32–33, 35–36, 40–41
   in tragedy, 78, 100, 102, 104, 107, 109
tyranny, as metaphor, xi, 71–72, 123, 198,
   202
   for Athenian demos, xvii, xxiii, 59, 78–
      79, 117–118, 121, 135, 156–157, 195–196
   for Athenian empire, 72, 117–119, 161
   in comedy, 163–164
   in Thucydides, xxii, 81, 159

wanax, 2, 4, 5, 7, 8, 12, 18
wealth (*see also* money): 127–128, 132, 142,
   158, 185, 260
   of Athenian demos, x, xix, 127–131,
      133–135, 137, 143
   as cause of tyranny, xi, 1, 11, 25
   as characteristic of tyrants, xiii–xiv, xx,
      17, 37, 62, 99, 122–124, 126, 135–136,
      140
   in tragedy, 105, 107, 110
   in comedy, 137, 139, 142, 165

Xenophanes, 99–100, 142
Xenophon, 74, 78, 254, 262–264, 266
Xerxes, 63
   in Herodotus, 33–36, 41, 43, 49
   in tragedy, xv, 17

INDEX LOCORUM